THE COMPLETE
BOOK
OF DOG CARE

REVISED EDITION

THE
Complete Book
of Dog Care

REVISED EDITION

Leon F. Whitney, D.V.M.
George D. Whitney, D.V.M.

DOUBLEDAY
NEW YORK LONDON TORONTO SYDNEY AUCKLAND

PUBLISHED BY DOUBLEDAY
A division of Bantam Doubleday Dell Publishing Group, Inc.
666 Fifth Avenue, New York, New York 10103

DOUBLEDAY and the portrayal of an anchor with a dolphin
are trademarks of Doubleday, a division of Bantam Doubleday
Dell Publishing Group, Inc.

PHOTOS BY JONATHAN TAYLOR

Library of Congress Cataloging in Publication Data
Whitney, Leon Fradley, 1894–
  The complete book of dog care.
  Includes index.
  1. Dogs. 2. Dogs—Diseases. I. Whitney,
George D., 1918–   . II. Title.
SF427.W43   1985   636.7   84-28763
ISBN 0-385-15547-6

4   6   8   10   11   9   7   5

To the memory of the senior author, who was a road builder, mentor, and inspiration to many, including his son.

Contents

THE COMPLETE
BOOK
OF DOG CARE

REVISED EDITION

1

You, Your Dog, and Your Veterinarian

Years ago, when we began veterinary practice, we often wondered why some people seemed to get so much more pleasure than others out of owning and handling dogs. As we talked with them, listened to their problems, and tried to answer their questions, it seemed to us that the difference lay largely in their general attitude toward animals, in their understanding of the nature of their pets and their relationships with them. All these things were important factors in the choice of their dogs, in the way they handled them, and in the care they were able to give them. Having worked with thousands of pet owners, we are now more than ever convinced that a proper understanding of the nature of animals is the first and greatest need of most dog owners.

WHAT YOU SHOULD KNOW ABOUT YOUR DOG

The capacity to feel love for animals is a gift—for many people, a gift as rewarding as any. There are those unfortunates—comparatively few, we think—who lack the ability to feel affection for animals just as surely as there are those who cannot distinguish red from green. They will never understand the pleasure and the gratification that every dog owner experiences, for the love of animals can never be truly taught. But most people, even those who have never owned a pet, do not have the sympathy and warmth and patience that it takes to get the most enjoyment from association with a dog. What they lack more than anything else, in our opinion, is a realistic conception of what they are to the dog and what their dog should be to them.

Just as so many humans feel the need of some higher power or individual to look to for support or guidance, so your dog looks to you, the provider, for its support. To it you are a god, you are Providence. Your dog looks to you for leadership and food, even as its feral ancestors looked to their pack leaders and to nature for guidance and sustenance.

To have the most fun from owning a dog, perhaps nothing is more important than learning to accept your pet for what it is, to cultivate the proper mental attitude. A dog is a dog. Thinking of it or treating it as a human being is the source of many of the difficulties some people encounter in dog owning. You must learn to refrain from the natural tendency of projecting yourself onto the dog. It is poor logic; it will make your pet unhappy and you dissatisfied.

Though most people are willing to accept the laws of nature as they apply to wild animals, some of them are still reluctant to extend the same reasoning to the animals they keep as intimate pets. In principle, there is no difference. You should always try first to understand the nature of the species you are interested in, not just that of a particular animal. We learn our best lessons, particularly about food and feeding, from nature, and we would all be much better providers if we could bring ourselves to rely more on such guidance.

Take feeding, for example. Because we have learned to enjoy a great variety of food, we are inclined to project our tastes on pets. A horse will quite contentedly eat hay, oats, and a little salt for an entire life-time. Wild dogs survive by eating what appears to be a single item, animal bodies. Even today, when cats become wild, they exist primarily on rodents. From a study of the natural habits of animals we can and should learn a great deal about the kind of food that is best for them. It would, of course, be foolish to suggest that we slavishly follow the natural diet of animals. Dogs have evolved with us for so long that they can exist on any food that a human can digest.

In every aspect of animal care it pays real dividends to know the natural requirements of the species—their breeding habits, the diseases they are subject to, the exercise they need. If every dog owner understood the natural needs of all canines and had the courage to treat his or her dog accordingly, we surely would never see fat, turtlelike dogs; we would see no hopelessly sick dogs being allowed to drag out their miserable existences; deformities would not be perpetuated. Dog breeders would refuse to breed another dog whose defects caused it or us inconvenience. Boston Terriers unable to whelp normally would never be bred again, and only Bostons with large pelves would become progenitors. What suffering could be eliminated! Suppose no Bulldog that snored because of its contorted nose would be used to sire another snoring pup? Or suppose that strains of terriers were bred to be resistant to skin disease? How much more pleasure all dog owners would find in caring for their pets!

Nature does not perpetuate defects; humans do it in defiance of nature. Nature allows only hibernating and estivating animals to become fat and lazy for the purpose of storing food. We would be wise indeed to use the examples that nature has given us as our guides.

It is not too much to expect an owner to raise a dog that won't bite under almost any provocation: it can be done and is done by people who have the proper feeling for animals. From the time a puppy is weaned it should be handled at arm's length and not too often so that it begins to understand that it is on its own, an independent creature as nature meant it to be and not an extension of a human's anatomy. A good way to start is to place a new puppy on a table. Put it at arm's length; stand it up. Brush it. Set it down. Make sure that it has nothing to lean against. Pose it in a show position for ten or fifteen minutes at a stretch, brushing and combing it all the time. If it tries to lean against you, move away. Open its mouth and feel around its little teeth. Let it know you mean no harm, and after a while you will find you can hold its mouth open for several minutes. Reward it from time to time with a tiny tidbit. If you do this, you will have a dog and not a nuisance—a dog that you can trust and one that will trust you.

Speculation as to why the dog holds such a unique position among all animals in relationship to man leads to interesting conclusions. It is the only lower animal on earth that will work for a master, play with a master, guard and even give its life for a master, and demonstrate affection even to the point of mourning when a master dies. Perhaps there is a historical genetic basis for this phenomenon.

Perhaps when early man was emerging from the cave the tamer precursors of our present canids followed him for his leftovers after a hunt and may have survived because of the availability of those leftovers. During the passing thousands of years those canids may have joined in the hunt, helping primitive man to survive. And those humanoids who used the dogs to help in the hunt may have recognized their value and permitted them to share the campfire. This evolving sharing could have been a significant factor in survival of both early humans and dogs, for at a time of great peril the dog could have sounded a warning for and/or protect its master.

So since it is possible that modern dogs' reaction to mankind and humans' reaction to dogs have a genetic basis, and since we are talking about an attitude, that attitude in humans could be applied to any creature, such as a cat, a bird, and in some cases even a lowly snake.

Exciting new discoveries in brain chemistry suggest that the dog or another kind of pet could be one of the initiating or triggering factors in chemical change in the brain. It is well accepted that most people will experience a five-point drop in blood pressure just by petting a dog (or observing a tank of tropical fish for that matter).

In recent years a whole new branch of science has evolved in the study of pet therapy, as well as of the effects of pets on normal people.

HOW TO SELECT A DOG

The following are four possible answers to the question, "How can I find the best dog for me?" Which do you agree with?

1. Go to a dog show and ask the exhibitors.

2. Find an active breeder of a breed you are interested in, and inquire.

3. When you see someone walking a dog you admire, strike up a conversation and ask about the dog.

4. Find a book that describes the breeds and read about them.

If you disagreed with all four responses you may go to the head of the class. People are defenders of their possessions, with children and pets heading the list. It is a rare exhibitor, breeder, or pet owner who does not extol the virtues of his or her animal's breed.

Our advice is to read the breed books that praise the favorable traits of a breed, make a list of those you're interested in, and ask a veterinarian about the problems presented by that breed. Pose those same questions to an impartial consultant, such as a local animal control officer, dog trainer, or kennel operator. And remember that ultimately only you can decide whether or not you can live with the drawbacks of a particular breed or animal.

We are frequently asked about mongrels, or mutts, or curs (the latter should not be confused with the Mountain Cur, a breed of coonhound). The disadvantage in getting one of these lies in the fact that it is difficult to predict what a mixed breed pup will turn into as an adult. On the other hand, mongrels are free of many of the inherited problems that plague purebreds (ironically, since many of these problems are recessive, it is often difficult to predict what a purebred will look like as an adult, despite the purebred's controlled parentage). There is some evidence that hybrid vigor in the mongrel produces more disease-resistant offspring. In our practice we find a larger percentage of trouble-free mongrels than of purebreds.

When we are asked, "What kind of dog do you recommend, Doctor?" we reply with a series of questions.

Do you want a giant, large, medium, small, or toy size?

Do you want a long, medium, or short coat?

Do you have a color preference?

Do you want a companion or a dog that will perform some function, such as hunting, racing, pulling a wagon, and so on, or both?

One elderly gentleman who called us for advice said he wanted a dark, shorthaired, toy dog under five pounds as an *attack* dog. We thought he was joking and said we couldn't imagine why anyone would want a five-pound attack dog. He told us he had always wanted a dog who would attack on command, and as he was now old he thought he couldn't cope with a larger pet. We told him we knew of no such breed. Two weeks later he struggled into our office with a twenty-pound Great Pyrenees puppy, a long-hair, gentle giant breed. Eventually, the new owner would learn the folly of his choice when six months and a hundred pounds later his puppy knocked him down a flight of stairs, which fractured his hip. That apparently did it. We found a good home for the dog; the gentleman recovered and, taking our advice, now owns a parakeet.

YOUR OBLIGATIONS AS A DOG OWNER

The obligations of dog owning are few, but you must fulfill them. All that the animal requires of you is *food, water, comfort, exercise, health, affection,* and *protection.* If you can't supply these simple needs, it would be better for you not to have a dog, for it will only be a burden.

For example, veterinarians will often see a Poodle whose coat is solidly matted and thick with fleas. No one could possibly comb it. The owner laments, "Oh, why didn't somebody tell me what he would be like when he grew up!" A dog allowed to get in such a condition poses a medical problem and a nuisance to the owner as well. When the dog has been clipped all over, defleaed, and the owner made to understand that from then on he must spend some time on the dog's grooming, he's likely to say, "But that's so expensive!" The owner should have known before he bought the poodle that a dog with a shorter coat is cheaper to keep.

Too often the prospective dog owner overlooks his or her own desires and tendencies when selecting a pet. The sedentary man of studious disposition not infrequently makes the mistake of selecting a dog that requires much more exercise than he is willing to give it. Let's say he has a Foxhound. Every day he takes it for a walk around the block—thereby satisfying his own conscience but providing practically no exercise for the dog. All the owner has done is to give the animal a chance to relieve itself. He should know that sometimes a foxhound will run on a trail for as long as forty-eight hours. At 10 miles an hour, it will have traveled 480 miles in that time. The hungry wild dog may run 100 miles to get a single meal. In the face of such facts, the owner's walk around the block to exercise the dog becomes ludicrous. What the animal really enjoys is a 10- or 20-mile hike once a week—an outing that would probably do the owner as much good as it does the dog.

Beyond the few simple obligations that pet owners assume, there are a few things they learn to avoid. They soon find that it doesn't pay to let their pets roam anymore than they can help. It costs less to feed a dog on neighbor's garbage—but not for long. Sooner or later the animal eats some "tainted swill," sickens, and perhaps dies. Animals that roam are in constant danger of being injured in accidents or hurt in fights. They may even join others and ravage the neighborhood. A pair of German Shepherds in our community killed nineteen little pigs on one farm, seven sheep on another, three calves on another, and fifty-four rabbits on still another—all in one night. One of the dogs was shot and the other poisoned by the irate farmer who had lost the calves. Thousands of sheep are killed every year by dogs, and the dogs are in turn destroyed by the authorities. And in northern locations where snow is deep, dozens of roaming dogs are shot every year by wardens to prevent their killing the deer that can't escape from them.

A final word on the danger of letting a dog run loose. Sooner or later it will be picked up by the dog warden and put in a truck with other strays. It will be lodged in the dog pound, and if there is any disease among the other dogs there, your dog is sure to be exposed. It is true that the dog can be recovered from the warden, but it may well die or go through a long, expensive illness because of an infection it contracted in the pound.

Still another obligation of the dog owner is to help prevent the canine population explosion by the judicious use of a leash which is the cheapest contraceptive available. Of course, this does not mean the tethering on a leash of a female in heat where males are around. There are contraceptive additives to food as well as pills and injections to prevent heat, but these preparations are usually given to prevent no more than two heat periods. Unless you must use your pet for reproduction, it is wise to have it spayed or castrated as the case may be. Many states have or are in the process of legislating higher license fees for unspayed and uncastrated canines in the hope that the numbers of unwanted animals will be reduced.

HOW TO CHOOSE A VETERINARIAN

The failure to understand the simple processes of life and the basic body functions is to blame, we think, for the many people who take a dog to the veterinarian and say, "Kidneys out of order, Doc, fix her up." Or, "He's got kind of wobbly in the back end, sort of paralyzed. He's the only dog we have. We don't want anything to happen to him. Fix him up. When'll we call for him?"

A body isn't like an automobile. You don't replace parts by taking something out and putting something else back. You remove causes and supply adequate nutrition; you may remove growths, but you must wait for the body itself to do the regenerating. Physiologically a dog is not *much* different from a human, and you don't take *Grandpa* to the hospital and leave him with the admonition, "Fix him up, Doc. He's the only Grandpa we have and we don't want anything to happen to him."

People are inclined to expect either too little or too much of their veterinarian. Perhaps they have been misled in part by seeing too many movies in which the vet is depicted as a dirty, messy, careless drunk with a large cigar in his mouth, spilling ashes over his patient. The old gent who is perfectly content to sleep in the hay beside a sick horse, and his boon companion is always Dickie, the stableboy.

Most people today know that veterinarians neither look nor act like this caricature. They are men and women who have spent a good many years of their lives in rigorous study in order to be able to help you and your dog. Their skills and their abilities are of the utmost importance to the welfare of your pet and to your comfort and enjoyment. It is well worth spending some little time and thought in selecting the veterinarian who can best help you care for your pet.

What is the most important factor in your choice of a veterinarian? In our estimation, it is *confidence,* and before you place your confidence in a veterinarian the question you want to answer is, How much does he or she know?

In choosing a veterinarian, there are certain obvious criteria. You must not fail to notice the cleanliness and efficiency of the office or hospital. You will probably see the vet's credentials hanging on the wall; they must include a certificate of study at an accredited college of veterinary medicine and a state license to practice.

The ideal veterinarian should be completely honest, with conduct guided by the code of ethics of the American Veterinary Medical Association. The ethical veterinarian will not give unnecessary injections at exorbitant prices, using five cents' worth of vitamin concentrates. He or she will not exaggerate the seriousness of an illness nor claim a cure in a single visit. Not only does he or she do whatever is possible for the patient during an office visit, but you should be provided with instruction in the care of the patient as well. If repeated visits to the office give you a sense of security, that is a matter for you to decide. The wise veterinarian, however, knows that the pet that costs the owner too much is a burden rather than a pleasure.

The ethical veterinarian charges moderate fees. There are, unfortunately, a few who callously feel that it's not unethical to charge all the traffic will bear. It is. To be ethical, the veterinarian should consider all the factors involved. If a bill is too large for the value of the animal, or if it is beyond the owner's ability to pay without hardship, that person will find that the very purpose of owning a pet—namely, to have an enjoyable companion—is gone. Veterinarians who overcharge do infinite damage to their profession by reducing the number of pet owners.

The ethical veterinarian is democratic. He or she does not exclude from his or her attention the laborer in work clothes or the person from a different ethnic or racial background. Yet there are doctors who do exclude people on the basis of their appearance, and this is wrong: when a pet needs care, the pet is the patient, not the owner.

The modern veterinarian shares any discoveries freely with other members of the profession. Through the presentation of studies at association meetings and in veterinary journals, these observations are made available to others so that they can be used to relieve suffering.

In our opinion, the veterinarian who does not continue learning by attending lectures and symposia, or by extensive home study, might well be guilty of malpractice in five years. As a matter of fact, many states require evidence of continuing education for relicensing. Others have academies that require many hours of study each year for members to remain in good standing.

The veterinarian in whom you can place your confidence may not wear all these qualifications like shining armor. They represent the ideal, and, happily, today's conscientious veterinarian is approaching this ideal. The profession is distinguished by many truly magnificent characters—men and women with utterly unselfish attitudes, who sacrifice themselves for their patients just as willingly and unstintingly as the family physician shares his or her strength and knowledge. Which should not be surprising to anyone: a veterinarian must of necessity have an abiding interest in animals.

If you are new to an area and you have not obtained the name of a local veterinarian from your previous one, there are many ways to find one. Consult the local boarding kennels, pharmacists, and any neighbors who have a pet similar to yours. When you have settled on a name and have visited the establishment, you should then evaluate the premises and the doctor's personality. If confidence is inspired by the visit, your problem is solved.

You should know there is a reverse side to the coin, too: the veterinarian will be evaluating you. He or she will wonder whether you will "gild the lily" or tell it like it is (many people do tend to exaggerate some symptoms and minimize others). He or she will hope you both will work well together to help your dog when and if a problem arises.

The more recent veterinary school graduates have the advantage of knowing the newest theories and approaches to problems. And we have yet to see a woman veterinarian who hasn't equaled or surpassed her average male colleague in this profession, so don't let gender influence your decision.

THE BENEFITS OF OWNING A DOG

The abundant literature about dogs is full of examples of the benefits of owning a dog. One recent study examined 100 human cardiac patients, half of whom owned pets, for the most part dogs. One year later many in the group without pets had died and over 50 percent had suffered repeat attacks. Of the pet-owning half, few had died and under 20 percent had experienced attacks. Why this is so is still a matter of speculation, but the statistics are significant. It is also well documented that dogs have brought patients out of deep depression where shock treatment, drugs, and psychiatry have failed. In fact, several mental institutions across the country maintain kennels of dogs for patient therapy.

The dogs used by the blind do more than lead blind people, they are bosom companions. And now we find dogs for the deaf that let their owners know when the telephone or doorbell is ringing. There are also dogs for the handicapped that are trained to fetch articles difficult to reach, as well as dogs specially trained for the elderly, the infirm, and the retarded. For the rest who enjoy good health and are not disabled in any way, a dog is an invaluable friend, comfort, or companion. And even if a pet is taken for granted, which may become obvious only when its life is threatened, it is usually more important to us than most of us will admit.

2

The Dog's Body and How It Functions

So many high school and college graduates have not had courses in human/animal physiology and anatomy that we have long ceased to be surprised at the number of dog owners lacking any conception of animal physiology. If you are to get the most out of this book, it will be necessary to review briefly the structure and function of your pet's body. Even though the study of the mechanism of the living body is to us one of the most fascinating in the world, the general attitude toward the subject is such that we feel we must warn you that you are not in for an in-depth dissertation. All that will be necessary here is to learn enough about your dog's body so that you may treat it sensibly.

The science that deals with the functions of living things or of their parts is called physiology. That which is concerned with the structure of the body and the relationships of its parts is called anatomy. Let us combine the two and see how the body is formed and how its parts function.

The body of every animal grows from a single cell. What is a cell? It is a unit of life smaller than the eye can see. The whole body of some tiny animals is a single cell: the amoeba and paramecium, for example. Other animals consist of colonies of cells. All the visible animate creatures we see are immense colonies of cells, and each cell has some special function. Every one of these cells is composed of a covering, within which is some protoplasm, a substance not unlike egg white, and a nucleus, which carries the genetic material.

The first cell, which results from the uniting of a male cell (sperm) and a female cell (ovum) and is thus the beginning of an animal, is complete in every detail. It is a favorite academic paradox to say that a cell multiplies by dividing, and it is, of course, quite true. If one cell divides into two cells, it has divided, but because it is two, it has multiplied. The two become four; the four, eight. As they go on dividing and thus increasing, different cells become specialized at certain stages. Some may become skin, some liver, some heart, some germ plasm, some tonsils, and so forth. There are cells that may never renew themselves: brain cells, for example. Then there are other very specialized cells, like those in the hair and nails, that are constantly renewed. They all live together in a happy community or colony, doing their work unless hindered by improper nourishment or crowding (from overfatness), or disease.

And that's what our dogs are—big colonies of cells.

THE BODY'S COVERING

The skin covering the body is composed of several layers, each made up of innumerable cells. Two main layers are recognized: the outer layer, *epidermis,* the lower layer or true skin, the *dermis.* Sometimes we hear the epidermis called the cuticle or the scarfskin and, colloquially, the scurfskin. The true skin, in turn, consists of two layers. The skin is constantly shedding and renewing itself, a fact that has an important bearing on the treatment of skin diseases.

Under the skin we find subcutaneous connective tissue, an interesting part of the body made up of very elastic cells. Through it run nerves, lymph vessels, and blood vessels; fat is often deposited in it.

Out of the skin grow the appendages we call hairs in mammals, feathers in birds, scales in fish. Hair grows out of the skin from follicles (sacs or sheaths). In the follicles are little muscles which at times cause a dog's hair to stand on end.

Sweat glands are found in certain places on the bodies of dogs and everywhere in the skin there are sebaceous glands that usually discharge their waxy secretion into the follicles. As the hair grows, it comes out coated with this sebum, an acrid-smelling substance in dogs that partly accounts for the doggy odor. This is the substance that gums dogs' collars brown, over time, with so heavy a coating that it can actually be scraped off with a knife. Other glands secrete oil that helps the dog to shed water.

These protective coats, plus its natural resistance to water, make the

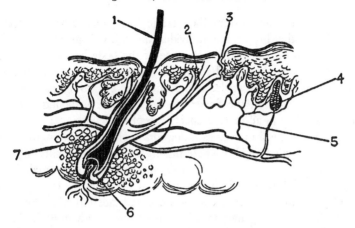

(1) Hair growing out of follicle. (2) Erector muscle. (3) Sweat duct. (4) Nerve end organ. (5) Blood vessels. (6) Bottom of hair follicle or papilla. (7) Subcutaneous fatty tissue.

skin waterproof. It is not, however, resistant to all oils, some of which can soak through it. In fact, the skin can absorb a good many drugs and substances that can be toxic (poisonous) to the dog.

The skin heals by growing outward from the lower layers if it is not wholly destroyed by a gash, scald, or other injury. (Blisters usually are pockets of fluid between layers of skin.) When all the layers are destroyed, growth occurs from the sides. In case of injury to your pet, it is for this reason that your veterinarian will want to bring the sides of the destroyed area as close together as possible, so that the space to be covered over will be as narrow as possible. Moreover, if the injury is left open, the newly generated skin will be devoid of glands and hair. Great scalded areas become covered with skin, but not skin with the usual accessories.

THE BODY'S FRAMEWORK

The Skeleton. The skeleton serves as the framework of the body and provides protection for the organs. The ribs cover the lungs, heart, liver, stomach, kidneys, and pancreas; the skull covers the brain and such delicate organs as the hearing mechanism and the organs of scent.

Each species differs from the next in form; breeds within species differ from other breeds, and individual animals vary in some respects. The skeleton on which the soft tissue of the body hangs is the basic cause of these structural differences. In some animals, for example, the mere shortness of certain leg bones can cause a startling difference in appearance—contrast the Basset Hound with the Foxhound, the two breeds are alike in all major respects except leg length.

The skeleton is a marvelous framework replete with strength where strength is needed, rigidity where rigidity is needed, flexibility, swivels, and hinges where stretching, bending, and rotating are required. Some bones are solid, others are hollow or filled with marrow in which red blood cells may be generated. Some are mere beads and others long and strong. The way they are joined is an interesting study in itself. There are ball-and-socket joints (hips), hinge joints (knees), others made by one bone abutting on another with a cushion between (vertebrae), and modifications of all three kinds. Some animals are more agile than others; some have difficulty turning around in a short radius, whereas others, because of their skeletal construction, can "turn on a dime."

Each long bone is made up of a shaft of hard, brittle material with a soft center of marrow and has ends of spongy material with a covering of dense, hard bone. Around the whole bone is a sort of skin called the *periosteum*. On top or on the bottom of the spongy end—if the bone terminates at a joint—is a springy, cartilaginous pad which takes the shocks. All through the bone small spaces form tunnels that carry blood and nerves; nourishment is also furnished by the periosteum.

Some bones are flat: ribs, head bones, and shoulder blades are examples. They are not as solid as they seem but are well fortified with nourishment. The ribs join at the lower extremities with cartilages. These look like true ribs but are only extensions upward from a flat "bone"—the *sternum*, or breastbone—to which all but one or two of the last ribs in some species are joined. The sternum is not actually a bone but is composed of springy, tough cartilage. The breastbone needs to be flexible, considering the strain it undergoes.

Muscles. Skeletal muscles help hold the framework together, cooperate with it in locomotion, and are easily detected beneath the skin. There are two kinds of muscles: the skeletal and the others, not visible outside of the body, called the *smooth muscles*. When seen under a microscope, fibers of a skeletal muscle appear to have bands or stria-

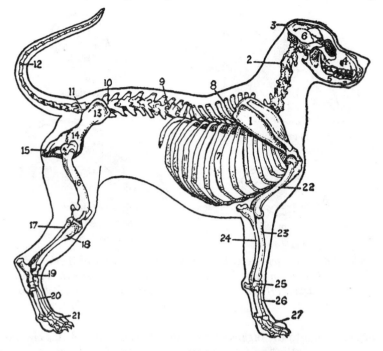

Skeleton of a dog. (1) Shoulder blade. (2) Neck vertebra. (3) Occiput. (4) Nasal bone. (5) Mandible. (6) Cranium. (7) Ribs. (8) Thoratic vertebra. (9) Lumbar vertebra. (10) Lumbar vertebra. (11) Sacrum. (12) Tail vertebra. (13) Ilium. (14) Ischium. (15) Pubis. (16) Femur. (17) Fibula. (18) Tibia. (19) Tarsus. (20) Metatarsus. (21) Rear toes. (22) Humerus. (23) Radius. (24) Ulna. (25) Carpus. (26) Metacarpus. (27) Front toes.

tions that do not exist on the smooth muscles. The striated muscles are under voluntary control. The duties of the smooth muscles are generally restricted to the functioning of organs and the digestive tract. The gullet, intestines, bladder, blood vessels, and sphincter muscles, which act more or less involuntarily, are all smooth.

THE CIRCULATORY SYSTEM

Heart and Vessels. The body is nourished by the blood, which delivers to the cells the substances they need and picks up their wastes and

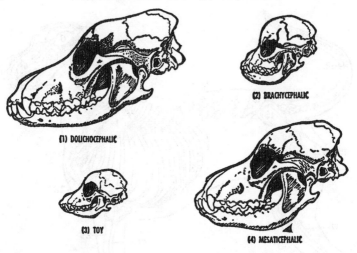

Skulls of dogs of different breeds. (1) Skull typical of Collie or Greyhound. (2) Skull typical of Boston Terrier. (3) Skull of midget or toy breeds such as Pomeranian or Chihuahua. (4) Average skull type characteristic of hounds, Dalmations, and others.

delivers them to the organs of excretion. At the center of this circulatory system is the heart, a natural pump which for efficiency is not excelled by any man-made device.

The heart receives blood via two veins, the anterior and posterior vena cava, then squeezes or contracts so that the blood is driven first into the lungs, where it liberates a gas, carbon dioxide, takes up another gas, oxygen, and is then hustled back to the heart to be pumped around the body via the arteries to distribute the oxygen and pick up cell wastes.

The great arteries, which carry the blood from the heart, start dividing into smaller arteries, which in turn divide into smaller and smaller ones, called arterioles, and thence into capillaries. From the capillaries the blood returns to the heart via venules, veins, and finally large veins. It also returns in lymph vessels. (The lymph may be thought of as concentrated blood without red blood cells.)

The pump keeps up its contracting squeezes and relaxations rhythmically for the life of the animal. It sounds like a continuous lubb, dubb, lubb, dubb in the chest and, in an eight-pound dog, pumps about a quart of blood every minute. Everything about it is a marvel—the

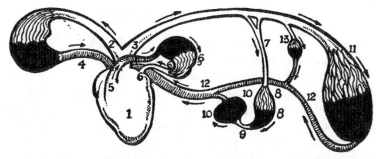

Heart and circulatory system. (1) Heart. (2) Anterior aorta, supplying front end of body. (3) Posterior aorta, supplying rear of body and organs. (4) Anterior vena cava, returning blood from front of body. (5) Pulmonary artery, carrying blood to lungs. (6) Pulmonary vein, carrying blood from lungs. (7) Celiac and mesenteric arteries carrying blood to (8), (9), and (10) stomach, spleen, intestines, liver, and other organs. (11) Blood supply to rear of body. (12) Posterior vena cava returning blood from rear of body. (13) Kidney circulation.

delicate valves, its strength, its four chambers, the skin around it, called the pericardium, the nervous mechanism that causes it to beat.

Spleen and Lymph Nodes. All along the path of the blood and lymph are filter organs, the chief of which is the spleen. A dog's spleen weighs about one ounce for every twenty-five pounds of body weight. It is a flat, long, narrow organ which lies close to the stomach. The spleen's function is chiefly to help purify the blood. It destroys great numbers of bacteria, and when red blood cells become aged the spleen breaks many of them down into liquid. In addition, the spleen manufactures a certain number of red and white blood cells. Since the blood spaces in the spleen are very large compared with ordinary capillaries, when the organ is ruptured in an accident a major hemorrhage into the abdomen may occur—and this can be fatal.

The spleen, a part of the lymphatic system, is the principal filter organ of the blood. Other smaller glands situated along the lymph vessels also serve to remove solid impurities, such as bacteria, from the blood fluids. Lymph does not move about by blood pressure, but rather by the body's movements. Muscle movement, the expansion and contraction involved in breathing, intestinal movements, and others, all force the lymph through the nodes and along its course. Valves in both lymph vessels and veins permit flow in only one direction.

THE RESPIRATORY SYSTEM

A pair of organs situated in the chest, one on each side, the lungs function in cooperation with the blood in the oxygen-carbon dioxide transfer and, to a certain extent, in body temperature control as well.

In all mammals a partition—strong in some and gossamer thin in others—divides the chest cavity so that the lungs are separated. In the dog this membrane is extremely thin, which means that if the chest cavity is broken open on one side so air enters, not only does the lung on that side collapse but its companion usually follows suit. In humans, where the partition is stronger, if one lung collapses the other may not.

From the upper throat a tube called the trachea, made up of many rings of tough cartilage, runs down into the chest and branches into two bronchial tubes, one for each lung. (Bronchitis is an inflammation in the linings of these tubes.) They in turn branch and subdivide into bronchioles and finally into air sacs, each of which is surrounded by a network of blood capillaries so thin that gases can be absorbed or escape through them.

THE EXCRETORY SYSTEM

The Kidneys. Blood disposes of certain chemical substances other than gases through the kidneys. It travels through their intricate mechanism, disposing of excess water and wastes such as urea (the end product of the breakdown of proteins in the body), sugar, poisons, and carbonates.

In most animals the kidneys are located on either side of the body close to the backbone and are partially protected by the ribs. They constitute one of the most delicate and ingenious filter plants imaginable. Anyone who has eaten kidneys or fed them to animals knows in general what they look like. But few have observed, microscopically, the minute inner workings or wondered at their remarkable construction. If you slice a kidney lengthwise, you see the so-called pelvis, a pocket for collecting urine which is then conducted via a tube—the ureter—to the bladder. The microscope, however, reveals the really interesting features of this organ: the blood vessels, which divide to become capillaries, in tiny containers called *glomeruli* and minute collecting *tubules* into which the urine filters and is conveyed to the pelvis. These are beautiful and clever arrangements to effect the transfer and reabsorption into the blood of certain useful substances and the rejection of the useless ones—all of which are accomplished while the blood is passing through the kidneys, entering under high pressure and emerging under much lower pressure.

Diseases can easily upset the normal function of the kidneys so that they cannot retain useful nitrogenous substances like albumin. Under certain circumstances the kidneys may lose their absorptive capacity so that too much water is secreted from the blood, causing great thirst. Albumin in urine and excessive thirst are both indications of kidney disease or dysfunction.

Kidneys that function properly regulate the amounts of blood ingredients to a considerable degree. If too much sugar is present, some will be found in the urine. The same may be said of salt. Urine is composed mostly of water (95 percent). Urea constitutes about 2.3 percent, salt 1.1 percent, and the balance, 1.6 percent, is composed of other solids.

The bladder is a reservoir with remarkably elastic walls. We have removed as much as seventeen ounces of urine from the obstructed bladder of a thirteen-pound dog and seen the dog recover.

Other Excretory Means. Other impurities and surpluses from the blood—some mineral salts, for instance—are also excreted into the intestines; some gases are excreted by the lungs, and still other substances by the skin in sweat, although this is minimal in dogs. Thus the excretory system actually is composed of four parts.

THE DIGESTIVE SYSTEM

As we have seen, one of the functions of the blood is to transport nourishment to the body's cells. The nutrients are prepared for the blood by the digestive system.

The Teeth and Mouth. Mouths of animals differ markedly among the several species, yet there is a general similarity. The lips are the portal to the mouth. They are also remarkably sensitive organs of touch for some animals, such as the horse, which can, with its coarse lips, feel among a lot of debris in a manger for a single oat grain! Monkeys too use their lips with singular effectiveness. Fishes rely on them. Dogs, cats, rabbits, guinea pigs, mice, and rats, on the other hand, seem to use their lips almost entirely for their primary purpose—to retain the food as it is chewed and the mouth juices, or secretions.

In each species of pets the teeth are unique in some respect—number, arrangement, length—yet in major respects there is an unusual similarity. Whereas humans frequently need dental care for cavities in their teeth, dogs develop very few. Nearly all their tooth troubles stem from bacterial infections or defective diet. What accounts for their sound teeth? Chewing hard foods can't be the reason, because many dogs are fed soft, mushy diets all their lives, and their teeth, though covered with tartar, do not decay. And most dogs' teeth are never cleaned. The difference is to be found in the structure of their teeth.

Many years ago to investigate the effect of sweets on dogs' teeth we fed several litters of puppies 20 percent corn syrup in their diets. When they were two years old the experiment was terminated since none of the dogs developed even one cavity. Nevertheless, it is assumed diet and heredity determine the quality of teeth.

A dog has two sets of teeth. The first, or the milk teeth, fall out after their roots are partially resorbed by the body at about halfway through the puppy's growing period. The eruption of the new teeth takes place so rapidly that it often causes loss of weight in growing animals and fever may sometimes accompany the teething.

Anatomists and students of natural history have a method of representing the number and arrangement of teeth of a species. Examples of the dental formulas of all our common pets follow.

The front "biting-off" teeth are called the incisors. A dog and a cat have three on each side of the midline of the upper jaw and three on the lower. Observed from the front, there appear to be six even teeth in a row in the upper and lower jaws. So the formula for these incisors is $I \frac{3-3}{3-3}$. Behind the incisors on each side is a long, strong canine tooth in both upper and lower jaws: $C \frac{1-1}{1-1}$. Next we find premolars: $P \frac{4-4}{4-4}$. Finally there are the molars $M \frac{2-2}{3-3}$. We write the whole formula:

$$I \frac{3-3}{3-3} \quad C \frac{1-1}{1-1} \quad P \frac{4-4}{4-4} \quad M \frac{2-2}{3-3} = 42.$$

The part of the tooth above the gum is called the crown, the part between the crown and root is called the neck, and the part embedded in the socket is called the root. Some teeth have one straight root, some several. More than half the length of each canine tooth is embedded inside the gums; the roots of the teeth are strong and exceedingly difficult to extract. Animal teeth are remarkably tough. When one sees a dog crush a large, hard, flinty bone, or a squirrel gnaw through a hickory nut, or a raccoon crack a nut that few of us would want to risk our molars on, our respect for animal teeth deepens.

Enamel adds to the hardness and strength and covers a softer substance called dentine. The root has no enamel covering. Inside each tooth we find the pulp, a structure with nerves and blood vessels. These structures seldom give way, but pets can and do have tooth and gum troubles even though these rarely have anything to do with cavities.

If a dog is sick with a fever-causing disease during teething, the enamel fails to deposit on the teeth. By observing the pits or rings on the canine teeth, for instance, anyone can tell at what time the puppy was sick. The whole period of replacement is not more than forty-five days. In dogs the upper-middle incisors erupt at close to fourteen weeks of age; the canines at about eighteen weeks. Thus, if we see a five-year-old dog with just the tips of the canines devoid of enamel and the lower part of the enamel missing on the incisors, we know it was sick at about four months of age. The teeth may thus form a chart of puppy sickness.

It used to be said that pitted teeth in dogs were "distemper teeth." Today we know that is not necessarily so. Pitted teeth can be caused by any one of several diseases, some quite mild.

The teeth of no two species are exactly alike. It has been said that the natural diet of any species of animal can be told by examination of the teeth. This is probably true. Long, sharp tusks like those of cats or raccoons would indicate that the animal's natural prey was some small animal easily killed and eaten. Dog's teeth are those of carnivores. The long, powerful tusks help a dog pull skin off a carcass, tear muscles loose, or rip out organs, while the arrangement of the back teeth for cutting or shearing would suggest that they were once meant to cut off pieces that the canine teeth had torn loose. The molars also have some flat surfaces that indicate usefulness in crunching grains.

A dog bolts its food, usually without making any pretense of chewing. It will swallow anything small enough to go down its extraordinarily elastic gullet. We once threw a piece of tripe three feet long, eight inches wide, and over half an inch thick to a fifty-five-pound male hound. A few minutes later we saw him swallowing it; only a few inches had not disappeared. We pulled it out to see how much chewing had been done and found it whole. He swallowed it again—all the way—and the next day his stool was normal. That huge piece of tripe had been well digested.

It is because a dog does bolt everything we give it that it may not digest some foods very well. All other pets, except fishes, do a much better job of mastication. Some fishes swallow other fishes whole. Birds, of course, have no teeth, so the problem doesn't arise.

Glands below or behind the mouth of all animals secrete a fluid called saliva which in some animals contains a starch-digesting substance. Dogs and cats have very little. This explains in part why it is so important to cook foods such as potatoes—to break up the starchy granules—before feeding them to these pets.

The roof of the mouth has a hard surface, the hard palate, going as far back as the last teeth and made up of ripples, or bars, extending across the mouth. Behind the teeth the roof (soft palate) is flabby. By the time a pet's food reaches the soft palate, it is practically in the throat.

The Tongue. The tongue, the principal organ for moving food into the mouth, is also the primary taste organ. Taste is experienced by the reaction to chemical stimuli of "taste buds," or sensitive areas, which stud this organ and produce the sensations of saltiness, sweetness, bitterness, and acidity. The taste buds are situated all over the tongue but are more abundant in the tip and at the back, in the throat proper.

The Throat. The delicate business of getting food correctly started down the esophagus and not the windpipe is accomplished in the throat by the pharynx and larynx. The esophagus is located above the windpipe (trachea). An arrangement called the epiglottis, which is part of the larynx, closes over the windpipe as food and fluid descend the esophagus, then drops down to allow the passage of air.

Peristalsis. In order to explain how food moves along through the body, we must refer back to the smooth muscles mentioned earlier. The only so-called voluntary muscles involved in digestion are in the lips, throat, and anus, and even these are partly involuntary. Physiologists regard the inside of the alimentary tract, a tube with valves and enlargements, as continuous with the skin of the outside of the body.

Once food is swallowed, a constriction in the esophagus starts behind it and, as it progresses, forces the bolus (lump) of food into the stomach. The progress may be upward. A dog drinks with its head downward, and the fluid is moved upward for some distance before it goes down into the stomach. The contractions that pass along the tube are called peristalsis.

The Stomach. The ingested food travels down the gullet and into the stomach, which has walls sufficiently elastic to accommodate the varying amounts of food swallowed, and this wavelike movement continues and mixes the stomach juices with the food. Here some digestion of food takes place through the action of glands that pour into the stomach an acid liquid that helps digest proteins and fats. Starch digestion, begun by salivary enzymes, stops when the food in the stomach becomes acid, but few animals rely on this kind of digestion.

The Intestines. When the exit valve of the stomach, the pylorus, opens, the food passes into the small intestine in sausagelike gobs produced by the constrictions of the stomach. Soon other constrictions may start and cut the sausages in half, but persistently this process pushes the intestinal contents along through the whole length of the intestine as digestion continues.

The duodenum, a thickened area of small intestine that starts at the stomach, receives via two ducts, or tubes, two important substances. One of these is bile, which is made in the liver and stored in the gallbladder. Bile breaks up fat into infinitesimal globules that have laxative effect on the food. The yellow substance that an animal vomits is both the stomach contents and the bile that has been forced backward into the stomach by regurgitation.

The second duct transmits more starch-digesting substances manufactured in the pancreas. These enzymes turn starches into dextrin, which, as the food is pushed along, is further broken down into glucose by another substance excreted by the small intestine itself. The glucose is then absorbed through the intestines and winds up in the bloodstream. Glucose is also the sugar of grapes and of corn syrup. And so in this way digestion transforms the carbohydrates in the food into a form transportable by the blood. Proteins and fats are also reduced to their component parts, amino acids and fatty acids; as such they too can pass through the intestinal walls and into the lymph and blood.

Absorption of materials from the intestine is increased by a unique arrangement. The velvety inner surface is studded with microscopic, short, hairlike projections called villi. Each one, while minute in itself, increases the surface of the intestine a little, and in the aggregate these tiny projections increase the area of the intestines immensely.

How the inside of an animal's intestine appears when magnified to show the villi. This arrangement increases the absorbing surface of the intestine enormously.

This efficient "factory" of the digestive system is like an automobile assembly line running backward, with the cars being taken to pieces bit by bit, instead of being built up. As it passes through the digestive system the whole mass of food that entered the mouth is reduced to its essential parts—fatty acids, glucose, and amino acids—and these disassembled products are absorbed into the blood.

The Liver. The liver is the largest solid organ of the body. It lies in front of the stomach and just behind the diaphragm, which is the partition separating the abdominal cavity from the thoracic cavity and is constantly massaged by the regular inhalations and exhalations caused by breathing. The healthy liver is dark red with a glistening surface and several lobes, the number depending on the species.

The activities of the liver are not limited to digestion; it is also a prime organ of regulation and manufacture. Bile, as we have said, comes from the liver. Besides aged red blood cells, bile contains bile salts, cholesterol, lecithin, fat, mucin, and pigments. Urea, another liver product, is made by converting ammonia left over from protein metabolism (chemical changes). Bacteria are destroyed in the liver to some extent, too, as they are in the lymphatic system and spleen.

The liver is essential as a sugar regulator for the body. If, for example, glucose were absorbed from the intestine in greater quantities than the body could use, the liver would then change it into glycogen (animal starch) and store it. When the blood sugar level drops too low, the liver obliges by releasing glucose from the conversion of the glycogen.

When the gall duct, or gallbladder, becomes obstructed or the bile cannot escape, the pigment gets into the blood, causing the skin to turn a yellow color. Jaundice, as it is called, is not a disease but a condition or a symptom.

Another function of the liver is the absorption of fat, which is deposited in the tissues of the body to be used when needed.

The Pancreas. We cannot leave the subject of digestion without mentioning important functions of the pancreas. Besides furnishing enzymes (digestive ferments), the pancreas regulates the power of the body to handle blood sugar. In this task it functions with the liver, which, as we have seen, stores up or liberates glucose. Tiny cells called the islets of Langerhans in the pancreas manufacture insulin, a substance that in some unknown way regulates the percentage of glucose in the blood. If there is too much, it causes the liver to store it; if too little, the pancreas sees that glucose is called out. A lack of insulin causes *diabetes mellitus*, or sugar diabetes. The excess sugar escapes into the urine and may be measured. The disease also causes an increase in thirst and in the amount of urine excreted.

Final Steps in Digestion. What remains of the food after it has traveled through the small intestine is deposited through a valve into the large intestine. Here excess water is absorbed, and a huge growth of bacteria takes place. In some species it has been estimated that over half the feces is living and dead bacteria. The more unassimilated food ending up in the colon, the more there is for bacteria to work on. There are also more products of bacteria to be absorbed by the body along with the surplus water. This is another good reason for not overfeeding and underexercising pets.

THE GLANDULAR SYSTEM AND REGULATION OF BODY FUNCTIONS

Blood also acts as a vehicle for transporting substances known as hormones, produced by the body regulators, only one of which we have thus far considered—the pancreas. For the most part, these regulators are ductless glands, that is, glands lacking an outlet except back into the blood. Though the spleen and lymph glands are also ductless, they do not, as far as we know, secrete hormones. The important, strictly ductless glands are the pituitary, adrenal, thymus, thyroid, and parathyroid. Salivary glands are good examples of ordinary glands because they have ducts that lead their products away from the glands; in this case, saliva is secreted into the mouth.

Some glands, like the pancreas, are a combination of ductless and ordinary glands and are considered body regulators. The important mixed ductless and ordinary glands are the pancreas, ovaries, and testicles.

The Pituitary. Probably most important as a body regulator is the double-lobed pituitary gland located at the base of the brain, to which it is attached by a stalk. It is incredible that such a tiny organ could be capable of performing the feats it does. Yet its direct and indirect chemical influence on other glands and organs directs them to extraordinary accomplishments. Among its capabilities, it can

cause an animal to come into heat;
make an unmaternal animal become maternal;
affect the shedding of the coat;
cause a pregnant female to commence labor;
stimulate growth and cause giantism, if overactive;
cause stunted growth, if underactive;
cause sexual development;
help regulate metabolism of carbohydrates;
cause overfatness, if underactive;
raise blood pressure.

Because it is so potent, the amount of pituitary hormone required for these tasks is very small.

The Adrenal Glands. The adrenal glands, situated near the kidneys, are also known as the suprarenal glands. They produce epinephrine— also called adrenaline—a potent chemical that regulates blood pressure by its effect on the heart and blood vessels right down to the capillaries. These glands also determine in some manner the amount of salt in the urine and affect the use of fat and sugar. Their outer layers secrete a substance now being used in the treatment of arthritis.

The Thyroid. The thyroid gland lies in the neck on either side of the windpipe. It is attached to the larynx, so that with every swallowing movement the thyroid is also moved. It secretes an important chemical regulator, thyroxin, which is known to contain about 60 percent iodine. Animals whose diets are low in iodine content become sick, and some young animals develop cretinism—a peculiar abnormality not often seen among pets—they become dwarfed, stupid, slow, dull, and gross in appearance.

Thyroxin regulates the metabolism, or speed of living, in any animal. Slow, sluggish animals, overweight and phlegmatic, respond with quicker actions, more rapid pulse, restlessness, and sleeplessness when given this hormone. When the gland secretes too much of its regulating substance, the animal becomes nervous, develops a ravenous appetite, wastes away, and exhibits protruding eyeballs and usually an increase in the size of the gland itself. (Any such increase is called goiter in man or in animals.)

Parathyroids. Located beside the two parts of the thyroid are two small glands, the parathyroids, whose function is the regulation of calcium metabolism. If they are removed, a condition known as tetany, involving violent trembling, is established and death ensues. It has been thought that they are also concerned with eclampsia, characterized by trembling and rigidity in nursing mothers. Injections of parathyroid extract increase the percentage of calcium in the blood, even when none is fed, by forcing the body processes to draw it from the bones.

The Ovaries. Located behind the kidneys in bitches are the ovaries, small organs with several functions, the most important of which is the perpetuation of the species. But we will discuss this more fully in Chapter 5. Here we are dealing with the secretions that regulate the animal's behavior.

The ovaries influence body development even before reproductive functions begin. They control even such a thing as mental interest. If the ovaries are removed long before sexual maturity, an animal grows somewhat ungainly and tends to put on fat more than a littermate whose ovaries have not been removed. This propensity continues through life. The animal also tends to become an intersex. A female chick grows hackle feathers like a cock; a female puppy loses some of the charm and grace of the whole bitch; a female kitten tends to grow larger and lazier than her whole sisters.

Working in cooperation with the pituitary, the ovaries initiate the sex cycle (though there is some question as to which gland is of greater importance). Once the cycle begins, the behavior of the female in heat is determined by an ovary-secreted hormone in the blood known as the follicular hormone. This hormone produces the swelling of the vulva, the bleeding well known in bitches, and, after several days, the desire for mating.

The Testicles. Besides producing sperm, the testicles secrete the male hormone, testosterone, which functions in connection with the pituitary gland. Some grave errors were made in the use of testosterone in the mistaken notion that it stimulated the testicles to greater activity. It was administered in great quantities until it was learned that the use of testosterone actually lessened testicle activity and caused the deterioration of the testicles. It was found that the pituitary gland's secretions caused testicle activity and production of testosterone, which in turn affected the maleness of the animal. Some good stud animals have been at least temporarily sterilized by the indiscriminate use of testosterone.

THE REPRODUCTIVE SYSTEM

The sex organs exist as a means of producing the next generation. Eggs are produced by the female, sperm by the male. When an egg and a sperm unite a new being is started. The process of multiplying and dividing begins. Mammals are arranged so that the fertilized egg or eggs develop within the female.

Female Organs. The female's ovaries contain her heritage—the germ plasm of which she is the custodian and that created her. At certain intervals the ovaries produce eggs in blisterlike follicles. The eggs are conducted to a resting place, the uterus, but before they arrive they can be fertilized by the sperm, a tiny tadpolelike cell containing the male's heredity. This heredity from the male is in a form so small we would have to magnify it a hundred times to be able to see even its crudest details.

The uterus in which the fertilized eggs rest is an organ of various shapes in the different species. In the bitch it consists of a short stem and two long horns, something like the letter *Y*. At the lower end of the uterus is a muscular ring known as the cervix. The cervix also constitutes the upper end of the vagina, that part of the reproductive tract into which the penis of the male is inserted during copulation. Close to the opening of the vagina (the vulva) is the clitoris, a small glandular organ known to be the female equivalent of the penis. If a female puppy is regularly injected with enough male sex hormone, this clitoris will grow to be almost as large as the penis of a male of the same species. The function of the clitoris in mammals is not known. Being of erectile tissue, it becomes somewhat enlarged at times. Probably it assists in making the sexual act pleasant for the animals and, if so, is helpful in stimulating procreation.

The vulva, which is located below the anus, is the termination of the reproductive system of the female. Into it urine is discharged, so that the organ actually serves two functions. During the mating cycle, the vulva enlarges considerably.

The breasts of the female mammal are the milk-producing glands of the skin. The process of milk production, or lactation, has given rise to a number of misconceptions. Except for a small amount held in a reservoir, milk is not made up in advance and then drained out. Rather it is produced by the breasts from blood while the young are nursing. Otherwise the breasts could not possibly contain the amounts of milk required to feed the average litter. At first, little or no milk may come forth, but eventually it may come so fast in some animals that it actually has been known to flow freely from teats to which no young are attached. This is because the mother exerts an involuntary pressure that forces the milk out easily.

Bitches have been known to produce up to five quarts of milk a day, proportionally outproducing the world-champion Holstein cow, who would have to give three hundred quarts to equal a five-quart-a-day bitch (the best cow on record has given no more than eighty). When it comes to butterfat, the bitch's milk is nearly three times as rich, so she is an infinitely better producer.

Male Organs. The male organs are pairs of the following: the *testicle*, in which the sperm are produced; an *epididymis*, in which they are stored and which is connected directly on the outside of the testicle; and a *vas deferens*, through which the sperm are transported to a common duct. Unlike humans, most male pet animals have no seminal vesicle. The vas deferens from one testicle joins the one from the other

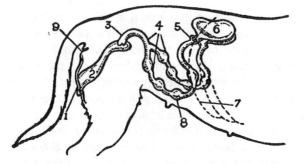

Reproductive system of a bitch. (1) Vulva. (2) Vagina. (3) Cervix. (4) Uterus. (5) Ovary. (6) Kidney. (7) Location of ribs. (8) Lump consisting of embryo and placenta. (9) Anus.

side, and the *urethra* forms the passage by which the sperm are discharged during copulation. The penis runs out through the pelvis, under the anus, bends around between the hind legs, and emerges through its covering, the sheath. In mammals, the testicles must be located outside of the body since body temperature is sufficient to prevent the production of sperm. A strong muscle draws the testicle up close to the body if the external temperature is too cold, and lets it down when it is hot.

In puppies, the testicles are descended at birth, which is not the case in some species—humans, for example—in which they descend considerably later through two slits in the abdominal muscles. Each testicle, besides having the vas deferens leading away, has a vein and artery and a muscle (the cremaster), which together compose the spermatic cord. This enters the body through the same opening in the abdomen through which the testicles descend.

Many mammals, including dogs, have a bone in their penis. Called the os penis, it adds rigidity to an erection but it can be the cause of problems if a bladder stone, or calculus, descends the urethra to become lodged at the os penis. The urethra passes through part of this bone and at that point the urethra cannot expand. This bone very occasionally is fractured by an injury.

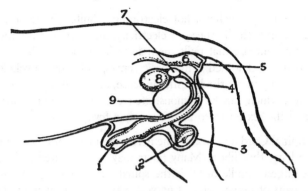

Reproductive system and related organs of a male. (1) Penis. (2) Testicle. (3) Scrotum. (4) Pelvis. (5) Anus. (6) Rectum. (7) Prostate. (8) Bladder. (9) Vas deferens.

THE NERVOUS SYSTEM AND ORGANS OF PERCEPTION

The nerves may be thought of as the telegraph wires of the body. Thousands of miles of these fibers control the body's activities. They stimulate the muscles to contract, and each of even the tiniest muscles has its nerve supply. The brain is the central station from which the nerves radiate through several pathways, the principal one being the spinal cord. Most of the conscious body movements are regulated by the brain and spinal cord. These two organs are exceedingly well protected, entirely enclosed in bone—the skull and spine.

Nerves carry impulses to the brain from distant parts of the body, such as the delicate nerves in the skin which telegraph messages via other nerves to the brain. Feeling is a function of these nerves of the skin—sensitivity to temperature, to electrical stimuli, to wetness or dryness, to sharpness, as in the case of a pin prick. Some diseases— rabies, for example—may destroy the skin's sensitivity, so that a rabid animal may not even feel the bites of another animal.

Whereas telegraph wires carry messages both ways, nerves conduct impulses in only one direction, some *to* the brain and some *away from* it. Suppose a dog touches a hot electric light bulb. The sense organs alert the brain with the speed of electricity, and instantly the muscles are given an impulse that pulls them away from the hot object.

We used to acknowledge five basic senses, but today psychologists recognize many more: the kinesthetic sense, or muscle sense; the sense of balance, which can be demonstrated even while animals are embryos; and the sex sense, to mention only a few.

The Spinal Cord and Brain. The nerves are unlike other cells in that they are long, thin fibers. Many fibers may be associated in bundles, and the largest bundle of all is the spinal cord, which gives out and takes in pairs of nerves (cranial nerves) between every vertebra of the backbone. The bundles of fibers branch here and there (the trunk divides into branches) until the final divisions are tiny individual fibers innervating some small area of the body.

In addition to the spinal cord there are other nerves that leave the brain and extend to organs and other parts of the body. All of the body —organs, muscles, glands, the intestines—is controlled by the spinal cord and by these cranial nerves.

For every sensitive area in the body there is a corresponding center in the brain. When a dog has a twitch in a leg, it is difficult to realize that the origin of that twitch is a part of the brain or spinal cord. Nor, when we see a pet scratch, do we think that a nerve somewhere in the skin telegraphed the brain, which set in motion the pet's hind leg. Have you ever scratched a dog on its back close to the tail and observed the animal immediately scratch its shoulder? This is due to the so-called reflex action. A human knee jerk is a reflex, and animals are not unlike us in having such areas. Anyone who has groomed a Scottish Terrier knows that there is a large patch on each of its sides that, when combed or clipped, makes the dog scratch involuntarily.

Contrasted to that of a human, the brain of a dog is very small, chiefly because the fore part, called the cerebrum, is relatively so much smaller in all lower animals. The positive, willing, conscious actions are evolved in this portion of the brain. Involuntary living is a concern of the rear part, called the cerebellum. There are other parts, most of which, like the two already mentioned, are arranged in pairs.

Without the cerebrum, animals can function mechanically but have no memory, can't learn, and lack the will to do anything. Their existence is almost like that of what we consider a human vegetable. They can breathe, eat if their faces are held over the pan, defecate, urinate, sleep, wander aimlessly around, bite or growl when hurt. But by the way some of our pets are trained (or not trained) one might conclude that all they had were cerebellums.

The cerebrum is the part of the brain that responds most to training. Let no one think a pet can have its brain "cluttered up" by training. Once a pet learns what is wanted of it and is properly rewarded, each succeeding act or trick is easier to teach than the previous one. The most highly educated dogs find learning easier and easier. Unfortunately our pets do not live long enough: just as they become "almost human" mentally, they break down physically and die or must be destroyed.

The Eye. The eye is, surprisingly, far less complex and much tougher than most people believe it to be. Its parts include the cornea, the large, round, transparent area. Surrounding this is a ring of glistening clear white tissue, the sclera. In the lower part of the eye socket some animals, including dogs, have a third eyelid, the nictitating membrane. Inside the socket, next to the nose, dogs have glandular tissue that often becomes inflamed and causes the membrane to protrude and exhibit a swollen, red, spongy-looking tumor. This usually has to be removed surgically.

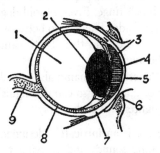

Cross section of the eye. (1) Vitreous humor. (2) Lens. (3) Iris. (4) Aqueous humor. (5) Cornea. (6) Lids. (7) Sclera. (8) Retina. (9) Optic nerve.

In the middle of the eye we see the pupil. This is only a name for an opening between the two chambers of the eye. The pupils get larger or smaller, depending on the amount of light the eye needs for vision, or by drug action, or brain disease. An animal looking at a bright light shows a very small pupil; when there is less light or darkness, the pupil enlarges. If its vision is unimpaired, a dog shows a round spot. The colored tissue around the pupil is called the iris. It ranges in pets from pearl, yellow, green, and blue in some to blood color in albinos and dark brown in still others; a dog may have two different-colored eyes, but this is rare.

Behind the pupil lies the lens. It is tough, fibrous, and crystalline. Through it light rays are bent so that the image comes to rest on a sensitive nerve-laden area behind the lens, known as the retina. The retinal nerves in turn transmit visual images via the optic nerve to the brain.

People so often think that scratches on the cornea constitute a cataract that it should be stated that a cataract is an *opacity in the lens.* When you look at the pupil and see a cloudy or white area it may be a cataract. As the normal pupil should enlarge and contract with a change of light, the cataractus pupil will react to light also, but it appears white no matter how dilated or contracted the iris is. Really all we see is the white lens, since, as we have said, the pupil is actually an opening in front of it.

The color of the pupil is a good indicator of a dog's age. The pupil of a young dog will be a dark clear blue whereas a very old dog, free of cataracts, will have nearly white pupils. Dogs of intermediate ages show gradations of the whitish tinge. Five-year-old dogs show enough white so the blue is a lighter shade. There is no better way of roughly approximating a mature dog's age than this. Teeth cannot be relied upon to reveal the age of the adult.

Dogs, like most domesticated mammals, are color-blind (that is, they see colors as shades of gray) and so can distinguish a bright red from a dark green as only lighter and darker gray.

The Ear. As the eye is an intricately designed organ, so is the ear, the device for catching sounds and carrying the impressions to the brain through nerves. The four-legged animal has cupped erect ears to enable it to pick up distant or faint sounds. When the head is turned, the sounds can be picked up in the same manner as by a trumpet or radar antenna. The sounds are conducted downward through the external canal. Surely most pet owners have looked down into their pets' ears, probably cleaned them, and know the projections to be found there. And that is all of the ear most people know about. They may often wonder about the possibility of piercing the eardrum when they are cleaning the canal. As long as they clean downward, they do no harm. The canal becomes smaller at the bottom, then turns inward slightly and terminates in a very delicate membrane, the eardrum. The rest of the ear is within the solid bone of the skull.

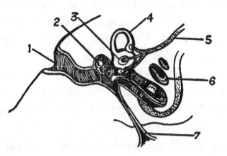

Cross section of the ear. (1) Auditory opening and canal. (2) Middle ear with mechanism for feeling vibrations. (3) Tympanum. (4) Semicircular canal. (5) Auditory nerve. (6) Cochlea (a spiral represented in sections). (7) Eustachian tube.

Behind the eardrum are three tiny delicate bones which constitute a remarkable mechanism activated by sound vibrations. The three bones transmit these vibrations, via the semicircular canal, to nerves which in turn carry them to the brain via the auditory nerve. From the small cavity (the middle ear) in which the three bones are found, a tube called the Eustachian tube runs into the throat. Its function is to equal-ize pressure on the eardrum. If we travel up a mountain, or under a river in a subway, we may feel a sensation in our middle ear. If we swallow, the pressure is relieved or, in other words, equalized. If it were not for this provision, the delicate eardrum might be broken by abrupt changes in atmospheric pressure.

Suppose some ear medicine is dropped into the ear canal of a dog. The canal is rubbed and squeezed by the fingers to mix the wax with the medicine. While that is being done, the pet sticks out its tongue as if it has experienced an unpleasant taste. Perhaps we open its mouth and smell its breath: there is the odor of the medicine. This is a certain indication that the eardrum is broken. Some of the worst cases of ear disease, and the hardest to cure, are due to infections in the middle ear.

When the eardrum is broken, special medicines are required to effect a cure.

The Nose. That part of an animal's face that we call the nose is only a small part of its smelling apparatus; all the important parts are out of sight. These consist of a complicated pair of cavities with a partition, or septum, between. The front part is called the anterior nares; the back part, the posterior nares. The bones of the face cover the anterior nares. This cavity is called the vestibule.

In warm-blooded pets the inspired air passes through the vestibule and thence through a convoluted, shell-like arrangement made up of turbinate bones covered with erectile tissue that can become engorged with blood. A mucous membrane overlies this tissue.

When the air is cold, the erectile tissue fills with extra blood, which helps to warm the air before it passes to the lungs. The arrangement of bones and erectile tissue also filters the air at all times, removing dust and bacteria from it.

Before an animal can smell anything, an odor (which is actually a gas) must be dissolved in the watery secretion that is present in the olfactory organs. A chemical stimulus received by large numbers of nerve fibers terminating in olfactory hairs in the mucous membrane goes to the brain via the olfactory nerve. At the first stimulus or acknowledgment of the new odor, most animals begin to sniff, which, of course, brings more of the odor into contact with the mucous membranes where it dissolves. The stimulation is thereby increased.

It is difficult for us to realize how minute an amount of odor is required to effect this extraordinary recognition in dogs. When we see a Pointer smell a bird perhaps fifty yards away or a Bloodhound follow a three-day-old human foot track, we know that the smelling ability of these animals is of a different order from ours. Not a little research has been done on scent and the conditions under which scenting is most efficiently done. Wind direction and velocity, moisture content of the air, and the strength of the stimulus are all important factors. So is heredity; it is quite well established that certain breeds excel in scenting ability. How much of this ability is actual scenting keenness and how much is tenacity has not yet been determined.

Even dogs with a poor sense of smell must live in a world of aromas much different from ours. When exposed to an aroma diluted until people could no longer smell it, Labrador Retrievers could identify it immediately when diluted twenty thousand times.

3

What You Should Know About Food and Feeding

Animals are usually divided into three classes—flesh-eating (carnivorous), plant- and seed-eating (herbivorous), and those that eat both plant and animal matter (omnivorous). These classifications are made not only on the basis of the food the animals eat, but also on the characteristics of their teeth and digestive apparatuses as well.

The distinction between these three general types of animals is not so sharp and clear as most people think. There can be no doubt, of course, about the group to which some animals belong. Having observed large numbers of rabbits and cavies without finding a single instance in which they ate food of animal origin—even crickets—the scientist can be certain that they are as herbivorous as the cow or deer. But the classification of most household pets is a different matter. The layperson is likely to think of dogs, cats, rats, and raccoons, for example, as carnivorous animals. The zoologist, however, very properly considers them omnivores, because he has observed that they eat *every part* of the animals they catch—including the partially digested vegetable matter in the intestines. Despite the fact that dogs' teeth are typical of carnivorous animals, well-adapted to tearing the flesh and puncturing the skull and vital organs of the smaller animals on which they may prey, studies have shown that dogs, as well as many doglike animals, are nearly as omnivorous as we are. With one notable exception, there is practically nothing that humans eat that these animals cannot digest as well as humans. This one exception is, as we have seen in Chapter 2, that, since dogs bolt their food, they must have certain starchy foods crushed for them. When wild dogs consume the stomach and intestinal contents of their prey, they are getting the benefit of the chewing and mastication that has already occurred.

Today we are beginning to doubt whether any of our pets, in fact, can live on flesh alone without deficiency diseases developing sooner or later. It is fortunate that our dogs *can* assimilate foods of vegetable origin. It may become increasingly important in the future, when the earth has more people and less to feed them.

Nearly all the information we have about nutrition has been provided by the great laboratories of the world since 1900. And much of our knowledge of food values and human nutritional needs has resulted from feeding experiments with pets. Yet we have been extremely slow in applying this knowledge to the care of household animals. As we read through a volume on dogs published in 1872, we found that the directions given in the section on feeding are just about what many dog owners think is the proper way to feed a dog today! There is no excuse for not keeping up-to-date. We have put into daily practice innumerable scientific findings with regard to our own food requirements, but we still cling stubbornly to outdated ideas in feeding our dogs.

No one should assume, of course, that because we are interested in adopting scientific methods in the feeding of animals that we intend to depart from their natural habits and tendencies. We have previously stressed the point that if we want to keep pets healthy and happy, it is essential that we understand and consider their native inclinations. A dog is a dog, we said, not a human being. Nobody would want to take an old meat-covered bone, scratch a hole in the ground, bury the bone, and later dig it up and eat it. It might not hurt us to eat it; it seldom hurts a dog. But, being human, we have other preferences. To a dog, however, that old bone is a delicacy which it finds much more tasty than breast of chicken or devitalized dog biscuits. Whereas it is true that we should interfere as little as possible with an animal's natural mode of life, it is also true that when we refuse to use what knowledge we have of its care we are being foolish and wasteful.

We know that modern dogs differ from their remote ancestors because human selection of certain odd characteristics has made them most unnatural in many respects. Their mildness and ease of domestication are the most interesting illustrations of that fact. No similar form of animal can be domesticated to such a degree of dependability as the dog. Many of what we consider the finest characteristics of dogs and many of those most useful to us are the very ones that would make them unable to survive if they were suddenly dropped back into a wild existence. Can you imagine a sweet, lovable, long-haired Japanese Spaniel living and reproducing if it were raised by a she-wolf in the natural environment of wolves?

Dogs have been evolved to be useful to man, and while they were being developed they lived closely enough to man to share his food. They became accustomed to it as time went on, and those that could not manage it died off, while those that could lived and reproduced. Partially as a result of that selection, we find that dogs, large and small, today thrive on an almost unbelievable variety of diets—such a wide variety of diets, indeed, that we may safely say they can digest anything a human can digest. So the problem boils down to how to feed our pets *best* and most *completely* with the foods we have available, rather than to consider what they *must* be fed.

DIGESTION AND DIETARY NEEDS

Let us see first how our dogs' digestive apparatuses differ from our own. Starting at the mouth, we find that the teeth are different. The teeth useful for ripping an animal apart and cutting the tissue off are longer and sharper than the equivalent teeth in our mouths. Our back teeth (molars) are flatter and more useful for grinding foods into powder. Dogs' habits of eating consist of tearing their food apart, cutting off pieces with the back teeth, and gulping them with only sufficient chewing to make them small enough to swallow.

The next difference is in the saliva. We have a starch-digesting enzyme, *ptyalin*—now called *salivary amylase*—which contributes to the conversion of starch into sugar. Dogs, on the other hand, have very little of that enzyme. It was this discovery years ago that caused people studying dogs' eating habits to say that they couldn't digest starch. Probably these people never saw a human wash down a huge mouthful of a doughnut with a gulp of coffee—and stopped to think that that too is digested.

Let's see how starch digestion works both for man and for our dogs. Our pets' stomachs secrete somewhat stronger juice than do ours. For example, a bone ingested into a healthy dog's stomach becomes soft and pliable in less than an hour. This bone is acted upon by this stronger juice which is rich in hydrochloric acid and pepsin, and it actually dissolves in the stomach. Actually the same thing might happen in the human stomach, but it would take much longer.

Upon leaving the stomach the food in a dog is mixed with the same kind of juices—pancreatic enzyme and bile—which affect our food. Here, then, is where most of the digestion of starch takes place. The human who washes down the half-chewed doughnut and the dog who gulps its starchy meal both live and thrive because digestion takes place in the small intestine. But this is the important difference: we usually chew our foods, so that we crack starchy grains and nuts into a fine paste, but the dog doesn't. When the pancreatic enzyme (amylase) works on these starches in our case, they are so fine that the enzyme has little trouble breaking them down. In the dog, when the starchy foods are fed in too large lumps, the enzyme cannot do its work effectively. To some degree the same thing happens in the human digestive tract if a person fails to chew a nut or a kernel of sweet corn—neither is digested anymore than it would be by a dog. Occasionally a dog will regurgitate any such indigestible material, but more often it will not.

In feeding dogs it has been found that it indeed pays to feed either very finely ground raw starch or precooked starches. Cornmeal fed raw is an inefficient food, but cornmeal that has been boiled until the starch granules have been cracked open, so that they are vulnerable to the attack of the amylase, is an efficient, if incomplete food. Another point of difference between dog owners and their dogs is the length of the small intestine. Food travels through it more quickly in dogs and there is less time for absorption—another reason for feeding easily digested foods. Cereals, vegetables, and fruits should be cooked to facilitate digestion. Meats are digested as easily raw.

Now, there are certain known requirements that must be met in the diet of every dog of every breed. These are the essentials without which our pets develop nutritional deficiencies. First of all it is obvious that a dog must have *enough* food. This is another way of saying that there must be sufficient food to furnish energy for its daily life. We measure this energy in the food by burning it in a device called a calorimeter to see how many heat units it holds. The heat units are called *calories*. It is now known how many calories any resting animal of a given size requires. An animal needs more, of course, as it exercises or works more. Living, exercise, or work all require energy, and this energy is extracted from the food. If a dog gets too few calories it will live on its fat; in other words, it'll get thin. If it gets too many, it may discard the surplus in the feces or use some to make fat to store for a time when its food will be scanty. Laypeople often forget that the pet doesn't have to consume food to obtain nourishment when it is carrying it around in the form of fat. We will discuss this further when we take up the very common problem of how to reduce a pet's weight.

When we read charts indicating how many calories a dog must have, we are reminded of the old adage, "The only consistent feature of nature is inconsistency." The charts are an average of thousands of animals studied and, moreover, are studies done on research animals maintained in kennels. The caloric requirements of most house dogs are often at considerable variance with the suggestions on the dog food containers. We have clients with both a giant breed and a shepherd-size dog in the same house and both eat exactly the same amount of food. Both are walked on leashes, which is no exercise, and both are the same age and normal weight.

Instead of using charts, there is a simple way to determine the amount of a given food your dog needs. Look at the dog—is it too heavy? Too thin? Needless to say, if it is too heavy you have too heavy a hand with its food. If too thin, increase the total amount fed or add a little animal or vegetable fat.

Speaking of fat, all too many dogs are fed fat-deficient diets. We know puppies drink their mother's milk which contains three times the fat found in cow's milk. They are often weaned on cow's milk and may be kept on low-fat diets all their lives. Many dogs with unhealthy skin and coats show marked improvement within two weeks when adequate fat is added to their diets. On the other hand, some cannot tolerate much fat.

FOOD FALLACIES

Anyone who is really interested in feeding his or her dog properly should discard the notions that dogs can't digest starches or sugars; that they can't digest fats; that they must have lean, raw meat; that if a dog doesn't like something it is bad for it and, conversely, that whatever it likes is good for it. Along with these should go other common misconceptions, such as "milk makes worms," "potatoes cause skin rashes," "garlic eliminates intestinal parasites," "raw egg white makes a dog's coat shine," certain foods "overheat the blood," and "sulfur in drinking water keeps dogs healthy." None of these is true. They are all fallacies that for years have prevented people from feeding their pets intelligently.

VARIETY IN DIETS

The average one-dog owner whose pet is fed canned or dried foods, or table scraps with some meat added, will scarcely credit some of the "diets" on which dogs have been maintained in good health. Here are a few, showing simply the diversity of foods that dogs *can* digest.

In Scandinavia a dog breeder feeds his dogs mostly cooked whole fish with a little cooked grain.

In Kentucky a fox hunter leads an old mule or worn-out cow over the hill, shoots it, and lets his hounds live on the carcass until only the larger bones remain. Usually the organs and intestinal contents are first to disappear.

At a large university the physiology department feeds its dogs cane sugar, lard, bone ash, casein, vitamin concentrates, and a mineral mixture.

A certain chick hatchery owner feeds his dogs infertile cooked eggs and stale doughnuts from a nearby bakery, with alfalfa-leaf meal mixed in.

A Maine potato farmer gives his dogs boiled small potatoes in their jackets, mashed and mixed with hamburger and alfalfa meal.

We have fed our dogs a diet of dehydrated dog food in meal form and nothing else but water.

During World War II many United States Army dogs were fed on horsemeat and cornmeal boiled together.

Stray dogs live after a fashion by rummaging through garbage pails.

And then again we know of one overzealous dog owner who prepared the following menu for her pet: *Breakfast:* two crumbled zwieback slices, yolks of two raw eggs, one glass of milk, one vitamin capsule, one calcium gluconate tablet, and two yeast tablets. *Lunch:* one half cup of kibbled dog biscuit soaked in a cup of warm soup made with parsley and fresh, canned, or frozen spinach, together with one jar of baby's liver soup, and one fried lamb chop trimmed of all fat, diced in cubes with one teaspoonful of cod-liver oil added. *Supper:* six tablespoonfuls of diced top round, two ounces of tomato juice, one tablespoonful of limewater, one half cup of cooked vegetables, and one half cup of kibbled biscuits soaked in warm water. *Late evening:* two puppy biscuits, two lumps of dog candy, and a bowl of milk. Though the dog flourished, it was very overweight.

A neighbor of this woman buys kibbled dog biscuits, soaks them, mixes cooked vegetables and meat with them, and feeds the mixture to her dog once a day with good results.

Another dog owner on the same street opens cans of dog food, spoons out the contents, and her pet thrives on it.

Besides having enough food, our pets need these essentials: water, minerals, amino acids, fatty acids, fiber, and vitamins. Some species can live without consuming certain essentials that other species must have. (Cavies need vitamin C; dogs make their own.) Knowing what the requirements are makes feeding simpler and at the same time permits us to ensure that our dogs get enough of everything.

WATER

That water is essential to living is obvious. Blood, the all-important carrier of nutrition to the cells, consists mostly of water. And the absence of water leads to dehydration, dry mouth, dry skin, sunken eyes. Besides its internal uses, the evaporation of water helps regulate body temperature.

Fortunately, supplying water is so easy that it is usually not a problem. A bowl of water from which the pet can drink at will is all it needs. If there is enough water in the pet's food, it is satisfied; if the food is of such a type that the pet must have additional water, it drinks from the bowl.

A dog drinks to replenish water lost by its system. Normally about 20 percent of this loss (more in hot weather) passes out as vapor with the breath. Almost all the rest is eventually passed in the urine.

Seventy percent of our pets' bodies is water. Here are the percentages of the individual parts:

Teeth	10	Brain	79
Cartilages	55	Blood	88
Bones	60	Urine	93
Skin	72	Lymph	96

| Muscles | 75 | Gastric Juice | 97 |
| Ligaments | 77 | Saliva | 99 |

The water content of foods varies greatly. The juiciest meat contains about 75 percent water. So do many brands of canned dog food. Dehydrated meals and baked biscuits contain about 7 to 10 percent water. If they are dried below that level, they often absorb enough water from the air to build back up to the 7 to 10 percent level. It follows that some feeding schedules require a greater water intake than others. High water consumption, rather than indicating kidney disease or diabetes, as some pet owners surmise, often means that the diet is too dry. Conversely, dogs fed soft-moist products containing about 25 percent water will drink less than those dogs on dry diets. Since canned foods contain about 74 percent water, dogs on this diet need little supplemental water. But remember the inconsistencies of nature and be assured some healthy dogs in similar environments eating similar diets will consume different amounts of water.

And we have been asked by dog owners whether it is harmful if their dogs eat snow. Not at all. Some dogs prefer it. In the Far North dogs eat snow as they would food. Even in areas where water and snow are simultaneously available, dogs often prefer snow.

MINERALS

A chemical element is a substance made up of atoms and cannot be decomposed by chemical means. Some of these elements are minerals, some gases. Most of a dog's nutrition is in combinations of elements, very complicated combinations, chemically.

Minerals make up about 6 percent of an animal's body in these proportions

Calcium	40	%
Phosphorus	22	%
Potassium	5	%
Sulphur	4	%
Chlorine	3	%
Sodium	2	%
Magnesium	0.7	%

with many trace minerals in lesser amounts. Among these are: iron, manganese, copper, iodine, zinc, cobalt, fluorine, boron.

Table I THE FUNCTIONS AND SOURCES OF MINERALS

MINERAL	FUNCTION IN BODY	PRINCIPAL SOURCES
Calcium		
90% is in the	Bone building	Bones and bonemeal
bones	Rickets preventive	Alfalfa-leaf meal
1% in circulation	Blood component	Milk
Stored in body	Reproduction	
	Lactation	
	Muscle function	
	Nerve function	
	Heart function	
	Tooth component	
Phosphorus		
Bones, blood, mus-	Bone building	Cereals
cles, and teeth	Rickets preventive	Meat
	Tooth component	Fish
	Carbohydrate metabo-	Bones
	lism	Milk
	Fat metabolism	So abundant in pet
	Blood component	foods it should be
	Liquid content of	of little concern
	tissues	to pet owners
Potassium		
	Body fluid regulator	Blood
	Helps regulate blood	Potatoes
	Muscular function	Vegetables
Sulphur		
Minute amounts re-	Body regulation	Meat
quired but needed		Egg yolk
regularly		Any food that when
Combination in		decomposed smells
salts as sulfates		like bad eggs
Chlorine		
Found in combina-	Component of gastric	Table salt
tion with sodium	juice	Blood
and hydrogen	Blood regulator	
	Regulates body fluids	
	Component of urine	

MINERAL	FUNCTION IN BODY	PRINCIPAL SOURCES
Sodium Found in combination with phosphorus, chlorine, and sulphur	Regulates body fluids Blood regulator Component of gastric juice Component of urine	Table salt Blood
Magnesium Needed only in minute amounts	Muscle activity Bone building Normal growth Nerve function Blood function	Bones Vegetables Epsom salts
Copper Needed only in minute amounts	Forms hemoglobin with iron	Blood Copper sulfate
Iodine Most is found in thyroid gland	Thyroid health and normal growth Regulates metabolism Prevents goiter and cretinism In formation of thyroxine	Foods grown in iodine-rich soils Iodized salt Fish meal made from saltwater fish Shellfish
Iron Composes only .004 of the body weight 65% is in the blood 30% is in the liver, bone marrow, and spleen 5% is in muscle tissue Needed in minute quantities Stored in body	Component of red blood cells Transports oxygen in blood	Egg yolk Liver Kidney Gizzard Heart Bone marrow

PROTEINS AND AMINO ACIDS

A second general group of essentials for every diet is proteins. These complex chemicals always have the element nitrogen as a component. All proteins are composed of amino acids, which contain the nitrogen hydroxide (NH_2) group in varying combinations.

There are twenty-two amino acids, each of which has been studied both for its composition and its essentiality. Of these, ten are absolutely essential to life and as far as is known must be part of the diet of all pets. These are: arginine, histidine, isoleucine, leucine, lysine, methionine, phenylalanine, threonine, tryptophane, valine. In Table II you will find some of the commoner proteins listed.

Two amino acids, cystine and methionine, contain sulphur. The most satisfactory way to feed sulphur is not as the element, because as such it is not absorbed, but as one of these two amino acids from which ample sulphur is available. Wheat, meat, fish, milk, yeast, and egg are excellent sources of both cystine and methionine.

The proteins found in various foods have unequal properties. Milk proteins possess all of the essential amino acids, and all are digestible. But corn, with its protein called zein, is not complete and is less valuable to feed to pets. Here, taking milk as a standard, are the relative values of the proteins found in some common animal foods:

Beef	104	Yeast	71
Milk	100	Casein	70
Fish	95	Peas	56
Rice	88	Wheat flour	40
Potato	79	Cornmeal	30

Most proteins contain more than one amino acid. Some proteins have one complete amino acid and others incomplete ones. Proteins, with their different assortments of amino acids, can be mixed to produce complete rations of amino acids. Cornmeal and horsemeat, milk and cereals, alfalfa with wheat or oat flour—all are compatible mixtures. Even meat protein can be supplemented to advantage. It is the mixtures of proteins that produce the almost limitless variety in diets, varying flavors, aromas, and appearances.

Protein Requirements. If we could feed just the minimum of complete proteins, the average adult dog of any breed could probably get along on a diet that included 4 to 6 percent of available protein, and the growing animal on 15 percent. Nearly all pet foods and rations contain over 20 percent of protein mixtures, some complete, some incomplete, some supplementing others so the results are excellent.

Protein is used primarily in building the body. Some is burned as energy, the nitrogen passing out in the urine, but protein foods, such as meat, are not primarily energy foods. Hunters mistakenly think they must feed their dogs great quantities of meat while the dogs are hunting but, as we shall see, all species get their energy best from fats and carbohydrates.

Table II lists the most important proteins together with their most common sources and some of their properties. It will be useful to those interested in checking the protein content of their pets' diets.

Table II SOME COMMON PROTEINS AND THEIR SOURCES

PROTEIN	RICH SOURCES	PROPERTIES

Albumin	Egg white
	Milk
	Meat
	Blood
		Soluble in water
		Does not precipitate
		  by dilute acids or
		  salts
		Coagulates when
		  boiled

Casein	Milk Cheese Cottage cheese	Does not coagulate when boiled Coagulated by renin Coagulated by pepsin Coagulated by acids

Fibrinogen	Blood	Soluble in weak salt
		  solutions
		Coagulated by heat
		Forms scabs
		Elastic
		Dissolved by weak
		  acids

PROTEIN	RICH SOURCES	PROPERTIES
Myesin	Muscle meat	Dissolved by weak acids Flexible only while alive Semifluid in consistency Coagulated by heat Shrinks Easily digested
Syntonin	Muscles and organs End product of digestion of other proteins by gastric juice	Dissolved by weak acids Step in digestion before a peptone
Peptone	End product of protein digestion by gastric juice	Leaves stomach and enters intestines after protein digestion Can diffuse through intestinal walls Has more hydrogen and oxygen than other proteins
Gelatine	Well distributed throughout animal body	Precipitated by tannic acid and alcohol 3% or more solidifies a batch of food; trick ingredient often used in dog food to give appearance of solid goodness Becomes solid by boiling
Chondrin	Ligaments Cartilage	Similar to gelatine in properties Requires longer boiling of the tissues that contain it to bring it out

PROTEIN	RICH SOURCES	PROPERTIES
Keratin	Horns Hair Nails Hoofs	Tough fibrinous indigestible, useless in pet feeding but sometimes found in foods Manufactured in hair follicles Contains much sulphur
Vegetable proteins	All vegetable matter Richest in seeds, especially legumes	Very similar to animal proteins In legumes one protein is found like albumin is in milk Some are like fibrinogen, some like albumin with similar properties

CARBOHYDRATES

All carbohydrates are derived from plants. The chlorophyll of the plant leaf (much like the hemoglobin in the animal's body) is able to take six parts of carbon dioxide (CO_2) from the air, combine it with five parts of water (H_2O), and produce starch, $C_6H_{10}O_5$, then have some remaining oxygen that it passes into the air. (Aquatic plants do the same thing but pass the surplus oxygen into the water, where it may be used by fish.) Starch granules are built up, layer on layer, the primary factor in nutrition. Plants add nitrogen to starch and make proteins.

The starch granule has two substances in its composition: cellulose and granulose. The cellulose is fiber and gives plants their rigidity. When boiled it becomes soft but does not dissolve. Granulose will dissolve in boiling water. We find the starch diffused all through plants, some in seeds, some in tubers or roots, and so forth. Some starchy food has large amounts of water (potatoes), some very small amounts (grains). When we buy starches we compare them on the basis of their dry components.

As a practical matter, it is important to remember this: raw starch is not soluble in cold water but it does dissolve in boiling water. However, about twenty times as much water must be added for the dissolving to take place. Mixed with an equal amount of water, it does not dissolve. Dissolving starch does not materially alter its composition, but when dissolved starch cools it becomes solid. This unimportant change explains why pet food canners like to add some starchy foods to their products before processing. Many of these products are excellent food but are not the solid goodness the buyer might think, since they are at least 70 percent water.

In order to make starch digestible for some species—dogs and cats—it is necessary to crack the granules by cooking. The starch can then be handled quite easily. Rabbits, cavies, and other animals digest part of the cellulose by enzymes in their bodies and liberate the soluble starch. Because lumps of potato were sometimes found in dogs' stools, it was once commonly believed that dogs couldn't digest starch. We now know, however, that when potatoes, carrots, or any other starch food is cooked and mashed, dogs can utilize it perfectly well.

Baking starch to 400° F changes it to *dextrin* (not dextrose)—a gummy, sweetish substance, not unlike sugar, that dissolves easily. Biscuits taste good to animals because the heat has converted the starch to dextrin. They are sweeter but actually very little different from starch; they have one more molecule of water (H_2O), $C_6H_{12}O_6$ where starch is $C_6H_{10}O_5$.

Starch is found in the animal liver and muscles as *glycogen* or animal starch. It is soluble in hot or cold water. Animals quickly convert vegetable starch into animal starch, and they are able also to convert protein into glycogen.

Fasting uses up stored glycogen, eating replaces it, and quickly. Within a few hours after a meal of starch there are abundant stores to be found in the liver. As it is circulated for the nourishment of the body, glycogen is converted into blood sugar, *glucose*. And, as the blood leaves the liver, it may contain as much as 3 percent glucose. Sometimes animals are fed so much sugar they cannot store it. The excess is found in the urine; allowances for this must be made in tests for diabetes.

Besides the starches there are several carbohydrates common to most diets.

Milk sugar (lactose) is found in its only natural liquid form in milk. It is not, as a matter of fact, particularly sweet. Lactose is the food of acidophilus bacteria in the intestine. Many very difficult cases of intestinal trouble have been greatly helped by the simple expedient of adding milk to the diet or some food like bread which has considerable milk in its composition. Lactose is easily dissolved by the acid digestive juice. Its action on the bowel is laxative, which explains the effect of skim milk.

Cane sugar is good for animals but spoils their appetites as candy spoils those of children. It is, of course, usually fed in artificial forms. Honey is composed of cane and fruit sugar. The latter is the sugar sweetest known to taste.

FATS

Fatty acids are carbohydrates in a sense—being composed of carbon, hydrogen, and oxygen—but they have much less oxygen and more carbon than starches.

Unlike proteins, fats contain no nitrogen. Like proteins, they too are combinations of components, known as fatty acids. Only three of these are essential as far as we now know—*linoleic, linolenic* and *arachnidic* acids, all believed to be concerned with our pets' health in several ways. All are so very common in nature they may be almost neglected in our thoughts of nutrition. Some other nonessential ones are *butyric, caproic, lauric, oleic, palmitic, stearic acids.*

Fats melt when heated; they are smooth, lubricating when warm. Some fats like tallow are comparatively hard and crystalline; some, like vegetable oils, are extremely soft and fluid. All are made by plants and the animal bodies.

Fats have a number of interesting properties which should be remembered by the dog owner.

Fats are able to emulsify; when acted on by bile salts, for instance, they can split into tiny invisible particles that remain in suspension in water or gastric juice.

Fat acts as a vehicle for carrying some of the vitamins—A, D, E, and K. Because of this, mineral oil can absorb them from food in the intestines and prevent their absorption.

Fat slows digestion and renders it more complete. It reduces the availability of vitamin B in the diet and is concerned with fertility.

A balanced diet should contain not less than 20 percent fat. An animal living on prey often eats 30 percent or more fat. The amount of fat animals can utilize depends on the amount of exercise they are getting. Sled dogs can eat pemmican consisting of 70 percent fat which would sicken a house dog. Bitches giving huge amounts of milk fat to their puppies need higher percentages in their food to remain in good condition while nursing a large litter.

Cows' milk, with the water omitted, contains about 25 percent fat; and milk is an excellent food for many pets—almost a criterion of what a food should be. But note that it contains a goodly amount of milk sugar. Feed milk sugar alone and the pet's stools become almost liquid. Feed fat alone and the same thing happens. Feed the two as whole milk and the stool is perfect.

Physiologists say that *fat burns in the flame of carbohydrates*. When you feed fat, always see that there is sufficient carbohydrate present. On the other hand, if you fail to provide enough fat, the pet has to manufacture its own from proteins and carbohydrates in its diet—a less efficient and more costly process.

The economy of fat in pet food can be easily and conclusively demonstrated. One pound of rendered suet contains about 4,000 calories; one pound of the best dehydrated foods contains about 1,550 calories; and the fat costs less than the dog food. Fat in the diet contributes two and one quarter times as much energy as either proteins or carbohydrates.

For those who wish to compute the calories in any food formula, this is how it is done. Consider only the protein, carbohydrate (which may be expressed as nitrogen-free extract), and fat. Disregard the rest. Multiply the protein and carbohydrate by four, because a gram of protein, when burned, yields four calories. Multiply the fat by nine; a gram of fat burns to yield nine calories. This will give you the number of calories in 100 grams of food. Since there are 454 grams in a pound, you can convert the answer to pounds by multiplying by 4.5.

How many calories in a one-pound can of a certain canned fish food? The guarantee says:

Protein	9%
Carbohydrate	11%
Fat	2%
Fiber	2%
Water	74%
Ash	1%

Protein	9 × 4 equals	36
Carbohydrate	11 × 4 "	44
Fat	2 × 9 "	18

98 × 4.5 equals 441 calories in a pound.

How many calories in a pound of top round? It contains about 21 percent protein, 10.5 percent fat, and the rest is mostly water.

Protein	21 × 4 equals	84
Fat	10.5 × 9 "	94.5

178.5 × 4.5 equals 803.25 calories in a pound.

How many calories in a pound of a certain dehydrated dog food? It has 25 percent protein, 57 percent carbohydrate, 4.5 percent fat.

Protein	25 × 4 equals	100
Carbohydrate	57 × 4 "	228
Fat	4.5 × 9 "	40.5

368.5 × 4.5 equals 1,658.25 calories per pound.

It is also necessary, however, to consider what part of the total caloric volume is actually usable, because sometimes the protein and carbohydrates may not be as completely available as those in other foods. Even so, a dehydrated ration that furnishes 1,600 calories certainly should recommend itself for consideration, especially since some fat could readily be added to it.

LAXATION

We now come to the subject of residue. There often is considerable residue in the indigestible fiber and in part of the proteins and ash in many ingredients of pet foods. For a long while it was thought that the amount of this fiber determined how laxative a food would be, and tables containing this information were published. It is now known that it is more a matter of the presentation of the fiber than the amount. If alfalfa meal is powdered like flour and used in food, it is not laxative; if it is ground coarsely like fine bran, it is exceedingly laxative; but if the same amount is fed as whole leaves, then it is constipating.

The question of residue in animal food is of considerable practical importance to the dog owner. Dogs eating mice pass much of the hair and stomach contents and skin, but are not constipated by it. Some pets—rabbits and cavies—eat only vegetable food, which if fed alone to dogs would produce loose stools. The natural food habits of the canine species have to be considered. In general, however, it is quite well established that animals are kept in better health where the stool has considerable bulk. It is unwise, therefore, to try to figure diets with as little indigestible residue as possible. Some residue is definitely an advantage.

VITAMINS

Another class of essential elements in food is vitamins. It may sound like heresy, but there is good evidence that far too much stress has been placed on this subject. Too many people drew rash conclusions from the scanty information available to them. We are now finding that we will need a great many more facts before we can speak with the confident tone many adopted some years ago. New vitamins are in the process of being tested daily, and there will be many others. Our knowledge will be incomplete and inconclusive for some time to come. Table III gives a brief review of the vitamins about which we do know something.

The definition of a vitamin is: one of a class of substances, existing in minute quantities in natural foods, necessary for normal nutrition and growth, whose absence produces dietary diseases. Some vitamins can be produced synthetically. Some are soluble in fat and are found only in foods containing appreciable amounts of fat. Others are water soluble. Some are destroyed by heat, some by rancidity, some by age.

Vitamins are necessary only in minute quantities. With a few exceptions, all the essential vitamins are present in a normal diet. What is sure about the information we have now is that it seems certain that our dogs can get all the vitamins they need if their diets contain yeast, fresh alfalfa-leaf meal, and some form of vitamin D. This may be fish liver oil, in tiny amounts, irradiated yeast, and so forth. It is as simple as that.

Many vitamins have individual but very similar functions. In maintaining health some are useful only in conjunction with others. It is often difficult to break down the better sources into their individual components. For our purposes it is quite unnecessary to discuss each of the vitamins individually in order to understand the effects of the groups in which they occur and in which we handle them. The B complex is an excellent illustration. It comprises many essential B vitamins. All may be found together and are used together medicinally. A veterinarian seldom gives thiamine, rather he or she gives the whole complex when using vitamin therapy.

Table III gives in outline form the major properties, functions, and sources of the principal vitamins and vitamin groups.

Table III THE FUNCTIONS AND SOURCES OF VITAMINS

VITAMIN	FUNCTION	SOURCES
A (and carotene) Fat soluble; body stores it, spills with air exposure; stable at boiling temperature	General metabolism growth, skin health, muscle coordination, fertility, calcium utilization, vision, hearing; prevents infection	All green and yellow vegetables, butter, fortified milk, liver
Requirements:	Adults 110 I.U.*/kg†/day Puppies 220 I.U./kg/day	
B Complex B₁ (thiamine)	Growth, appetite, digestion	Meat, milk, cereals
Requirements:	Adults 22 ug‡/kg/day Puppies 44 ug/kg/day	
B₂ (riboflavin)	Heart functions	Liver, milk, yeast, cereals, cheese
Requirements:	Adults 48 ug/kg/day Puppies 98 ug/kg/day	
Niacin (nicotinic acid)	Carbohydrate digestion; prevents blacktongue or pellagra	Meat, liver, poultry, cereals, wheat germ, rice
Requirements:	Adults 250 ug/kg/day Puppies 500 ug/kg/day	

VITAMIN	FUNCTION	SOURCES
B_6 *(pyridoxine)*	Blood generation, growth; lack of causes epilepsy, anemia, seborrhea, nerve damage	Fish, liver, legumes, whole wheat, milk, wheat germ, yeast
Requirements:	Adults 22 ug/kg/day Puppies 44 ug/kg/day	
Pantothenic acid	Nerve health, digestion, growth; prevents gum disease	Organ and muscle meat, yeast, cereals, eggs
Requirements:	Adults 220 ug/kg/day Puppies 220 ug/kg/day	
Biotin	Growth promotion; prevents dermatitis	Yeast, peanuts, milk, eggs, legumes, organ meats
Requirements:	Adults 2.2 ug/kg/day Puppies 4.4 ug/kg/day	
Folic acid (folacin)	Blood cell development, reproduction	Organ meats, leafy vegetables, yeast, grains
Requirements:	Adults 4 ug/kg/day Puppies 8 ug/kg/day	
Choline—lecithin	Digestion	Organ meats, eggs, yeast, soybean oil
Requirements:	Adults 26 mg/kg/day Puppies 52 mg/kg/day	
B_{12} *(cyanocobalamin)*	Protein metabolism, blood regeneration; alleviates need for cobalt	Eggs, meat
Requirements:	Adults .5 ug/kg/day Puppies 1 ug/kg/day	
C (ascorbic acid)	Aids digestive processes; prevents scurvy; aids wound healing, tooth, bone, cartilage, skin development	Citrus fruits and many vegetables
Requirements:	Dogs produce their own	

VITAMIN	FUNCTION	SOURCES
D	Aids mineral absorption, calcium and phosphorus in blood, bone formation, growth, reproduction	Fish, liver and oils, some animal fats
Requirements:	Adults 11 I.U./kg/day	
	Puppies 22 I.U./kg/day	
E (tocopherols) Fat soluble; body stores it, perishes with air exposure; stands cooking temperatures	Protects vitamin A and carotene, muscular coordination, fertility in some species, muscular development, sound hearts, growth; prevents muscular dystrophy	Seed germs, green plants, liver, vegetable oils
Requirements:	Adults 1.1 I.U./kg/day	
	Puppies 2.2 I.U./kg/day	
K Fat soluble	Blood clotting, young puppy health; prevents liver damage	Alfalfa, leaf meal, cabbage
Requirements:	Adults 22 ug/kg/day	
	Puppies 44 ug/kg/day	

(Antivitamins—rancid fat destroys vitamin E; an enzyme in raw fish destroys thiamine; raw egg white inactivates biotin; high temperature cooking destroys many vitamins; excesses of some vitamins such as vitamin D are dangerous.)

Although not specifically vitamins, unsaturated fatty acids perform many of the same functions, and so we list them here:

Linoleic acid	Coat and skin health	Corn oil
Linolenic acid	Young puppy health	Linseed oil
Arachidemic acid		Rapeseed oil
		Many seed oils

* I.U. = international units;
† kg = kilogram (2.2 lbs.);
‡ ug = microgram

Scientists have made careful studies of what they often call "nutritional wisdom" in animals. In doing so they expose animals of one species or another—children, rabbits, dogs, cattle, poultry—to separate dishes of all kinds of foods. Each day they measure what is left and keep track of what the appetite dictates the animal needs. In making these studies the scientist tries to rule out "conditioning." He knows that once an animal is conditioned or habituated to eat only certain foods it is almost useless for experimental study of nutritional wisdom.

If dog owners had only a little realization of the effect of food habits on animals, those who judge the value of a food by how greedily a dog eats it would revise their opinions completely. Investigators have consistently found that the taste test is nothing but a test of previous conditioning. It is difficult to understand why dog owners should sometimes be so reluctant to accept this fact. Anyone working with humans knows that undesirable habits in food selection are amazingly difficult to eradicate. A man is asked, "Why don't you eat cabbage? It's good for you." "Because if I ate it I might like it, and I hate the stuff" is his reply.

How many people prefer bread made of white flour to whole wheat bread! And yet it is distinctly inferior in value. Most of the better proteins, iron, manganese, magnesium, copper, calcium, thiamine, and riboflavin are removed. But white flour keeps better, so flour and bread manufacturers have conditioned the public to prefer it. Fish is as valuable a food as meat and costs much less, yet many people refuse to eat it—and some have even trained their omnivorous pets to reject it.

A remarkable number of people project their own peculiar food habits on their dogs. Animals can't reason, even as poorly as the man who won't eat cabbage, but it is extremely easy to build up likes and dislikes by habit formations that are difficult to break. We have seen many dogs, raised on dehydrated dog foods, that had to be starved several days so that they would eat meat, and vice versa.

The point is that every pet should be trained to "eat what we set before it," as long as we know our provisions are wholesome and nutritious. All experience indicates that, given a very large assortment of foods, any unconditioned puppy will settle down to a certain diet of foods it likes, mostly what is good for it. Among these might be the smelly contents of a steer's intestines or overripe meat. But since most of us can't offer such tidbits, or live in the same house with a dog that has eaten them, it behooves us to remember how important training is in the cultivation of appetite. A puppy reared on a diet of just one dehydrated-meal dog food mixed with water, and given nothing else, enjoys every meal.

GENERAL FEEDING PRINCIPLES

There are some general principles of feeding that are important to the health of every dog regardless of breed. Next to our consideration of what to do when the end comes, this is the most ticklish subject we have to tackle.

Nobody should have any difficulty understanding the fundamental rule: *In feeding mature pets, the less they eat,* compatible with keeping them in sound condition, *the healthier they'll be and the longer they'll live.* It goes without saying, of course, that they should have a complete and balanced diet. They should not be allowed to get too fat or too thin. If you try to keep them too thin, they may get too little of some essential ingredient; if you permit them to get too fat, you will shorten their lives.

In growing pets, the faster they grow the cheaper it is to raise them. *But*—will they live longer, be healthier? Probably the best rule for sound health and longevity is to grow them moderately fast, but not to force them.

Nearly everyone overfeeds his or her pet. And almost every animal will eat 20 percent more than it needs. There are some animals, like some people, that never get fat even though they are chronically overfed. The way to feed your pet—the way people who are good feeders do—is to find just the amount that will maintain its weight and then give it no more. No rule is as important as this one. Your dog is happier if not burdened with unnecessary fat.

If only pet owners who allow their animals to become obese knew a few truths about food storage in the body and something about fasting —which some people mistakenly call starvation—how much better off their pets would be. Starvation is the long-continued deprivation of food. Fasting is short-term, total, or partial abstinence from food.

Starvation is forced; fasting is voluntary. A sick animal fasts; an obese animal must be starved but not necessarily deprived of all food. When an animal is too fat it won't really starve, even though it takes no food until its own fat is consumed. We say that "it lives on its fat." In winter the raccoon fasts. Not that it reasons what it is doing; it just lazily lives on its fat. It has stored sufficient vitamins and minerals along with the fat and moves about very little except during the warm spells of winter. No one need feel sorry for raccoons. Why, then, pity your fat dog when it has to forgo the habit of overeating for a while?

Most of this feeling sorry for pets that are put on reducing diets stems from the idea that starvation is painful. But it is not, as long as there is a reservoir of food in the stored fat of the body. If you give them a little protein and a little carbohydrate—say, a slice of bread a day—to help burn the fat, there is no danger of acidosis developing. If a vitamin-mineral supplement is added, there is no danger of starvation at all.

Anyone who thinks starvation is painful need only try it. One of us once lost forty-two pounds in less than two months and smaller amounts on many other occasions, and never felt a pang of anything but hunger. And we knew someone who lost twenty-five pounds in fourteen days from infectious hepatitis, and there was no pain. Hunger pangs are habit pangs—not pain at all.

There are many instances of dogs living with only water for two months. One dog lived 117 days. So don't think your pet is going to die if it doesn't eat for a few days while you are accustoming it to what is good for it. Its taste can become reeducated to like the diet you choose, and your pet will thrive on it if it is complete.

Clients whom we have advised to feed a certain diet ask if a dog doesn't need variety. How can a certain canned food or dry food that is fed day after day still be palatable? The reason is that our pets can smell each ingredient in a food. You and I smell hash. The dog smells separately each of the ingredients of which hash is composed. If you doubt this, watch a finicky pet trying to separate finely ground ingredients from each other in a mixture of foods. It isn't difficult to understand this ability if one thinks about it for a moment. A Bloodhound can smell a man's track a day after he has walked down a path, even when that track has been trampled all over by many other people. Why should we doubt that it is as simple a matter for any dog to smell the ingredients of a dog food and to enjoy its various components?

It is far crueler to overfeed than to underfeed. It is a disservice to the pet and a discredit to the owner. Obesity shortens the life of an animal and makes it sluggish and no longer fun to have around. It often brings great misery and suffering to pet and owner alike, because of the paralysis that so frequently sets in as the pet grows older.

DIETARY ESSENTIALS

The important thing to keep in mind is that in order to be balanced a dog's diet requires protein, carbohydrate, and fat, just as do the diets of human beings and all other animals. A safe general rule is to have 14 percent protein as a minimum (dry basis); 20 percent fat, and the balance carbohydrate and minerals with some indigestible residue. These essentials, in their proper proportions, can be supplied easily and inexpensively without figuring percentages with paper and pencil, as we will see when we consider the specific foods available for our dogs.

Fat in the Dog's Diet. Let us stress again the fact that dogs can handle to advantage much more fat than most people give them. Idle dogs can utilize as much as 25 percent fat in their diets, whereas hard-working dogs, such as those drawing heavy loads in the Arctic, are often fed diets with 70 percent fat.

"Fat burns in the flame of carbohydrates." Fat and protein alone are not as well tolerated by a dog as fat and protein with carbohydrate. Everyone knows that a fatty steak eaten alone soon becomes sickening, but that when bread or some other starch is taken along with it much more fat can be enjoyed. If all starchy foods are omitted, the proportion of fat should be lower.

Breaking Down Starch for Digestibility. Carbohydrates are so often locked up by nature that foods containing them need preparation if they are to be of most value to any dog. As we have said, starch granules are broken down by heat; heat also reduces starch to dextrose—one further step in the digestive process. It is amusing to hear dog owners say that they never feed their dogs starch and in the same breath announce that they give them lots of dog biscuits—which are mostly baked starch.

Carbohydrate is found in liver in the form of glycogen (animal starch), and this, too, is digestible. Many starches are locked up in cellulose (the chief component of the cell walls of plants). Heat helps break down cellulose so that dogs can digest the starch. Carrots, potatoes, turnips, and other vegetables; apples, pears, and other fruits are often relished in their raw state by dogs, but much of what is eaten is found in an undigested state in the stool. Boiled or baked, and then mashed, these foods are assimilated almost entirely.

GENERAL TYPES OF FOODS

The following are general types of food available nearly everywhere in the United States, any of which can be fed to dogs. Prepared foods will be considered later.

Meat and By-Products of the Slaughterhouse. There are few parts of any meat animal a dog cannot eat and digest. Hair, skin, bones, and blood have little value to it, but all the rest has, even the intestinal contents.

Most dog owners think that meat is a must, but this is not so. Other proteins are equally good. But meat and its by-products in general constitute readily procurable foods. Muscle meat is in itself no better than organs, such as the liver, lungs, tripe, udder, brain, and in some cases is not as valuable.

Needless to say, meat is less expensive when cut from poor-grade animals, such as old cows, bulls, or horses, and it has almost as much nutritional value as meat from prime steers, except that there is usually less fat. There is little choice between beef and horsemeat from the standpoint of value, though some sentimental people can't bear to think of feeding a noble horse even to a noble dog.

Now, as to how to feed the meat—cooked or raw, ground or in hunks. The answer is that it makes little difference in its digestibility if it is cooked or raw, but boiling meat brings flavor out into the water which can then be mixed, fat and all, with other foods, such as bread and cereals. Meat in chunks small enough for a dog to swallow is digested better than meat ground into hamburger.

Bones occasionally cause trouble by splintering. Raw chicken bones splinter badly, whereas well-cooked bones snap at right angles. Once a healthy dog gets a bone in its stomach the bone is quickly dulled and digested. If a dog crunches through a soft rib bone it usually pushes a good deal of tartar off its teeth, thus cleaning them. These kinds of bones are the best kind to give your dog, if you give it any. They contain worthwhile nourishment in protein, fat, and minerals, including iron.

However, you should keep in mind that dogs will often drag large bones about in places where they or other dogs have defecated. Worm eggs that are in stool stick to these bones, are ingested by the dog, and thus infect it.

Milk. Research shows that milk is as good for dogs as is meat. Both contain a high percentage of water—meat has about 65 percent and milk about 87 percent. Meat has approximately 800 calories per pound and milk about 250 per pint. A dog, therefore, needs three times as much milk by weight as meat to produce the same nutritional effect. Milk has much more calcium than meat, and more vitamins. This is one of the very best dog foods. It does *not* produce worms, as too many people believe.

Fish. Raw saltwater fish fed over a long period produces a form of paralysis in dogs. Cooked fish is fully as valuable a source of protein as is meat and will keep dogs in sound health. Almost all kinds of fish eaten by humans make excellent dog food. The whole fish, including the bones and intestinal contents, is better than fillets alone, and what is left of the fish after the fillets have been removed is too high in bone content for efficient dog food, although it contains much good protein.

Fish bones. More fish could well be fed to dogs than is now being fed to them. Nearly everybody wonders whether the bones will stick in the dogs' throats and, without knowing the answer, decide "when in doubt, don't feed them fish." There have been instances of fish bones that have actually done serious damage by sticking in the throat or between teeth, but such instances are rare. It might be dangerous to feed a dog a pan of fish bones left over from the family meal. If it chewed and swallowed them, the stomach fluids would soften the bones quickly; the danger would be to the mouth and throat.

Fish bones subjected to the 250° F temperature of the canning process become harmless, as anyone will remember from having chewed bones in canned salmon. Whole fish with the bones embedded in the meat seldom do harm. In fact, whole cooked fish constitute a substantial part of dogs' diets in many parts of the world.

Cereals. Many cereals, such as corn, wheat, oats, soybeans, barley, rice and their by-products, make worthwhile dog food when cooked. The protein of corn is zein, which is incomplete. Wheat is more nearly complete. Oats are especially valuable. Brown rice is useful—much better, in fact, than white polished rice. All furnish calories, or heat units, and many nutritional essentials. Bread is one of the most valuable dog foods; not by itself, to be sure, but as composing a large proportion of the diet it may be put to good advantage. Besides well-cooked wheat or rye flour, it contains skim milk, salt, and yeast. The devitalized white bread has almost as much value as whole wheat, since much so-called whole wheat has a large proportion of white flour.

Vegetables. Since vegetables contain such great quantities of water, most of them are low in caloric value, but dogs can be taught to eat large amounts. Potatoes in their jackets and other vegetables grown in the ground can be utilized admirably if they are cooked and fed with meat, fish, or milk. Green vegetables are especially valuable as sources of vitamins and minerals and furnish some calories if they are well cooked but not overcooked.

Probably the best vegetable available for dog food is alfalfa-leaf meal. This is generally ground so fine that much of it is digestible without cooking. However, in the raw state it is very laxative, almost like raw bran in this respect, so it must be fed sparingly. Only the highest grades (20 percent protein) should be used to feed a dog, the lower grades being too laxative because of the large amounts of woody stems they contain.

Fruits. Fruits are a canine luxury and more in the nature of trick foods. Dog owners delight in showing how their dogs eat even apples, pears, peaches, or bananas. Too little of these fruits is digested to make them efficient dog foods, but they do no harm.

PREPARED DOG FOODS

There are hundreds of conscientious manufacturers of dog foods earnestly working to turn out products that, when fed exclusively, will nourish dogs from weaning throughout the rest of their lives. There are also charlatans turning out foods that have no other qualification than that dogs like them. We have tested scores of these foods. Some were deficient in half a dozen essentials. Dogs fed these foods developed bone problems, showed vitamin B deficiencies, failed to reproduce, developed sore eyes characteristic of vitamin A deficiency, and became anemic because of iron deficiency. And every one of these foods was eaten eagerly by the dogs. Appetite is definitely no guide to the goodness or completeness of a food. Good or bad, prepared dog foods fall into four general classes.

Canned Foods. There are many brands of canned foods on the market. The chances are good that, if you patronize a large market where many brands are sold, there will be at least two made by one packer from the same formula. That packer and the proprietor of the store know that most dog owners buy on the basis of what a dog likes, so that you may buy one of each of the two brands. At noon you might offer your pet food from one of the cans. Suppose it does not happen to be hungry then and turns up its nose and leaves it. At suppertime you try another can of the same formula, but packaged under a different label. Naturally your pet is hungry by that time and eats it, and you think, "This is wonderful food." Don't judge the food on these grounds. The taste test is no test at all of a nutritious dog food.

The best canned foods on the market today are known to the trade as *pudding foods.* They are poured into the cans as a thick soup that contains enough gelatinizing substance to make a solid cake after processing. Most of them are 70 percent or more water and about 450 calories, which is just about enough food for a dog weighing fifteen pounds. An active, medium-sized Cocker Spaniel requires two one-pound cans a day if fed canned food exclusively. An English Setter weighing sixty pounds needs four cans—and that is correct no matter what the directions on the can say.

Dog Biscuits, Cakes or Kibbled. Nearly all dog biscuits, which are composed mostly of flour, are palatable to every dog. The baking process by which they are manufactured—heating to sometimes 450° F for an hour or more—destroys the heat-labile vitamins and some amino acids of which proteins are composed. Some biscuits are not baked as long as others, and the insides do not become as hot as the crust, so that some of these destructible essentials are preserved.

In all of the nutritional tests we have conducted, dog biscuits stood at the bottom when compared with other foods and judged on the basis of growth promotion. Earnest efforts are being made to improve them. Kibbled biscuits—those broken into small pieces and often referred to as fillers—are usually fed along with meat and vegetables. Manufacturers know this, and some of them have been less eager than others to make their products complete foods, realizing that the dog owner will provide the essentials.

Years ago fits and paralysis in dogs were often attributable to too many biscuits made with bleached flour processed by a method that produced a toxic chemical. But now that the cause is known, manufacturers use flour that will not produce such troubles. It is still true, however, that dog biscuits, if fed in too large amounts, are constipating —especially when they are supplemented only with meat and bones.

The claim is often made that dog biscuits are essential for good teeth. This is not true. Teeth are made from the inside, not by rubbing the outside, although chewing hard foods may remove a certain amount of tartar. We have had a number of very old dogs with beautiful good teeth though they have never eaten anything but mushy food.

Frequently dogs are made overweight by the constant feeding of dog biscuits between meals. These pathetic creatures—canine "five-by-fives"—are the victims of their owners' indulgence or ignorance or lack of willpower. They can't say no when a dog begs, and the easiest thing is to hand their pet a dog biscuit.

Biscuits have their place but should be used sparingly, as treats. Because Fifi begs for it is no more indication that she *needs* a biscuit than a child's teasing for a lollipop is an indication he or she should have one. Both biscuits and lollipops, when given more than occasionally, spoil the appetite for more complete foods essential for health.

Dry Foods. During World War II some manufacturers dehydrated mixtures of wet dog foods because tin cans were not available and sold the new product in cardboard containers. When water was mixed with this food the resulting mixture was much like the canned dog foods, except that it contained less meat and more cereals. Many dogs thrived on these foods, which were truly *dehydrated* foods.

But before, during, and since World War II, other dog foods, made by mixing separately dehydrated ingredients, have been available. These have come to be known as *dry foods.* They usually consist of approximately half cereal ingredients and half foods of animal origin. The cereals may be corn flakes, wheat flakes, bread meal, soybean meal, or peanut meal. Such mixtures often include raw cereal products, such as middlings and cheap flour, and some manufacturers who make dog biscuits include the crumbs of broken biscuits in the mix. The products of animal origin may be meat scrap, fish meal, liver meal, or mixtures of organs dehydrated, skim milk powder, and other such items. Vitamins and minerals are added to make doubly sure that every known dietary essential is included in the food mixture.

Dry dog foods are usually called "complete foods." All they require is the addition of water. Actually, despite the fact that dogs will thrive on them, most are low in fat content, seldom having over 4 percent. As we have seen, a balanced diet requires approximately 20 percent fat. The wise dog owner buys dry food, melts any wholesome edible fat—used lard, margarine, chicken fat, roasting fat, bacon drippings, or fat skimmed from the soup kettle—and mixes it with the dry food. House dogs should not be fed a richer mixture than one part fat to four parts of dry food. In the average household there is usually enough fat left over from cooking to furnish all the dog needs and relishes. It is not essential to the digestion of dry dog foods to add this fat, but it makes for good nutrition, economy, and palatability. If we were feeding a dry dog food that we had not tested, we would add fat to it and mix it with milk and water. Then we could be sure that the dog had every essential.

Semimoist Foods. In recent years the semimoist chewy foods prepared to resemble hamburger or chunks of meat have gained justified prominence in the dog food world. They are palatable, nourishing, and convenient. No cans, can openers, or containers to mix food with water are necessary. Just open a package and give the ingredients to the dog. This type of food has been unjustifiably criticized, however, for the high amounts of sugar used as a preservative.

More years ago than we care to remember we added 20 percent corn syrup to moistened dehydrated dog food that we fed to weaning puppies until they were two years old. The object was to study the effects on the teeth. Not only did their teeth remain sound but they were as healthy as any dogs in the kennel.

Since the advent of the semimoist foods, many dogs have been fed this exclusively with no ill effects, even when raising litters of puppies. They are more expensive than the dehydrated foods but a satisfactory solution to feeding smaller pets.

Do bugs in dog food cause worms? Are they poisonous to dogs? These are frequently asked questions. The answer to both is no. Inquiry into the natural food of foxes, coyotes, and other doglike animals indicates that bugs are often eaten from preference. All the meal bugs and larvae are harmless.

Table IV COMPOSITION OF TYPICAL DOG FOODS
(in percentages)

	AS PURCHASED	WATER REMOVED
Canned		
Water	75	
Fat	5	20
Carbohydrate	6.5	26
Protein	10	40
Ash	2.5	10
Fiber	1	4
Soft moist		
Water	25	
Fat	9	12
Carbohydrate	35	46
Protein	21	28
Ash	8	11
Fiber	2	3
Dry		
Water	10	
Fat	8	9
Carbohydrate	47.5	53
Protein	21.5	24
Ash	8	9
Fiber	5	5

ECONOMICS OF FEEDING

Now for the economics of dog feeding. Disregarding for the moment the time and trouble that may be spent in the preparation of some foods, suppose we consider only the cost of feeding a pet.

If you buy a little more food for the family to feed the dog, as so many do, it will cost you about six times as much as a good dehydrated dog food.

If you feed canned or semimoist food to your pet, it will cost about three times as much as a poorer kibble-type food to which even the cheapest meat is added.

By adding leftover cooking fat to a dehydrated food you will save even more and we doubt there is a better way to feed a dog. Such a diet provides three times as many calories per pound as meat so that only one third as much needs to be fed. Of course, the added water increases the bulk.

All these methods require only common sense, and most dogs can be made to thrive without digestive disorders on any of the foods we have discussed or on combinations of these different types of food.

In spite of the higher cost, you may decide to feed your dog the foods you eat yourself. If you do, remember that feeding a forty-pound dog in this manner is practically equivalent to feeding half of another adult member of the family. Table V gives you, in round numbers, the approximate caloric value of many foods fed to dogs. From it you can decide on the proper amount to feed.

Table V APPROXIMATE WATER CONTENT
AND CALORIC VALUE OF SOME HUMAN FOODS FED TO PETS

	PERCENTAGE OF WATER	CALORIES PER POUND
Beef		
Round	68	800
Hamburger, lean	74	520
Heart	63	1,100
Liver	65	550
Lungs	80	410
Marrow	3.5	3,800
Suet	14	3,400
Pork		
Ham	55	1,350
Leg	60	1,210
Veal	65	720
Lamb		
Leg	51	1,350
Flank	46	1,900
Chops	50	1,570
Poultry		
Chicken	65	1,000
Turkey	55	1,300

	PERCENTAGE OF WATER	CALORIES PER POUND
Soups		
Beef	93	116
Chicken	85	265
Meat stew	84	355
Bouillon	98	5
Milk products		
Whole milk	87	310
Evaporated	73	635
Skimmed	90	167
Cream, 20%	70	990
Cream, 40%	55	1,600
Whey	93	120
Cheese		
Cheddar	34	1,850
Cottage	72	490
Cream	38	1,700
Ice cream	63	930
Butter	12	3,450
Margarine	5.5	3,750
Cereal products		
Bread	36	1,150
Bread, dried	7	1,760
Frosted cake	18	1,700
Doughnuts	18	1,900
Rolled oats	11	1,700
Corn flakes	12	1,550
Macaroni	10	1,600
Vegetables		
Dried beans	12	1,500
Beets	87	190
Cabbage	91	121
Carrots	88	180
Onions	87	200
Lettuce	97	75
Potatoes, boiled	75	400

ACCUSTOMING YOUR DOG TO A SPECIFIC DIET

As we have said, a dog accustomed to any specific diet that satisfies it and keeps it healthy will generally have a difficult time becoming accustomed to any other diet. In making a change, the point to remember is that once you have decided on a sound diet, every member of the household must cooperate to see that nothing is fed to upset the schedule you have adopted. If Toby is put on a diet of canned food when he has previously been eating chicken with buttered broccoli, he must be starved, if necessary, until he eats the canned dog food. Any member of the family who feels sorry for him and gives him even a scrap of chicken or broccoli will defeat the whole plan and will be punished by having a spoiled pet continually begging for more of the same.

We give our dogs only a good type of dehydrated dog food. There are a number of excellent ones on the market. Sometimes when we have bought new dogs that have been brought up on fancy diets, it has been most difficult to change their feeding habits to the food of *our* choice. One large dog lost eighteen pounds before it accepted the change. It was seven days before it would touch a morsel of the meal-type food. Now it gulps it with evident enjoyment and is healthy and sleek.

HOW OFTEN AND HOW MUCH TO FEED

Once a day is often enough to feed a grown dog, no matter how much it begs between meals. It is all right to let a growing puppy eat all it wants. But an adult house dog on this kind of schedule soon becomes overweight. It is much simpler to keep a dog's weight down than it is to reduce it. If a dog seems famished when it has finished its meal, give it a little more. If it doesn't eat it all, it has been given too much. If it is gaining weight, or losing, the owner should provide more or less food appropriately to keep the dog in proper condition.

HOW TO REDUCE A DOG'S WEIGHT

If you don't give your dog more to eat than it needs, it won't be overweight. If it is already too fat, you can get it back into shape by regulating its diet. If you have a reasonable amount of willpower, reducing your dog's weight will be a fairly simple matter. We have worked out a chart that should provide all the information you need. The left side of the graph is divided to show weight in pounds. On the baseline you will find a series of figures representing the number of calories necessary to maintain a given weight in a dog.

Weigh your dog. Let us say it weighs sixty pounds. Find the sixty-pound mark on the left side of the graph. Follow this line until it strikes the curve. From that point on the curve, drop straight down to the baseline. There you will see how many calories it needs—1,900 for a sixty-pound dog.

Or you can work the graph backward from the calorie line to see how the diet your dog is getting compares with its actual needs. It is getting two cans of a good grade of dog food, plus three large dog biscuits, three candies, assorted tidbits from the table, and a bowl of milk every night. Let us figure just the first two items. Two cans of food have 900 calories, three large dog biscuits (one half pound each) have 2,200. That makes a total of 3,100 calories, when only what is necessary is 1,900. Add the table scraps, candy, and milk and your dog is getting nearly twice what it requires. This will explain why it weighs ninety-three pounds when the correct weight for its breed is sixty pounds.

How are you going to reduce your dog's weight? There are two or three ways. First, you can feed it 1,900 calories and—knowing that a working dog needs many more calories than an idle one—exercise it enough to take off the excess weight. By exercise we don't mean walking around the block. You can easily find ways of real exercise. Hitch your dog to a wagon and give the neighborhood youngsters rides; take it for ten-mile hikes, if you yourself are energetic; or make it retrieve. If you throw a stick or rubber ball only fifty yards and the dog runs after it and brings it back, remember that seventeen retrieves will mean it has run for a mile. If it is very fat, you will have to accustom it gradually to this exercise, a little more each day. But if you do make your dog exercise, the fat will melt away—provided you and the rest of the family all see to it that it gets its 1,900 calories a day and no more. The dog won't be starving until it has used up the energy stored in its excess weight. When it is down to sixty pounds it still will have plenty of fat.

The second method is underfeeding. Switch to a totally different diet, say, dehydrated dog food. You know it is good for your dog but so different that it won't eat at first. Fine! The less the dog eats, the more

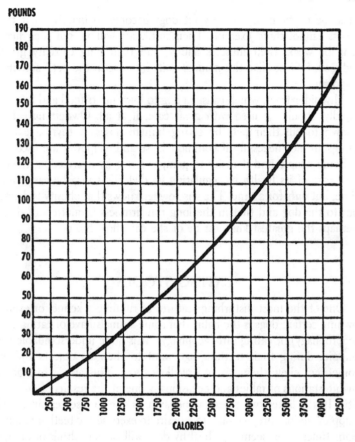

Approximate caloric requirements of dogs by weight. Find the weight of your dog on the left-hand side and follow the line toward the right to its point of intersection with the heavy black line. Then drop downward to the baseline, where you will find the daily caloric requirement.

of its own fat it consumes. By the time it is eating the new food well, considerable weight will have been lost. Then feed your dog half its daily caloric requirements and its fat will melt away by this method too. It is well to give a complete vitamin capsule with the food once a day while the dog is losing weight, because it may not have sufficient vitamin content in its restricted diet.

A combination of exercise with a restricted diet is good. But one must be cautious. Some very fat dogs become so inactive that their hearts cannot stand exercise. Their spirits are willing, but their hearts may be weak, their muscles flabby, and their lung capacity greatly reduced. In cases like this *gradual* daily increase in the pets' activity is important.

Thyroid extract, which causes a dog to burn up its food and fat more rapidly, should be used with great care, if at all. Owners have been known to kill their pets by giving human doses of thyroid extract. Drugs are not necessary if common sense and willpower are used.

Some people find it easier to pamper a dog by overfeeding than to take care of its health by regulating its diet. This may be easier for a time, but *only* for a time. The wise owner knows that obesity is dangerous to the dog and that in the long run firmness in matters of diet is perhaps the greatest kindness he or she can show the pet.

EATING STOOLS

One of the most disturbing features of running a kennel or even of owning certain dogs is the habit that some animals have of eating dung (coprophagy) or eating dirt (geophagy). It is quite understandable how puppies during their teething age want to chew on objects and will sometimes chew them up and swallow them. This also is one of the manifestations of rabies and occasionally one of the results of encephalitis. In the latter two cases the behavior is due to disease; but mainly puppies' actions are due only to a desire to exercise the teeth and gums. Sometimes other seemingly healthy dogs will eat mouthfuls of dung or dirt. The owner immediately wonders what is wrong, as well he should.

In the old days, when there were horses in the city streets, it was not at all an uncommon sight to see house dogs eating horses' droppings. Farm dogs, too, will eat horse and cow manure, and many dogs will eat their own or other dogs' stools. Some dogs display a passion for eating cats' stools. What is behind all this? Probably many causes, some of which we do not as yet know.

Undoubtedly nutritional deficiency is one cause of both coprophagy and geophagy, but it is not the only cause. When it is the cause, the dog is trying to conserve nutritional essentials. If you visit rat laboratories where nutritional tests are in progress, you will find all the rats kept in cages with wire bottoms elevated so high that the animals can't reach down and obtain stools to eat. If they could, some tests would be invalid. Another cause is some odor in the stools that attracts dogs. An important cause, especially in kennel dogs of a retrieving nature, like Cocker Spaniels, is their desire to retrieve. They will pick up stools, carry them around in their mouths, and eventually eat them, thus more or less training themselves to this obnoxious habit. Another cause is underfeeding. Some dogs get so hungry that they become stool eaters. Parasites, especially hookworms, which may cause anemia, are also a cause of the habit.

If a dog secretes an inadequate amount of one of the digestive enzymes it soon learns that by eating its stool it adds some of the needed enzyme. For this condition the addition of a meat tenderizer containing papain is corrective. Papain is also found in the fruit of the papaya tree.

Cures are effected by first considering the causes of the condition and eliminating them. Nutritional deficiencies can be overcome by feeding complete diets. It must be remembered that a great many vitamins are manufactured by bacteria working in the intestines, and it can easily be that dogs need vitamins when you find them eating stools. They may also need essential amino acids or minerals. Consider everything carefully and supply what you think your dog or dogs may need. You may quickly cure your pet.

The use of chlorophyll, which will eliminate some peculiar stool odors, sometimes produces dramatic results. This can be supplied by a lot of dark green vegetables boiled lightly and added to the food. Alfalfa-leaf meal may also be added to the food, but not in large enough quantities to physic the dog. Chlorophyll pills, obtainable in any drugstore, may also be given.

In the case of retrieving breeds, if the dog is given something to carry, coprophagy usually ceases immediately. We have seen a whole kennel of Cocker Spaniels miraculously cured by putting a rubber ball in each pen. The ball gave them something to carry and play with, and that was all it took. Sometimes house dogs can be cured by having a bone to chew on.

If the trouble is parasitic, especially hookworm infestation, see that the dog is dewormed. After deworming, the pet will retain enough iron in its body to help replenish its blood supply and will not feel the urge to conserve the mineral by eating dung or dirt.

Of all these explanations, we think the most probable one is that the dog smells something in the fecal material it likes. Perhaps it is a by-product of the bacteria in the colon. This requires a change of diet over weeks of time to change the bacterial flora of the intestine but it is worth the effort. Try adding 25 percent yogurt or cottage cheese to the diet for two weeks.

If the situation has become a repugnant habit, a hot pepper sauce may be added to the stools, and if this fails, gentian root powder in gelatin capsules the size of an antibiotic capsule may be given with each meal. The dose is one for a small dog, two for a medium size, and so on. If one is not adequate for your dog, double the dose until it works. The powder is so bitter it cannot be mixed with food. Gentian root powder may be obtained from a health food store and should be administered for two weeks to break the habit.

4

Sanitation, Hygiene, and Health Hazards

Your first concern as a dog owner must always be the maintenance of your pet's health and well-being. To be able to care for a pet in sickness is a necessary skill, but for many obvious economic and humanitarian reasons the prevention of disease is even more important.

The proper care of a pet requires that you have a fundamental knowledge of animal hygiene and sanitation, that you recognize the necessity of keeping the animal clean, that you provide quarters that are free not only of visible dirt and debris but also of disease-carrying agents. In short, it is essential that you have a thorough and realistic understanding of how to establish and maintain environmental and personal conditions that actively promote and preserve your pet's health.

Let us start first with the care of the animal itself and then consider its surroundings and how to manage them.

COAT CARE

When you think of the condition of an animal's coat, you must consider both its hair and the skin under that hair.

You undoubtedly have noticed that when dogs are brought into the warmth of a house in cold weather they have a doggier odor than they do in warm weather. That is due largely to the greater secretion of sebum, a protective substance emitted by glands embedded in the skin and deposited mostly against the shafts of the hair. To some extent it coats the skin, acting as a waterproofing agent helping it to shed rain and dampness, and it also serves as a protection against some types of bacteria. The sebum serves several useful purposes, but when it is allowed to accumulate on the dog's coat it may produce a strong odor that must be removed by bathing.

The animal's skin functions as an organ of the body, just as do the kidneys or liver. Its exposure subjects it to all kinds of abuse which better-protected organs never experience. In a healthy animal, glandular secretions of the skin keep the coat shiny. But a coat must be combed often. Dead hair must be removed and snarls untangled in all long-haired breeds. Only a comb or wire brush and elbow grease will accomplish this. Burrs must be removed by hand. Hard mats have to be cut with scissors. To do this, push the scissors under the wad, pointing them away from the body, and cut the wad in half. Large wads may be cut into many sections which then comb or brush out with the least pain to the pet. It is almost never necessary to do the easy thing—snip across the hair. With patience, all the dead hair can be separated from the wad, leaving a lovely coat.

Combing of long-haired dogs should be done as frequently as necessary to keep the coat in good condition. Animals should be taught from puppyhood to stand or lie on a table or, in the case of a large dog, on the floor, and expect and abide combing.

Shorthaired animals need less attention. Some people take a hacksaw blade and drag it, like a comb, over the coat. The teeth catch the loose hairs and pull them out. The bare hand, moistened and rubbed over a shorthaired dog's coat, will pull out many loose hairs and leave the coat looking glossier.

Soft-bristle brushes should not be the mainstay of grooming. Running brushes over the outside of a long-haired animal's coat accomplishes little in the way of loose hair removal. It does sweep out some of the finest skin scales, accumulated dust, and a few loose hairs. There are many kinds of specialized brushes. Thousands of elaborate grooming brushes, with wire bristles on one side and fiber bristles on the other, are available. You can get along very well with (1) a comb with very strong teeth, ten to fourteen to the inch, which can pull out snarls and do rough work; (2) a fine comb with twenty teeth to the inch; (3) a strong brush; and (4) a pair of scissors.

A tried-and-true method of producing a natural sheen on many coats is to rub the coat briskly with a handful of green grass.

If the animal is a small, smooth-coated pet, a fine, strong comb plus a small scrub brush will suffice.

Once we had to groom an Old English Sheepdog for a dog show. He was a fine specimen but had never been groomed during his two years of life, which meant that one solid three-inch-thick mattress of hair completely enveloped him. Twenty hours of hard work were required for that job. Ever since then we have suggested that long-haired dogs belonging to owners who don't want to spend the necessary amount of time grooming them be clipped clean in the spring and fall. Coats grow slowly in the summertime and rapidly in the fall. This kind of clipping can be a disaster for a show coat; but if you are interested in comfort for your pet and a minimum expenditure of time and energy on its coat, haircuts are the answer: comfort in the summertime and a beautiful coat by December.

PLUCKING AND CLIPPING

Should wirehaired breeds be plucked or clipped? Wirehaired Terrier breeders who show their dogs express dismay at the mention of clipping. A clipped terrier does not have a typical show appearance. But those who are not interested in showing their dogs will find that the dogs like clipping better than plucking. The clipped coat is smoother, the dog is not subjected to the annoyance of plucking, and the job costs only about half as much. A dog may be clipped every three or four months for a year and be in trim condition all the time at a cost no greater than that of two pluckings.

Summer clipping is advisable for long-haired dogs for hygienic reasons as well as for the dog's comfort. At one time it was generally thought that since dogs have few sweat glands in the skin it was unnecessary to clip them in hot weather. Some people even insisted that the long hair served as a protective insulation against heat. Our own experience with hundreds of long-haired dogs has convinced us that this reasoning is fallacious. Clipped dogs are definitely and obviously much more comfortable in extreme heat. In addition, a clipped dog is more easily cared for. It requires less combing, keeps cleaner, and does not shed long hair throughout the house. It is also much less likely to get fleas or skin disease since many parasites prefer skin that is under heavy coats of long hair. If, in spite of clipping, your dog should get a skin disease, it is more readily curable and requires less medication than would be the case without clipping.

Most dogs are groomed by professionals who know how to do it correctly. Great skill in grooming is required to turn out a Poodle, for instance, in style. It generally pays to have the work done by those who know how. An amateur cuts off the hair all right, but sometimes the result resembles a moth-eaten garment. Professionals with efficient clippers do a much smoother job.

However, you can learn to do this as have many experienced non-professionals when properly equipped. If you have never clipped or plucked a dog, the following brief instructions should enable you to make a workmanlike job of it. In addition to the equipment mentioned above, you will need, depending on the breed you're dealing with, a stripping comb, a dog razor, and an electric clipper. The Oster clipper, made especially for trimming dogs, comes with several kinds of replaceable blades. Blades # 10 and # 5 will be adequate for almost any work. The # 4 blade is perhaps the most useful attachment. It cuts hair approximately plucking length but does not pull out the loose hair. The short stubs, when they do fall out by themselves, are not noticeable about the house.

Some experts deplore the use of electric clippers. Most people who have had experience with both methods, however, feel that a clipped dog looks as good—to the owner, at least—as a stripped one. Certainly clipping is a much quicker way of removing surplus hair and obviously it is much easier on the dog. Among thousands of dogs clipped at one grooming establishment, there were hundreds that had previously been plucked. In almost every instance the owner was so well pleased with the appearance of the clipped dog that he changed to that method exclusively. In any event, the choice between clipping and plucking seems relatively unimportant since a clipped dog soon has hair long enough to look plucked.

If your dog is one of a breed that is ordinarily plucked and you intend to show it, by all means have it plucked. For example, if you own one of the wirehaired breeds and have lots of time, you will probably want to groom it with a plucking comb, available at any pet shop.

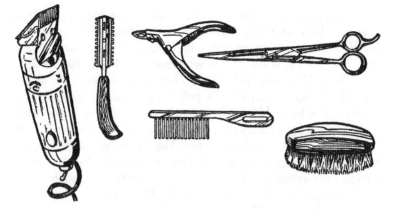

Grooming and plucking equipment. Electric clipper, stripping knife, nail clippers, shears, steel comb, and brush.

HOW TO CLIP AND PLUCK

The Wirehaired Breeds. The illustration of the Wirehaired Terrier on this page will serve as a clipping guide for that breed as well as for Airedales, Irish and Welsh Terriers, and Schnauzers.

Sealyham Terrier and Wirehaired Terrier.

The dog to be clipped should stand on a table over which there should be hook of some kind to attach to a leash from its collar. By placing your hand under its crotch you can make the dog understand that it must stand, and it will eventually learn to pose like a statue.

When you are plucking, hold the handle of the plucking blade in your right hand with your thumb at a short distance from the serrated blade's edge. Press the edge against the hair, apply thumb pressure, and pull. The hair cut is released by removing your thumb. Repeat these steps for another comb full. The motion becomes quite rapid as you learn the method. Pull, pull, pull, pull as quickly as you can make your hand go. The long, old hair gives way quite easily and, in a short time, you can pluck out a good-sized patch, leaving only the curly undercoat.

All of the neck and body is stripped. The legs are left as they are, and only the very longest hair is pulled out to make the legs look large, straight, and cylindrical. The hair on them is left considerably longer than the body coat. This is shown in the illustration.

The head receives different treatment. Showmen often clip the head with electric clippers, trimming the cheeks, the top of the head, and the ears. If you have no clipper, however, you can safely use a safety razor. The guard will prevent shaving the hair too closely. Cut the hair on the top of the nose to the same length as that on the top of the head but, starting at the brim, allow the hair down along the lips to be increasingly longer, to form the beard. From the rear angle of the mouth backward and underneath the eye, the hair is short. The only long hair is on the eyebrows and beard. When you have finished with the head, the long hair of the beard should produce a line under the face, parallel to the line from the eye to the top of the nose. The hair on the feet should be cut with scissors to give them the appearance of round cat feet.

There is no reason to make grooming a chore. You need not try to complete the job at one session. If your dog is uneasy or gets tired, stop for a while and let it rest. After you have finished, look at another dog of the same breed which has been groomed by a professional—at a dog show if possible. You will soon see where you have gone wrong and learn how to improve your technique.

Scottish Terriers and Sealyhams. Dogs of these two breeds are especially easy to clip or pluck, and their appearance is greatly improved by proper grooming. After you have finished clipping and look at the dog from behind, it should have the shape of a half circle whose edges drop straight to the ground. More beard is left on the foreface of these breeds than on the Wirehaired Terrier, but otherwise the clipping is similar. The eyebrows are also usually left a little longer. No hair should be removed from the underbelly. The trimming line ends halfway down the dog's side and the hair below allowed to grow progressively longer so that it appears to be continuous with that on the legs.

West Highland Whites, Cairns, and Others. Although owners often mistakenly think that some terrier breeds should be trimmed or plucked, "tidying up" is a better description of the kind of grooming they need. Certainly no clipping is necessary, only the pulling out of stray or long, unruly hair is needed.

Cocker Spaniels. Cocker Spaniels include the old and new types of American Cockers and English Cockers. The old type of American Cocker is the one that in the past made the breed so popular. The illustrations on pages 85 and 86 show how it and the English Cocker should be clipped. All the long hair is removed from the top of the head and from the top third of the ears (the insides are trimmed out too). The back, the top, and the sides of the tail and both sides and the front of the legs are also trimmed, as are the feet all around and for an inch up the back of the leg. The hair that forms the "feathers" on the backs of the legs and the belly hair are left long. When the clipping has been finished, the whole coat should be combed to remove snarls. When that has been done, scissors may be used to trim away any scraggly hair to enhance the clean-cut, jolly appearance of the dog.

Old type of American Cocker Spaniel.

New type of American Cocker Spaniel.

The new type of American Cocker is clipped on the head and back the same way as the old type, but the long hair on the legs is left uncut. The feet are clipped all around and the hair combed down straight. This bushy-legged clip, though preferred by some people, has undoubtedly done much to harm the popularity of the Cocker Spaniel. Those who advocate it also breed for a heavy coat. This huge coat gives the owner more to work with in grooming the animal, but the average pet owner will also discover that such long, abundant hair has an unfortunate tendency to become a snarled mass of burrs and twigs and an ideal breeding place for parasites. Not only does the long hair on the legs become matted and unsightly, it also collects dirt which the dog distributes about the house.

The Bedlington Terrier. When properly groomed, the Bedlington has a unique appearance, which can be developed only because the animal has a peculiarly thick, linty coat without a wiry texture. The coat of the show dog stands straight out and should be about one inch in length. It can be encouraged to grow in that manner by frequent combing and brushing toward the head.

The head of the Bedlington is clipped in a most distinctive way. The hair on the ears is clipped short except for a flat tassel an inch long at the tip of each ear. The topknot on the head should be the highest at the occiput and from there permitted to taper to its shortest length just behind the nose. It should be rounded over the head, starting from the eyes and the point where the ears are attached.

Bedlington Terrier.

The leg hair is somewhat longer and straighter than the body hair and should be trimmed to give the typical terrier appearance—cylindrical. Some experts use only scissors and combs for the entire job, some use a razor, and many laypeople simply clip the body close and let the hair grow again but leave the leg hair, which they trim with scissors and comb thoroughly.

Poodles. Trimming Poodles is not nearly as difficult as the fancy styling might lead one to believe. Still, clippers, combs, scissors, and razors will all prove useful. The hard part is knowing the basic designs and then being able to start with a great ball of hair and give the dog that spiffy French appearance. Many poodle owners prefer to have the dog clipped in a more masculine fashion, without decoration, maintaining that poodles are really hunters and general-purpose dogs.

There are four most popular clips, and for each there are variations.

THE FIELD CLIP: Usually the whole coat is clipped in the field clip with the #10 blade, leaving long hair only in a pompom on the top of the head and another on the tail. Tassels on the ear tips are sometimes left also. Clipped in this manner, the poodle is comfortable, easy to care for, and ready for action.

THE PUPPY CLIP: As the coat lengthens on a growing puppy it is necessary only to keep it combed and clean. The only parts that really require trimming are the face, the tail where it's close to the body, and the feet and legs up a few inches from the ground. Then when the dog

Continental clip and English clip.

is ready for its first fancy clip, the coat is all there to trim in whatever style the owner prefers.

THE DUTCH CLIP: In the Dutch clip, the distinctive features are the pantaloon effect, the whiskers, and the head pompom. The whiskers are left to form a long fringe about the face. The head, feet, part of the

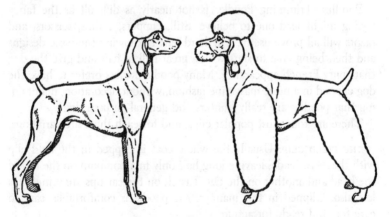

Field clip and Dutch clip.

tail, and body are clipped short, and the pantaloons are trimmed with scissors only. There is considerable variation in the clips. Some owners prefer the top of the long hair to start high up on the body with only four inches of the back separating the two sides. Some clip the chest clean while others leave it covered, with the long hair running from one "pants leg" to the other. Considerable combing, brushing, and scissor trimming are required to produce the proper cylindrical legs.

ENGLISH AND CONTINENTAL CLIPS: In the English and Continental clips there are three distinct hair lengths. However, a good deal of variation is permitted. A number of experts clip the ears and leave the eyebrows with a bare area between them and the pompom on the head. Others leave the hair on the ears long and the hair from the eyes continuous with the pompom. Show dogs need the full topknot and feathers on the ears to give the essential Poodle expression.

The feet are always kept clipped. In the Continental clip a pompom is left on each hip only, but in the English clip there is a blanket of medium-short hair. A modification of the English clip omits the upper bracelet on the front legs, and instead the long hair over the shoulders and chest is left unclipped down to the position of the bracelet. Follow the design, study Poodles groomed by experts, and each time you clip you will come closer to perfection.

The Kerry Blue Terrier. The Kerry's soft wavy coat should be trimmed so as to leave the body well covered but neat. In the proper trim, the head is clipped on the cheeks, ears, and forehead, but long bangs are left over the eyes and down the nose. The whiskers are full and flare out. For house pets, it is most practical to reduce the whiskers by shearing them short. If they are left long, they will require too frequent washing and combing. The legs are trimmed cylindrically.

Setters and Springer Spaniels. For showing, English, Irish, and Gordon Setters and Springers are clipped on the head and part way down the ears. The hair on the neck and shoulders is smoothed and all scraggly hair removed from the back. The sides and top of tail and the feet should also be carefully trimmed. The finished dog must look sleek. Such meticulous and careful trimming is unnecessary with pets or hunting dogs. Some hunters do, however, remove a goodly part of the feathers and long hair when they hunt with their dogs in rough territory, especially where burrs are present.

Kerry Blue Terrier and Cairn Terrier.

CARE OF THE SKIN

The skin of many species of animals, including humans, has large numbers of sweat glands. Dogs, however, have them in restricted areas —under the tail, for instance, and fewer about the rest of the body. But if dogs do not sweat, how is the skin cleaned? Cleaning is accomplished by the renewal of the outside layer, which is constantly being sloughed off by growth in the layers beneath, and by the shedding of the hair itself. There is always a fine scaling of skin going on, more at some times than at others. Healing skin often sheds large, flaky, dandrufflike scales which must be combed or brushed out of the hair. Sometimes the shed scales will stick to hairs and you may find little disks of skin clinging to them, an eighth of an inch out from the body.

Because nerves are everywhere in the skin, it takes very little—only a fleabite, for example—for a pet to show its annoyance by scratching. With the other basic information necessary to care for an animal's coat properly, you should learn something about the nerve patterns in the skin. If you scratch your dog in certain places on the back, your dog will scratch but may not come within ten inches of scratching the spot where you are scratching. When groomers use an electric clipper on the backs of some dogs, particularly the members of wirehaired breeds, they find areas along the sides that cause a dog to scratch so violently that they often have trouble clipping. Clipping in other parts causes no such reaction. The dog's hind leg may not even reach the sensitive area and the dog doesn't try to chew at that area—it merely scratches in a random sort of way. We mention this reaction only because dog owners frequently do not realize that when their pets scratch their shoulders it is no indication that they are itchy there. A better indication in locating an itchy spot is to watch where they chew most.

NAILS

The nails are appendages of the skin. Each nail has a hard outer crust protecting it, and inside there is a blood and nerve supply. Nails, being organs of defense and aids in locomotion, as well as being useful in holding food while the teeth tear it apart, are strongly attached to the toes—much more so than our nails.

Dogs' nails are constantly growing to make up for the loss of nail which, in a wild dog, would be worn off by contact with rough surfaces. House pets seldom have the opportunity of wearing down the nails sufficiently. Dogs running the streets keep their nails filed off by the pavements, but dogs walking on carpets or sleeping most of the time have no such opportunity and often their nails curve back under the foot until they press into the toes. Various dogs differ markedly in their rate of nail growth. In some the rate of growth is so rapid that even running on city streets fails to wear their nails off.

When nails get too long they cause painful feet and sometimes real lameness. If the tips are below the pads of the feet, the pads have no traction on smooth surfaces like linoleum or hardwood floors and the dog slides on the kitchen floor, has trouble climbing stairs, and often appears to get lazy. Nails of house dogs need trimming or filing regularly. Some dogs object so strenuously that they must be muzzled. If you cut too close to the quick and the nails bleed, the capillaries will soon close if the dog is kept off rough surfaces for a while; there is no danger of infection. Silver nitrate styptic pencils are helpful in controlling such bleeding.

SHEDDING

"Doctor," thousands of people ask their veterinarians every year, "what makes my pet shed the year round?" The answer is—light. All our kennel dogs live outside, subjected to the light of the sun only. That's the way nature intended them to live—without electric lights. It has been found that as the days get noticeably longer the influence of these lengthening days on the dog's body (probably via the eyes) causes the hair to stop growing and fall out. New hair replaces the old. If, now, the day is suddenly made much shorter, the new coat will grow faster and reach the acme of its beauty far sooner than if the days gradually shorten. Pets that are not subjected to the normal light cycle shed a little all the time and heavily in the late spring. Combing helps remove the loose hair before it falls out or is rubbed off on clothing, rugs, or furniture.

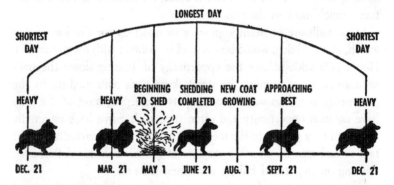

How the length of the day influences the shedding of a dog's coat when it is kept outside.

BATHING

Dogs and cats are the only pets ordinarily bathed, and they are bathed simply to remove dirt and odors. There is no best way to bathe a pet, and no way has yet been found to eliminate the need for elbow grease. For bathing a pet the human fingers are far more efficient than any mechanical device yet developed.

Because the coats of dogs are water-resistant, the help of a chemical is needed to wash a dog with ease. A liquid detergent used to hand wash dishes is our first choice and liquid soap with either a 20 percent (or a diluted 40 percent) coconut-oil base is excellent. To dilute 40 percent soap, simply add an equal amount of water. Cake soap can be used instead of liquid, but it requires considerably more work.

By whatever method the soap or detergent and water are applied, the solution must be well worked into the coat and rubbed until the dirt has been loosened or dissolved. After the lathering, the suds must be thoroughly rinsed from the coat. This is best accomplished by working the fingers through the hair, just as one does in applying the soap solution. Usually one soaping and rinsing is enough, but if necessary, the process may be repeated.

There are soaps that contain vermin poisons. If one is used, no further medication is required. However, there are several very efficient vermicidal dips and rinses available that are well worth using to finish off your pet's bath. Prepare the solution just before the bathing starts. After the pet has been washed and rinsed, pour the dip or special rinse all over the coat, allow it to saturate the coat for a few minutes, squeeze out the surplus with your hands, and dry the pet.

A loosening of hair generally follows any bath. After the pet is dry, considerable combing is generally necessary to free the coat of the loosened hair and give it a sheen and tone.

Bathing small dogs or puppies may be easily accomplished by using a basin and towels. The whole animal may be dipped in the basin, leaving only the head out. The soiled water can be allowed to run out and fresh water quickly drawn while the pet sits on a towel, waiting for the next immersion.

One of the questions about bathing most frequently asked is whether it is safe in winter. It is safe in winter provided the pet is well dried before being allowed outside in the cold air. For that reason many pet owners bathe their pets at night, knowing they are sure to be dry by morning.

Another common question concerns the age at which it is safe to bathe a young animal. There is no rule about age. Young puppies that have become soiled and foul-smelling must be bathed if they are to be kept in a house. We have never seen a bath harm a pet, provided it was properly dried. The fact is that puppies of all breeds frequently suffer from parasites and diseases. When one gets sick shortly after being bathed, the bath is all too often assumed to be the cause. Most of the harm that supposedly results from bathing has actually been caused by a preexisting condition.

There are several dry shampoos available that are quite effective cleaning agents. These should be used according to directions, which vary with the type. There are also several harmless detergents on the market that remove dirt without lathering.

Removal of Road Tar. Dogs often run in newly tarred roads and return with a ball of tar and sand around each foot. The safest removal method is to massage lard into the tar and wash with a detergent. Repeat this procedure until all the tar is washed away. Kerosene will dissolve the tar but it also irritates the skin. In cases where kerosene has to be used it is necessary to rinse each foot in several washings of kerosene and then quickly wash off the kerosene with strong soap and water each time—it is as necessary to wash out the kerosene as it is to remove the tar. The discoloration on the dog due to the tar is hard to eliminate completely but does no physical harm.

Removal of Paint. Most of us are cognizant of the dangers of lead in oil-based paints. Since some of these oil-based paint pigments are poisonous they should be removed immediately. If the dog comes home with still wet oil-based paint on its coat, turpentine will remove it, if plenty is used without allowing too much to come in contact with the animal's skin. The turpentine must be removed by thorough washing with soap and water after each application.

If the oil-based paint is dry, first try to dissolve it. And if your dog's skin is especially tender, use linseed oil to do this. When you have diluted the paint greatly, wash it and the oil out with soap and water. You may, however, have to cut the paint out with scissors as a last resort, even though this may make the dog look less attractive for a while. Of course, water-based paints can be removed by washing with water.

Animal Odors. The sources of animal odors, aside from excrement of course, are ear canker, lip-fold or other infections, anal gland secretions, sebum from thousands of body glands, and dog collars, which absorb sebum. All of these can be eliminated by cleaning the ears, by treating the infections, by expressing the anal glands, and by thorough bathing.

Parasite Control. Bathing in itself will not eliminate parasites, as many people seem to think, but preparations of excellent efficiency for use with bathing are readily available. Some are used as a rinse or dip following the bath; others are liquid soaps or soap cakes with insect killers added. Some manufacturers claim that their products will prevent fleas and lice from reinfesting dogs for several days to a week after use. Some claim their products will kill the eggs of lice (nits).

In eliminating lice, it is necessary to apply the killing agent every eleven days, as this breaks the generation and so eliminates the lice. If there is any doubt about the thoroughness of the treatment, apply the preparation once a week for three weeks.

The more effective way to control pests is to use a liquid dip, soap, or rinse to kill all the insect pests during the bath and then keep the dog well powdered with a nonpoisonous flea powder. Flea collars that were once effective are less so now, thanks to the emergence of resistant fleas. We will discuss flea and tick control in Chapter 23.

THE MOUTH AND TEETH

An animal's unpleasant breath is often caused by dirty, broken, or infected teeth. Tartar an eighth of an inch deep is not uncommon. Your veterinarian can remove the tartar and further clean the teeth, which will do much to sweeten the breath. Cleaning many animal's teeth is not difficult. You can do it yourself with a tartar scraper available from a dental supply house. Otherwise your veterinarian can do the job.

Examine your pet's teeth at least once a month. Look for tartar and loose or broken teeth. Animals fed soft foods tend to have more tartar than those fed on hard foods. All animals enjoy chewing soft raw rib bones, which help to keep teeth clean and prevent tartar from building up. Most dogs will not permit teeth brushing but damp cotton dipped in pumice powder may help remove tartar. Healthy teeth and gums seem to be a genetic trait.

Many dogs will not permit anyone to clean their teeth, and if that is the case with yours, a veterinarian will have to administer an anesthetic to accomplish the task. Of course, serious teeth and gum problems must be treated by a professional.

THE EYES

Our dogs' eyes require very little attention. The only hygiene necessary is the removal of surplus hair that may curl inward and irritate the eyes, and the removal of exudate from the inner corners where the tears of the eyes overflow in many breeds. Spaniels and Toy Poodles are two breeds that often exhibit soiled spots below the inner corners of the eyelids which may discolor the hair. Pekingese dogs with large wrinkles of skin close to the eyes need to have the hair on these ridges kept short to prevent it from touching the eyeballs. Such hair may be kept matted down with Vaseline.

Most people believe that dogs such as Poodles, Old English Sheepdogs, Kerry Blue Terriers, and many mongrels will become blind if the hair is clipped from in front of their eyes. This is not true. The hair may be harmful. These dogs sometimes have mats and caked areas where the eyes' secretions have built up a mass of material under which the skin is generally irritated. Only very fastidious owners who groom their dogs frequently should let hair grow long over the eyes. Even then the eyeballs may easily be injured.

Every hunter knows how dogs' eyes look the day after a hunt. Hounds hunt with heads to the ground, plowing through reeds, brush, and tall grass. Seeds, dust, and vegetable fibers that fill their eyes are sometimes too coarse to wash out with tears and wind up caking around the eyes. In such cases, the eyes should be washed with warm water and dried with a soft cloth. Tears are a better antiseptic than boric acid. For comfort, administer a mild antiseptic like a nonprescription human eye irrigating fluid or ask your veterinarian for a prescription. It is wise to keep a supply of these drugs on hand for all dogs that have a tendency to sore eyes.

THE EARS

Ears are often a source of problems in dogs. Examine them occasionally under a good light. Dirty ears may have a foul odor which pervades the animal and may cause it to shake its head and dig constantly at the ear with its hind paw. If you see a pet moving its front paw over an ear that seems to itch badly, it probably has canker or ear mites. Propylene glycol (*not* ethylene glycol, which is toxic) from the drugstore is a helpful agent to clean ears with and many dog owners use mineral oil with good results. Flood the ear and massage the base of the ear and wipe out the debris. If it is a persistent problem see your veterinarian.

COLLARS AND HARNESSES

An animal's health should be the top consideration when you buy collars and harnesses. Unfortunately, salesmen do not always bear this in mind when making recommendations. Round collars for long-haired dogs, strap collars for shorthaired dogs are usually the most satisfactory. Harnesses are used for all small dogs, but it is sometimes difficult to hold a large dog with a harness. Big dogs tend to do less pulling than small ones because they are more often properly trained. Yet it is easier to train a small dog than a large one because it requires less strength. A properly fitted collar isn't cruel on any dog, and harnesses could be dispensed with, except in cases of medical or anatomical problems, if all dogs were trained not to tug on their leashes. Washable woven nylon and solid plastic collars have the advantage over leather in that they are easier to keep clean.

Every collar or harness should be examined to see that no sharp points or rivets protrude to scratch the animal's skin or wear off the hair. It is most important not to get a lot of hardware on these accessories that can injure a dog's ears. When a hound shakes its head and its ears flap against a heavy buckle and license tags, the ears are often damaged. A dog that has worn a heavy combination of hardware sometimes has the hair entirely worn off its neck.

Small chains used for collars can be cruel if a dog is kept chained. It is not uncommon to find these chains cutting deeply into the necks of the poor wearers.

BEDS AND BEDDING

Bedding for pets can also be a problem. For indoor dogs you have a choice of several different kinds of mattresses, canvas stretched across metal or wooden frames, and all sort of beds. You can make beds out of pieces of thick carpet or cast-off mattresses cut down, or you can allow pets to sleep in old chairs. An old blanket that can be laundered when necessary is a simple solution.

Some people like the smell of cedar in bedding, but the smell of stale cedar mixed with dog odors is unpleasant. After a while the smell pervades a whole house—even the clothing hanging in closets. Ordinary pine shavings can be bought for a fraction of the cost of cedar and actually makes a better bedding, especially if you add some flea powder to the shavings.

Some dogs refuse to sleep on soft beds. Great Danes often develop large elbow joint swellings from irritation caused by sleeping on hard surfaces, and almost everyone has known at least one dog that insisted on lying right by the crack under the door. Heavy dogs that refuse to sleep on the softer bedding provided for them sometimes develop sores or stiffness. Light dogs usually show the marks only at their elbows.

In outside kennels, oat or wheat straw is as satisfactory as any bedding. Marsh grass is also excellent. Wood shavings are likely to be tracked out, create an untidy appearance, and are difficult to rake. If straw is placed in a kennel, there should be at least four inches of the packed material under a dog in cold weather. In summer less is needed. It is seldom necessary to dust outdoor dogs for fleas if a liberal amount is shaken in the bedding each time it is changed. In wet weather the bedding may have to be changed every few days, whereas in dry weather it may serve a month. If it stays over a week, flea powder should be dusted over it every six or seven days.

RUN SANITATION

In a dog run, sanitation can keep a pet in sound health, whereas the lack of it may be responsible for its death.

Runs for pets of every kind are made of wire, concrete, sand, soil, gravel, grass, or of various combinations of these materials. Wire runs elevated from the ground permit all excrement to drop out of the cage and can be cleaned and hosed readily. Kennel dogs kept in these accommodations are relatively free of parasites. Dogs kept on rough concrete suffer the most from parasites, since concrete is a splendid incubator. Highly polished concrete kept clean is successful but, being slippery, is not an ideal surface for the dogs.

Grass is also objectionable. It is impossible to do even a halfway successful job of removing stools where grass grows. Worm eggs stick to the leaves as they grow, and dogs may eat the leaves and become infested or reinfested. Even when grass is started in a run, it soon dies out, leaving bare topsoil which then becomes muddy.

Washed builder's sand makes an excellent run floor. It costs little, is easily removed and discarded, and is easily replaced. It shakes off a dog's feet even when wet. In addition it doesn't track into the kennel as much as soil with clay in it does.

Sanitation, of course, consists of removing stools and replacing the run material. Proper stool removal requires that not only the stool itself but also the layer of sand under it be lifted out with a shovel. If rain has washed some of the outside surface of stool off, any worm eggs may be carried down a fraction of an inch into the surface, since these eggs are much smaller than the pores between even the finest kinds of soil granules. A little soil or sand should always be hoed up with the stool to be certain that all contamination is removed.

In cleaning a dog run, do not rake all the stools into a pile and then shovel them up together. When a stool is even partially pulverized by raking or sweeping, its parts, including worm eggs, are scattered and washed into the soil, which soon becomes thoroughly contaminated. Worm eggs that have become embryonated may resist the elements for years, waiting to be consumed by dogs. When hookworm eggs hatch and the larvae have reached the infective stage, they move upward from fairly deep in the soil with capillarity. They will be found close to the surface of the soil, even somewhat above the surface if they can find a little stem or stalk to climb.

Too much care cannot be exerted in gathering stools. Stools cannot be gathered efficiently from cinders, gravel, or grass. They cannot be removed from rough concrete without leaving eggs in the pores. Only by burning or daily scrubbing can rough concrete be freed of parasite eggs or larvae. Some kennel owners use flame-throwing oil burners which heat the soil surface sufficiently to kill worm eggs and hookworm larvae, but such methods are, of course, impractical for the owner of one dog.

It is difficult to clean any kind of dog run in winter. The problem is not as serious as it might be, however, since worm eggs do not incubate in cold weather, nor do fleas develop. How is this problem managed in kennels where runs are full winter and summer? All spring and summer the sand runs are cleaned with hoe and shovel. A summer's cleaning removes at least two inches and sometimes four from the run's surface. In the fall this is replaced so that the surface is an inch above surrounding ground. Since the sand will pack down an inch, six inches of sand should be added if four are gone. If a dog has infested a run with eggs or parasites, deworm the dog, shovel off the top two inches of sand, and fill the run with fresh sand.

In cold climates during the winter little run covering can be removed, except on balmy days when the surface may melt enough to enable shoveling. When snow covers the run the owner does the best he or she can, which usually isn't satisfactory even from the standpoint of appearance. As soon as the surface has thawed in the spring, the top two inches should be removed and replaced with fresh sand.

In a dog run the stools are generally deposited within a few square yards. It is easy to dig away this soil and replace it with sand. But don't merely turn it over for a depth of a few inches and think that the whole problem has been solved. Dogs dig holes, and when they do they will scratch old buried worm eggs to the surface. Even the necessary removal of bits of earth with the stools will in time dig away enough soil to reach the eggs again. Whipworm eggs have been found to live for eight years in the ground.

There are few disinfectants that will kill worm eggs. Roundworm eggs can stand even carbolic acid. But hookworms can be destroyed by a very strong salt solution poured over the surface of the runs until it stands in pools. It has also been found that a 2 percent solution of household lye applied in the same manner will destroy hookworm larvae. Neither method works very well on a slope. In addition, dogs must be kept off the lye until after a hard rain.

A more efficient method than either of these is the use of borax (sodium borate) made into a strong solution (two pounds per gallon) and poured over the run's surface at the rate of two gallons per hundred square feet. Borax may be procured from kennel supply companies and wholesale drug distributors. It does have the disadvantge of killing all vegetation not only where it's applied but many feet around that area.

OUTDOOR ACCOMMODATIONS

If a dog is left outside from spring on, it will be healthier than if kept indoors. It will have a better coat, shed less, and be in less danger of being overfed. A majority of hunters believe that making house pets of their dogs ruins them for the sport.

Scientific studies on acclimatizing animals show that they should not be exposed to sudden changes in temperature. An animal that might die of exposure when taken suddenly from warm to cold can stand much lower temperatures if it is introduced to them gradually. One reason is that cold stimulates the growth of the coat, which in time becomes much thicker and so provides better protection. When dogs from the south are brought north, their coats are so much heavier in their second winter in the north that they look like different animals. An animal that has become accustomed to cold can endure a great deal.

Northern outdoor dogs often prefer to be out in the snow when they might sleep inside of a comfortable doghouse.

Every fall outdoor kennels need to be prepared for the winter. There should be no cracks for the wind to blow through, and the doors should have a blanket or other substantial material hung over them. A single dog's body heat will keep a good kennel at 60° F on a night when the outside temperature is 15° F. These burlap front doors do not always stay in place, however, since dogs seem to pull them off. Because of this habit, our own dogs have spent nights with the temperature being 10° below zero curled up on straw beds open to the wind. As far as we could see, they showed no ill effects from the cold. In fact, many dogs prefer sleeping curled up in snow on bitterly cold nights even when they can sleep inside in what would seem to be far greater comfort.

DISINFECTANTS

Disinfectants must be chosen with care. Dogs are quite resistant to most of the ordinary forms, whereas cats and foxes cannot tolerate phenol derivatives.

Odorless deodorizers are excellent and can be purchased at reasonable prices. "Phenol coefficient" on a label may not mean a phenol product. It simply compares a product with phenol in its germ-killing ability. Some of the odorless deodorizers do have high phenol ratings.

Some pet owners like the odor of pine oil; others prefer phenols, which often simply outsmell the odor to be removed. Good soap-and-water cleansing is usually adequate around pets, and if there is an odor left after scrubbing, it is a safe assumption that the area is not clean. Disinfectants that give off chlorine are good but are also bleaches and must be used judiciously on that account.

ENCLOSURES

Dogs allowed to run loose are least infested with intestinal parasites, except for the rabbit form of tapeworm. (Country and suburban dogs kill and eat rabbits and thus become infested.) Dogs on small runs or on short chains have the most intestinal parasites.

A fenced-in yard is perhaps the best enclosure as far as safety and convenience are concerned; if the area is sufficiently large the parasite problem is minimal. It need not necessarily be a great and expensive project to fence a large area unless large, agile dogs are involved, in which case the six-foot height required may be a problem. For a five-foot fence, steel posts can be driven into the ground with a sledgehammer and the fencing wired to the posts. A similar fence using chain link fencing with pipes set in concrete accomplishes the same result but at many times the cost.

A tight wire stretched from the back door to a tree some distance away and eight feet off the ground is a preferred device for many owners. One end of a chain slides along the wire and the other is attached to the dog's collar. A word of caution is appropriate here. The end of the chain should, when hanging from the wire, extend about a foot from the ground. A long chain might entangle the dog's legs.

An outdoor doghouse should not be palatial but rather should be small enough for the dog's body heat to warm the area in cold weather. It should be constructed to permit ventilation in the hot weather. A piece of carpeting attached as a flap to the top of the entrance helps to keep flying insects out as well as to keep heat in during cold spells.

Most dogs have a few intestinal parasites off and on and they are equipped to live with them. When a dog with a few worms is confined to a small area that is not or cannot be properly cleaned the dog's chances of reinfestation are greater. It may still thrive with a moderate number of parasites but eventually the surface will be so contaminated that the dog may develop an overwhelming number which, untreated, can kill it.

The dog on a chain defecates, then runs around dragging the chain through the stool, spreading it over so wide an area that it is usually impossible to pick up. Dogs hitched to overhead wires have a better chance to remain parasite-free because they generally drop their stools at one end of the wire and spend most of their time away from the dirty sections of their runs.

Long, narrow runs are preferable to square runs with the same number of square feet. The dog usually defecates at one end of a long run, generally at the end farthest from the house. But if that is the end where the dog first sees you, it will spend most of its time in daylight hours there watching for you, and thus remain in the filth. If possible, the arrangement of the run should be such that this is avoided.

If enclosures are built, the wire needs to be of sufficient strength that dogs cannot chew through it, and it should be of a mesh that is difficult to climb. The wire should be buried at least eight inches in the ground —a foot is even better.

RAT CONTROL

Rats should not be allowed to remain as kennel parasites anymore than insects should be permitted to infest the kennel inhabitants. It is generally easy to eradicate them. Rodenticides, nonpoisonous to pets other than rodents, will keep rats at a minimum. When rats are known to exist on the premises, put out a small bowl of dog food and let them eat it. Do this every night until the rats are bold enough to eat it all and then you know how much they will take. When you have succeeded in making them to feel at home, mix the rodenticide with the food and leave it for them as usual. As a rule, four meals will eradicate the rats and no more will be seen for a month or more.

Some of the rat poisons are extremely effective but dangerous to pets. If they are used, they must be covered so there can be no possible chance that the pets can dig them out or uncover boards or boxes to get them. With these poisons the dead or dying rodent is also toxic to dogs.

PERIODIC HEALTH EXAMINATION

One of the best bits of advice veterinarians can give to their clients is that they keep most careful track of the health of their pets, especially those that have passed middle age, by periodic physical checkups. Your veterinarian can make some tests that may be instrumental in prolonging your pet's life by many years.

In many areas heartworms have become a problem requiring yearly tests. This is a good opportunity for booster inoculations, the heartworm test, as well as a physical examination. In most cases you as a concerned owner will recognize the telltale signs indicating a problem before the veterinarian even with his or her thorough examination. All too often an owner brings in a pet with a problem observable only at home, such as drinking or sleeping excessively. The animal is presented with no information given from the owner, who wants an examination to be done. In this situation veterinarians have learned not to ask,

"What seems to be the problem?" since the reply is apt to be "That's what I brought my dog here to find out." Instead, we ask what the purpose of the visit is and if the dog has been acting normally. We have always appreciated the owners who jot down questions to ask us or things to tell us. Some come in with a veritable list. This is great. This way they are less apt to forget signs that seem unimportant but may be extremely important.

All too often one member of a family brings in the family dog for one problem and fails to mention several others. This results in another member phoning to ask other questions or to supply other information, which at times indicate a problem more serious than that for which the dog was brought in.

The veterinarian can determine the presence of some diseases by temperature readings and other signs. He or she can detect external parasites, intestinal parasites, heartworms, skin disease, ear canker, kidney disease, bad teeth, overweight and underweight conditions, eye defects, and deafness. All these defects need correcting, if possible.

Any of these conditions can shorten an animal's life. When you take your pet to the veterinarian for a periodic health examination, take along a small sample of stool and a urine specimen. To catch the urine from a dog, take it for a walk on a short lead and, for a male, hold a cup under his penis when he lifts his leg; for a female, push a small shallow dish under her when she squats.

Let us consider how a periodic health examination can prolong the life of your animal. Suppose you know of nothing wrong. All you notice is that Rover hasn't the pep he used to have. You take in samples of his urine and feces and ask your veterinarian to examine him. But don't expect the whole examination to be worthwhile unless you have brought the urine and stool, because so many facts may be learned from them.

The veterinarian also may draw a blood sample. Then screening tests are performed on these three samples—most often in a laboratory on the premises—by the veterinarian or his or her technician/assistant. The urine is checked for protein, blood, bile pigments, and many other factors. The blood will give an indication of the presence of blood parasites as well as relative numbers of the many types of cells that are present. The stool is able to indicate parasites. The veterinarian might also suggest other tests which, depending on his or her facilities, may have to be run in an outside laboratory. X rays, cardiograms, and hosts of other procedures may be used as necessary. Then from the information you have supplied coupled with a physical examination and the laboratory findings, the veterinarian can be assured of a problem or suspect a problem or find the dog to be normal.

Even if a pet appears to be in excellent condition, we would urge any concerned owner of a middle-aged dog to have a series of tests performed in anticipation of problems in the future. When a problem occurs as the result of aging, another series of tests will, on comparison with the results of earlier tests when a dog was normal, be helpful in a diagnosis. Most tests have a spread so that any value in that spread is normal. If your dog runs a very low normal and then, due to disease, it shows a very high normal or even slightly above normal, it may be of great importance.

The number of diseases that can be uncovered in dogs is legion. Fortunately the majority of them can either be eliminated or relieved by proper care and medication. A proper examination, which reveals many diseases in their early stages when treatment is most effective, is one of the surest ways to ensure the health and longevity of your pet.

BOARDING

Dog owners sooner or later face the question, "What shall I do with my pet when I have to leave it?" There are a number of other questions closely related to this one. "If the dog becomes sick, shall I keep it at home or leave it in a veterinary hospital? Should I exhibit my dog in a show? Should I take my dog to a training class? Is it safe to allow my pet free access to neighborhood animals?"

Actually all of these general questions are part of a still larger one, "To what extent should I isolate my dog?"

In order to answer these questions intelligently, there are certain basic facts you should know. Every proprietor of a veterinary hospital or a boarding kennel, every dog warden and humane society officer, knows these facts. If every pet owner knew them as well, sickness among pets might be greatly reduced. Omitting for the moment any consideration of the emotional side of the question, let us discuss only the purely physical factors, the health hazards that "mingling" entails.

Let's assume that every dog owner and every dog handler is honest, and that every person owning an animal he or she knows is sick will isolate it. Let's assume, too, that no dog warden knowingly puts a sick animal in the pound. And last, but not least, let's assume that no veterinary hospital exists without isolation wards where dogs with each kind of disease are separately segregated. It is obvious that none of these assumptions can be completely true. Pet owners are no more and no less ethical than other groups of people. Certainly not all of them are sufficiently concerned about the health of other people's pets to isolate their own when they know it to be sick.

But suppose that all these things are true. Could you even then be certain that your dog could be safely placed with a lot of other healthy animals and never contract a disease? You could not.

The average dog show probably furnishes the best example of the risk involved whenever animals are brought together, in spite of the fact that every dog exhibited is supposed to be a healthy animal. Even if veterinarians examined all dogs at the entrance gate and rejected those that were sick, dog shows would still be one of the prime means by which disease is spread. Here is a case in point from our own experience.

Many years ago, just after one of our Bloodhounds, Barbara of White Isle, had weaned a beautiful litter of puppies, she was shown at the Westminster Kennel Club Show in Madison Square Garden. Twice a day she was walked to the exercise space. In that space one day there was a Dalmatian bitch from Texas. She looked sick to us, but her owner refused to keep her leashed and when she walked up to Barbara we were unable to shoo her away. On the following Saturday, six days later, we were showing Barbara at the New Haven, Connecticut, show when we noted she was squinting. A little later she vomited. Her temperature was only 102° F. Car sickness can produce vomiting. Dust in the eyes can cause squinting. But distemper can cause and was causing both symptoms. It so happens that on the sixth day after infection a dog's temperature drops when it has that disease—which accounted for Barbara's 102° F—and rises again the seventh day. Barbara's puppies and seventy-five other dogs of ours contracted distemper.

The Texas Dalmatian—via a dog show—had spread distemper to Connecticut and probably to many other localities, and who knows but that the Connecticut Bloodhound spread it to California, since there were dogs from California on the circuit of Eastern shows. Yet who was to blame? We had no means of conferring immunity at that time.

Today we have the means, and distemper is rapidly disappearing, but distemper is only one disease. The dog show remains a good example of the hazards of "mingling" because, if we face the facts honestly, we must admit that it is impossible to recognize disease in animals when it's in the incubation stage.

Here is another example of the way disease is spread. A kennel owner accepts a Mrs. Williams's dog in good faith. The dog is placed in a room in a building with many others. All of them appear to be in good health. After three days the kennel owner notices that Mrs. Williams's dog is gagging. She segregates it in another room. But suppose your dog had been in the first room? Many of the dog diseases are spread by droplet infection. A day after you take your dog home it starts to sneeze. You telephone the kennel owner immediately to complain. She tells you your dog was contented and well on its first visit. But the chances are she remembers Mrs. Williams's dog, and when two days later she finds that most of the dogs in that room are sneezing, what is she to do? Whose fault is it? Is the kennel owner under obligation to take your dog back and keep it until it is cured or dies? Unfortunately legally such an occurrence is considered, along with lightning, wind, and fire, as "an act of God."

Perhaps your dog contracts a disease while being boarded, and when you return it is dead. The owner of the kennel, half sick with worry over what has happened, has spent hours trying to nurse the dogs under her care to health. You are hurt, indignant, and furious that your dog has been lost. Perhaps you even refuse to pay for the board. Actually, considering the work and worry involved, you owe the kennel owner for more than if nothing had happened. If negligence is involved you should be irate.

Although rare, this does happen in dog-boarding establishments. Everyone with a lot of experience could tell of many similar instances. Owners will bring in their dogs, stating they don't want them kept close to other dogs because of the possibility of contracting a disease. They choose an outdoor run. The dog goes home infected with coccidiosis. Who's to blame? More than likely a fly. Did the fly first feed on an infested stool of a dog in the same kennel or did it fly from a kennel five miles away? Flies may easily travel eight or ten miles in a single night. You cannot call this an act of carelessness.

Needless to say, no boarding kennel owners ever *want* such things to happen. It hurts them every time it does. It causes worry, anguish, extra work, loss of money, and loss of reputation. So what, then, should be one's attitude? Should pet owners say, "I left a well animal; now it's sick. You're to blame"? Or should they try to look at it from a reasonable point of view, difficult as that may be, and to understand the circumstances?

It is impossible to assemble a large group of animals of any species and be 100 percent certain that not one is infested with parasites or is incubating some disease. And since this is true, you can't board a pet and be 100 percent sure the pet will be well, uninfested with parasites, and neither incubating a disease nor showing signs of a problem when you call for it.

The best and safest approach is to leave your pet in a kennel where veterinary attention is given or where the owner knows diseases well enough to be able to recognize the first signs and is willing and able to treat them properly. It is, of course, essential that there be a segregation ward in conjunction with the boarding facilities.

Dogs corralled by the city dog wardens may be placed in a truck with half a dozen others, taken to the pound, and there put in a cage or a pen with many other dogs. Some of these will be dogs from homes where they have received the best of care, but in general people who think so little of their pets as to allow them to run are not the citizens who have fine dogs and take good care of them. In fact, many cruel or irresponsible owners purposely abandon sick or mangy dogs, and when your pet is picked up by the warden it is subjected to all the infectious diseases available to the dogs of your area—all concentrated in one room.

If your healthy male dog knows where a bitch in heat lives, you may be sure he will be camped near her home, and so will all the other male dogs that know—another potent source for the spread of infection.

Unquestionably dogs can contract diseases in veterinary hospitals. The most careful veterinarian, in the best of faith, accepts animals, apparently free from disease, for operations. Two days later those same animals may be sneezing and filling surgical wards with invisible virus-filled droplets. Even though ultraviolet lights and germ-killing vaporizers may have been installed, they cannot guarantee that a few healthy dogs will not be infected. We have never known a veterinarian to tell us that no disease was ever contracted in his or her hospital. But neither can the superintendent of a hospital for humans make that boast. Who doesn't know of at least one case of a patient in a hospital contracting virus pneumonia or some other contagious disease: What of the diseases that sweep through the infant wards, or the women who even today are infected with "childbed fever"? We believe the risk of leaving a pet in a scrupulously clean veterinary hospital, complete with segregation wards, is less than the risk of contracting a disease yourself while in a hospital.

Just as children in a certain school and community who have measles, mumps, and chicken pox and are then immune to them are glad they don't get these diseases later, so pet owners can be glad their pets can be protected by inoculation against all the diseases it is possible to be protected against and then can build up natural immunity to others. This much is certain: animals can't assemble in large numbers and remain free from disease anymore than children can be expected not to contract the infectious diseases from their classmates in school.

Remember that not everything that happens to your pet in a hospital or kennel happens *because* it is there. Many of these things are the result of normal health hazards; many are the direct result of age, habits, idiosyncrasies, food, and appetite of your pet.

You may have left a very fat pet and return to find it thin. You should be pleased that it has lost dangerous excess weight. Or a comfortably fat pet may have grown too fat by the time you call for it. A few days' attention to its diet will correct that.

Remember the characteristics of the breed and of the individual animal. If you own a Great Dane, you can expect it will brood, be homesick, refuse food, and may lose twenty pounds in a week if left in a kennel. And when it does, this will be your fault for ever having allowed the dog to become so dependent upon you. The cure is to leave it more often and to use the same food at home as the kennel uses (if it is a wholesome brand) so that your pet won't have to be starved to eat this food every time you board it.

If you own a lively pet, the first day after you take it home its stools will probably be quite loose. This does not necessarily mean the dog is sick. Any hunter will tell you that, though dog's stools may be perfect when in the kennel, the dog won't have run a quarter of a mile before it may be passing liquid stools. Excitement after confinement—not sickness—often causes loose stools. Your pet was probably in a small run or even a compartment; at home it has the outdoors to run in and it jumps and frisks. Expect loose stools until your dog gets back into its old regime.

After leaving boarding establishments most pets seem thirsty. They have had pans of water in their runs, but upon returning home seem to drink a lot of water. Expect this too. Your pet may also act starved. This is not strange: it had been learning to know a new food and you take it back to the one it was accustomed to. Of course it enjoys its old food! Try to be reasonable about the food and care you expect for your dog while it is being boarded. If you want your dog fed fancy things, it is best that you supply them. For the average pet, where the cost of everything is considered, the boarding kennel owner is lucky to clear 10 or 15 percent a day on the average dog. Would you, for the average boarding charge, assume the responsibility of keeping a neighbor's setter for two weeks, feeding it, keeping it free of external or internal parasites to the best of your ability, changing its bedding regularly, cleaning its droppings twice a day, renewing its water twice or three times a day? We doubt it. The reason the kennel or pet shop owners are willing to do this is because they are equipped to keep large numbers of dogs.

If you find a boarding accommodation for your pet that suits you, continue to use only that establishment. In time your pet will become acclimated and your troubles are over.

One precaution you can and should take: consider the age of your pet. Young puppies are far more likely to die in a new environment than are grown dogs, because they have less resistance. Intestinal parasites are more harmful to young animals than to older ones. Virus diseases are much harder on younger dogs. Knowing these facts, you will be wise to keep your puppies—and all your young dogs—isolated, as far as it is in your power to do so, until they are over a year old. Thereafter the ravages of diseases will be less severe.

After you have read this book you will be in a better position to judge where your pet contracted any disease, because knowledge of an incubation period will help you. If you know the distemper incubation period is five days and you have had your pet home from its boarding place for ten days, you may be sure it "caught it" while in your hands. By the same token, if you are informed by the boarding kennel owner that your dog started to be sick a few days after it was accepted to board, you may know it was infected before you left it.

One other factor or risk in boarding pets is that they may run away. Don't expect the kennel owner to be responsible if your dog chews a hole in a sound fence and escapes. You owe the kennel owner for the damage. If your dog jumps a six-foot fence and you didn't tell the owner it could jump, or perhaps you didn't know it, that is your misfortune. Don't neglect the viewpoint of the owner of the establishment where your pet is left, be it a boarding kennel or veterinary hospital. We think you would be appalled if you knew how often people who were aware that their dogs were sick tried to leave them "to board" at a veterinary establishment. Every hospital and kennel owner has had this experience. Veterinarians with "weather eyes" out for such animals are not often fooled, but proprietors of boarding kennels who fail to recognize a diseased animal (and who are grateful to have another boarder) often have illnesses introduced into their kennels by unscrupulous dog owners.

The risk to health where pets congregate or are congregated is unavoidable. But it can be greatly reduced. Nothing does more to minimize the hazards than proper vaccination. Neglecting to take this simple precaution is not only unethical, since it affects others, but is also irresponsible—you must take the most obvious step to protect the health of your pets.

5

Breeding

Thousands of people breed and raise animals. Some enjoy breeding to improve a species, to originate a new strain, or even to originate an entirely new type of animal. For thousands more, breeding a dog may be more trouble than it is worth. In crowded city areas, in small homes, for busy people, breeding new litters of animals is out of the question. For this to be done you must have adequate space, conditions, and time.

FIRST HEAT MATING

Many people are convinced that a bitch should never be bred during her first mating cycle, but there is no scientific support for such a belief. All animals more closely related to canines than to humans are capable of rearing offspring from a first heat mating. Foxes, wolves, and raccoons are examples of this.

We cannot find any rationale in skipping the first heat. We have always mated bitches the first time they were in season and have yet to see any harmful results. A bitch does not come into heat until she is mature, full grown, and well able to look after a litter. In a young bitch, the bones that surround the birth canal are not fused together as they are in an older animal, so this pelvic girdle of bones may actually stretch with the birth of a large puppy. In older bitches, fusion of the bones precludes this stretching. A first litter produced when the bitch is under a year of age may make her subsequent litters easier.

In our experience, the first litter, regardless of the bitch's age, is not as successful as subsequent litters. Of course, the first whelping is to- tally instinctive but its appears that some conditioning is apparent at the second litter: there are not as many prelabor restless periods and the whelping seems to proceed with more deliberation.

HOW OLD CAN A FEMALE BE WHEN BRED?

There are well-sheltered intact females that have been isolated with great care all their lives until carelessness and ensuing pregnancy at an advanced age occurs. One case was a ten-year-old virgin Cocker Spaniel —rather, she had been a virgin. When examining her for an abdominal distension, we felt the puppies moving in her abdomen and announced the news to her owners, who were adamant that it could not have happened. We planned a cesarean section but then she went into labor and surprised us with a puppy in two hours. Just as we were about to perform a cesarean, almost as if she had got the message, she had another puppy. She had five in all over an eighteen-hour period. She, the owners, and we were all exhausted when the last puppy arrived and in retrospect surgery would have been easier on the dog than such a protracted, difficult labor.

How old a female can be bred for the first time? We think eight years old is the limit and, since she has never whelped a litter before, that age is not without a greater element of risk than an earlier age.

Many well-meaning pet owners tell us they did not have their female spayed because they wanted her to have a litter someday but it had not yet been convenient. Then, when the beloved pet begins to show signs of aging, there is a temptation to breed her and keep a puppy just like the mother.

Such thinking presents two problems. First, bearing a litter for a female showing signs of aging is risky or at least riskier than one she would have had when she was young. Second, with the infinite number of possible gene combinations it is unlikely that one pup from a litter will be just like the mother. If you are tempted, take your pet to your veterinarian and have a heart-to-heart talk covering the pros and cons of such an undertaking before making a decision.

How old is too old to breed a female? Each female should be considered separately, but in general we don't advise breeding the average female after eight years of age. With the giant breeds and a few others, six years old is about the safe limit. However, there appears to be no reason not to use a male at stud at any age.

WHY BREED?

A few words concerning the desirability of breeding a female are in order because too many owners breed their animals for the wrong reasons.

Some say it is natural and healthy for a female to have pups. No doubt it is natural but healthy it is not. The females spayed at a young age outlive the unspayed littermates by at least two years on the average, and two years is one sixth of the life expectancy. Although we do not have statistics to prove it, we believe the altered male outlives the unaltered.

Many well-intentioned people will breed a female that has endeared herself to so many friends and neighbors that good homes are assured for a large litter. A word of caution here: all too often those who rave about your dog and say they would like one of her puppies change their minds when the pups are available. If you do plan to sell the puppies, place ads in newspapers giving information sufficient to rule out many shoppers who want a five-dollar pup—unless you have five-dollar pups for sale. Mention price, age, breed or type, and your phone number or a box number for written requests for information. Screen the prospective purchasers so that the puppies will have good homes. The wife of one of us breeds Gordon Setters but never will she breed unless she has a small cash deposit on at least four puppies, or half the expected litter.

Another reason to produce puppies is allegedly to make money. A friend of ours overheard one of our clients state that the reason he was breeding his Poodles was to send his children through college. Our friend remarked that the client would send the veterinarian's children through college, not his own. There is more truth than fiction in that remark since it is a rare breeder who can make money breeding dogs.

Then there are those naïve enough to think they can improve the breed with scientific breeding. The problem with that proposition is that there are few with the scientific background, the objectivity, and the money to make an impression on a breed. In such a program, all offspring must be raised to maturity to select the individual animals to continue the program and those that do not measure up must be eliminated by altering or destruction. It is difficult to sell an adult of many breeds, making such a program an expensive venture.

In spite of charity spaying, neutering facilities, and educational campaigns, hundreds of thousands of unwanted dogs are destroyed yearly in our country. It is sad but true that half of them are misfits because of heredity or mistreatment and few as adults can be rehabilitated. The other half would make acceptable family dogs if there were enough families for them. So before you breed be sure you can place all the puppies in good homes. And it is a wise idea to educate your children about the surfeit of unwanted dogs. Talk to them about it and if you have any unwanted puppies that have to be destroyed—and if your children can handle it —you might bring them along when you have it done. Be part of the solution and not part of the problem of the pet population explosion.

THE MATING CYCLE

Biologically speaking, the basic reason for the existence of any animal or plant is to pass along the germ plasm of which it is the custodian for the next generation. Everything about a plant or animal that helps it to live in harmonious relationship with its environment is working toward that end. A creature is a bundle of natural adaptations designed to ensure its own perpetuation. One of the most interesting tricks or arrangements is the female mating cycle.

At maturity a female animal usually is said to come in heat or come in season. Most animals come in season in what are called mating cycles. The primary influence that causes different species to start their mating cycles is the length of the day. We do not understand how light accomplishes these changes, which vary from one species to another. Dogs have a mating cycle in summer and winter, and that is usually all. There are canids that regularly come in heat only once a year. This is the case with wild, doglike animals—the wolf and fox, for example— that have litters only in the early spring. How long ago it was that the dog developed the propensity to come in heat twice a year, we do not know; nor do we know whether the dogs that come in heat once a year inherit this idiosyncrasy.

As we pointed out when we discussed body regulators, the pituitary gland initiates the mating cycle. The follicular hormone carries it through, and when the follicles rupture and discharge their eggs, the luteal hormone ends it. At the same time a rather complex series of changes is going on in the animal's body. The mating cycle of the dog is fairly typical. An understanding of this process will help you handle your pet intelligently—and may save you embarrassment if you own an unspayed bitch.

Outwardly, the first signs of the season are the slight swelling of the vulva and increased appetite. For perhaps five days this swelling continues until a few drops of blood drip from the vulva. Some bitches bleed scantily and clean themselves so that no blood is ever seen. Others bleed fairly copiously. The first, or bleeding, period lasts from four to fifteen days. By the end of this period the discharge is pale red, almost straw-colored.

Inside the body the ovaries, which appeared smooth at the start, are showing the protrusion of the follicles as they enlarge. The uterus is growing longer and larger in diameter.

The second stage is initiated by a willingness on the part of the bitch to copulate. There may be a long teasing and playing period with the male dog, but eventually she will accept him. This is considered the first day of the second, or acceptance, period.

The follicles continue to enlarge on the ovaries, and the uterus and blood vessels are greatly increased in size. By about the sixth day of the acceptance period the follicles of the average bitch have ruptured and liberated their eggs (ovulation). It is possible to find bitches that ovulate the first day of the acceptance period, and others will be found that ovulate toward the end. If copulation has occurred, the sperm from the male (thousands of them) will be waiting around the ovaries for the discharge of the eggs so that one may fertilize each egg. Then the fertilized eggs move down the fallopian tubes and eventually come to rest at fairly even spaces from each other.

As soon as ovulation has occurred, a blood plug forms in each follicle. This changes into the luteal body that secretes the hormone whose presence in the blood effectively stops the mating cycle and mating behavior. Luteal bodies remain throughout pregnancy. If they are dislodged, the bitch aborts. After birth, the luteal bodies last for several months and their presence prevents another mating cycle.

During the copulatory, or acceptance, period the bitch mates repeatedly, if allowed, but toward the end she "goes out" rather suddenly. As the luteal hormone takes effect, her behavior changes. She may fight off willing males, and then just when the owner is sure the period is over she may play with and be teased by a male until she accepts him. These late matings often result in large litters, certainly larger than those of very early matings.

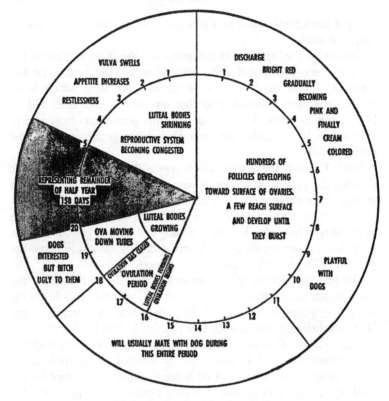

VULVA SWELLS

APPETITE INCREASES

RESTLESSNESS

LUTEAL BODIES
SHRINKING

REPRODUCTIVE SYSTEM
BECOMING CONGESTED

REPRESENTING REMAINDER
OF HALF YEAR
158 DAYS

DOGS
INTERESTED
BUT BITCH
UGLY TO THEM

OVA MOVING
DOWN TUBES

LUTEAL BODIES
GROWING

OVULATION HAS CEASED

OVULATION
PERIOD

LUTEAL BODIES FORMING
OVULATION BEGINS

WILL USUALLY MATE WITH DOG DURING
THIS ENTIRE PERIOD

DISCHARGE
BRIGHT RED
GRADUALLY
BECOMING
PINK AND
FINALLY
CREAM
COLORED

HUNDREDS OF
FOLLICLES DEVELOPING
TOWARD SURFACE OF OVARIES.
A FEW REACH SURFACE
AND DEVELOP UNTIL
THEY BURST

PLAYFUL
WITH
DOGS

Mating cycle of average female dog.

When dogs are mated the first day of the acceptance period, the sperm must live several days, waiting for the eggs. But when mating occurs late, the eggs are ready and the sperm find them waiting.

A frequent question asked is whether or not a litter of puppies can have two fathers. Yes, a litter of pups can have two and sometimes three fathers. Some of the ova may have been fertilized by the sperm of one male, other ova by the sperm of a second or third male. The majority of the puppies are likely to resemble the male that mated with the bitch nearest the fourteenth day.

Gestation is the time from fertilization of the eggs until birth, not the time from mating until birth. This period in a bitch lasts sixty-three days. On occasion we find a female with a "dry" heat. As the term suggests, there is little or no bleeding and such an animal may show so little indication of estrus that her owners do not confine her—and sixty-three days later she presents them with a litter of mongrels.

COPULATION

How is copulation accomplished?

The doglike animals accomplish mating by a unique physical device. In the dog's penis there is a bone. It is thick at the base and tapers toward the point. Through it runs the urethra. The penis is of a spongy tissue which, when an exit valve in a large vein is closed, fills with blood under pressure from a large artery. Right behind the bone there is a plexus of nerves that is very sensitive. Pressure on this point causes a violent thrust reflex. At the same time, the valve regulating the exit of the blood from the penis closes and the dog develops an erection, which is a distension of the penis with blood.

Unlike the penis of any other group of animals, the canid's penis has a large bulbous enlargement at the base. When the dog's penis enters the vagina of the bitch, it must go through a muscular ring or constriction of the external opening of the vagina. The bitch must elevate the vulva to make a straight tube of the vagina. As soon as the penis is pressed through this restricted opening, it passes into the vagina, which is much larger and very elastic. The moment the penis is through, the pressure of the tube on the reflex nerve center causes a violent thrust and the dog clings to the bitch with all his strength. And in that moment the penis swells to large proportions, three times its normal diameter in the smaller part and five or six times at the bulb.

The swelling of the bulb prevents the dog from withdrawing his penis. At this time he ejaculates semen and the sperm it contains. A pressure is built up and the semen is forced through the cervix and up the horns of the uterus, through the fallopian tubes, and into the capsule which surrounds the ovaries. In twenty minutes after copulation starts, the semen will have ascended that far.

Dogs remain "hung" in this manner from one minute to two hours. The average time is slightly less than twenty minutes. The male turns around and faces the opposite direction from the bitch. While the two are hung in this manner, they may get their nails into the dirt and pull with far more than their own weights. No one should be alarmed when they pull this way; neither dog is being hurt. As the valve relaxes, the blood leaves the penis, usually from the bulb part first, and allows the enlarged penis to slip out.

Very little has been written about copulation in dogs. We have made notes on hundreds of matings, including data about the length of time the dogs were hung, the number of times various dogs copulated in a day, and certain idiosyncrasies about individual dogs and breeds of dogs.

There have been many instances where a pair of dogs have been raised together, in the same home, and the owner has wanted puppies from the pair. While the bitch seemed to be willing to mate, the male showed no inclination. Then, toward the very end of the acceptance period, the owner has found them copulating, and good-sized litters of puppies have resulted. One pair of Boston Terriers that were kept together never mated until the seventeenth day. A pair of Great Danes were mated toward the end of the period only. Another pair of dogs, when kept away from all other dogs, behaved in this manner; but once when they were placed in a kennel where there were other dogs close by, their sexual behavior pattern changed and they copulated every day during the whole acceptance period.

Some dogs are never willing to mate more than every other day if left alone with bitches in the acceptance period. At the other extreme, one Foxhound we owned mated five times one day and three times the next and was hung at least twenty minutes each time

There are females that are very selective about the male they mate with, while others will accept all comers. After repeated unsuccessful attempts to mate to a selected stud, a female may permit the neighbor's mongrel the privilege.

Before breeding it is wise to have a veterinarian examine a female to be sure she is in good health and has a normal pelvic opening for the breed or type. If she has a small pelvic opening she may require a cesarean section, which might influence your decision to breed.

It is also helpful to phone your veterinarian a few days prior to the impending delivery date to alert him.

Normal Mating. Watch first for a swelling of the female's vulva and then for the first day of bleeding, which you record as day one for future reference. You observe the vaginal discharge change from bright red blood gradually to a faintly pinkish straw color by about the eighth day. If the stud is readily available, try the first exposure on the ninth day. If mating takes place permit them to breed every other day thereafter until she refuses him. If the male is not available breed on the tenth and twelfth days.

On palpating the vulva it will be firm until quite suddenly it loses this firmness and undergoes a detumescence—and becomes somewhat flabby. This is the time to breed if you plan only one mating.

Slightly before and during the acceptance period the bitch is said to "flag." The term flagging refers to a bitch in heat twisting her tail to one side when she is receptive and when either the male is smelling and licking her or even when a hand is rubbed over her hips on either side of the tail. And when she does permit the male to try, she flips her tail or flags to remove the tail from her vulva for the mating.

When two willing animals try repeatedly without the male gaining entry, the following is a proven method of success. With the male mounted on the female and you kneeling on the left side of the animals, gently grasp the male's penis so that the thumb and index finger are on either side behind the bulb of the penis. With the left hand reaching over the male's back hold the vulva so that the penis in the right hand can be directed into the vulva in the left hand. When you gently squeeze with the thumb and index fingers of the right hand, the male will thrust with a reflex action and gain entry into the vagina, where the bulb distends and the "tie" is accomplished.

Years ago, when Leon Whitney first described this reflex action, the renowned animal psychologist from the University of California, Frank Beach, entered the discovery in veterinary literature, calling it the "Whitney Reflex." Dr. Whitney was both pleased and embarrassed about his fame in this area; the younger Dr. Whitney basks in glory by close association.

Problems in Normal Mating. The most common problem is the female who tries to bite the male when he makes advances. Even when muzzled she becomes so violent she must either be raped or artificially inseminated. We are against even muzzling such an animal to say nothing of passing her genes on to future generations by artificial insemination.

When a normal mating cannot be accomplished it may be that the bitch is not ready to breed or has passed her acceptance period. In either case she is unlikely to conceive by rape or artificial breeding. A bitch may have a vaginal opening inadequate to accept the male. Or she may have a structural weakness that causes her to collapse with the weight of the male. She may also have a false heat: she will have the normal signs with bleeding and swelling but not as pronounced as with a normal heat. Moreover she is not as receptive to a male. As she does not ovulate, neither a normal nor an artificial breeding will produce pups.

All too often a prized show bitch will be shipped a thousand miles to be bred to a famous stud only to come into a normal heat two months later. Although there are many tests to determine the proper time to breed a bitch, the only one worth much is that performed by a veterinarian. Vaginal material is stained and studied under a microscope; at ovulation cell changes are observed that indicate the proper time for mating. A female usually ovulates at the same time in subsequent heat periods.

Of course, a problem in accomplishing a mating may be due to the male. He may have weak hindquarters or he may have infections that dampen his desire and prevent the act. Or, in the presence of strangers, he may not even try. Some males have a web or tendonlike tissue from the tip of the penis back up the sheath that causes great discomfort with an erection. This web may be snipped to correct the problem.

Some breeders have had their bitches artificially inseminated for so many generations some of their offspring seem to lose the sex drive.

There are few redeeming features of and few cases in which artificial insemination can be justified. When performed properly on animals that have produced from natural matings the success rate is almost as good. But owners usually request help when help is not in the best interest of future generations. One exception may be the selective bitch that will permit only a male of her liking to mate with her. The neighbor's mutt passes muster but not the famous international champion you would like to sire her puppies. Another possible acceptance situation for an artificial breeding is when animals are virgins. It is always wise to mate a virgin bitch with a male that has had at least one mating experience before or to use a virgin male only when the female has had a successful mating previously.

6

Pregnancy and Birth

After the female's ova have been fertilized, they nest against the uterine wall. As they grow, each fetus is surrounded by amniotic fluid which is enclosed in an amniotic sac. Each has a placenta attached to the lining of the uterus from which nourishment is carried to the fetus through the navel.

It is difficult to predict the size of a litter from the appearance of a pregnant animal. If she is very large, it may mean that she is carrying a small litter of large young or that she is carrying a large litter of small young. X rays are the only dependable means of determining the number, and they are easily employed if advisable.

THE MOTHER'S HEALTH

Few things that can be done to attain success in raising a healthy litter of puppies are as important as ensuring the mother's (or dam's) health before the puppies are born. This insurance must go back to the period before she is bred. She probably would not have come in season unless she had been in good health. Your primary considerations, therefore, are preventing disease and providing good nutrition. Parasites are enemy number one of the puppies to be born. If the dam is infested, her puppies are almost certain to be infested either during the embryonic period or after birth. Infestation after birth can result from contact with the mother's breasts or feet or with the infested run.

Puppies under three weeks of age can have worms in them old enough to be laying eggs; that can only mean that the puppies were infested while still embryos. Because this condition is not readily apparent, the pups may become so unthrifty (the veterinary term for unhealthy) that death occurs very soon after birth. It is most important, therefore, to make sure that the dam is free of parasites of all kinds, both external and internal, and that the exercising area is free of worm and flea eggs. Fleas and lice make the mother scratch and increase the danger of injury to her offspring. Fleas spread tapeworms also, and lice may cause anemia in both dam and puppies.

One of a litter of six Beagle puppies died and the owner was asked to bring the dead puppy in for necropsy. The puppy was thin but not emaciated. It had a large abdomen as it necessarily would with 179 adult roundworms. The puppy weighed one pound and twelve ounces or 784 grams. We presume death was due to toxins released by the developing worms; the toxins increased as the parasites matured. The other pups were treated successfully.

Be sure the mother is well fed but not allowed to become fat. One of the better grades of dry dog food is probably the best choice if economy as well as quality is any consideration; if economy is not a consideration, good canned food or table scraps are satisfactory, provided they include enough calcium, phosphorus, iron, and vitamins. Too many table-scrap diets are low in calcium and iron. Milk will furnish calcium; meat, phosphorus and iron; vegetables, some of the essential vitamins. We have found that a little alfalfa-leaf meal of 20 percent protein content or higher will do more to ensure success in pregnancy than any other one supplemental ingredient of diet. Most dry commerical food contains an ample amount of this.

If there is reason to suspect the pregnant female needs more calcium than her normal diet provides, add half a can of undiluted evaporated milk daily for a forty-pound dog. This is a natural source of available calcium. Dried egg shells powdered in a blender is a more economical source; give a forty-pound dog a level teaspoon of the powder daily. Start these supplements two weeks before the delivery date and continue until the weaning process begins.

FALSE PREGNANCY

Novice owners can do a lot of expecting. They may even sell expected puppies on the basis of outward signs in the dam. They will be disappointed when no puppies arrive. If a bitch is fertile and ovulates, anticipate that she will behave like a pregnant bitch even though she is not bred. There will be appetite increase, deposition of fat, increased weight, swelling of breasts, milk production, and often a tendency to want to mother. At the time when she would have produced her litter had she actually been pregnant, she may act for all the world as though she were going to whelp. For a day or two she may refuse food, make a nest, and apparently experience every sensation of birth—without result. This is called a false or phantom or pseudopregnancy. It is entirely normal.

HOW TO DIAGNOSE PREGNANCY

The dam may actually become pregnant and then resorb her fetuses —a not uncommon phenomenon. To be able to distinguish between a case of this sort and pseudopregnancy, it is helpful to know how to tell at an early stage if the dam is actually pregnant.

This is done by *palpation*, or feeling. (Page 30 in Chapter 2 shows the female reproductive organs.) Note how the lumps in the uterus lie. Unless your bitch is overly fat, you can feel these solid lumps along her uterus. If you have a keen sense of feeling, you can tell almost to the day how old they are. These lumps grow rapidly. In a forty-pound dog they feel as large as a pea at twenty-two days, as large as an English walnut at twenty-eight days, and as large as a small hen's egg at thirty-three days. After that they become so soft that palpation is difficult.

When you are sure you are not mistaking a lump—which consists of fetus, fetal membranes, placenta, uterine walls, abdominal walls, and skin—for a piece of feces, you can be certain that the bitch is pregnant. As you follow the development of the lumps by making these gentle and frequent examinations, you may one day note that they are smaller. If so, the dam is resorbing them; the uterus is virtually digesting them back into the circulation.

Unless the litter is small, after thirty-five days there will be sufficient distension of the abdomen so that palpation will not be necessary; the condition will be obvious.

The time from fertilization of the ova until birth is sixty-three days. The day before the dam whelps, her temperature usually drops one degree or thereabouts. Her actions, too, indicate that she is soon to whelp. She becomes restless, somewhat apprehensive, makes a nest or seems to be searching for a place to make one, often stops eating, and

Table VI
SIZE OF LITTERS BY BREEDS

	AVERAGE	LARGEST*		AVERAGE	LARGEST*
Hounds			Irish Wolf-	6	15
Bloodhound	9	17	hound		
Beagle	6	13	Greyhound	7	12
Foxhound	7	23	Whippet	5	11
Basset	8	15			
Dachshund	7	13	*Toys*		
Otter Hound	8	12	Italian Grey-	4	9
			hound		
Bulldogs			Chihuahua	3	11
English	6	11	Pug	6	11
French	5	9	Pomeranian	3	9
Boston Terrier	3	8	Pekingese	4	10
Bull Terrier	7	13	Toy Poodle	4	7
			Japanese Span-	4	5
Bird Dogs			iel		
Setter	8	17	Toy Terrier	4	7
Pointer	7	13	Brussels Grif-	4	8
Spaniel			fon		
Cocker	5	12	Schipperke	5	11
Springer	7	13	Papillon	4	7
Irish Water	7	11	Yorkshire Ter-	3	8
Retriever	7	13	rier		
Giants					
Great Dane	9	17	*Miscellaneous*		
Newfoundland	8	15	Elkhounds	7	13
Mastiff	8	21	Samoyeds	7	13
St. Bernard	9	22	Chow	5	9
Great Pyre-	9	16	Eskimo	7	11
nees			Boxer	7	13
			Dalmatian	7	13
Sight Hounds			Doberman	7	15
Russian Wolf-	9	15	Pinscher		
hound					
Scottish Deer-	8	15			
hound					

* Represents not necessarily the largest ever, but the largest ever to come to our attention. Knowledge of larger litters will be appreciated for the next edition of this book.

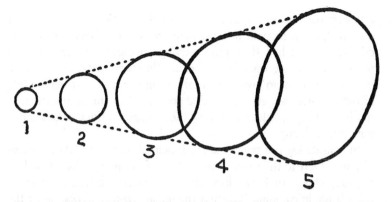

The size of the uterine lumps in a forty-pound bitch at various stages of pregnancy: (1) 22 days, (2) 25 days, (3) 28 days, (4) 31 days, (5) 34 days.

demonstrates in general the same behavior mentioned in the case of a pseudopregnancy.

Prelabor. The prelabor period may present a confusing set of signs to the inexperienced owner. All too often, due to hormonal changes, the prospective mother becomes restless, refuses food, and scratches a rug or the cushions of an overstuffed piece of furniture. Anticipating an imminent delivery, the humans involved may spend three or four sleepless days and nights during their vigil. As a rule of thumb, we suggest a veterinarian be contacted if a puppy has not been delivered in two hours from the onset of true labor, although some suggest three hours.

THE WHELPING NEST

If a nest is not provided as the whelping time approaches, an animal will make her own. If she is a house pet, she may fix it in a closet, on a bed, or out in the garden. As time of birth draws near, she will settle in her nest and appear to strain. The frequency and intensity of her uterine contractions increase.

It is wise to prepare a nesting area about a week before the anticipated whelping and to encourage the expecting mother to use it. The nest should be located in a convenient place if in a house but not in an area strange to her. A kennel dog should whelp in the kennel and not in a strange new environment, such as a residence. We have seen kennel dogs that, when brought into the house for their delivery, felt so insecure they spent half their time carrying puppies to a sofa from the nesting area. Once back in the kennel they were excellent mothers. Also, it is best not to invite the neighbors in to see this fascinating feat of nature since strangers and undue noise create a threat to some new mothers. Many females will destroy their puppies if the environment is not to their liking.

In considering the proper nest it is helpful to examine those typical of females left to their own design. We have seen farm dogs as well as city dogs choose their own locations and have their litters, and there is one feature in common. The nest the female creates may be under the edge of a haymow or under the back porch, but invariably it is not unlike a giant bird's nest in its concavity. Bitches dig and scratch, circling constantly in the depression until it is deep enough to their liking. We can benefit by this observation and provide a concave nest for a planned litter. Corrugated boxes with sides tall enough to prevent puppies from crawling out during their first three weeks of life but not too tall for the mother to jump over are useful and disposable when soiled. The corners should be packed with cloth to make the nest concave and a blanket should be placed over it.

Whelping Facilities in the Kennel. As is true in the house, be sure that everything is ready for the puppies. The ideal whelping box is square with the sides a foot high. It should be prepared with the proper bedding made of an absorbent material. Rye or oat straw and dehydrated sugarcane are all excellent. Whatever is used, be sure there is an ample amount of it. Fill the box with the material and then trample it down until it is saucer-shaped rather than flat. Those who have had little experience with bitches whelping often copy the whelping boxes built for sows. These have bars up a few inches from the side under which the piglets can roll if the mother tends to lie on them. However, bitches do not lie down in this fashion. A good mother hollows out a nest by walking around and around, pushing her puppies into a pile in the lowest part of the hollow. Then she lies down with all her teats available.

There are bitches so clever and petite that they can make a nest in a haymow barely large enough to turn around in and in it whelp and raise to weaning a large litter of puppies. The majority of house dogs, however, are incapable of such an expert and natural performance. If left to herself, every bitch will hollow out a nest in which the puppies tend to roll into a pile in the bottom, where they keep each other warm. If left on a flat floor, the puppies are more apt to be killed by their mother lying on them.

The preparation of a nest has a great effect upon the success of a litter. Avoid using loose material that is likely to get into the mouths of the young and interfere with their nursing. When you use dehydrated sugarcane for bedding material in kennels, you should put cloth under it, so that it will not irritate the puppies' navels should it be pushed aside.

Whelping Facilities at Home. For house dogs, we prefer cloth stuffed into the corners of the box with a blanket spread over all. During the labor the expectant mother may tear the blanket to shreds but sometime during the labor she stops shredding and another blanket may be added. Much of the cloth will be soiled by fluids from the birth process and it may be removed and laundered for future use. Some of the synthetic fibers such as nylon may wrap around a pup's extremity with tourniquet action resulting in the loss of a limb if not discovered in time. If the nest box becomes too soiled have a second one on hand with clean bedding to substitute.

If the litter is whelped and to be raised at home, a six-foot-high stack of newspapers will be about right for ten Setter pups. During the weaning period the mother stops eating the puppies' excrement and the keeper of the puppies has a constant job of cleaning up after them. A playpen-type enclosure or a small room covered with newspapers is the conventional and good way to handle this problem. In warm clear weather they may be taken out to an outside enclosure for part of the day, but keep stray dogs away since young puppies are particularly susceptible to many diseases.

THE BIRTH OF THE PUPS

As the puppies start to pass through the birth canal, there is an even greater effort of expulsion, which is probably due to a reflex occasioned by pressure on the upper part of the vulva. This is true labor and is a useful fact to know in helping a bitch to whelp. If you want to make her strain, insert a clean gloved finger in the vulva and pull upward and backward. She will nearly always strain and assist you. The average whelping time for dogs is five hours. Small dogs, such as Cocker Spaniels, usually finish whelping in three hours, but large dogs, such as Great Danes and St. Bernards, often take seven or eight hours. Twelve hours is the limit of normal time for a large dog, although bitches have been known to take thirty-six hours with no particularly abnormal aspects to the whelping.

The contractions of the uterus push the young animal out through the vagina. The puppy appears in one of several ways. It may still be in the amniotic sac. If so, the sac must be broken or the newborn will suffocate. If the mother doesn't do this, you should do it for her. The puppy may still be in its sac, but the sac may have ruptured. Or the young may be born with the sac remaining inside the mother. In this case the umbilical cord is still connecting it to the sac. The mother may chew this cord to break it, and the sac and placenta will be discharged later. But you can wrap a cloth or tissue about the cord and pull gently until the sac comes out with the placenta.

If a placenta is not discharged it may or may not become a problem. We have examined uteruses that had one or more placentas well walled off and in the process of absorption two weeks and more after delivery. Other retained placentas may cause serious infections and even peritonitis.

How do you know when the mother has delivered her last puppy? When is she ready for an examination and perhaps an injection? The birth process is a natural one happening often in dogs all over the world. Most deliveries are simple, normal events requiring only the mother's help. But for the owner, the experience of a first delivery is fraught with healthy concern that results in more difficulty for him or her than for the dog. To relieve the anxiety, it is wise to contact your veterinarian in advance of the accouchment, both to alert him or her and to ask advice. The veterinarian will tell you of any potential problems of your breed and will decide, depending on the individual case, if the female should be brought in after the whelping. If so, your vet may suggest bringing the puppies in for an examination, too. The trip will be disturbing to the new mother and is to be avoided in most cases, in our opinion.

The first puppy, frequently the most difficult to be birthed, may be the largest in the litter. This may occur because the first pup develops at or close to the bifurcation of the uterus, where there is a rich blood supply to the developing fetus. A good many contractions may be necessary to force this puppy's head or hips through the pelvic girdle. Sometimes the mother tires at this point and this is a time when you may help her by donning a disposable examination glove, lubricating your first and second fingers, inserting them in the vagina and gently pulling that part you feel. She will then contract and gradually you will be able to bring the head or the rear legs out of the canal.

Now, if the membranes have not ruptured with the head exposed, tear them and dry the puppy's nose. Then wrap a dry cloth or tissue around the head and continue gentle traction—as the shoulders squeeze through the pelvic girdle the puppy suddenly slides out with ease. If the delivery is breech, or hind legs first, and the legs are out of the vaginal canal, the umbilical cord will be under pressure, preventing the blood exchange circulation to and from the mother. In this situation there is no time to rush to a veterinarian for help. To save a breech puppy it is better to grasp the rear legs with a cloth or tissue and exert enough traction to deliver it. Sometimes you must pull so hard you may hesitate, but if you wait too long there is the danger of possible damage or death to the puppy.

When a female is delivered of a puppy that appears dead or if you find one during the whelping still in its sac, tear open the sac, dry the nose, and holding the puppy in a towel in one hand, imitate the mother's licking motion by rubbing it with the towel with your other hand. If there is still no motion gently swing it through the air in an arc to force blood into the head, then continue to stroke its sides firmly. Roll it over and stroke the other side. Rub it roughly but not roughly enough to damage it, and don't give up easily.

We have even tried mouth-to-mouth resuscitation but in postmortem examination found we had inflated stomachs but not the lungs.

If you lose a puppy or two, remember that for creatures of multiple births it is natural for some to die. Some have birth defects and some are very tiny by virtue of an inadequate blood supply to the uterus during development. Studies of wild wolves in Michigan find an average of only one pup from each litter grows to maturity and this is adequate to perpetuate the species.

It would appear we may be overzealous in saving puppies that would die without our help. Some of these animals must contribute defective genes to the gene pool of all breeds. This may account for the seemingly fewer problems of mixed breed dogs that as a group are not given the attention expended on our valuable purebred dogs.

It also appears that a female may regulate the number of puppies she has, provided, of course, she has been bred at the correct time. We had occasion some years ago to perform an exploratory operation on a champion English Setter female to determine why she had not had a heat period in four years. She had cysts on one ovary and all along one horn of her uterus. Half her uterus was thick walled and diseased. The offending ovary and horn of the uterus were removed. There had been an agreement between the breeder and a prospective English purchaser that if she came in season and was bred they would purchase her. She did indeed come in season two months after the surgery, was bred, and shipped to England where she had twelve beautiful pups while in quarantine. Twelve pups from half a uterus! Although we doubt she would have beaten the world's record of twenty-three puppies with twenty-four pups if she had had both horns of her uterus.

Birth defects are common problems. We have seen a collection of examples that include a puppy with an extra rear leg; one with one eye in the middle of its forehead; puppies with harelips and cleft palates; a mummified pup; and several with open heads with little or no brains. The list is longer but the point is that defects are common. Don't be discouraged if you encounter one from time to time. If you do find such a puppy, take it to your veterinarian for euthanasia. He or she may send it to a pathology department where records are kept of these happenings. It seems to us there may be an environmental basis for some defects and although we have urged different groups to collect and classify birth defects, each declares there are no funds available for it. It would seem that monitoring our dogs might disclose environmental problems that can also affect mankind.

In our experience delivering thousands of puppies we estimate about 20 percent are born with a breech presentation. There is nothing abnormal about it. We should mention that in only a few cases has it been necessary to tie an umbilical cord to prevent bleeding.

Normally a female will chew off the cord at varying distances from its attachment, then eat the placenta and lick her young dry. This is unpleasant for most people to accept, but it is part of a natural function and there is no indication that interference is called for. However, it may be necessary to crush the navel cord with blunt scissors two inches or so from the body if the mother is unable to do it efficiently.

There is good evidence that the ingestion of the fluids, placenta, and membranes by the mother in some way helps the mother produce in her first milk immune bodies that increase the puppies' resistance to disease. This milk is called the colostrum.

If you attend an animal giving birth you will find that your assistance and affection are reassuring and that she will trust you with her young. If she has a large litter, it is a good idea, when she is not looking, to hand the first ones to a helper, who can put them in a warm, dry place to stay until the mother is relaxed and ready to take care of them. In this way she can attend each one as it is born, without injuring others from whom her attention has been diverted.

Healthy newborn puppies are perfect examples of the inheritance of instincts when, blind, deaf, and still wet, they seek out a nipple and attach themselves to begin nursing—even while the mother is chewing their cords. It is a remarkable sight to behold, no matter how many births one observes.

Why a bitch decides to eliminate a certain puppy from her brood is difficult to ascertain. Perhaps a given pup has an odor she does not appreciate so she pushes it out of the way with her nose. You find it and return it to her breast and come back later to find it once again excluded from the litter. A pup like this should be removed to a container with a heating pad or heat light and returned to the mother every two hours when it must be placed on a breast for nursing. After a few days most bitches will then accept the previous reject.

Two postparturition infections in bitches are not common but do occur—uterine infections and infection of the breasts. Infection of the uterus is unlikely if no placentas remain in the uterus. Normally a female discharges from her uterus the lining to which the placentas were attached during pregnancy and through which the young were nourished. This takes the form of a dark red discharge and may last for ten or twelve days or even longer. Infected breasts are extremely serious to both a mother and her young, and they require immediate attention (see Chapter 16).

What Not to Do in Whelping. One often reads the most ludicrous directions for helping bitches to whelp, especially those about the need to be sterile. These warnings—"disinfect the scissors and hands"; "tie the cord with sterile silk"—are overzealous applications of the human birth precautions. With dogs you need pay no attention to such nonsense. Every puppy is a bacterial flower garden almost as soon as it is born. It comes, bacteriologically speaking, into a filthy world. If its mother is left to herself, she may allow it to drop into a manure pile; and even if this happens it will be unaffected. You can be as sterile as you wish and in spite of your efforts the puppy will be an ideal breeding ground for bacteria. Its mother's breasts and legs, its nest, hair, and intestines are teeming with them. Fortunately most of these bacteria will be benign, and nature has equipped the puppy to combat the others. The most important precaution for you to observe is to avoid handling puppies after you have been handling sick animals. You have far more to fear from viruses and coccidiosis spread by flies than from contamination from well-washed hands or clean home instruments.

The End of Whelping. One by one the puppies are pressed through the birth canal until the last pup and the last placenta have been expelled. Then, and not until then, will the bitch become relaxed and calm.

Using the method of palpation, it is possible to tell a great deal about birth just as it is possible to diagnose pregnancy. One fact that can be ascertained is when a cesarean operation is necessary. By reaching up from underneath and placing the fingers on one side of the belly and the thumb on the other, you can clearly feel a puppy entering the pelvic opening. If you find that the puppy is in the birth position and the bitch is straining but accomplishing nothing, check the situation again in a few hours. If the puppy is in the same position, get the dam to your veterinarian. He or she may be able to extract the puppy with special forceps or may have to perform a cesarean section.

Palpation can also be useful in determining whether or not the bitch has finished whelping. If you have not had practice in this technique, hold one of the newborn puppies in your fingers and then feel through the abdomen to see if there is a similar object contained within it. Some persons prefer to feel with both hands, keeping the fingertips of each opposite the other. This is particularly helpful in the case of large bitches.

Birth can take a few minutes for one or two puppies to perhaps twenty-four hours for a large litter. If, after having a puppy, the mother relaxes and does not appear to be having contractions, take her out of the nest for a walk. As she pulls to return, release her and she will run back. This exercise will often start strong contractions. Walking the female up and down a staircase a few times has the same effect. If you choose to walk her outside at night take a flashlight. Many bitches, appearing to urinate, are passing a puppy.

When you think the last puppy has been born, wait a few hours before you let the mother out. The great pressure on her bladder and other organs has relaxed and she can and naturally does go a long while without elimination. If she refuses to leave her pups twelve or sixteen hours after birth, take her for a walk, unless she is in a pen where she can go out at will. If she is in a pen, she will wait until it is dark and very quiet before going out.

Before the young are born, the mother should be prepared for suckling by being carefully cleaned and having long hair cut away. It often prevents the young from reaching the teats.

Breasts often cake because a mother produces more milk than her young need. This is inevitable when her litter is small. Caked breasts are normal and the symptoms usually disappear without medication.

Sometimes a mother dies during parturition or when her litter is very young. Although it is not easy to save the orphans, you can probably raise them successfully if you understand their needs. This means that you have to understand what their mother would supply if she were living (see Chapter 7).

A wise dog owner will look carefully at the puppies' navels every day to see that they are healing. The dried-up umbilical cord drops off sometime during the second day, although occasionally puppies will have it much longer. After this, healing should progress rapidly.

7

Raising Puppies

Having attended many of the eight thousand puppies that have been born in our kennels and hospital, we find that we have a natural tendency to assume that dog owners are more familiar than they really are with the details of puppy raising. To avoid making such an assumption in this chapter, we are going to suppose that you are expecting your pet to whelp a litter of puppies and that you know nothing whatever about how to raise them—what to do, how to plan, what to arrange for, or how to feed the little fellows when they are ready to be weaned. This may be tedious to a lot of readers, but it is one way of making certain that this section will include all the facts dog owners need to know in order to raise a sturdy litter of pups.

FOSTER MOTHERS AND ORPHANS

Every year we see newspaper pictures of queer foster parents—adopted pet combinations—a cat nursing a young rat or tending a chicken, a mare caring for a puppy or a goat, a bitch nursing a kitten. Behavior of this sort is because of an excessive "mother complex." In the case of a bitch that has not had pups and has no milk a hormone can be injected that will make her into such a good mother that she will steal other bitches' pups in order to have something to love and protect. She'll curl up with them and accept them as her own.

Almost any female with enough prolactin in her blood will try to mother some animate thing. Perhaps it is a bitch mothering a duckling, or a rat mothering a young mouse. The trouble with getting a foster mother to adopt young not her own is generally that she already has got used to her own and then it is difficult to make the substitution. Most people have heard what pains a shepherd must take to get a ewe that has lost her lamb to accept an orphan.

The best way to encourage an adoption is to smear the orphan all over with vaginal fluids and milk from the foster mother. This makes the orphan smell like one of the mother's own. She licks the fluids off and this licking tends to make her want the orphan. There is no quicker way. Persistence will win over a foster mother even if she at first refuses an orphan. It may be necessary to hold it to her breast, remove it so she can't bury it or kill it, and bring it back at the next nursing. If you are there, she won't harm it, but if you are not, she may kill it. However, once a foster mother starts licking an orphan it is usually safe to leave them alone.

If no foster mother is available, the greatest difficulty in raising bottle-fed orphans is to arrange for a nipple of the right size, and then to induce puppies to nurse from it. Some people use medicine dropper rubbers through which they punch holes; others use children's doll bottle nipples. Puppies will usually thrive on rubber nipples for infant humans.

Many small orphans are killed through the careless use of medicine droppers. Unless you are very careful to put a drop at a time on the puppy's tongue and see that it is swallowing, its mouth may fill with the milk. Then it may cry or wheeze and inhale some of the milk. This often causes pneumonia, and from this the little thing dies. Few of those using medicine droppers know how much milk to give. A day-old puppy of a small breed needs five dropperfuls six times a day, one from a large breed needs twenty.

Table VII gives an approximation of the requirements of puppies for their weights. As in humans, it varies with the individual animal.

People who are desperate to save an orphan often rush to buy goat's milk. Most people think there is something magical in it that will save the young of any species. Actually goat's milk is very similar to cow's milk and much more expensive. It is richer in fat than most Holstein milk but not as rich as Jersey milk. About the only important difference is that in goat's milk the fat is broken up into much finer particles than in any cow's milk. It is not the formula of choice for newborn puppies.

Table VII BOTTLE-FEEDING
REQUIREMENTS FOR
ORPHAN PUPPIES

WEIGHT OF PUPPY	AMOUNT OF MILK REQUIRED	FREQUENCY OF FEEDING*
3 oz.	3 cc†	Every 3 hours
5 oz.	5 cc	Every 3 hours
8 oz.	1/2 oz.	Every 4 hours
12 oz.	1 oz.	Every 5 hours
1 lb.	1 1/4 oz.	Every 5 hours
2 lb.	2 oz.	Every 6 hours
3 lb.	2 3/4 oz.	Every 6 hours

* All orphans under one week old do best on 4-hour feedings
or oftener.
† A cubic centimeter (cc) is 1/5 teaspoon.

FEEDING

Animals in a litter should be watched carefully to see that they are all
getting enough milk. When they are a few days old they can starve in a
very short time. Frequently old animals have some teats so large that
the young will suck from the side or be unable to suck at all. They
sometimes have to be helped so that they can find the teats small
enough for them.

A healthy puppy struggles in your hands, attempting to find the
proper environment for survival, namely, its littermates and its mother's breasts. Sick puppies are noisy puppies until they become so weak
they are limp to the touch and have little strength when picked up.
Hungry puppies are also noisy. The litter cries a pathetic chorus as it
seeks food, and if the mother has inadequate milk a puppy nurses on a
nipple, releases it, and tries for another, crying between efforts.

If the litter is a large one and all the puppies are to be raised by the
mother, remove half the puppies as they are born by stealing them
away without the dam's knowing what is being done. Stroke her head
and, as you cover her eyes with your hand, quickly take a puppy and
place it behind you in a box. This can usually be done most easily while
the bitch is giving her attention to the latest arrival. On the other

Table VIII COMPOSITION OF MILK
IN DIFFERENT SPECIES OF ANIMALS
(in percentages)

	FAT	PROTEIN	CARBOHYDRATE	ASH	WATER	TOTAL SOLID
Dog	11.2	5.7	3.1	1.3	78.7	21.3
Cow	4.0	3.8	4.9	0.7	86.2	13.8
Goat	4.1	3.7	4.2	0.8	87.1	12.9
Cat	5.0	7.0	5.0	0.6	82.0	18.0
Rabbit	16.0	14.0	2.0	2.2	65.0	35.0
Guinea pig	7.0	5.0	2.0	1.9	85.0	15.0
Rat	15.0	12.0	3.0	2.0	70.0	30.0

hand, it is possible to wait until all the pups are born and then take half of them away. The mother cannot count and will be content with the puppies you leave, provided the absent ones are placed so far away that she cannot hear them.

The two groups of puppies can be switched for feeding every two or three hours for the first few days and every four hours for the next few. To have them grow satisfactorily, however, you must change them at not more than five-hour intervals.

If the dam's milk is infected or insufficient, or if she is nervous and even seems afraid of her pups, it may be necessary to feed them from a bottle or by stomach tube. Supplementary feeding may also be advisable if the dam has too large a litter.

Bitches' milk is naturally slightly acid. Many people blame the death of puppies on acid milk, but they should look for other causes. If a formula is used as a substitute, do not try to modify cow's milk so that it approximates the chemical composition of human milk, even though you have read that this should be done. Bitches' milk is not at all like human milk. It has more fat, less sugar, more protein, and more ash. Most of the old formulas advise adding limewater, glucose, or dextrose. These formulas, however, are modified in precisely the wrong direction, as you will see from Table IX.

There are specially prepared modified milks on the market today for puppies. If these are unavailable in your neighborbood, try one of the spray-dried baby milks. Mix one ounce with six ounces of water by volume and add one ounce of fresh cream. This can make a stock

Table IX MILK COMPOSITION
(in percentages)

	BITCH	COW	HUMAN
Water	78.7	86.3	87.4
Protein	5.7	3.8	1.3
Sugar	3.1	4.7	7.0
Fat	11.2	4.0	3.5
Ash	1.3	0.7	0.2

solution which serves admirably, although it is high in sugar. Keep the solution refrigerated. It should be shaken and warmed before being fed to the puppies.

We have tried many feeding devices and find a small bottle with a small human infant anticolic nipple best for one or two puppies. If a 20-gauge hypodermic needle is inserted through the hub of the nipple next to the bottle's lip, the air can run in while the puppy is sucking and the nipple will not collapse. Start with two small holes and increase the size of the holes if the puppy is not able to suck with enough strength to withdraw the formula.

If there are more than three puppies, the stomach tube method is preferred as a time saver. The formula is drawn into a syringe attached to a premature human infant stomach tube. Before inserting the tube down the puppy's throat hold it alongside the puppy so that the tip is just behind the rib cage. With the puppy's head extended, mark the tube at the puppy's nose. This will be the mark to reach before injecting the formula. Such a tube is premarked for humans but disregard that mark. Insert the tube down the throat until the pup swallows and then pass it until your mark is even with the nose and inject the formula and withdraw the tube.

There are two dangers to avoid. First, if the tube is introduced into the windpipe, or trachea, it can be inserted only halfway. If formula is injected into the lungs the result will be death. Second, if the end of the tube is not down into the stomach some of the injected formula will follow the tube back up to the entrance of the trachea where the puppy may inhale it and die a few days later.

The overzealous owner decides a young puppy should have supplemental feeding, purchases a bitch's milk substitute, and administers it with a bottle and nipple—usually with poor results. There is no milk substitute that tastes to a puppy like its mother's milk and the puppy will often refuse it. If the puppy's mouth is forced open and a nipple is placed in it, the puppy will usually chew it, fighting to resist the unusual flavor. Some of the formula may be inhaled with disastrous results since mechanical or foreign body pneumonia may result, and for these there is little effective treatment.

There is an obvious way to determine if puppies are not able to get enough milk from their mother and that is to hear them crying between trying one nipple after another. When hungry enough they will then take a formula with gusto. Many females have little milk for about six hours after whelping but an adequate amount thereafter.

The supplementary milk must be close to body temperature at first. Even five or six degrees of variation in either direction will inhibit sucking. Feed the puppies before returning them to their mother. At first puppies will take about 1 cc of milk for each ounce of weight. You can increase the amount proportionately as they grow. They must be nursed at least four times a day if they are to thrive, and five times a day is preferable.

Since young puppies are stimulated to urinate and defecate by their mother's licking, a puppy fed by other means than its mother must be stimulated by gently rubbing the genitals with cotton after each feeding. They may not defecate but will urinate at each feeding with the proper stimulation.

When puppies reach as little as three weeks of age their mother does something for them of which many people strongly disapprove—she eats food, lets it partially digest, and then vomits it for them to eat. This is their first natural food. The mother's actions are probably under hormone control. Do not be alarmed if you witness this phenomenon. Learn a lesson from it and start supplying the little pups with solid, easily digestible food at this time. There are several puppy foods on the market specifically formulated for the requirements of this period of explosive growth just as there are human baby foods geared to the needs of children. If such food is not available, offer the pups cooked meat and cereal foods. Concoct a stew of ingredients such as protein, lots of vegetable matter, and fat. Let it cool, then watch them eat it! The addition of such foods to the puppies' diets spares the mother the burden of furnishing huge amounts of milk, and she is thereby kept in good condition.

WEANING

Weaning refers to that period between the first solid food and the end of nursing. With commercial puppy foods available, weaning should start at about three weeks of age. A large litter extracts a tremendous amount of energy and nutrients from the mother during the third and fourth weeks and the more the puppies take from a dish the less they require from their mother.

Mix the puppy food of your choice with water in a shallow dish. A pie plate is about right. Allow the food to soak up as much water as it will and then crush it with a fork, adding more water to make a gruel-like consistency. Place the dish on the puppy pen floor and push the puppies' noses in it. At first the puppies appear to be trying to draw it up with a nursing action. They lick their chops and poke their noses in it again. After they have eaten as much as they want and have walked through the food and become a general mess, permit the mother to come in and lick them clean. She will finish the puppy food too.

Feed the puppies three times a day and let the mother clean up each time. After the third day the puppies will look forward to each meal. Puppy foods have extra milk solids so additional milk is unnecessary. We like to feed our puppies three times a day until they are three months old, always using the same formula.

By the time the puppies are five weeks old they can be on their own, although it may be kinder to a mother with a large milk supply to permit a few puppies to nurse once daily after the five weeks for another week.

When weaning has been completed, from five weeks onward, you will have eased the puppies off dependence on their dam and her milk secretion will diminish naturally. But if you suddenly have to remove the puppies, or lose them, she will still dry up in a natural way. You need not bind her breasts, rub them with camphorated oil, or massage or milk them. As a normal transition, the udder will become inflamed. A hormone action stops milk secretion, and after a time the inflammation will gradually decrease. If you do rub the breasts with oil, the secretion will subside—but not because of the medication. We have tried massaging and oiling only one side of a heavy milk producer's udder and have found that both sides dry up at the same rate.

The Newly Weaned Puppy. We believe that puppies weaned at five weeks of age are ready to be placed in new homes. This is particularly important in breeds such as Shetland Sheepdogs, where socialization at a tender age with people results in an outgoing, well-adjusted pet. But if not given this early exposure they may be shy all their lives. And many shy, fearful, biting adult dogs became that way because of inadequate handling and affection when they were a young impressionable age.

Some states have enacted legislation making it illegal to dispose of a puppy under eight weeks of age. We feel that this is the result of misguided if well-intentioned legislators. Puppies cannot receive as much individual attention as parts of a litter as they can in new homes, where each is the center of attraction. Not only is this legislation a disservice to the puppy but also to the person who has to clean up after it for two or more unnecessary additional weeks.

A shy puppy needs more than handling, cuddling, and kindness; it needs exposure to strange noise and activity as often as possible. Taking it along on trips to noisy, busy places on a regular basis underscores your frequent reassurances that there is no danger. For any four- to sixteen-week-old puppy, we cannot overemphasize the importance of handling and affection.

IMPORTANT POINTS OF GENERAL CARE

As puppies grow older the bedding in the nest box can be leveled by bringing it down from the sides. This keeps the puppies in. Much of the bedding material will have to be changed soon after whelping is over because of the large amount of amniotic fluid present which accompanies the birth of each puppy.

The floor of the area where the puppies are is of great importance. If it is of concrete or rough wood, it should be covered with several thicknesses of burlap or cloth before the bedding is put down. If the rough surface is not covered, the pups will wear away their navels, infection will creep under the skin, and the puppies will die unless treated promptly. Indeed thousands of puppies die each year from infected navels.

Treatment for this consists of cleaning away the infected parts and injecting an antiobiotic. An antiseptic powder or ointment should be applied and worked under the skin, which should then be covered with a gauze pad bound in place by adhesive tape. It is best to keep the puppy under treatment isolated and carry it to the mother for nursing five or six times a day. The puppy should be treated until the skin has grown across and healed. Another method is to dissect the infected area away and suture the skin together. Healing may require five days or more.

As soon as puppies begin to crawl about, a pen must be made for them. They can use sand runs. Grass and concrete are the devil's own devices for spreading worm infestation. The best plan for small kennel dogs—one that has everything to recommend it and few drawbacks—is to provide a wire-bottom pen. A picture of its construction is shown. The wire for the bottom of the pen, one-inch square mesh, should be 9- or 11-gauge, preferably welded. Lighter netting soon breaks, unless the puppies are a light breed. Smallish bitches can be kept in this kind of pen and allowed to whelp in the hutch.

When the puppies crawl out on the wire and defecate, there is no chance for contamination. If the droppings are removed under the pens every day, even flies cannot transmit infestations of embryonated worm eggs. The only serious objection to the use of these pens is that puppies raised in them often cannot successfully be introduced into houses with hot-air floor registers unless these registers are screened from the pups. Having trained themselves to defecate over the wire flooring in the pen, the puppies search tirelessly for a similar surface to use for the same purpose in the house. When a pup finds the furnace register, the owner often feels that the idea of a wire-bottom pen was all a mistake.

Raising puppies in cool or even cold weather is generally more successful than when it is too hot. When they are cold they will pile up to keep warm, and their mother is less likely to lie on them than she is if they have spread out to keep cool. The best temperature is that which will induce the puppies to remain huddled together to keep warm.

If a little pup gets chilled—by falling out of its box, for example—but is still alive when found, heat may revive it. Never give up. As it becomes more animated, let it suck some warm formula and watch the quick change.

Hiccoughing in healthy puppies is common enough to call normal but why they hiccough we do not know. A puppy settling into sleep as well as a wide-awake playing puppy may hiccough for a few minutes.

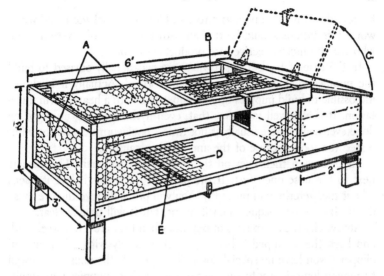

Details of construction of a wire-bottom pen. (A) Sides and top of 14- or 16-gauge, 1½-inch, hexagonal fox netting. (B) Door covered with same. (C) Hutch cover. (A piece of flat rubber can be tacked over the crack where the cover hinges.) (D) Wire bottom of 9- or 11-gauge, 1-inch-square mesh, preferably welded. (E) Angle-iron brace.

We asked a group of veterinarians if they had ever seen an adult dog hiccough and not one of us could recall a single case.

As little puppies grow, they occasionally twitch. You may see this jerking in one after another and think it means that they have fleas or are sick. It doesn't; instead it means that they are healthy and doing well. If they *fail* to twitch, they are unthrifty, possibly underfed, or anemic. It has been suggested the sleep a puppy experiences while twitching is similar to the REM (rapid eye movement) sleep of humans.

How early may little puppies be dewormed? Since they may be born with intestinal parasites, it pays to have fecal examinations made starting at three weeks of age. If they are infested, they can safely be dewormed at any age.

Consult your veterinarian for a fecal analysis and the proper medication for the type of worm present. Capsules of Piperazine may be obtained where animal medicines are sold, and are safe and efficacious for roundworms when used as directed. However, hookworm and whipworm infestations should be treated with the advice of a veterinarian, who has the most effective safe products available.

In the case of hookworms, owners are occasionally advised to build the puppies up before having them dewormed. Actually it is almost impossible to build puppies up in competition with a heavy worm infestation. It is also well to realize that, even if this building up could be done eventually, there usually is not time—hookworms cannot be eliminated too soon because of the anemia they cause.

Puppies open their eyes on the tenth day after birth. The corners next to the nose open first. If the puppy's eye bulges before it opens take it to a veterinarian promptly. You will probably save the eye by so doing. It may be opaque when it opens, but it will usually clear.

Always clip the sharp nails of puppies when they are a few weeks old, and keep them clipped. This may be done safely with a human nail clipper if you have no special dog nail clippers. If the nails are allowed to remain long, injury to the eyes of one or more puppies may result. Hundreds of puppies have scars or, worse, are blinded every year by failure of the owners to take this simple precaution.

8

How to Train Your Dog

The subject of training has been of great enough interest that a small library of books has been written about it. Many are specialized, such as how to train a Gordon Setter to hunt birds or a Beagle to trail rabbits. Then there are step-by-step books on training for obedience work. The list is long and impressive but all are based on principles that many of the authors don't acknowledge.

The training must take into account the personality of the animal to be trained. A sensitive Toy Poodle may be trained more easily with rewards than the overexuberant Boxer, which may respond better to training with force. The discipline necessary for a Poodle may be a harsh word, something often completely disregarded by a Boxer.

The age of the dog is another important consideration since it is easier to train one with some maturity than a devil-may-care puppy. However, the objective of the training is an important matter and may have little to do with age, as in the case of housebreaking.

Many professional trainers recognize German Shepherds or Alsatians as being more easily trainable than other breeds and will accept them at six months of age in their training programs. Most other breeds must be ten or twelve months of age for professionals to accept them for training.

Some breeds inherit aptitudes to perform functions by developing and training themselves. Just give them the opportunity and with virtually no training by the handler/owner they do what their breed is supposed to do. The Beagle is a good example of self-training. All that is necessary is to take one into a field that has rabbits and, if the inherited genes are there, its trailing and barking develop naturally. The sight hounds, such as the racing Greyhound, are other good examples. The bird dogs, including retrievers, also inherit their aptitudes but usually require some training by handlers to perform their functions properly.

Rather than delving into all the specifics of training, we will describe the systems or methods that have proved successful over the years. We will also discuss some common behavior problems.

THE REWARD METHOD

With the reward method a dog is never disciplined but rewarded only when it responds to your satisfaction. A reward may be offered either as affection or food; when the latter is given as a treat now and then, the dog accepts it as a form of affection. This method is used by many pet owners, and it requires the patience of Job. We find it frustrating.

"I feed and walk our dog. I bathe and comb it and spend most every day with it and it likes my husband better than me. Why?" This observation is a common one, and the obvious answer must be that the husband probably disciplines the pet. The person who makes the dog toe the line is its master.

THE NEED-REWARD METHOD

In our opinion, the need-reward method is the most effective one. The need created is that for food. Most dogs are fed once daily so the training must take place twenty-four hours after the last feeding; for difficult trainees, thirty-six hours later.

Training to Come. Let's say you want to train your dog to come when you call it. Tie the end of a twenty- or thirty-foot cord to its collar and take it outside. Use the same command each time with the same tone of voice, which is usually the word, "come." Say "come" and pull the dog to you with the cord and offer it food as a reward. Being hungry, it will take the food with relish. Then walk on and when the dog is some distance from you, repeat the procedure. Repeat it a dozen times, which is enough for one session. Wait a few days and go through the same paces, and in a surprisingly short period of time you will have conditioned it to come on command.

Discipline with No Reward. About the only time the no-reward method is used is to break an established bad habit. One example might be a dog that barks excessively when there is no good reason for it, such as an apartment dog that barks and doesn't stop when you leave for work. Before the neighbors call the police, try this solution. Cut two ten-inch pieces of one-inch-wide adhesive tape from a roll and stick them on a convenient surface in the apartment. Leave, but wait where you can hear the dog start to bark, then return, sounding your choice of command—perhaps "quiet" or "be still"—that you will use later without the discipline. Remove one piece of adhesive tape and wrap it around the dog's muzzle and leave again for thirty minutes. We suggest you do leave, as the dog will go through all sorts of contortions in an attempt to remove the tape. In half an hour return and remove the tape, repeating your command to be still. Leave once again and wait for the barking to start over, which it will; return and wrap the second piece of tape around the dog's muzzle. With all but the most stubborn dogs, two treatments will train the dog to obey the command. A word of caution: do not use this technique in a hot environment since the dog, not able to pant to maintain a normal temperature, could develop heat exhaustion.

Leash Pulling. Another problem to correct with the discipline-with-no-reward method is that of a dog constantly pulling on the leash. This is an alternative way to the more normal methods and is not recommended if you have tennis elbow or bursitis. Cut a sapling about eight feet long and remove all the leaves except those at the end. As you walk your pulling dog, lower the sapling so that the dog is walking into the leaves on the end. In a short time most dogs will back off and walk with a slack leash rather than constantly pull into the "bushes."

TRAINING BY ROTE

To illustrate the training-by-rote method we will use the example of housebreaking a puppy. This requires a good deal of time, for a week or two, but the rewards are great. The puppy is to be housed in a crate or cage just large enough for it to curl up in. Place a folded blanket in the bottom as a bed. Take the puppy outside every few hours, and above all a few minutes after a meal, but when the puppy's back in the house it should be in the cage when you don't have the time to watch its every move. It is a rare puppy who will soil its own bed, and once the habit of relieving itself outside is established most every puppy will remain housebroken for life. That puppies have the ability to hold out for long periods is exemplified by a six-week-old Gordon Setter we delivered to a friend. We drove eight hours through a blizzard with the puppy sleeping in a box on the backseat. It slept all the way. Even puppies have the ability to hold out but usually they won't be bothered.

To test rote training, we selected a one-year-old Miniature Poodle that had had no training except leash breaking. On a cold, wet day chosen by choice we walked the dog on a lawn and gave the command "sit" and gently pushed its hindquarters down until it was sitting. Then we walked the dog a dozen feet or so and repeated the performance. We continued this effort for almost an hour until suddenly when we said, "Sit," the dog sat, and for the rest of its life, every time we gave the command, it sat. The dog was taken from the kennel to our house some months later and it lived out its life as a house dog. Dogs avoid sitting on wet surfaces, but by our training this dog to sit on wet grass it would plop down anywhere anytime it was given the command. Of course, there was a reward associated with this training and that was for the dog to see that we were pleased. Most dogs try for a favorable reaction from a person they like.

Car Chasing. Chasing cars is an especially dangerous bad habit. An ancient method of stopping a dog from doing this is to hang a stick on a rope or chain from the dog's collar so that it dangles three quarters of the distance to the ground. When the stick is balanced properly it becomes an encumbrance when the dog tries to run. Of course, the proper method is to leash or pen a dog up in the first place.

TRAINING BY FORCE

The last method in any list of techniques to try is training by force. We will not dwell on it except to say if we were to have to beat, use electric shock on, or otherwise abuse a dog to make it perform or to correct bad habits, we would get rid of the animal first. We are not against a well-timed slap when it seems important and if the dog is not too sensitive. We often suggest rubber flapper fly swatters for such discipline. If a puppy barks and cries at night when you need your sleep, take the swatter in hand and give the culprit a whack on the head with a sharp command. We're not suggesting you use a club—the fly swatter will make an impression without inflicting any real pain. It has the effect of an unwelcome surprise.

LEASH BREAKING

Many dogs are brought to veterinarians' offices without leashes and the owners seem pleased that they could not leash-break the animal. What they are really saying is that they *would* not leash-break it. We have never seen a dog that could not be leash-broken. Some learn in a few minutes, whereas others take more effort on your part.

First, place a collar on your pet, young or old, and let the dog get used to it. That may take a week. Then, if the dog seems to be a difficult one to train, snap a chain on the collar and leave it on, dragging about, until the dog becomes used to it. Then pick up the end of the chain and walk where the dog wants to walk. Finally, restrain the dog ever so lightly and change its direction by leash tension. With this effort even the most difficult shy dog can be leash-broken.

Another quick method but one that may unduly stress a pet is to tie it to a fence and leave. The dog will jump and pull and go through all sorts of contortions until it finally gives in. This may take fifteen minutes. Repeat this daily until your pet is used to it.

If you analyze the training methods we have outlined, you will recognize they are what is called conditioning. If your dog wants to please you, your job is simple, but if the dog doesn't seem to care about your reactions you have a more difficult time of it. It takes patience and understanding to make the difference between an average dog and a great companion.

UNTRAINING

As a practical expediency, many dogs are trained to relieve themselves in the house because of weather conditions or schedules or apartment living. When it becomes desirable to relocate that habit to the outdoors, frustration enters. A dog can and does hold out for hours of walking to return to the confines of the house to perform.

Instead of walking the dog the interminable hours necessary, there is the successful albeit indelicate trick of inserting two wooden matches rectally when you reach the area selected for the dog to defecate. Of course, this should be at the time you expect the dog normally to defecate in the house. If in a few minutes you get no response, insert two more. When the desired results are achieved give the dog a treat immediately, pet it, and let your approval over the event be obvious.

A word of warning: if the neighbors see you they may send two men in white coats.

9

The Physical Examination

Let's consider the physical examinations that dogs should have: the exam you should do at home, the one your veterinarian does, and the one a specialist does. The quality of the examination is not proportional to the knowledge of the examiner—it's the application of the knowledge that is all important.

THE HOME EXAMINATION

Any concerned person can and should do the simple, straightforward home examination. First, consider how the animal appears in general. Is it gaining or losing weight? Is its fluid and food intake and output normal? Are there any personality changes? Does it limp, cough, sneeze excessively, or have halitosis? Have there been any changes since its health was last evaluated?

If everything appears normal you have passed the first hurdle. Next make a closer examination of the animal's eyes, ears, nose, and mouth. Do the whites of its eyes look normal and not inflamed? Do they squint or have an ocular discharge? Look in the ears: Are they clean with a minimum of brown waxy substance and with no excess hair? Smell them. Any unusual odor? Then examine the nose, lips, gums, tongue, throat, and teeth. Are the membranes a normal pink? Look at the teeth for plaque or tartar. Fan the hair and look for blemishes and parasites such as ticks, fleas, and lice. Lice look like motorized dandruff of the biting variety.

Next check the nails, pads, and between the digits.

Check every inch of the skin by feeling with your fingers. Feel for swellings and rough areas.

Now, if you started at the west end, check the east end by raising the tail. Does the anal area appear normal? The vulva in the female and the testicles and penis in the male should be examined. It has always been interesting to us that veterinarians find so many growths in testicles that were unobserved by owners. A small swelling in a testicle can upset the dog's hormone balance, so check them. In Chapter 27 dealing with cancer we mention the frequency of mammary tumors, particularly in the unspayed female, so the mammary area should be given special attention by touch and sight for any swelling.

Now this home physical examination may sound like quite a chore, but we just placed our fourteen-year-old Poodle, Rosie, on a desk where the light is bright and gave her such an examination. The procedure took three and a half minutes. Tomorrow we will take one minute to clip her nails. Otherwise Rosie is in great shape.

THE VETERINARY EXAMINATION

The veterinarian's examination will depend on the reason you brought your dog in to be checked. If you want your veterinarian to do the things you should be doing routinely at home he or she will gladly do everything we have mentioned above. The vet will in addition listen to the heart and lungs and perhaps take a rectal temperature. Blood may be taken for a heartworm test and an examination of feces for intestinal parasites may be performed. Also your dog may be given its routine inoculations.

If on the other hand your dog has a problem, the vet dons a Sherlock Holmes hat and becomes a detective. He or she must have clues to arrive at a solution of the problem. And this is when you must give clear, concise information in answer to many questions. Then come laboratory tests of blood, urine, and stool, and even other body fluids. And X rays may be desirable.

Since most dog owners have to be concerned with economics, veterinarians do not usually call for the dozens of tests that are frequently and routinely run on people. We call only for the tests that we think will be helpful in a diagnosis of the specific problem. If the results are inconclusive, repeat tests and additional tests may be called for until a pattern is observed that leads to a diagnosis.

THE SPECIALIST'S EXAMINATION

There are specialists in the veterinary field just as there are in human medicine. Economics dictates that there are many times fewer individuals as well as fields of specialization in veterinary medicine.

To become a specialist a graduate must spend years of study in his or her chosen field and then pass a comprehensive examination before being admitted to a small but distinguished group. Those most important are concerned with pathology, radiology, dermatology, ophthalmology, surgery, and orthopedics. If there is such a person in a given area that person is called upon when the problem has not been solved to the satisfaction of the general practitioner. If a patient is not responding to treatment and if there is a specialist in your area you should ask for that person's advice. More and more veterinarians call on this small but effective group to help solve some of their more perplexing cases.

The specialist's examination is more in-depth and, coupled with knowledge and experience, results in superior diagnosis and treatment.

The specialist depends on and is usually interested in the more perplexing problems which are referred by a general practitioner. The practitioner is kept advised of the diagnosis and the progress of the patient.

10

What You Should Know About Restraint, First Aid, and Emergencies

Adequate care and intelligent handling are usually sufficient to keep a dog in good health. But even a healthy animal—like a healthy child—cannot be perfectly guarded against every eventuality. Accidents do happen. Emergencies arise in spite of every precaution. The most conscientious owner cannot know that his dog will surprise a porcupine on a particular country path; he cannot prevent his dog from killing and eating a poisoned rabbit that wanders across the backyard.

Two things owners *can* do. By exercising reasonable and humane precautions, they can avoid the accidents resulting from carelessness. They can learn how to cope with emergencies when they do arise.

Every year thousands of pets are needlessly lost simply because their owners have never taken the time to familiarize themselves with a few simple principles of first aid and emergency treatment. The owner who has never learned how to handle the common emergency situations becomes panicky and does nothing to help his or her injured pet—or does worse than nothing, the wrong thing. The person who has no understanding of the normal recuperative processes or powers of animals too quickly assumes that the best he or she can do for an animal that has been hurt is to put it out of the reach of pain and so destroys the pet when it might have recovered easily and completely.

Too many pet owners feel that since they prefer to have their veterinarian deal with all serious pet problems, there is no necessity for them to be able to handle difficult or unpleasant situations themselves. People who feel this way should remember, however, that emergencies have a way of happening at inconvenient moments. Even in metropolitan areas there often are times when a veterinarian is not immediately available, and in most sections of the country it may well take several hours to reach a veterinarian. As long as that is true, the owner who doesn't take the trouble to find out what he or she can do to help a pet in an emergency is risking the animal's life foolishly.

Any owner can be and should be prepared to administer first aid to an injured pet. He or she should know how to restrain an animal that is frightened or in pain so that it will not harm itself or others. An owner should know how to stop the flow of blood from a wound, how to relieve the pain as much as possible, how to protect the pet until the veterinarian is available. He or she should know *what not to do*. The skills and techniques are not difficult to learn or to apply. They are available to everyone—the cheapest and best insurance a person can get against the loss of a pet.

HOW TO RESTRAIN A DOG

Before you can attempt any sort of treatment for an injured dog, you must know how to protect yourself and how to keep the dog from doing damage to itself or escaping before you have taken care of it properly. Restraint of some sort is usually necessary to administer first aid and always necessary when pain is involved. With some unruly pets it is even necessary when the animal is being groomed.

Your dog's defenses consist of biting and clawing. Your animal must be held so that it cannot reach the handler. Its head must be covered or its mouth must be tied closed. An injured pet is often panic-stricken. Under such circumstances even the most gentle animal may bite and scratch when you attempt to help it. Don't blame it, and *don't destroy it because it's vicious.* Remember that biting is a normal reaction of a frightened or injured animal. Remember, too, that the pain may have subsided for the moment and that in handling you may have caused it to recur with terrible intensity. Don't expect the animal to respond as it usually does. Expect it to act like it is—an animal in pain.

What can you do when you see a dog lying in the street that has been struck by a car—probably surrounded by a crowd of sympathetic but helpless people? First, you can call a vet. Next you can move it out of the street. It has dragged itself several feet. It can move its tail, so you know its back is not broken. The pelvis may have been crushed. Approach the dog from the side, with its head at your left. Put your left hand near its head. If it makes no attempt to bite, grasp as large a handful of loose skin as possible, high up on the scruff of the neck, and hold tight. So long as you hold fast the dog can't bite because it can neither shake itself loose nor turn its head far enough to reach you.

The dog can be lifted by this grip until it is high enough so that your right hand can reach under the chest just between the front legs, thus encircling its body. The dog will not try to bite your clothing. It cannot reach your hand. It is being held too low to be able to bite your face. By holding it in this position, you can lift and carry even a large dog without much difficulty. Let us suppose you want to carry the dog into your house, or that you want to put it into your automobile. Just push your right arm forward and place the dog gently where it will rest, pulling your hand backward from under as it reclines. We have handled even setters, Collies, and hounds in this manner and have never been bitten doing it.

But suppose that the dog, when you put a hand near it, snaps viciously? What then? That is when a simple piece of cloth, three feet long and three or four inches wide, does the trick. Cross the ends and start to tie a knot, but instead of drawing it taut, let a large loop hang down, while you hold the ends in each hand. You now approach the dog from the front. Your hands are far enough apart so that it cannot reach either one. Slip the loose loop over the nose, about one and a half inches from the tip, draw it tight, and tie a knot. To prevent the dog's scratching the restraint off its nose, tie another single knot under the chin and then bring both ends around the neck, tying them in a bow-knot behind the ears. When you have done this you can safely lift the dog as described above.

But suppose again that the dog is badly lacerated about the face and chest, and savage. It would be cruel to place a tie around the muzzle. What can you do then? Obtain a blanket and spread it on the ground beside the dog. Then make a slip lasso, toss it around the neck, and drag the animal gently onto the blanket such that two men can pull the four corners taut and make a stretcher of it.

The blanket may be used in another way: fold it to the smallest size that will cover the dog's chest and head with enough extra to extend several inches in front of the nose. This will probably be eight thicknesses, and even if a large dog should bite through it, the bite can inflict very little damage. The folded blanket should be dropped squarely over the head and shoulders and the dog is to be grasped firmly from behind, with one hand in back of each shoulder. With this grip the dog can be lifted with the blanket wrapped around it and held securely in front of the handler.

When the injured dog is safely in the car or in the house, the mouth tie may be used for restraint while you examine any broken bones, gashes, bruises, internal bleeding, or other injuries.

Suppose you are handling a dog dazed from a head injury inflicted by a glancing blow of an automobile bumper. You have cornered it, tied its mouth, and started to carry it. Everything goes well until the dog wriggles out of your grip. Then you remember that you neglected to snap a leash to the collar. When you have a hold of the dog again and fastened the leash, remember to take the time to tighten the collar. In struggling the dog will probably slip the collar over its head unless the collar is drawn tighter than usual.

If the dog is too large to carry and won't be led, run the leash backward, encircle the chest behind the front legs, and loop the leash through as if it were in a giant knot. You can then pull forward with a lifting force. Usually this will make the dog walk, even when it is not leash-broken. By grasping the rope so positioned just above the dog's back, you can move the animal along almost as you would a suitcase.

The double-lasso method is effective for powerful animals that can inflict damage if not restrained. Two lassos are thrown over the head and around the neck and pulled in opposite directions until the dog is thoroughly subdued. The pullers must be careful not to strangle the dog.

The dog warden's loop on a pole, or through a pipe, is excellent for bad fellows, because the dogs can't escape and can be held at a distance.

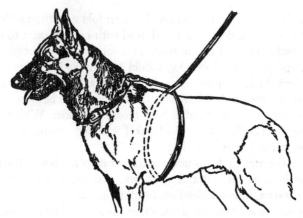

A useful hitch for a stubborn dog.

HOW TO STOP A DOGFIGHT

There are times when you may find your dog engaged in one of those occasional natural affairs which some dogs seem to enjoy—a dogfight. Your dog may be the aggressor or it may be the victim of a bully. In either event you will want to stop the fight or the mutilation. *Don't reach for the collar of either dog!* You are almost certain to be bitten. Quickly catch hold of a hind leg or the tail of the more aggressive dog and pull. If you are strong enough, lift it off the ground and throw it as far as you can and then use your voice and scold. It must be a severe loud tone or the dog will pay no attention to you. Get between the dogs and hold the weaker behind you until help arrives. Once extricated the loser will beat a retreat.

Household pets are ordinarily affectionate and gentle, but there are emergencies when even the mildest of them must be dealt with firmly and even severely. We remember once seeing a small Bullterrier attacking another dog ferociously. As we approached, the Terrier growled but still held fast to the other dog. People stood about the fence, the owner of the attacked dog was screaming, a policeman was ready to shoot, and the Terrier's owner was pleading with him not to shoot. We grabbed the Terrier by the tail close to the body. It let go of the other dog and tried to attack us. There was only one thing to do—swing it around and bodily throw it away from the other dog.

FIRST AID

The principles of first aid that the dog owner needs to master are simple and relatively few, but they are of vital importance in handling emergencies. Whether an animal that has been injured is to recover quickly or slowly, whether it is to be completely restored or marked or scarred—indeed, whether the animal is to survive at all—often depends upon the treatment it gets immediately after it is hurt. The balance of this chapter is intended to give dog owners the general information needed and at the same time to provide a reference manual of the specific ways to handle any emergencies that may arise with their pets. We suggest this list of basic things that pet owners should have on hand.

First Aid Accessories

3"- and 6"-wide rolled bandaging
1"-wide adhesive tape
cotton
antiseptic powder
antiseptic ointment
hydrogen peroxide
scissors
thermometer

Shock. Any severe injury—being hit by a car, burned, hurt in a struggle or a fight—or even severe fright may bring on shock. The animal usually seems to be prostrate in a semi-oblivious state, yet apparently anxious. The nervous system is in depression, sometimes so severe as to cause complete immobility. On the other hand, occasionally an animal may suffer the opposite effect, so that it seems to be in a state of nervous excitement. The pulse is slow and weak, the breathing is shallow. Often, as the animal recovers, the pulse becomes too rapid and the temperature may drop well below normal.

First aid consists in covering the dog so its temperature will rise to normal. High artificial heat is not necessary if the animal is at home in familiar surroundings. Administer a stimulant, such as coffee, then let it rest. Occasional fondling is often reassuring and helpful. Recovery may sometimes take an hour or more.

If a veterinarian is available a more effective treatment is the administration of steroids and fluids to increase the fluid volume in circulation. Too, a veterinarian may discover internal bleeding which often accompanies injury and which may have to be controlled by surgery.

Heatstrokes. Of all pets, dogs are most subject to heatstrokes. English Bulldogs and fat dogs are the most frequent victims. Dogs with heavy coats of fine fur suffer most, of course, and for their protection and comfort they should be clipped in the summer as a preventive measure.

We are all conscious of the refreshing sensation of a breeze in hot weather. This is due to evaporation of moisture from our bodies and the consequent cooling of the surface of the body. The bodies of animals are cooled by the same process, which is aided by evaporation in the throat and mouth when the pet becomes overheated and pants. Dogs have few sweat glands in the skin compared with those of humans and horses, but they do have some. When an animal is sufficiently cooled by bodily evaporation, it stops panting.

In itself, panting is a normal method of reducing body temperature. It may sometimes be an indication of thirst. A hot, panting dog is obviously evaporating an abnormal amount of moisture from its body and needs to replenish the loss.

In a heatstroke, however, the panting is sharp and continuous. The dog seems to be "burning up," its tongue turns purple, and it finds it difficult to catch its breath. You know the animal has been exposed to great heat, possibly to excitement. What should you do?

Remember the principle of cooling we have just discussed: the evaporation of water reduces body temperature. Lay the dog on a flat surface and pour cold water over it until it is thoroughly soaked. Set up an electric fan a few feet away, turn its blast directly on the dog, and keep on adding water as it evaporates. Take the dog's temperature occasionally. Usually the fever will drop in less than half an hour from about 108° F to 101° F. When it has come down to normal or nearly so, dry the dog with a towel and keep it out of the heat.

If an electric fan is not available, a cold-water enema is advisable. If this is impossible, immersion in cold water is a satisfactory method of reducing the temperature quickly. A great many animals have been saved in this manner.

Dogs are frequently afflicted by heatstroke in cars. If this should happen, stop for water and lay your dog on the floor in front. As soon as you have the water, drive on with the ventilator open so that the draft will blow directly on your animal. Keep it wet, and before many miles its temperature will have dropped to normal.

Anyone who takes a dog on a long trip in very hot weather should be aware of the danger of a heatstroke and be careful to avoid it. Carry a pan and water for the pet. The animal that is losing an unusual amount of water by evaporation needs to replace it by drinking frequently. If the dog has enough water, it is much less likely to succumb to the heat.

Accidents. The most common cause of accidents among pets is the automobile. So common is it that companies that insure dogs' lives often exempt death by automobile from their policies. Dogs will dash across the street, for example, to get to another dog. Even dogs that are so well trained that they will wait for a car to pass will walk across the street behind it only to be struck by a car coming from the opposite direction. The brightest animals have not learned to look both ways, to anticipate so far into the future.

When a pet is struck by an automobile, you must first restrain it and then treat it for shock. Look at its gums. If they are pale it may be an indication of internal bleeding or shock. If its gums appear gray or white, it has probably suffered an internal injury and is bleeding internally. Roll up long strips of bandage—an old sheet may be torn in strips for this purpose. Have an assistant stretch the pet out and hold the front and hind legs. Then wrap the bandage around its body tightly, in a corset fashion. Keep on wrapping until you have made a good firm support. Be sure that the bandage will not pull together in a narrow roll around the animal's abdomen when it moves. The bandage must form a long tube which holds the animal's abdominal organs relatively immobile, so that a clot can form and remain in place. Without this firmness and pressure, the organs can move freely and disturb the blood clot. Do all you can to keep the animal quiet. The veterinarian will administer drugs and may decide upon surgery or a transfusion. Whatever you do, move an animal gently after an accident if there are indications of internal bleeding. It can bleed to death very quickly. It may be saved if you keep it quiet and get veterinary help in time.

If an animal does bleed internally, what becomes of the blood that escapes into the abdomen? A large percent of the red blood cells are absorbed back into the circulation. A clot also forms at the injury site. This is composed of red and white cells, plasma, and fibrinogen, which causes coagulation. As it forms, the clot squeezes out a fluid or serum. This serum can be, and is, soaked up by the peritoneum (the lining of the abdomen and covering of the organs). Obviously the serum gets back into the circulation and thus helps to increase the blood volume. Many of the red cells which transport oxygen through the body are in the clot. This clot does not persist permanently as a liverlike lump. Instead a process called lysis occurs. The cells simply dissolve into the fluid in the abdomen. Their covering disintegrates and releases the contents. The fluid is now circulated, but only a small amount is utilized by the body; most of it, including the red pigment, is passed out of the body through the urine as waste.

When you see your weak but mending animal urinating what appears to be blood, don't presume it is passing blood from its kidneys and bladder; this is probably blood-colored matter. Indeed, anticipate this happening. This fact is sometimes used as a diagnostic means of demonstrating internal hemorrhage that occurred several days before the red color is seen.

Rabies. The cry of "mad dog" is no longer heard in America as it used to be, or as history tells us it was in Europe. Nevertheless, it *does* occur. An animal that manifests *any* symptoms of rabies is suspect. Rabies is discussed in detail in Chapter 24, and here we need only concern ourselves with the problems of first aid—first aid to the dog and to the animals or humans it has bitten—and the subsequent management of the incident.

For the suspected rabid dog, isolation must be provided. Shut it in a yard or room and call your veterinarian immediately. Keep people and animals away from it. Your veterinarian and the health authorities will diagnose its condition. Either the local authorities or veterinarian will provide isolation until the diagnosis is clearly established. If an animal *is* infected, the local authorities will determine its disposition. Frequently they prefer to let the disease progress until Negri bodies have developed in the brain at which time a positive diagnosis can be made.

Any pet that has been bitten by a rabid animal should be quarantined. Since a high proportion of all animals—perhaps 75 percent of all unvaccinated dogs, for example—are susceptible to rabies, no other course is safe. The period of isolation is long. An exposed dog must be confined for six months. Will it pay to maintain the dog so long at a costly boarding fee? Will you ever have complete confidence in it? Rabies is such a horrible disease that we feel it is advisable that all rabid animals and most animals bitten by a rabid animal be destroyed.

Needless to say, if a human is bitten, call a doctor immediately. Only a physician is qualified to decide on the treatment or prophylaxis for the humans involved.

Lacerations. Dogs hustling through barbed-wire fences, stepping on broken bottles, scratching in ash piles, and stepping on concealed metal scraps come home gashed, bleeding, and torn. They seldom bleed to death.

Most of the cuts that occur on animal skins are triangular tears or clean, straight cuts. In either case only a limited kind of first aid should be administered. In animal saliva there is an enzyme that combats bacteria. The surface of an animal's tongue is made up of small, tough scales so strong that it can wear flesh away if it wants to. There is no better way of cleaning a cut than allowing the animal to lick it. It will lick away all dead flesh or debris and kill germs as it does so. Eventually it will heal its own wounds.

First aid consists not of strapping the cut together with adhesive tape, nor of binding up the wound, unless it is bleeding badly, but of allowing the animal to clean its wounds, then having the veterinarian treat them. Though it may not be an emergency, let the veterinarian advise the proper treatment. He or she may cut away any dead edges on the flap and suture the wound in place, so that when it has healed no ugly scar will remain.

There are cuts that dogs cannot reach to lick, however. In long-haired dogs these may be covered with hair, which should be trimmed off about the area. Or they may be on areas of the body, such as the neck, head, face, and shoulders, which the dog cannot reach. In these cases, clean the cuts yourself (hydrogen peroxide is excellent for this purpose) and take the animal to the vet as soon as possible.

Cuts in the feet usually cause profuse bleeding, since this is a vascular area. A cut of this sort should always be examined to see if a foreign object has remained in it. After the examination it is necessary to stop the bleeding. A plug of cotton pressed against the opening and a pressure bandage that holds it there will quickly check the bleeding. If a serious hemorrhage is observed, apply a tourniquet immediately above or below the joint above it. It must be loosened and reapplied every ten minutes. (On the trip to the veterinarian take along some cloths to absorb blood, which may stain your clothes or the car.)

The most dangerous cuts are those made by filthy objects. These cuts may heal or mat over with hair that becomes part of a scab, and tetanus (lockjaw) germs may infect these wounds. Since they can develop only in a wound that the air cannot reach, cuts or punctures of this sort must be opened, cleansed, and kept open until they have been disinfected and sutured. There are some wounds that are best left unsutured for a considerable length of time. These must be flushed daily while they heal from the bottom out, and they are sutured to avoid unsightly scars only when the healing process has reached the surface layers of the skin.

Animal Bites. Animal bites and venomous snake or insect bites need very different treatment, so we shall consider them separately.

It is sometimes important to determine the kind of bite to be treated. The bite of a dog or cat, or even that of a rat, can usually be distinguished by the number of teeth marks. When a large dog attacks an animal, if one tooth mark is found, three others can nearly always be located. The distance between these skin punctures, as well as their size, gives some idea of the size of the attacker. Little dogs sometimes open their mouths wide and leave impressions of their upper and lower canine teeth perhaps four inches apart, but the distance between the two upper canines will still be small. Large dogs may happen to get hold with only a small nip, but the distance between their upper canines may be as much as three inches in some breeds.

Because of their size and strength, large dogs inflict greater damage than do small dogs. Ordinarily a dog attacking another animal does not simply attack, hold on, and squeeze; it shakes its head and thus drives its fangs deeper. These teeth wounds can be cleaned by shaving the hair away and filling them with antiseptic from an inserted medicine dropper. The attacker may have freed the skin from the underlying connective tissue over a large area. In such cases your veterinarian will flush this area clean and bind it down and perhaps apply a drain for a few days.

Cat bites on dogs often become seriously infected. The skin should not be allowed to heal quickly over them. First aid often consists in hurrying the animal to the doctor. If infected, the punctures become large abscesses which burst, carrying with them large areas of skin which has been killed in the process of abscess formation. A bite that has been allowed to abscess takes much longer to heal than does a properly treated bite, and the new skin which eventually covers the open area will scar and never have hair.

Snake Bites. First aid in snake bites is extremely important. When you suspect a rapidly increasing swelling to be the result of a rattle-snake, copperhead, or water moccasin bite, there is usually sufficient time to reach a veterinarian. If there is not time, try your family doctor. Many physicians have saved animal lives in emergencies. The great majority of venomous snake bites in dogs occur on the head. The curious dog ventures too near the reptile and is not aware of the speed of a striking snake. In order for the snake to deliver much venom it is necessary for it to strike and bury its fangs deeply enough for pressure to be exerted on the venom glands. Since much of a dog's head has mostly skin over the bone of the head, the snake cannot bury its fangs deeply enough to deliver very much poison. Nevertheless, even a small amount causes an alarming reaction in the swelling, which is usually extreme enough to double the dog's head size, close the eyes, and triple the thickness of the lips.

Many veterinarians in venomous snake areas keep antivenin on hand and, with supportive treatments of antibiotics and intravenous fluids, are able to save most animals bitten by snakes.

If the bite is on an extremity the swelling may be so extensive that the skin acts as a tourniquet, resulting in gangrene. It then is some-times necessary to incise the skin longitudinally to permit circulation.

The time to act with a dog bitten by a snake is immediately! And if the dog is taken to a veterinarian within two hours the recovery rate is excellent. Unfortunately a venomous snake bite is not always observed by the owner; however, you may surmise that if your dog arrives with an area that is swelling even as you watch it, it may well be a snake bite.

Spider Bites. There are many spiders capable of poisoning by their bites. The black widow is perhaps best known. We think most venomous spider bites are never diagnosed since the actual bite is virtually never observed by the owner. The lips, nose, and even the tongue are the most common sites for these bites but the actual spot may be impossible to locate. Some cause a sudden intense itching which subsides in six to twelve hours as mysteriously as it started. The itching may be so intense that the dog is taken to a veterinarian who may, unaware of the cause, treat the symptoms with rapid results. We are not aware of fatal spider bites in dogs.

Bee Stings. It is not uncommon to hear of pets being stung to death by bees or yellow jackets. Dogs will frequently swell from single stings but more often come home drooling, their mouths partly open from the pain and swelling occasioned by snapping up a stinging insect—wasp, hornet, or bee.

The painful stings, the poisonous effect of the toxin, and, worst of all, the sensitivity to the foreign material developed by having been previously stung may produce a severe reaction.

Veterinary treatment gives prompt relief. Home treatment with antihistamines helps but is not as effective as prescription preparations given by injections.

We recall a frantic phone call from a client who described a bizarre situation. The dog had been tethered in a new location and the family had started their lunch when the dog was heard screaming in pain. The husband ran outside and, seeing the dog virtually covered with yellow jackets, rushed into the swarming insects and carried the dog into the house, brushing off the stinging insects as he went. The wife phoned me to ask if her husband could bring the dog into the hospital. I told her to send someone else in with the dog and to rush her husband to the emergency room of our local human hospital.

The dog was brought in but died two hours later. The woman phoned later in the day to tell me her husband had collapsed in the hospital waiting room from his fifty or so stings, and the doctors claimed he would have died had the reaction occurred away from immediate help.

Removal of Foreign Bodies. No first aid discussion could be complete without suggestions as to the removal of foreign bodies.

IN THE MOUTH: Dogs sometimes overestimate their ability to manipulate certain bones. It is common to find bones caught in various positions: wedged across the roof of the mouth between the back teeth; driven down into the gum beside a tooth; driven through the soft tissue below the lower jaw; stuck between two teeth; stuck on top of a molar tooth; or covering several teeth.

A T-bone from a lamb chop can sometimes become caught across a dog's mouth between the back teeth, with its sharp point sticking into the throat. The dog paws desperately at its mouth, and the owner often thinks that the end has surely come. Dogs sometimes chew two- or three-inch shank bones from lamb so that the rounded bone slips down over their teeth and they can't close their mouths without forcing the sharp edges of the bone farther down against the gums. They become frantic.

Many other kinds of foreign bodies become wedged in the teeth or stuck in the mouth. Any dog may have accidents in its mouth. The mouth must be opened and the object pulled out. Whenever possible, it is wise to rush the pet to the veterinarian, who has the instruments to remove the obstruction without difficulty.

IN THE STOMACH: If you do not actually see a dog eat a foreign object, you can never be sure that the dog does have it in its stomach. You may have seen the dog eat gravel or sand, or chew on an old doll. But circumstantial evidence is usually all that is necessary. If a small item the dog was playing with is missing and the dog begins to show evidence of stomach pain, it is time for action.

Suppose you suspect that your small dog has swallowed one of your child's iron jacks, the little crisscross gadget the child picks up when bouncing a ball. The dog will probably show some evidence of stomach pain, and you should act at once. For a twenty-pound dog, mix about two ounces of peroxide with two ounces of water and pour it down the dog's throat. Use more if it is a large dog. If vomiting does not occur very soon repeat the dose. When it begins, lift the pup by the back legs so that its forepaws are touching the ground and its head is down. In almost every case the jack will be regurgitated the first time.

You may be surprised sometime to pick up your dog and hear stones rattling together in its stomach. Don't be too astonished, for this is a fairly common occurrence and it shouldn't worry you very much. Stones can usually be recovered with the peroxide treatment. Puppies with gravel impactions in their stomachs can be relieved by the same means. Mineral oil should be given fifteen minutes after the peroxide, to help move along the gravel that has entered the intestine.

Remedies of this sort for the removal of foreign bodies are properly classified as first aid. More difficult cases should be left to the veterinarian. With X rays he or she can locate bullets, needles, pins, spark plugs, and any of the hundreds of other odd and dangerous objects that dogs have been known to swallow.

IN THE RECTUM: If your dog squats, strains, cries, and possibly exudes a little blood from its anus, it is possible that it has a foreign body in the rectum. If a constipated mass is considered a foreign body, surely it has. Not infrequently the stoppage is caused by sharp bone splinters, which were not properly softened and digested in its stomach. Poultry, pork, and lamb bones are the most likely to cause such difficulties. Since any movement of the sharp bones is extremely painful, the dog refrains from defecating. In time the fecal material piles up behind them and soon a solid, dry mass with sharp bones sticking out of it precludes all passage.

First aid consists of enemas to soften the mass, though they often are not sufficiently effective to allow passage of the material. Humane considerations indicate a prompt visit to the veterinarian, who will probably first soften the mass and then gently reach in with an instrument and crush it into small particles. Occasionally an oily enema is sufficiently lubricating to permit the stool to be passed without great difficulty or pain. In difficult cases the veterinarian may have to pull out the sharp pieces with instruments to avoid lacerating the rectal area.

Needles are frequently found in the rectums of dogs. A thread hanging from the anus is a good indication of the cause of the pain. If the needle is just inside and can be felt, an ingenious person with a small wire cutter, such as electricians use, can snip the needle in half and remove the halves separately. Generally, however, this job is best left to the veterinarian, who will use anesthesia and a speculum to see clearly what he or she is doing.

IN THE SKIN: Foreign bodies in the skin or feet are usually splinters or bullets, although other objects, such as pitchfork tines, glass chips, and porcupine quills, are not as uncommon as most people think. Common sense dictates the quick removal of such objects, whenever possible, in order to relieve the animal. It also dictates the injection of an antiseptic into the wound. If a bullet has come to rest against a rib and it can be seen through the hole, you should—for once—do what your first impulse tells you: pull it out with the family tweezers and cleanse the wound.

Children often put elastic bands around the neck, leg, tail, ear, lower jaw, or even the penis of their pets. The hair covers the band and it goes unnoticed by adults until swelling and odor are observed. There is little that can be done by the owner after he or she has removed the band. If the skin gap is too wide, have the veterinarian suture it to prevent formation of a hairless scar. Ropes and small chains may also cut deeply through the skin. Most people have seen at least one animal with a hairless band of skin around the neck—mute evidence that some negligent owner left a rope or chain on until it cut the animal's neck. Having callously injured the animal, the owner failed even to have the gaping skin sutured.

Porcupine Quills. In many states in this country, and in all parts of Canada, porcupines are common. They tempt courageous dogs to attack them, and when they do, the unfortunate dogs find their mouths and bodies full of quills. A quill, which is only a modified hair lightly attached to the porcupine's skin, has small reverse barbs protruding from the shaft. Under a microscope the barbs look like the prickles on a thistle, with one scale overlapping the next. When a quill penetrates the skin, every muscle movement of the victim draws it inward, since the angle at which the barbs are set prevents its moving outward.

When attacked, porcupines often inflict severely painful and dangerous injuries. Strong dogs may pick up the porcupine and shake it from side to side, driving hundreds of quills into themselves on each side. For good measure, the porcupine thrashes its quill-filled tail from side to side and up and down, swatting the dog's legs and body. The tail quills leave a pattern, because they are small and black and usually half studded with barbs. To cap the climax, the poor dog, now feeling the pain, rolls and paws at the quills, driving them in deeper.

So many nonsensical ideas still persist about porcupines shooting quills that we must emphasize this fact: the porcupine does not shoot quills; the quills are loosely attached to the skin, and when they become fastened into the flesh of the attacker they are pulled free. The porcupine does not fight with dogs but only defends itself. To cut each quill to release a vacuum and somehow make quills easier to pull is also a fallacy.

If a dog were to attack a porcupine directly in front of a veterinarian's office, quill removal would be simple. The doctor would quickly administer an injectable anesthetic and pull the quills. It has never been our good fortune to have one of our dogs quilled within miles of any place where the quills could be pulled surgically. We have pulled thousands and thousands of quills from hunting dogs with electrician's pliers when we've been far off in the woods without surgical equipment.

When they have no pliers, some old hunters just take out their jackknives, cut the quills off, and lead the dog home. They say a cutoff quill is not particularly dangerous and does not work in. Perhaps not so much as with whole quills, but we have seen a dog blinded by a cutoff quill.

No one should take his or her dog into the woods where there are known to be porcupines without carrying a pair of pliers which have carefully machined jaws and tips. When a dog has been quilled, there may be no time to take it to a veterinarian. Chain it firmly. Get right to work with the pliers from the car if no others are available. With no halfway measure, *pull the quills*, blood or no blood. Here is a place where heroic methods are necessary.

If your dog is quilled in the woods, let it stand up while you pull the quills from the side on which you are going to lay it. Then pull the quills out of its mouth. Grab a handful of dirt from the forest floor and get hold of the tongue with it, covering your hand so the tongue won't slip. Pull the tongue out and remove the quills that have stuck into it. If the quills in the dog's lips have worked through far enough to feel the points on the other side, pulling them point first through the lips is less painful for the dog. Tie its mouth to prevent it nuzzling the quills and driving them in farther. Remove quills from around the eyes. Then go to work on the body, first behind the shoulders, where quills may work into vital organs. When quills break off, feel sorry, but go to work on others.

On many occasions we have extracted quills from dogs surgically while they were in shock from the severity of having been quilled. Anesthetics must be administered cautiously during shock. When they are used, the progress of any quill is stopped.

If quills are allowed to work in out of sight, they will continue to move about the body. Those that entered the front legs or shoulders generally move upward, and by the following morning the needle-sharp points of some can be felt emerging from the skin above the shoulder blades, whence their progress has been guided by the broad bones. Putting dozens or even hundreds of gashes over a dog's shoulders and legs is less satisfactory than letting the quills move themselves to a point where the tips can be felt through the skin. If the point doesn't emerge, nick the skin and pull it, thus removing a fresh crop every day, until they are all out. Feeling for quills is the only efficient method of locating them. X rays are useless.

FOXTAILS: Many bits of vegetation such as cactus spines, thorns, and weed seeds may gain entrance to the skin or mucous membranes of the mouth and penetrate, causing abscesses. Foxtails, a weed-seed spreading device, are perhaps the most common of these objects and must be removed to correct the problem.

MAGGOTS: It is hard to believe that every summer hundreds of dogs are killed by flies. And yet dogs die everywhere in the United States from being eaten alive by the larvae of flies—maggots. In the North only long-haired dogs are attacked.

Somewhere, for example, under the long bushy coat of a Collie or on the matted hair of an Old English Sheepdog, an abrasion may occur. Perhaps it is a small patch of skin disease. Flies are attracted by the serum that the body has exuded and lay eggs on or near the wound. Maggots hatch and live on the moist tissue which they kill by the toxins they secrete. The hair prevents the dog from chewing and licking off these enemies. The maggots continue to grow and spread in the area. Finally some migrate to other moist spots and begin to feed. More flies are attracted and soon the dog is a mass of maggots.

Even a badly infested dog can be saved by prompt action, but many dogs have died for the want of adequate and timely attention. The coat should be clipped, the holes, which may be an inch deep, washed clean of the pests, and antiseptic dressings applied. Often the first sign to the owner will be prostration of the dog, for the maggots give off a powerful toxin. If you don't discover the worms until that stage has been reached, get the animal to your veterinarian at once. Infusions may save its life.

Skunk Spraying. Skunk odor has chemically a rather simple formula —a mercaptan, a sort of alcohol-sulphur combination. It is a volatile substance. Volatile chemicals usually turn into gas with heat and maintain their liquid character in cold. The way to dissipate skunk odor, therefore, is to get what's affected by it hot. (Hang your clothes in the sun in the summertime, or in a garage attic—anywhere that is dry and hot—don't bury them.) The odor leaves quite quickly. A hot bath with lots of soap will usually remove most of the odor from a dog—or from an owner, for that matter. Several baths certainly will. If the dog is left where it is hot, the odor evaporates more quickly to a point where it loses its unpleasantness. Washing the pet in tomato or concentrated orange juice is most efficacious in removing the odor. The amount needed depends on the size of the animal.

Drowning. If a drowning dog can be pulled out of the water while its heart is still beating, it can almost always be saved. Slow, steady artificial respiration does the trick. Not as you may have been taught to work on a human. Place the animal on its side and push with the flat of the hand on its ribs. Then pull your weight up quickly. Repeat at regular intervals about once every two seconds. The animal will usually start to breathe very shallowly, then gradually breathe more deeply. Even when the heartbeat is faint, there is hope. It pays to try.

Some years ago we treated the Yale University mascot, Handsome Dan, as an emergency case. He had been taken out to a local river where the Yale crew was practicing, then fell off the dock. The students laughed and waited for him to surface to help him back on the dock but Handsome Dan didn't surface—he was walking on the river bottom. The students dived in and brought him up just in time. He did have a bout of pneumonia but recovered nicely.

Electric Shock. Since animals' bodies are such excellent conductors of electricity, the shock of 110 volts—which ordinarily merely jolts a human—may kill them. When shocked, they sometimes stiffen so rigidly that they appear to leap into the air. There is a great temptation for a dog to chew a dangling electric cord, and many have been badly injured when they tried it. One such experience is sufficient to teach a dog's owner the hazard of loose electric wires—often at the cost of the pet's life. If the shock has not killed the animal, artificial respiration should be administered immediately. If it cannot let go of the wire, be careful when you pick the dog up. It may have urinated; you may step in the urine and, in touching it, the current may pass through you. It is imperative to pull out the plug first or take hold of the wire with a wad of dry cloth and jerk it out of the animal's mouth. Visit your veterinarian immediately. He or she will probably administer drugs to stimulate the heart and breathing, and treat shock and the burns.

Burns. The seriousness of severe thermal burns must not be minimized—helpful initial treatment consists of cooling the affected areas with ice packs. Ice in a plastic bag works well, but this is no substitute for veterinary care, since shock may develop that can kill. Cooling the burned areas seems to help reduce pain and if done quickly may reduce healing time. If thermal burns are not extensive, phone the veterinarian for suggestions. He or she may suggest gently removing the hair in long-haired dogs with scissors and cleaning the burned area with a tamed iodine soap such as surgeons use to scrub with prior to surgery. A pharmacist will suggest the best soap and burn remedy if your veterinarian is not available.

Burns with caustics and acids can be as serious or even worse than thermal burns. In such cases the chemicals must be removed in all haste with copious amounts of water. If the base of chemical burns is an oil, add your own vegetable oil, massage it in, and bathe the animal as soon as possible with a mild detergent soap such as one that is used to wash dishes.

If as much as half the skin is severely burned by thermal or chemical burns, consider putting the animal to sleep, as the pain involved with this extent of damage is unbelievable and usually ends in death anyway.

Dogs are fortunate in having surplus skin so that large scars left from healed burns can be removed with excellent cosmetic results. If the scars are too severe for excision, veterinarians use grafts effectively.

Convulsions, Fits, and Seizures. Fortunately the so-called running fit, or fright fit, is rare today with the advent of proper nutrition. However, epilepsy is not rare and is observed in dogs as in man in all degrees of severity. If the seizure is mild and the pet does not lose contact with the environment, comfort should be the treatment. If, on the other hand, a dog has a grand mal seizure it will sometimes thrash around, flailing its legs and knocking down things, urinating, and defecating. At this time it is important to protect the dog by throwing a blanket over it. As the seizure subsides a dog will gradually regain consciousness but, not able to recognize even people familiar to it, may struggle to its feet and fall many times before it recognizes its surroundings. During this in-between stage a leash is helpful to restrain it. An afflicted dog does not become aggressively mean but may open and close its mouth involuntarily.

A dog with a low blood sugar may have a similar seizure which should be handled in the same manner—protect the dog from self-injury.

A veterinarian should be consulted for a differential diagnosis and preventive treatment. Don't put the trip to the veterinarian off as some poisons masquerade as epilepsy and, untreated, are fatal.

Let your dog alone until it has recovered from the fit and then look for the cause. Prevention of future attacks is the best first aid. Your veterinarian will help you to locate the cause and provide help. See Chapter 19 for more on convulsions.

Bruises. It requires a hard blow to bruise a dog. Even dogs that have been skidded along on a road until the hair was scraped off and the skin left bloody seldom swell as do some other species. Probably the looseness of the skin over the dog's body is one of its prime protections. When uninfected swellings are found they need only cleansing. They soon subside without further treatment.

If the hair is rubbed off but the skin not cut through, the chances are the healed skin will not be hairless.

Broken Bones. You may find, when you examine an injured pet, that it has a broken bone. You should be familiar with certain first aid techniques to prevent additional damage to the pet.

A broken leg is the most common animal fracture and requires immediate attention. Care involves straightening the leg and immobilizing it. Sometimes this takes courage. A splint is needed. A barrel stave, a tine from a bamboo rake, or a yardstick may serve as an improvised splint. The leg should be tied to the splint below and above the break and wrapped with anything suitable to hold it securely in place until you can get the pet to the veterinarian.

A splint should be applied at once. If the broken bone slashes about the flesh, it can easily cut a major vein, artery, or nerve, and then the area around the break will become a large pocket filled with blood, greatly complicating the task of setting. It is just as important to splint a greenstick fracture, which is what we call a partially broken bone. Movement or a fall may break it further.

If ribs are broken, keep the animal quiet. It is possible for ribs to puncture lungs, so lay the animal down with the broken ribs up and keep it as calm as possible until the veterinarian can look at the problem.

An untreated fractured pelvis heals slowly. No home treatment can be done to repair pelvic breaks or to hasten the natural process of reconstruction. Occasionally only one side is broken and the dog can continue to walk on three legs. More often the pelvis is fractured in such a way as to preclude walking until the usual numbness develops, deadening the pain in the area. Even after a veterinarian has treated the animal, for several days after the break it may be unable to raise itself without help. Gradually it takes a few unstable steps and soon is waddling about. Don't expect your dog to run for at least a month after the break. Even after the healing is well started you may have to help it up, carry it outside, and sometimes hold it in a position to defecate. Some animals learn why they are taken outside surprisingly soon and, as quickly as they are placed in position, will void. Standing the animal up and putting pressure on the bladder from both sides usually causes urination, and it is not uncommon to have a dog so cooperative that just touching its sides is suggestion enough for it to urinate. Since the nature of the fracture determines the treatment, X rays are a must in suspected pelvic fractures. Not unusually one or more of the six pelvic bones are fractured along with the femur; if the femoral fracture is overlooked, the dog could be a cripple for the remainder of its life.

Few broken bones are irreparable. Many broken backs are set and immobilized so that the dogs can live normally again. Palpation will usually determine where the tips of the vertebrae are out of line. If you suspect that your pet has a broken back, get it to the veterinarian as quickly as possible with as little jolting as you can. The spinal cord is a delicate structure. If the animal is to survive, the nerve damage must be held to a minimum.

Once again, X rays are a great help in predicting the possibilities for surgical repair if the cord is not severed, or for euthanasia if the damage indicates the pet will never walk again.

One of the most usual spinal fractures comes at the point inside the body where the tail vertebrae start. In such a fracture the tail hangs limp and lifeless. Sometimes there is enough muscular strength remaining to move it slightly. It is often soiled with feces because the animal cannot raise it to defecate. Even if the tail is not set, it may retain its life; but more often the tail loses all its feeling and dries up. In this case, the veterinarian will have to open the skin over the fracture and remove the useless appendage.

Poisoning. Pain, trembling, panting, vomiting, convulsions, coma, slimy mouths are all symptoms of poisoning. Any of these, except a caustically burned mouth, may also be a symptom of another malady. But if your dog should manifest any of these symptoms, you should investigate immediately to see if it has been poisoned.

Animals are very seldom deliberately poisoned. Usually they are poisoned either by chewing plants that have been sprayed, by gnawing at a piece of wood that has some lead paint pigment on it, by catching a ground mole that has been poisoned with cyanide, by consuming poison put out for other animals or insects, by eating infected garbage, or lapping antifreeze. Since none of the poisons is easily traced, you ought to know the procedure to follow *in case* your pet may have been poisoned.

An emetic *must be administered immediately.* The loss of a few minutes may give the poison time to do irremediable damage. Mix equal parts of hydrogen peroxide and water. Force your pet to take one and a half tablespoonfuls of this mixture for each ten pounds of its body weight. A pup needs less than one tablespoonful, a large dog seven to eight tablespoonfuls. If in two or three minutes the contents of the stomach have not been regurgitated, repeat the dose.

Either mustard or a strong salt solution can be used as an emetic, but hydrogen peroxide has proved to be most effective. If the poison was known to have been ingested hours before, an emetic may be too late.

Following the administration of this emetic, call your veterinarian. If you know the source of the poisoning and can look on the package it came from, you will find the antidote on the label. If you don't know the poison that your pet has ingested, your veterinarian may be able to identify it from the symptoms and give further appropriate treatment.

If there is any chance that poison can be the cause of intestinal trouble, it is imperative that all traces of the poison be eliminated before giving the animal drugs which will stop bowel movement and allow the intestines to become quiescent—paregoric, for instance. But if the intestines are badly irritated, it is dangerous to give physics. We know many animals are saved by inducing vomiting promptly. If the substance is suspected of having entered the small intestine, from which it cannot be regurgitated, we believe a through and through enema is a lifesaver. This is administered by a veterinarian, who introduces water rectally until vomiting occurs. It may require many quarts of water and patience.

Once the poison is removed, our job is to give such common home remedies as milk of bismuth, paregoric, or strong tea for its tannic acid content. Strangely enough, some cases are benefited by castor oil, which removes the cause and tends to be followed by constipation. Veterinarians will prescribe effective prescription drugs.

The same drugs that are useful in human care can be employed. Today a variety of mixtures containing kaolin, bismuth, pectin are available, and your veterinarian will advise you on their use.

GENERAL ADVICE IN TREATING POISONING. Immediate action is essential since some poisons are absorbed at once. Phone your veterinarian immediately for advice.

Table X HOUSEHOLD ANTIDOTES FOR COMMON POISONS

POISON	ANTIDOTE
Acids	
(Hydrochloric, nitric, acetic)	Bicarbonate of soda, eggshells, crushed plaster (1 tablespoonful)
Alkalies	
(Sink cleansers, cleaning agents)	Vinegar or lemon juice (several tablespoonfuls)
Arsenic	
(Lead arsenate, calcium arsenate, white arsenic, Paris green)	Epsom salts (1 teaspoonful in 1/4 cup water)
Food poisoning	
(Bacteria from garbage or decomposed food)	Hydrogen peroxide (give enema after stomach has emptied)
Hydrocyanic acid	
(Wild cherry, laurel leaves)	Glucose (2 tablespoonfuls dextrose or corn syrup)
Insecticides	
(Flea powders, bug poisons)	Hydrogen peroxide and enema

POISON	ANTIDOTE
Lead (Lead arsenic, paint pigments)	Epsom salts (1 teaspoonful in water)
Mercury (Bichloride of mercury)	Eggs and milk
Phosphorus (Rat poison)	Hydrogen peroxide (peroxide and water in equal parts, 1 oz. to each 10 pounds of weight of animal)
Sedatives (Overdoses in medicating)	Strong coffee (1 cupful for a 40-pound dog)
Strychnine (Strychnine sulfate in rodent and animal poisons)	Sedatives such as phenobarbital, pentobarbital sodium (1 grain to 7 pounds of dog)
Thallium (Bug poisons)	Table salt (1 teaspoonful in 1/4 cup water)
Theobromine (Cooking chocolate)	Pentobarbital, phenobarbital

EMERGENCIES

What is an emergency situation? Unlike beauty, which is in the eye of the beholder, many problems may appear to be panic-button problems that are not.

Late one night we received phone calls from two people: one wanted to rush his Boxer in as an emergency, the other wanted to wait until morning before bringing his Labrador in.

The Boxer was having a severe convulsion, and the owner, who had not observed the condition previously, decided the dog needed immediate attention. This dog had been diagnosed as epileptic a year before and averaged one convulsion a month even on medication. While we discussed the problem, the dog recovered from the seizure.

In the second case, the owner, a very considerate gentleman, apologized for disturbing us and described his old Labrador as having become suddenly weak. He would bring the dog in for an examination in the morning but he wanted advice as to what he might do in the meantime. We asked him to examine the color of the dog's tongue. He reported that it was almost white. We asked him to rush in with the dog and, by emergency surgery, saved its life by removing a ruptured spleen. The dog would have been dead by morning.

So we can state that a dog with sudden loss of color in its mucous membranes is an emergency. So is a dog with depression accompanied by a subnormal temperature, say, below 100° F. A sudden high fever with depression may indicate a problem with the temperature-regulating mechanism or the onset of an acute bacterial infection, such as pneumonia. Of course, heatstroke is a true emergency. An injury from an automobile or from a fall from a high place may or may not need emergency treatment, depending on the signs displayed. Lacerations that bleed profusely and cannot be controlled are obvious emergencies.

The known ingestion of a toxic substance is an obvious reason to seek emergency care, but usually this is not observed. If you should see a dog lapping the radiator fluid, ethylene chloride, that is an immediate emergency situation and not one in which to watch for signs a day or two later.

There are many problems that to a concerned owner are presumptive emergencies but for the dog less than critical. A puppy vomiting roundworms six inches long may seem an emergency situation, but it usually is not. A dog suddenly snorting with a reverse cough sounds serious but is not. Nor is the onset of kennel cough, where spasms of coughing are followed by a nonproductive gag.

Cuts and lacerations that do not bleed much are not emergencies and can wait until morning. A broken nail is uncomfortable and may cause limping but it is not a panic-button situation.

Dogs can survive about 75 percent of their problems without help, just as we can. The trick is to identify the remaining 25 percent, as it is in this group that lives can be saved and serious complications prevented. In questionable cases, veterinarians appreciate being contacted to make a value judgment.

Unusual Accidents. One reason for books such as this is to provide information in such a way that personally experiencing pitfalls is unnecessary. A few examples of unusual accidents may be helpful to forewarn.

Playthings should be too large to swallow and indestructable. We have surgically removed peach pits, baby nursing nipples, rocks, corncobs, rubber balls, and many other objects that had become lodged in the small intestines of dogs.

A dog was placed in a car and tied to the headrest. The driver left the area for a few minutes and the pet jumped out of the car window. Another member of the family, seeing the dog loose, ran out and snapped a long chain on the collar with the other end around a tree, not observing the leash leading into the car window. The driver returned and drove off. The dog died two days later from its broken neck.

A dog that jumped fences was tied to a fence and left. It jumped the fence and was found, hanged, on the other side.

A dog, tied halfway up the staircase, jumped over the hand rail and was found dead when the owners returned.

A dog chewed an electric cord. The children saw smoke coming out of its mouth and called their mother, who pulled the electric plug. (Never touch the electrified pet.) This dog survived, although plastic surgery was necessary to close the hole burned through the bone of the roof of the mouth.

A dog retrieved a large Fourth of July firecracker. It survived after weeks of intravenous and stomach tube feeding, but will never taste its food again.

A dog that leapt from a hotel's seventh story fire escape landed on grass and suffered only bruises.

A dog licking a can partially opened with the lid pushed inside nearly amputated its tongue.

An elastic band on tail, neck or leg cuts like a knife, only more slowly.

Acting as if in a seizure, swinging its lowered head from side to side, a heavy-coated dog was presented as a 2 A.M. emergency. Its lower front teeth were caught in a snarl in the long hair of its chest.

A ball large enough to enter the back of a dog's throat, but too large to swallow, blocked the airway, resulting in death.

A board was tossed for a dog to retrieve. It split and a splinter was forced beside the base of the tongue into the neck. The splinter was seven inches long.

Permanent radiator antifreeze, ethylene chloride, is sweet tasting. Beware of an overheated radiator that overflows on the ground; a lap or two of the liquid is often lethal.

And don't feed a dog from a car's hubcaps. They contain cadmium, which can kill dogs.

Experimenting with pills purchased from a drug pusher, some people poison their dogs, sometimes fatally.

A dog permitted loose and unattended in the neighborhood eventually found garbage with tainted food it could not vomit. It might have been a rodent killed with a toxic substance.

A hound was caught in a steel-jawed trap for forty-eight hours through the worst blizzard of the Connecticut winter and survived, and even uses the leg without toes.

11

Surgery

In general, we can divide surgery into three categories: necessary, elective, and vanity.

Necessary surgery is surgery to save life or improve the quality of life. Automobile injuries to the soft tissue and fractures are examples. The surgical approach to eliminate cancer is also necessary and successful more often than not.

In days gone by and occasionally today seriously injured animals were and are unnecessarily destroyed by well-meaning unenlightened people —people who do not realize how effective a veterinarian can be. For the novice to assume an injured animal is hopelessly injured is a mistake. Even we veterinarians surprise ourselves at times when a seemingly hopeless case recovers.

A three-pound adult Chihuahua ran out in front of a car that was traveling fifty miles an hour. The wheels straddled the dog but the undercarriage of the vehicle struck the little animal on top of its head, crushing the skull and indenting the head, forming a large depression. The owner rushed in with the unconscious animal, which appeared to be taking its last breath. Assuming, as we did, that this was a fatal injury, the owner left in tears as quickly as she had arrived. There appeared to be little to do but to operate immediately. However, when we grasped the skin with an instrument at the deepest part of the depression and pulled, we discovered that the fragments of the fracture had pinched the inner layer of skin between them so that when the skin was pulled with a surgical forcep the fractured skull returned to its normal position. The little dog recovered from unconsciousness in ten minutes, but the injury appeared to be so serious we waited for half an hour before phoning the distraught owner to come and get her dog. That Chihuahua lived another fourteen years to die at sixteen years of age of natural causes.

Injuries from automobile accidents present challenging problems to veterinarians all too often. Bone and joint injuries are amenable to repair, but only after the animal is safely out of shock and when it can tolerate the necessary procedures of X rays and surgery under anesthesia.

There is often a healthy hesitancy when surgery is suggested to the owner of a cherished pet. Will the anesthetic be too much for it? This is a frequent question, but the fact is that anesthetic deaths are all but unheard of in most veterinary establishments. In our experience performing all surgery with eight veterinarians at the New Haven Central Hospital, we doubt we have lost three dogs in five years from the anesthesia. As far as tolerating a surgical visit to a hospital, it should be pointed out that a pet is soon under anesthesia, then recovering for many hours. During those hours it is not capable of homesickness and if such a problem is anticipated that animal is sent home as soon as possible after surgery.

SPAYING

Most owners are not aware of the chain of events in a surgical procedure. We will describe one of the most common procedures, an ovariohysterectomy, known also as a spaying (not spading) operation.

Having found the dog to be in satisfactory health for surgery, the veterinarian may administer drugs to sedate, prevent excess salivation, and empty the stomach to prevent vomiting during the operation but this is not always advisable. The dog is placed on a prep table where a trained assistant holds and cajoles it while the veterinarian administers a short-acting anesthetic intravenously. An endotracheal tube is inserted in the trachea (windpipe) and anesthesia is continued with gas and oxygen provided by a gas anesthesia machine. When the correct level of anesthesia is reached, the patient's fur is clipped on and around the surgical site. The area is scrubbed and the pet is taken into a surgical theater. The surgeon, who is dressed in cap, mask, and clean garments (often called greens), scrubs his or her hands with a medicated soap, dries them, and dons a sterile surgical gown and sterile gloves. Sterile instruments, suturing material, drape, and gauze have been laid out by an assistant. After draping the site, the surgeon proceeds to make an incision through which one fork or horn of the uterus is delivered. It is traced to the end and the ovary attached is removed by first ligating the blood supply to it. The uterus is traced back to its bifurcation and this is ligated and severed. The second horn is traced to its end, where the second ovary is ligated and removed. If one of the three ligatures slips off, the patient may bleed to death, but this virtually never happens. The incision is closed by suturing the deep layers and finally the skin after which the patient is disconnected from the gas anesthetic machine and moved to a recovery area. Usually in five or ten minutes reflexes—the blinking of the eyelids and jaw movements—are observed. When she can swallow, the endotracheal tube is removed but the patient is closely observed until she is enough awake to be placed back in her compartment.

The same operation performed in 1916 was described to us by an onlooker. Each end of a three-foot cord was attached to the forelegs of the patient and another to the rear legs. The animal was raised by the rear cord, which was then hooked over a fence post. The doctor placed his foot on the loop of cord attached to the forelegs. This stretched the animal effectively, exposing the abdomen. The doctor reached in his pocket, produced a small pocketknife, and made a three-inch incision in the abdomen. He reached in and extracted the uterus. He severed the attachments and discarded the uterus and ovaries. Next came the suturing. He removed a prethreaded needle from the lapel of his coat and with it sutured the incision. He removed the binding cords, and the dog ran off. Since no anesthesia was used, the poor dog screamed all through the surgery. His charge for this service was fifty cents. The veterinary profession has come a long way.

For many years opinions of the results of spaying a bitch were bandied about by "experts" on a purely conjectural basis. Mr. James found his bitch became obese; Mrs. Jones found her dog did not change; Mrs. Wilson thought her Great Dane became timid after the operation; Mrs. Doe thought her Doberman became bold and ugly. Even veterinarians couldn't agree.

Considerable research now shows that spaying has little effect on the general characteristics of the animal. Spayed Greyhounds race as well as and have very little tendency to be fatter than unspayed sisters. Other species are not spoiled, except for reproduction purposes, by the operation.

It has been assumed spaying should be done when the female is approaching maturity, at which time glandular development has had a normal effect. If it is desirable to produce a chicken that will be large, awkward, lazy, and fat—a capon—you don't put the operation off until the bird is full grown. For then you would have merely a sterile rooster. The operation should be done in the early life of the bird because at that time it accomplishes precisely the changes which we want to avoid in spayed pet dogs.

The same example may be found in bovines where, when spayed as a calf the steer is quite different from the ox that is castrated as an adult.

More research is needed to be done in neutering both male and female dogs at young ages to be able to compare them with unaltered littermates. Many scientists believe early neutering may not be a disadvantage in the canine.

The fact that some spayed bitches get fat is not in itself a valid argument against spaying. Unspayed bitches, too, get fat. Some of the most grossly overweight dogs we know are whole animals. They are overfed. If they had been spayed and placed in the hands of the same owner, his or her explanation for the overweight condition would have been that the bitch had been spayed.

Spaying has little effect upon a mature animal. The animal does not have mating cycles and the urges that they bring. This may have a very slight effect on weight and personality. The reason for spaying some bitches young is to prevent the bitches of vicious breeds from becoming dangerous as they get older. If they are spayed as puppies, they tend to remain gentle.

In some remote localities, female puppies have almost no sale because of the expense of the spaying operation. Dog dealers refuse to buy puppies for resale unless they have already been spayed. In such areas, there is some justification for the operation; it is better to operate on young puppies than simply to destroy them.

Spaying a bitch has a number of definite advantages.

1. The animal is spared the risk attending birth.

2. The owner is spared raising or having to destroy unwanted animals.

3. The owner avoids the annoyance of males surrounding his or her house, killing shrubbery, breaking windows, and following members of the family.

4. The spayed female does not wander at certain seasons as the unspayed one does.

5. Spaying almost certainly prevents the formation of cancer in the

breasts, which sometimes occurs in bitches three or four years of age and commonly in older dogs. It also prevents metritis, the inflammation of the uterus, which afflicts unspayed bitches.

6. The owner can be saved many dollars a year for boarding the pet twice a year.

7. Money for food is saved, since a pregnant, or lactating, mother consumes more food than a spayed one.

8. In many places the license fee for a spayed bitch is less than for an unspayed bitch. Where this is so, the owner will save the cost of spaying many times in the course of a normal life span.

There are also disadvantages in spaying.

1. An owner may someday regret that his or her female can't reproduce.

2. As spayed animals grow older they sometimes lose control of the bladder sphincter. But this can be corrected by giving medication occasionally (see Chapter 16).

Does spaying harm a hunting dog? Some of the greatest hunters ever known have been spayed bitches. In fact, it helps hunting dogs, becaused unspayed bitches so often come into heat in the all-too-short hunting season. Because of this they often miss the training and experience that makes better hunters of the spayed bitches which are never incapacitated.

Months after a bitch has been spayed and returned home, dogs sometimes collect about the house as if she were in heat. The owner should first look to see if the bitch is bleeding and swollen. If she is not, she is not attracting the males. Occasionally a chip of ovary, or even a whole ovary, may have been left. Human gynecologists often spay their own animals, using the technique of removing the uterus but not the ovaries. These bitches have not been spayed in the veterinary sense. If ovaries are not entirely removed, a bitch will come in heat, copulate, but fail, of course, to conceive.

Very often spayed animals that are thought to be attracting males actually are not. Another bitch in heat is probably the basic attraction. She may have urinated in many places about the neighborhood. Dogs smelling the urine detect nothing of the keep-away odor of normal urine and therefore conclude that the bitch in front of whose house they find it is in season. When she appears, the dogs attempt to copulate. She thinks they are playing, and if she has a mild disposition, she will not fight them as a bolder animal would. Not being repulsed, they hang about until the dogcatcher comes in answer to a complaint and removes those he can catch to the pound. A bold spayed bitch will fight off any intruders and the dogs will stay away.

CASTRATION

Much the same arguments hold for castration as for spaying. Generally it is done to make males stay home. Those that congregate around the abode of a bitch come home torn or punctured with tooth marks from the frequent fracases attending these encounters. These wanderers are brought home by the dog warden, who collects his fee. They are expensive animals. Castration usually alters their wandering habits because the sex urge is often the cause of it.

There are many other reasons for castrating animals. Dogs of breeds whose members tend to become vicious with age are often rendered gentle and lovable when castrated when they are young. Castration also tends to prevent a good deal of male territorial wetting and thus saves shrubbery.

Whether or not castration will cause dogs who are chronic wanderers to settle down and stay home is a moot question. It definitely has had that effect in numerous instances but has produced no diminution of the wandering tendency in others. It is worth a try, however, if your choice is either to alter the dog or dispose of it.

It seems to be the opinion of many people that animals should not be spayed or castrated because copulation is essential to health. This is not the case. Any animal, whether whole, spayed, or castrated, is just as healthy if it is never bred as those that are used for breeding. Considering the risks of pregnancy, birth, and disease, a female's chances for longer life are actually greater. And as for males, only a small percentage ever copulate in their whole lives. This is true of many species, not of our pet animals alone.

Castration is elective and if a male is not going to be used as a stud it has great merit. What a dog doesn't know about sex won't hurt it and if altered at six months it will develop normally without the sex drive. An alarm, guard, or attack dog will be no less able to perform its functions and a hunting dog is no less a hunter for the surgery.

If a male has been used as a stud dog and is castrated at a later date he may continue the sex act for years afterward although, of course, he can't sire puppies. However, for a few weeks after surgery he may be potent.

We are told there was a male terrier who was so nervous at dog shows that he retracted one testicle. Some enterprising person operated on this show dog and placed a wax object in the scrotum simulating a testicle. At the next dog show, a judge upon checking found three testicles.

CESAREAN SECTION

Whether or not to perform a cesarean section is a value judgment on the part of one best equipped to make such a judgment and that is usually a veterinarian. With problem deliveries some veterinarians prefer to extract a puppy from the birth canal with instruments hoping the others will then be delivered normally. Others prefer to operate immediately so the female will not overtire herself straining. After a cesarean operation the mother and her puppies go home immediately if there are no complications.

DEVOCALIZATION

The devocalization, or debarking, operation, although an elective procedure, is performed usually as a lifesaving one. We have had clients tell us they will have to dispose of their dogs because they bark in their absence and may be of an age or type that cannot be placed in another home. In the spirit of a lifesaving operation some veterinarians perform this surgery. In our experience it is not as effective in medium and large dogs, but it is very effective in smaller breeds.

Many people are horrified at the thought of this, but the dogs have no problem. They bark away as usual except with a whisper rather than a normal voice.

One of our clients had a kennel of sixteen little look-alike Yorkshire Terriers, all of whom barked off and on, although they were not a noise problem. The family had to move to another city, where with great difficulty they located a house in a residential area that permitted only two dogs per household. She asked us to debark fourteen of the little fellows, which we did. That family lived for two years in their new residence without the neighbors discovering there were more than two dogs. The sixteen were smuggled in under cover of darkness and the family walked only two dogs at a time. The neighbors were heard to remark many times that those two dogs were walked more than any dogs in the state.

In the future, most surgery will be a thing of the past when we exclude vanity surgery since solutions other than surgery are in the future. The exceptions will be to correct inherited defects, injuries, and cosmetic surgery.

URINARY CALCULI

If your dog urinates frequently with or without blood, the problem may be the presence of calculi, or stones. These stones are rarely in the kidneys and most commonly found in the urinary bladder; they are not to be confused with gallstones which are in the gallbladder. Salts in the urine that normally remain in solution precipitate on clumps of bacteria and may grow to over three inches in diameter in the bladder. In an animal of normal weight they can be diagnosed by palpation by your veterinarian. X rays are necessary for an overweight pet with small stones.

The problem can be more complicated in the male. Small stones may lodge in the urethra at the bone of the penis called the os penis.

Surgery corrects the immediate problem. The recovered stones are analyzed and special diets with medication may prevent a repetition of the problem.

Kidney stones may require the removal of the affected kidney. Dogs survive well with one healthy kidney.

OTHER ROUTINE PROBLEMS AND PROCEDURES

It is a good bet almost every dog will have the need for at least one of the procedures during a normal lifetime.

Unusual Swellings Other Than Growths. Abscesses form from splinters, animal bites, gunshot wounds, or any other injury that breaks the skin. One of a host of different bacteria may be the cause but most abscesses are treated by lancing the lesion, draining it, and flushing it with an antibacterial material. If extensive, a drain may be necessary and hot compresses.

Cysts are usually smaller than most abscesses and are not usually infected. They are lanced, expressed, and if necessary their linings are removed.

Serum Pockets. After accidents great pouches of fluid often develop under areas of skin that has been loosened. Sometimes they fill with blood which clots and from which the plasma is absorbed back into circulation. If the injury is serious enough, bacteria may gain access to the pocket. After the skin is shaved, an incision at the lowest part of the pocket is made and the fluid and clots squeezed out. The area may be flushed with antibacterial solutions and the body bound to press the skin against the underlying layers to promote rapid healing with or without a drain.

Ear Hematomas. Hematomas are pockets of blood between layers of the skin. The most common location is in the ear. Dogs with ear mites bruise the ears by constant scratching. Dogs shaking their heads bruise the ear flaps on collar hardware. If the ear is not treated, the ear will heal with a gnarled deformity, sometimes called a potato chip ear. Let the veterinarian operate.

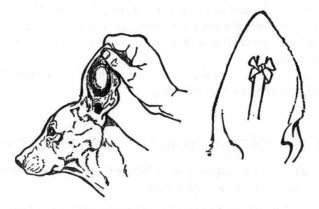

One method of surgical treatment of a hematoma in the ear, to facilitate rapid healing without puckering. The drain is moved back and forth to prevent the middle strip from healing, and is removed when the sides have healed down.

Lacerations should be cleaned and if the edges have skin without good circulation it must be trimmed away before suturing. It is wise to have open lacerations sutured promptly to prevent infection. The tip of the flap of some, such as a three-corner tear, may have an inadequate blood supply and must be trimmed before suturing. Commonly caused by barbed wire, this kind of tear will retract in a few days, making surgical repair more difficult.

More extensive lacerations usually require drains to prevent hematomas and seromas and to permit the drainage of purulent material from infection, which commonly develops.

Lacerations of the edges of the ear tend to become deeper as the dog shakes its head. Healing is often completely prevented, and even after the area has healed, the dog may open the tissue to blood flow by shaking its head incessantly. The bleeding can be greatly reduced by taking a stitch to encircle the blood vessel at the base of the notch. A fresh cut can best be repaired by your veterinarian, who will use an anesthetic and carefully suture layers of the skin of the ear together separately. One stitch through both skin layers and the cartilage is seldom entirely satisfactory, but if the skin is sutured neatly, the cartilage and layers will heal together evenly.

Warts. Simply cutting a wart off results in hemorrhage. To remove one successfully, the skin below the wart must be dissected along with the protruding part. A few drops of local anesthetic under the wart is enough to deaden the area. A single suture bringing the skin together usually results in perfect healing. Regardless of local anesthesia, many dogs are apprehensive and struggle. It is usually best to remove such lesions with a general short-acting anesthesia.

Polyps and Papillomas. Little toadstool-like growths on the body or in the mouth or on the lips of a dog may often be removed by simply tying them with a thread at the base with a surgeon's knot and letting them drop off. However, oral papillomas can be so numerous that much more extensive surgery is required. If there are only a few of these virus-caused oral papillomas, we prefer to do nothing as the dog will develop resistance, usually in four to six weeks, and the growths will disappear without treatment.

Eye Surgery. Most eye surgery, such as cataract removal, demands a high degree of skill and should be done by a specialist if one is available.

One lesion that appears serious is quite easily corrected, and that is the prolapse of a glandular tissue from the inner corner of the eye. It appears suddenly and is considered by many concerned owners to be a greater emergency than it is. We have lubricated the tissue and gently pressed it back under the third eyelid and have successfully treated the eye with ointment. More often it will not remain corrected and should be removed surgically. If the condition develops in one eye we can predict it will occur in the other eye one day.

Sometimes foreign objects must be removed from the eye. A light oil such as a few drops of cooking oil in the eye will lubricate it so that the object works toward the inner corner, where it leaves with excess tears.

Another minor problem that may appear worse than it is is a swelling, under an eye, that ruptures and drains down the cheek. It wouldn't appear that the problem is an abscessed tooth root but it usually is. One of the roots of the largest tooth, the fourth premolar, is the problem. After the tooth is extracted the abscess heals.

Two minor maladies requiring surgery. Left, abscess under the eye, which can be cured by extraction of infected tooth. Right, inflamed gland of Harder, which can be snipped off.

Dental Surgery. Unlike the human physician, the veterinarian is licensed to perform dentistry among his or her many services.

The most common culprit in dental problems is the buildup of tartar or plaque on the teeth, which causes receding of the gums by pockets of infection. Removing the tartar should be done if necessary to save teeth. Different types of food seem to have little effect on tartar buildup. In our kennels some of the dogs fed a mushy mixture had beautiful healthy teeth and gums all their lives, whereas others had to have the tartar removed every six months. Sound teeth and gums seem to be influenced by heredity.

You may be able to chip or scrape tartar from your pet's teeth but most dogs require a little anesthesia to reach all the affected areas. If the tartar is soft, a moistened cotton swab dipped in powdered pumice or even baking soda will remove it.

Some teeth become so loose they can be pulled out with your fingers. Many dogs in certain breeds lose most of their teeth before they are two or three years old. It appears to us that many dogs pass through a phase of a few years when, due to gum disease, they lose perhaps half their teeth and live the remainder of their lives with their remaining teeth in good condition. A dangling loose tooth does not require veterinary assistance to be removed—you can do it.

In older patients extractions may be difficult as with age the jaw bones become dense. Some teeth must be sawed or split before the roots may be removed.

Although it is rare, dogs can have cavities, in our experience always in the first upper molar teeth. Teeth with cavities should be extracted.

Removing Dewclaws. Some dog owners brag about their pet's extra toes and never have them removed. According to show standards, some breeds of dogs—Newfoundlands, St. Bernards, and all the retrievers, for example—need dewclaws, the surplus and often useless toes equivalent to human thumbs. Most owners, even show enthusiasts, have no objection to front dewclaws but think that on the rear legs they tend to detract from the neatness of the dog. Accordingly, they insist that these useless appurtenances be removed. Dewclaws tend to be inherited as Mendelian dominants. It should be remembered that two *days* of age is the ideal time to remove them. At that age dewclaws may be snipped off with scissors and cauterized with silver nitrate to control bleeding. Many puppies have been killed by unenlightened amputation taking place when the puppy is two or so weeks old, which results in excessive bleeding.

Hernias. A hernia is a protrusion of tissue, an organ, or organs through a normal or abnormal opening. Hernias occur commonly in dogs and are a hereditary tendency.

The most common hernia is located at the navel and is called an umbilical hernia. Some people wrongly claim this to be caused by the mother's chewing the umbilical cord too close to the abdomen. Umbilical hernias usually contain merely a small bleb of fat. In human infants they are commonly corrected by special bandages, but bandages do not work for a creature that walks on all fours with gravity exerting constant abdominal pressure. If in a young puppy the bleb of fat can be returned to the abdomen with digital pressure this may be done twice a day until the opening in the abdomen closes and the problem is resolved. However, it is rarely much of a problem since even with an opening large enough to insert one's thumb into the bulge is only unsightly. We advise the surgical correction of larger umbilical hernias in females that are to be bred. If your veterinarian suggests it, have the hernia corrected during the spaying operation.

Inguinal hernias are more serious. Located in the groin, they tend to enlarge over the years until there is an ever-present danger of a loop of intestine becoming trapped in the hernial sack, resulting in a condition known as hernial strangulation. Immediate surgical correction is imperative in such a situation and, of course, this type of hernia should be corrected before a life-threatening condition arises.

Scrotal hernias, rare in our experience, appear to be an inherited defect and require surgery if only for the comfort of the pet.

Perineal hernias, more common in males, are observed as bulges next to the anus. They may make the dog appear to be straining excessively when defecating. If these hernias are not treated by a veterinarian in the early stages, extensive surgery is required. In our practice, about half the males diagnosed as having perineal hernias respond instead to castration and require no further surgery. Invariably the prostate gland is enlarged, causing excessive straining in a futile attempt to pass it with stool. Castration results in a shrinking or atrophy of the prostate gland.

Diaphragmatic Hernias. The thin sheetlike muscle that separates the chest and the abdominal cavities is called the diaphragm. When this muscle tears, as it may from an injury, some of the abdominal organs may be drawn into the chest or thoracic cavity.

We have performed necropsies on old dogs and incidentally found diaphragmatic hernias, which we suspect occurred years before. More often the dog has shallow breathing and vomiting. To establish a positive diagnosis radiographs must be studied to locate the problem. Surgery is necessary to correct it.

Prolapsed Rectum. It is not uncommon to find a pet that from long, continued straining at stool has suffered a prolapse of the lower bowel. The name is not as accurate as it might be since the dog's rectum is only one half to three quarters of an inch long. The straining may have been caused by either constipation *or* laxatives, by improper diet, by foreign objects, by tumors, by infections, or by infestations. The cause must be established and corrected.

The tissue is returned to the abdominal cavity and a purse-string suture applied to prevent a recurrence. The suture is removed some days later.

Salivary Gland Cyst. If one of the ducts that conducts saliva from a salivary gland to the mouth is injured or obstructed, the saliva gradually accumulates, forming a pouch resembling early-stage mumps in people. Left untreated, it gravitates under the neck where it is unsightly though not life-threatening. Instead of pouching behind the jaw, some dogs gather saliva under the tongue, which is displaced to one side. This variation is called a ranula and requires surgical correction.

Laporotomy. A procedure performed more routinely in other countries than here and which has great merit is the laporotomy. This term describes the surgical opening of the abdominal cavity and is used in an attempt to find a problem.

The health of one six-year-old male Dalmatian had gone downhill for three months. He ate a small amount every third day or so and had lost his previous enthusiasm. Every test was repeated three times and every test was normal. X rays and a GI series were no help, so we suggested to the owner that we operate and examine his abdominal organs. It was frustrating to find everything normal and to have to tell the concerned owner we had failed to find an answer. However, almost as soon as the anesthesia had worn off, he ate his first good meal in three months. He made a rapid uneventful recovery. That case remains a mystery to this day.

Veterinarians recognize that a laporotomy is a therapeutic procedure but not why. Many animals are helped by it and many problems can be diagnosed by the operation.

Of course, we cannot discuss all the surgical procedures in this chapter but we hope you appreciate the potential for helping an animal when surgery is indicated. Above all, let us reassure you that the anesthesia is not a great problem and your veterinarian will give you a fair appraisal of the chances for a good result in any surgery.

Chapter 27 discusses the surgical approach for cancer and will help you make a decision as to its advisability.

ELECTIVE AND VANITY SURGERY

There are a host of operations performed on dogs that are termed elective because they are not necessary. Some are truly done for aesthetic reasons and change the dog's appearance for the benefit of man's personal values with little thought given to the discomfort inflicted on the dog. Of course, we are referring to ear cropping and tail docking in other than very young puppies. In a one- or two-day-old pup, tail docking is about as painful as the mother's chewing the umbilical cord but in older puppies the nervous system has developed. The operation results in pain we are not willing to inflict.

The British outlawed vanity surgery many years ago and we presume this country will follow suit in the future. There is no pain during the actual surgery, but the removal of half an ear *is* painful during the healing period for a week or more after the operation.

There are elective operations that may benefit the dog in the long run, such as surgery to sagging eyelids, which may predispose the animal to eye infections.

The removal of a retained testicle is preventive medicine since many become cancerous later in life. However, an operation to bring a retained testicle into the normal position in the scrotum is unethical since a dog with this condition can then be shown and used at stud. It usually requires three separate surgeries.

Docking Tails. Some breeds of dogs require tail docking either for styles set by breed fanciers or for health reasons. Some breeds will wag their long tails with such vigor that they damage the tips by striking hard objects. The infections and bleeding that result are difficult problems to control and in this case docking tails is good preventive medicine.

If you must have your pets' tails docked, we urge you, for two good reasons, to ask your veterinarian to perform the task. First, he or she will do it right. Second, excessive bleeding occurs infrequently, but still it does occur. Every puppy has a limited supply of iron. It can ill afford to lose any blood, because even though it will replace the volume, the new blood will not have quite the iron content necessary for good health. This retards development at a crucial time of life.

The initial loss of blood is not the only problem to consider. Many a litter has been cleanly docked and returned to the mother in excellent condition. She, however, may single out one or two puppies and lick the ends of their tails so that the blood cannot clot. If she is not stopped she may lick the pup to death. Every litter returned to the mother should be watched. If the mother will not let their tails alone, the pups should be removed, then returned to the mother only for nursing and only while the owner watches, to prevent her from unconsciously committing murder.

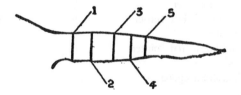

Points at which puppies' tails are usually docked. The lengths shown are those generally preferred, but styles change. If any doubt exists as to the proper length for your breed, consult the breed standard. (1) American Fox Terriers, Boxers, Doberman Pinschers. (2) Welsh Corgi. (3) All spaniels. (4) German Shorthaired Pointer, Lakeland Terrier. (5) Airedale, Wirehaired Fox Terrier, English Smooth Fox Terrier, Poodle.

You may have been told that the tail should be "disjointed" at a specific vertebra. People who give you such information have not docked young puppies' tails. You can't feel the vertebrae; you simply cut the tail to the proper length. Only in Doberman Pinschers and Boxers, where the tails are cut close to the body, does the skin slip to any extent. In these cases the skin should be pulled back toward the body before the cut is made. With other breeds, the cut is made according to the length the tail will be on the grown dog. Table XI shows the proper proportions to leave in all the breeds whose tails are docked. If you want an adult with a specific tail length, tell your veterinarian and he or she will oblige. It should be noted that some breeds are famous for producing puppies with varying tail lengths in one litter. In this case the percent removed, rather than the amount left, is the guide.

Table XI PROPER PROPORTIONS OF DOCKED TAILS

	PROPORTION TO LEAVE	ULTIMATE LENGTH (IN INCHES)
Airedale Terrier	5/8	6
American Smooth Fox Terrier	1/8	1
Boxer	1/8	1 1/2
Brittany Spaniel	3/8	3 1/2
Clumber Spaniel	1/4	2
Cocker Spaniel	3/8	3
Doberman Pinscher	1/8	1 1/2
English Smooth Fox Terrier	5/8	4 1/2
Field Spaniel	1/4	2
German Shorthaired Pointer	1/2	5
Lakeland Terrier	1/2	4
Old English Sheepdog	0	0
Poodle	5/8	5
Springer Spaniel	3/8	3 1/2
Standard Poodle	5/8	5
Welsh Corgi	1/4	2 1/2
Wirehaired Fox Terrier	5/8	4 1/2
Yorkshire Terrier	1/5	1

12

Drugs and Medications and How They Work

Not long ago a dog with pneumonia was practically doomed. Pneumonia was a killer; leptospirosis, streptococci, and meningitic diseases progressed unhindered; intestinal infections often proved fatal. Today we are able to treat all of these diseases with confidence. We have developed new uses and better methods of administering many of the older drugs. The development of the sulfa drugs and antibiotics has made it possible to cope with many of the most devastating diseases. We have developed new insecticides of great potency and seem to be on the verge of perfecting others in the near future. Equipped with a vastly improved arsenal of drugs and aided by an enormously expanded knowledge of the actions of those drugs, veterinary medicine has made astonishing progress in the last decade.

The value of these lifesaving drugs is too often taken for granted by the dog owner. All of them are actually of the greatest importance, for in a very real sense it is they that have made it possible to own pets and keep them healthy and vigorous. If dog owners are to be able to take full advantage of this new science of health, they must know some of the fundamental facts about drugs and their actions so that they can use them more intelligently and more effectively. Obviously there is no need for pet owners to understand the pharmaceutical intricacies of the various medicinal preparations, but they should certainly know the characteristics of the several general types of drugs and be familiar with their common uses.

With a very few exceptions, your veterinarian if asked will tell you exactly what he or she has prescribed for your pet. Your understanding of what is being given and why will make for more intelligent home care. And there is no reason why you should not be able to understand what your veterinarian tells you and what has been prescribed. There has been a small revolution in prescription writing. Latin names of drugs are being dropped and the metric system is being used. The U.S. Food and Drug Administration insists that the simplest names or the exact chemical names be used on labels.

In order to understand the uses of drugs, you must first understand that drugs work in several different ways. Some drugs do not kill germs outside of the body as well as they do those in the bloodstream; working in combination with the bacteria-destroying cells in the blood, they are highly efficient. Without the cells the drugs are of little value, and the cells without the drugs are helpless. This might be called a synergistic action. Phenols (such as creosol, thymol, and tars) and mercurial salts (such as bichloride) kill by causing the protoplasm of the cells to precipitate. Other drugs, such as arsenic, prevent the multiplication of bacteria. Still others combine chemically with some constituent of the protoplasm of the organism. Some have oxidizing properties and some interfere with the functioning within the bacteria themselves. There are drugs that may not be given together; they are *incompatible*. There are drugs that are incompatible with certain species; for example, phenol for cats and penicillin for guinea pigs. Still others produce odd effects; for instance, morphine when given to a cat may cause convulsions and death. Drugs likely to be given from the home medicine chest are few.

The success of all drugs depends on their being used in proper concentration. They must be strong enough to kill bacteria yet weak enough to cause minimal harm to the tissues of the animal. The required strengths for the various drugs have been worked out by long study and testing, and your veterinarian's instructions should be followed explicitly. When he or she gives you pills or tablets with instructions to give them at certain intervals, he or she has usually calculated how fast the drug will be eliminated in order to be sure that your pet always has enough in its system to accomplish the desired results. If you cannot give the prescribed doses at the prescribed intervals, it is better to leave the pet with the veterinarian, where the drugs will be administered as they should be.

Which brings us to the question of body repair. Always remember that the body of a pet is composed of many delicate organs. Its potential length of life is more or less determined at conception. With good care and nonexposure to some diseases against which it may not be resistant, the pet should live its normal life span. But when it becomes sick there is no certainty that, with the jab of a needle and a dose of medicine, it will recover. Life isn't like that. Recovery takes care—and time. Think how long it takes for a cut on your hand to heal. Cells slowly grow together, scar tissue forms and shrinks, and several weeks may pass before the area looks normal. Yet too often we expect pets to recover in a day or two from diseases more debilitating than influenza is to humans. Drugs can and do have marvelous properties but they can't abolish the element of time required for recovery.

Great care must be taken not to overdose, a common tendency on the part of laypeople. If a teaspoonful cures, then three teaspoonfuls should cure in a third of time, they often reason. Sometimes it kills. Doses have been worked out by pharmacologists with great care. The animal's size and the desired effect determine the dose. Overdoses are wasteful even when not dangerous.

One most interesting fact is that the larger the animal, the less of the drug is needed proportionately. Doses are proportional to surface area rather than to weight, but weight is easier to measure. Whereas you might think that a smaller animal is tenderer and should have less than its proportional weight might indicate, the opposite is true. Therefore, a fifty-pound dog of average weight receives the same dose as an eighty-pound dog which is thirty pounds overweight. The surface area may be stretched a bit in the overweight animal but it is comparable to that of the normal animal.

GENERAL ANESTHETICS AND SEDATIVES

The types of drugs used for general anesthetics and sedatives that allay pain and make surgery possible for pets include: those administered as a vapor, which is inhaled into the lungs, absorbed by the blood, and carried to the brain, where they temporarily deaden the sense of feeling and consciousness; those that are injected in liquid form; and those given by mouth.

Ether, chloroform, and nitrous oxide were the forerunners of modern gas anesthesia. Of the three, only nitrous oxide remains as an important agent used with newer agents to provide us with exceptionally safe anesthesia for our dogs.

Phenobarbital, perhaps too well known to laypeople, is one of the oldest barbiturates from the standpoint of use. Its introduction followed that of the first barbiturate, barbital. Given in both tablet and liquid form, it is one of the longest acting of this class of drugs.

Barbiturates of which phenobarbital is a good example, are composed basically of urea and malonic acid and have the following general actions:

1. *Depressant.* The size of the dose determines the degree of depression.

2. *Sedative.* Results are quickly accomplished, usually within an hour.

3. *Anticonvulsant.* Occasionally almost anesthetic doses must be given to animals convulsing severely, but they are effective even against the convulsions of strychnine poisoning. For this purpose, injectable barbiturates like pentobarbital are preferable.

4. *Anesthetic.* Phenobarbital is seldom used for this purpose. When overdoses are given, the blood pressure falls and breathing becomes slowed.

Pentobarbital was for years the most frequently used general anesthetic for pets and resulted in hours of surgical-level anesthesia. The problem with it was the length of time an animal was anesthetized and depth of anesthesia, which could not be controlled, as is possible with short-acting drugs and gas.

Pentothal and Thiamylal Sodium are short-acting general anesthetics and have many virtues for short procedures, such as the removal of small tumors and dental work. They are given in amounts necessary for the depth of anesthesia desired and when the procedure is completed the patient awakens over a relatively short period of time.

If your veterinarian is planning to use a barbiturate for an anesthetic, there are several things he or she should be told about your dog, if you know them. If your pet has had an increased thirst, this may suggest kidney disease. Animals with kidney diseases require much smaller amounts of barbiturates given by any route of administration. Dogs are partially poisoned by the wastes of disease in their systems. Liver disease and general debility also make a pet a poor subject for barbiturate anesthesia.

Animals terrified by thunderstorms, explosions from fireworks or blasting, or auto riding can safely be given small doses of pentobarbital for partial sedation and to produce a temporary loss of fear and memory. Your veterinarian can suggest a choice of medications for such problems for you to administer at home as necessary.

Alcohol is a "stimulant" that clients are forever telephoning their veterinarians to say they have just given to their dogs—a dose of brandy or a little whiskey. Somewhere laypeople have picked up the idea that alcohol is a great animal saver. Actually it has so few warranted uses in veterinary medicine that it need be mentioned only to emphasize the fact that it is actually a depressant, rather than the stimulant that most people believe it to be. It stimulates neither the respiration, the heart and blood systems, nor the muscles.

Alcohol irritates the skin, injures the cells, has an astringent action, and shrinks tissues; it causes irritation and inflammation to mucous membranes. When injected into tissue, it acts as an anesthetic but may permanently destroy nerve tissue. Alcohol anesthesia lasts longer than does ether or chloroform but, if given in large enough doses to anesthetize, it is too near the fatal dose for safety.

Alcohol has very little germ-killing power, and only at 70 percent by weight—a percentage difficult to approximate—is it worth using for this purpose.

The public has been so well educated in the use of alcohol to sterilize skin prior to an injection that members of the medical profession, both human doctors and veterinarians, choose to use it rather than explaining why it is ineffective.

Never give alcohol to "warm up" a pet. All it does is lower the body temperature by bringing the blood to the stomach and producing a false sensation of warmth. Nor should it be given as an aphrodisiac. We have known clients to use it in an effort to get shy breeding males to attempt copulation. They found it often makes them worse.

Alcohol does have one important use in veterinary medicine. It is used intravenously in the treatment of permanent antifreeze (ethylene glycol) poisoning.

LOCAL ANESTHETICS

Local anesthetics, which can be injected to cause loss of pain in a given area, are a great boon to animals, veterinarians, and pet owners. They may be injected over a main nerve trunk, around the area to be anesthetized—for example, around a bad gash that needs to be sutured —or around a small tumor that requires removal. When Adrenalin (epinephrine) is combined with any of the local anesthetics, the capillaries of the anesthetized area shrink and bleeding is greatly reduced. It is well to remember this if you take home a pet that has been operated on or sutured under a local anesthetic of procaine and Adrenalin. When you start for home from the vet's there may be no bleeding, but as the effects of the Adrenalin wear off considerable bleeding may ensue, so be prepared. It is nearly always better to leave an animal that has been operated on in a hospital for twelve to twenty-four hours.

Some veterinarians prefer combinations of local anesthetics, and there are many new ones coming along.

TOPICAL ANESTHETICS

Several drugs are also used to deaden pain simply by allowing them to soak through tissues. These topical anesthetics stop itching when they are incorporated in salve and rubbed in, and they relieve pain when they are ingredients of ointments used in cuts, sores, or conditions such as ear canker.

In using these anesthetics it is essential to keep them in contact with the tissue. If the dog persists in licking or rubbing them off, they must be replaced.

PAINKILLERS

Acetylsalicylic Acid (Aspirin) is something all dog owners want to give their animals. How many times have we heard on the telephone, "Doctor, how about an aspirin for my dog?" Then the client sometimes goes on to tell us that she has already given Fifi three aspirins but the little thing still seems to have a pain. Fifi is a twelve-pound Pekingese.

The derivatives of salicylic acid, a synthetic drug made from coal tar, are numerous, but only acetylsalicylic acid (aspirin) is of much interest to pet owners. The salicylates act to reduce fever slightly. No effect on heat production is noticed, but the heat loss is heightened by bringing the blood to the body surface where, in shorthaired animals, it tends to dissipate.

We can judge the effect of aspirin as a painkiller only by questioning human subjects. They assure us it does not relieve sore throat, or toothache, or pain in the intestines. It does afford relief from neuralgia or arthritic pains. In canine encephalitis, when dogs are bound to have headaches, aspirin may be effective. Salicylates do not exert germ-killing power in the blood, so should not be given to cure disease.

The dose for an adult human is five to fifteen grains (the usual aspirin tablet contains five grains). It is evident from this what a huge dose only one five-grain tablet is to a Cocker Spaniel, for instance, or to twelve-pound Fifi. If the Cocker weighs twenty-five pounds, it weighs one sixth as much as an average human being. One tablet for the dog is equivalent to giving a person six tablets—obviously an overdose, especially when given four or five times a day. Half a tablet is enough for a twenty-five-pound dog, while a grown St. Bernard can be given three with safety. This may be repeated every three hours.

Many dogs cannot tolerate aspirin and vomit from it. In overdoses, vomiting with blood is obviously a danger signal. Always give aspirin-containing tablets wrapped in food to prevent the pill from resting on the delicate gastric wall and causing local irritation.

Dilantin is one of the drugs used as an anticonvulsant and to lessen convulsions. Equivalent doses of it are far more efficient than phenobarbital. Doses of one grain daily for a forty-pound dog, or even as high as one and a half grains, produce excellent results. A St. Bernard needs only three or four grains. One has to experiment with Dilantin in slightly varying amounts on each pet to determine the proper dose.

Primidone is another anticonvulsant effective in some cases of epilepsy.

Morphine and the Opiates (Morphine, Paregoric, and Codeine) are derived from the poppy and are used in veterinary medicine. Morphine is being used less frequently today; many veterinarians no longer use opiates since they are convinced that other drugs work just as well or better. There are other vets, however, who still believe that it stands at the top of the list as a painkiller.

Morphine kills pain and brings sleep but produces constipation.

Paregoric (camphorated tincture of opium) is used to induce similar effects, but the concentration of the opiate is so slight that there is less danger in its use. In general, paregoric produces a quieting effect while at the same time relieving pain. Like morphine, it produces constipation. These drugs cause the pupils of the eyes to contract to smaller than normal, varying with the size of the dose given. Paregoric, which causes the mobility of the intestines to decrease, will produce a definite sleepiness in dogs but causes cats to become restless.

Paregoric with 0.4 opium is given in fairly large doses. When a forty-pound dog has been poisoned and is hemorrhaging bloody diarrhea, a drastic dose of a teaspoonful three times a day may be necessary. A giant dog with diarrhea can manage two teaspoonfuls. For small puppies with diarrhea from six drops in a little water up to one fourth of a teaspoon for a six-week-old Collie puppy has proved successful. Your veterinarian will tell you the safest dose for your pet. This old preparation is still useful in veterinary medicine.

Codeine in syrups is used considerably to control coughing. Opium or any of its derivatives accomplishes this result. Whether its use is sensible therapeutically depends on the kind of cough. If phlegm has accumulated in the pet's air passages and coughing helps to remove it, then why should the cough be stopped—except because it annoys the owner? Codeine is sometimes used as a drug of last resort to control heart cough which often accompanies chronic heart disease. But if the cough is a dry, useless, hacking spasm, opiates or any antitussives are definitely indicated.

STIMULANTS

Caffeine, besides having a slight stimulating effect on the peristalsis in the intestine, is useful because (1) it stimulates the general circulation by accelerating the heart, increasing its force and raising the blood pressure. It affects the heart muscle directly. Overdoses cause such rapid heartbeat that blood pressure drops; (2) it increases the rapidity and depth of respiration; (3) it stimulates the nervous system; (4) it increases muscular strength and power; and (5) it stimulates the production of urine by heightening the activity of the kidneys without irritating them, thus it is a *diuretic.*

Since caffeine is an effective, if mild stimulant, many dogs with a degree of cardiac insufficiency benefit from it. One level teaspoon of instant coffee contains about one grain of caffeine, which is helpful for a twenty-pound dog. It must be given frequently since the effectiveness lasts only a half hour or so. Very little coffee is required as a good-size dose for a dog. The error most people make is in giving their pets too much. In proportion to the human dose, when used as a stimulant, caffeine enough for a Cocker weighing twenty-five pounds is only one third to one half a cup, whereas a cup is enough for a great Great Dane. Yet an owner will often mistakenly give two cups to a small dog if the dog is hungry for it.

As a stimulant to counteract a narcotic or barbiturate poisoning, fairly large amounts of coffee should be given, but great care is necessary to prevent some from running into the lungs of the anesthetized animals. If coffee is not handy, strong tea is an excellent substitute. A cup of tea contains almost as much caffeine as a cup of coffee. Cocoa contains theobromine, which action is similar to that of caffeine. Ask your veterinarian before administering medications for potentially serious problems.

Ammonia in the form of aromatic spirits to sniff are often given to dogs and other pets, or it is given orally as a stimulant. A dog the size of a Cocker can stand one half a cubic centimeter in water, but very often large doses are given mistakenly. Ammonia has also been given to stimulate kidney action and to help an animal to raise phlegm from the trachea, but for these purposes it is inferior to other drugs that do this.

DIURETICS

Agents that increase the flow of urine are called diuretics. We noted earlier several drugs whose actions incidentally increase urine flow, although they are used primarily for some other purpose. In addition to these, certain drugs, such as salines, by increasing thirst cause the blood to absorb a surplus of water which later escapes through the kidneys.

Diuretics are occasionally useful to flush some circulatory toxin from the blood or to withdraw fluid from the abdomen and relieve pressure on the heart and lungs without resorting to tapping. When animals have bladder infections, sometimes copious urine formation and elimination help wash that reservoir clean. There are also times when the abundant flow of urine helps prevent formation of urine crystals and flushes out those which have formed.

It need hardly be said that while you are trying to eliminate part of the dropsical fluid by diuresis without tapping the abdomen, you must prevent the dog from drinking excess water. You are trying to make the animal soak this surplus fluid back into its blood vessels. To do that you cause it to urinate copiously, which reduces the water content of the blood, which in turn causes the dog to replenish it from the abdomen.

Water and the excretion of it are the bases of diuresis. Reducing the percentage of water in the blood is one thing that is striven for. This in turn creates thirst; more water is drunk, more eliminated. So your veterinarian may inject water with added salt to make a so-called "physiological solution." Or he or she can inject a small amount of common salt in solution, or even give it by mouth so that the pet will drink copiously.

Sugar—either glucose or cane sugar, or both—may be given as a diuretic, but in very large amounts a pet can't utilize it all. It must be given by vein, and when so given, especially in poison cases, helps detoxify some poisons. A 50 percent solution is generally used, a forty-pound dog requiring about 12 cc. Cane sugar is used intravenously in double the dose of glucose and in some ways is preferable.

Flurosamide has superseded the older and more dangerous drugs, such as the mercurials, and several new diuretics are in the development stages. When given flurosamide it is impossible for a dog to drink as much fluid as it eliminates. In the past water had to be rationed with drugs used to dehydrate but the restriction of fluids can retard the correction of the problem. Sometimes called "water pills," flurosamide is a lifesaver for treating many maladies, such as cardiac insufficiency in which the heart cough is caused in part by fluid buildup in the lungs.

HEART STIMULANTS

Digitalis exerts its action specifically on the heart and leads the list of effective heart stimulants. The dried leaves of the lovely garden flower, foxglove, are the source of this remarkable drug. Several other plants produce the so-called digitalis principles: squill, a sea onion; strophanthus, a tree whose seeds are used; and even the bulb of the lily of the valley.

Of the active ingredients of digitalis one is most effective for dogs and that is digoxin. Digoxin directly affects the muscle of the heart, whose force of contraction it greatly increases. The rate is also slowed. It is useful in many disturbances that result from heart failure—and heart weakness is heart failure. Dropsy and edema of the tissues may be due both to heart and kidney failure. Digoxin gives relief in some cases. It is not, however, the universal remedy some people think. Digoxin is not a useful stimulant when a quick one is needed, because it takes too long to establish the desired effects. It is useless in some forms of heart trouble, in pneumonia, and in shock. When your veterinarian establishes the fact that your dog requires digoxin he or she has two avenues to consider. Either he or she may administer doses that will build levels of the drug in the heart muscle rapidly and then reduce the dose to a maintenance dose. Or the maintenance dose, which will require five or more days for its full therapeutic effect, may be prescribed. The disadvantage of the first approach, which is called a loading dose, is that the patient may become so ill one wonders if the cure is worse than the disease. The loading dose should be done under the direct observation of a veterinarian. The maintenance dose may be administered at home.

Epinephrine (Adrenalin) in a small dose may be injected by your veterinarian into your dog to treat it for shock after an accident or severe intestinal bleeding because of certain lifesaving properties that this drug, produced by the adrenal glands, has demonstrated. Of its many effects, the desired one here is contraction of the capillaries and arterioles sufficient to cause a clot to form without being washed off the injured tissue or organ. When this occurs, blood pressure may increase enough to help the animal recover from shock, breathing may be easier, and oxygen absorption promoted. Epinephrine's effects are of short duration—only a matter of minutes—but those minutes may be all that are required to save the pet's life. This wonderful drug can be relied upon to produce all these effects.

Mixed with procaine and used as a local anesthetic in surgery, epinephrine helps prevent capillary bleeding. In cases of heart failure adrenalin, injected directly into the heart, may sometimes cause it to beat again. In acute bronchial asthma it brings relief. The dose is very small. Your veterinarian usually uses a 1:1000 solution and injects fractions of a cubic centimeter.

Ephedrine, a drug of plant origin, has similar properties. Unlike epinephrine, it has the advantage of being absorbed from the digestive tract; it need not be injected unless quick action is required. Moreover, it has much longer effects. Practically everything said regarding epinephrine applies to ephedrine, except that it is sometimes harmful when used in shock treatment. In pet medicine it finds use in emphysema in old, wheezy animals. Animals that cough constantly, apparently trying to raise phlegm from the lungs, often benefit from a little ephedrine. A mixture with atropine sometimes works wonders.

SECRETORY GLAND DEPRESSANTS

Belladonna, that wondrous panacea, used to pervade all the old veterinary books. It was a favorite remedy used by all sorts of people. The old horse jockeys used to give mixtures of it with arsenical preparations to give temporary relief to horses with heaves (chronic emphysema), so that they could trade them to some unsuspecting victim.

If a dog has been eating plants in a garden where this deadly nightshade (belladonna) grows, and you see it bumping into objects, trying to get into a dark spot; if you open its mouth and find it dry; if its temperature is high, heart very rapid, pulse weak, and gait abnormal; if it is restless and excited—call your veterinarian. He or she can flush out the offending herbage, inject preparations repeatedly until the pet's mouth shows moisture, and save the animal.

Atropine is derived from belladonna, which today is seldom used by small animal practitioners, and has many uses. Atropine does almost everything that the parent product will do. But other drugs with the same effects are also used. All are given principally to cause dilation of the pupils, as in eye examinations; to dry secretions, because they inhibit glandular secretions with remarkable efficacy; to aid in preventing car sickness; and to counteract overdoses of certain drugs.

DRUGS AND THE REPRODUCTIVE ORGANS

Nearly every pet owner has wondered what drug he or she could use to advantage in some particular phase of a pet's reproduction cycle. Could males be made to stay home if certain drugs were fed to them? Could other drugs cause a bitch to dry up? Could a female hunting dog have her heat period postponed by drugs? Could anything be used to stop the undesirable results of a mismating? In each case, the answer is yes, and in these matters the veterinarian can often be of great assistance.

In the Male. Male animals have had all manner of drugs fed to them and injected into them to make them fertile and eager to mate. Some drugs make matters worse. There was a vogue for using testosterone until it became apparent that it was making animals sterile instead of fertile.

Several preparations have been used in attempts to encourage retained testicles to descend to their normal locations. It should be mentioned that retained testicles are a genetic anatomical defect not influenced by medicinal products.

In the Female. Starting with preparation for breeding, we know that certain vitamins are essential for reproduction. Chief of these is vitamin A. Vitamin E is essential for rats; despite the testimonials you may have seen to the contrary, we believe it has not been demonstrated as necessary for other species. Vitamins are discussed in Chapter 3, since they are not drugs, but food. Here we need only repeat that no supplementary vitamins or drugs are apt to have beneficial effects on reproduction, provided the animal has been fed a complete diet.

What can you do if your bitch is bred by accident to an undesirable male? If she has been bred during the very first part of the acceptance period, breed her at once to the desired male. Then breed her every other day as long as she will accept him. The chances are good that her pups will be sired by the proper male. Of course, it will be necessary to observe the results for some months to be assured the resulting puppies are from the chosen matings.

But if she is bred too late to do anything, then have your veterinarian inject her with medication that will prevent the ova (eggs) from implantation in the uterus. Hormones may also be dispensed. You may douche her, but that can be risky; medication is preferable.

How can a pregnant female animal be helped at the time of parturition? Is she sluggish? Your veterinarian can inject an extract made from the posterior pituitary gland, one of many manufactured. Pituitrin is of great value. Oxytocin has been of even greater worth because it has its principal effect on the uterus and less nausea accompanies its use. Any of these drugs should be injected only by your veterinarian. None of them should be given to an animal with a constricted pelvis. If a puppy is too large for passage through the pelvis, it would be cruel to inject the mother. What she needs is a cesarean operation.

At weaning time should you rub the mother's breasts with camphorated oil or other substances? No, let them cake naturally and they will soon stop secreting. Drugs are unnecessary.

ABORTIFACIENTS

Pet owners have repeatedly attempted to cause abortion in their pregnant charges by using drugs that they think cause human abortion. Most of these drugs do not accomplish the desired result, and many cause sickness in pets just as their misuse does in humans.

Experimental preparations have been used with success but not without danger to the mother. A drug-induced abortion may result in disaster if some of the developing puppies are aborted while others die and decompose in the uterus. The classic dilation and curettage (D & C) procedure for humans is not applicable to bitches because of the difficulty in reaching each embryo. We prefer an ovariohysterectomy as soon as the uterus, on palpation, is found to have developing embryos. This is about twenty-four to thirty days after ovulation and mating.

DRUGS TO KILL INTERNAL PARASITES

Some of the worms that infest pets are flat worms (platyhelminths) and round worms (nemahelminths). The drugs used to eradicate these worms are called antihelmintics. This class of drugs is of vital importance to us all, since the most prevalent group of diseases which pets contract is caused by worms and external parasite infestation. We will consider the life histories of all of the common parasites in Chapter 23. Here we will discuss only the drugs used to eliminate the worms.

Most of the effective worm medicines cannot be purchased legally over-the-counter. They are prescription preparations that drugstores do not carry, which forces the veterinarian to maintain supplies to dispense. This is necessary since with one exception each of the more effective preparations has specific problems associated with it. Your veterinarian will explain them to you.

Several of these drugs are given by injection. As some must not be administered to a dog with heartworms, a blood test for these parasites must prove negative before the medication can be safely given.

No worm medicine is 100 percent effective 100 percent of the time, so don't be alarmed if one treatment is not successful. For example, tapeworm medication will digest the bodies of the worms but occasionally will not destroy the tapeworm heads. The remaining head requires about three weeks to develop into an eighteen-inch worm, which will start shedding terminal segments again, so it behooves you to watch freshly passed stools for new segments, the evidence needed to reworm the dog.

The one exception to prescription drugs for deworming dogs is one called Piperazine, which may be purchased at any pet supply counter. It is important to know that this safe and efficacious product is effective for only one common worm, roundworm, when found usually in dogs a year of age or under.

It is true that pet supply departments have many drugs and combinations for most common worms, but many including tetrachlorethylene are dangerous if not used properly. In our opinion some are of such low efficacy they are practically worthless.

We are reminded of the case of an eighteen-pound Boston Terrier we treated for tapeworms twelve times without results. The owner was as frustrated as we were until we stumbled on a suggested treatment that worked the first and only time it was needed. We had asked a visiting M.D. from Brazil if he knew of a treatment. He told us that people in his country treat the problem by eating raw pumpkin seeds. The dose was a half cup of shelled raw seeds chopped finely and eaten as a porridge. The owner of the Boston Terrier was willing to try anything and patiently shelled enough pumpkin seeds to make a quarter of a cup. She chopped them up and spooned them into her pet. There were no ill effects except to the worms. We note that raw shelled pumpkin seeds are available now in shops, but if you try them you're on your own as we doubt this has been researched and some dogs may be sensitive to them.

There is no evidence that garlic destroys worms, but without doubt that herb does stimulate tapeworms to produce segments more rapidly, and it must nourish the parasites. If you think you have seen a tape segment, feed one well-crushed garlic clove to your dog daily. By the end of a week you may see many well developed segments on each stool.

DRUGS TO KILL EXTERNAL PARASITES

Dozens of drugs can be used to kill insects, but some of them will kill mammals, including humans, if misused. The dangerous long-lived environmental polluters have been outlawed but many organophosphates are still around. They are effective and sometimes spectacular in the sudden death of fleas when applied. Ticks are difficult to kill and these products are useful; but for fleas we prefer an old product, rotenone, which has a short life. Although it does take longer to kill a flea, the flea is just as dead as if it were killed instantly by more dangerous drugs.

Rotenone and related resins are obtained from the roots of tropical plants, notably derris in the East Indies and cube in South and Central America; it is one of the most potent insect killers known. Pets can eat it in small amounts, usually with no ill effects. It is more poisonous if inhaled, and is especially so if it gets into fresh open cuts.

Rotenone also kills fish. If you use it, don't allow rotenone to blow into the water in a fishpond. And don't allow a dog dusted for flea infestation to swim in water with fish in it.

Rotenone in dusts, diluted to 1 percent, is probably as safe a flea and louse powder as anything one could ask for. No dog should be put in a closed box and dusted, since it is then forced to breathe the dust. It is hard to believe that pets could be so mistreated, but they often are—by people who want to keep the powder off their clothes.

With some people rotenone causes numbness of the lips and the tip of the tongue. The sensation soon passes. If you are sensitive, dust the pet in the open where the breeze blows the dust away from you.

Rotenone is an ingredient of some of our best dips and rinses. A 1 percent solution in pine oil to which an emulsifier has been added kills all insects except ticks. One percent rotenone dust may be obtained from garden supply establishments where it is sold for treating fruit and vegetable crops to destroy some of their pests.

Pyrethrum comes to our store of drugs from chrysanthemums. In pure form, the chemical agents made from it are called pyrethrins. They are mentioned here because they are so often ingredients of flea powder, but this is not an endorsement, since they merely stun the insects. The early powders were sold with the advice that you dust the animal, brush the fleas and lice onto a newspaper, and burn the paper. You burned it because the insects usually refused to "stay dead" and manufacturers knew it.

Pyrethrum has a wonderful psychological effect on the pet's owner. When it is used as an ingredient of a powder or rinse, the insects appear to die instantly. They drop off, and that is what the owners love to see. Mix in some rotenone and the bugs not only drop off but they stay dead! The combination of the two drugs makes a fine treatment for the owner as well as for the pet.

The Future. New drugs awaiting approval by the USDA appear to have great promise in killing all parasites in and on canines.

DRUGS APPLIED TO THE SKIN

Possibly because vanishing creams are supposed by many to be essential aids to beautify the human skin, many pet owners have come to the mistaken conclusion that there must be lotions necessary to animals' skins. Some think there are miracle drugs or vitamins which may be given to make an animal's skin and coat shine and his eyes sparkle. There are no such lotions, nor does a healthy animal need any.

What we are going to consider here are the vehicles, skin remedies, drugs used in burn treatments, antiseptics for cuts and scratches, and liniments.

Vehicles for Drugs Applied to the Skin.

WOOL FAT, also called lanolin, forms an excellent vehicle because it holds most drugs and, when it is absorbed into the skin, carries the drugs with it. It is coherent, sticking even to surfaces which are moist.

Wool fat of the ordinary variety contains about 25 percent water. It can also be obtained in an anhydrous form (without water).

PETROLATUM is available as a liquid (mineral oil), or as a jelly (Vaseline). When used as a vehicle, it is not absorbed, and drugs used with it remain more or less outside of the skin. Depending upon whether a liquid or solid nonabsorbable is desired, one or the other form is used.

LARD is still a standard base, as is suet. Everyone knows that it is usually advisable to mix some pleasant odor with them when they are used in medication.

GLYCERINE, a thick, sweet, syrupy material, is mixed with innumerable drugs for skin application where liquids are used. But glycerine absorbs water from the tissues. Because it finds so many uses in human medicine, one would expect more in veterinary practice, but pets often lick the sweet substance and may be sickened by the accompanying drugs.

PROPYLENE GLYCOL, one of our favorites, is a nontoxic water-soluble vehicle. Many medications may be added to it which are carried into the pores and hair follicles of the skin. This should not be confused with permanent antifreeze for cars, ethylene glycol, which is poisonous to dogs even in small quantities.

VEGETABLE OILS may be used as vehicles when a lightweight oil is necessary.

Skin Disease Remedies. Almost every veterinarian has a favorite remedy for skin nonspecific diseases. Some smell so unpleasant that the curing process seems almost worse than the disease. Some require such frequent application that treatment becomes a great bore to pet owners. Some irritate. It is unfortunate that one general remedy cannot be given that will cure all skin diseases, but since some are caused by mites, which require special drugs, others by fungi, and probably still others by bacteria and viruses—not to mention occasional cases resulting from some allergy—no one remedy can be suggested. Here are the common effective drugs and chemicals used today:

SULPHUR is one of the oldest and still one of the most reliable of skin remedies. Sulphur alone is useless, but when oxygen in the air combines with sulphur it forms sulphur dioxide, a gas deadly to fungus diseases and to some insects. It is this constant gas formation that cures. Sulphur, to be of value, must therefore be kept by some base that holds it in place and yet does not cover it to such an extent that air cannot reach it. The old lard-and-sulphur or axle-grease-and-sulphur treatments had some virtues, but they cured very slowly because the grease coated the sulphur particles.

The fineness of the sulphur particles, too, makes a great difference. Coarse sulphur crystals are not as effective as the sulphur which is close to the colloidal state. Colloidal materials are so fine they will stay in suspension as if they were in solution and never settle out. It is possible to obtain colloidal sulphur, but it is expensive and its results are not enough better than those obtained by the finest air-floated mechanically ground product to warrant the additional cost.

Sulphur mixed with vegetable oils produces better results than that mixed with heavy greases, but other drugs can be added which help materially.

A dermatologist (for people) told me if he had his choice of one medication to treat skin ailments he would choose not some high-priced fancy antibiotic but sulphur. When sulphur is added to corn oil and kerosene, believe it or not, it makes a messy but effective lotion for the itchy skin that occurs so often toward the end of summer and into the fall. We use equal parts by volume.

CALAMINE LOTION, a white liquid which needs shaking each time before application, cures some mild forms of skin disease. Calamine itself is a 98 percent zinc oxide preparation with a little iron rust mixed with it. Calamine lotion contains 8 percent calamine. It is effective in certain cases where only the surface layers of the skin are attacked. The ear is part of the skin, and quite good results have been obtained by pouring the ear canal full of calamine lotion and allowing as much to stay as possible after the pet has shaken its head. But it should not be used when the eardrum is broken, since it may cake around the delicate mechanism of the middle ear. Dogs are sensitive to heavy-metal poisoning and zinc is a heavy metal. With a dog's propensity to lick, calamine lotion must be used judiciously.

BORIC ACID has been prescribed by the medical profession for so many years for so many millions of people that it is the first thing some laypeople think of to cure almost anything. Boric acid and boracic acid are the same thing. In skin disease its value is questionable; it does not kill germs but does retard their growth.

SALICYLIC ACID is useful in skin remedies, for one reason, because it destroys the outer layers of skin but does not destroy the growing layers. It has been used for years as a corn remover along with collodium. When it is applied, the skin swells, becomes soft, and the outer layers slough off. Like boric acid, salicylic acid's action on bacteria is to slow their growth but not to kill them. It is seldom used stronger than as 10 percent of any solution or ointment.

POTASSIUM PERMANGANATE, a favorite water solution and a useful drug, is more valuable in human skin treatment than for animals. In humans, dressings can be applied and allowed to stay in place; animals often tear them off. Laypeople often apply overly strong solutions. One part to one hundred parts of water is as strong as it should be used when applied uncovered. If a wet dressing is used, a solution of 1:10,000 is strong enough. And don't forget that it leaves a purple discoloration.

GENTIAN VIOLET, speaking of stains, is a dye that will really leave its mark. Used with water at 1:500 parts, when applied to the skin uncovered, it kills many kinds of germs. Even a 1:1,000,000 solution will kill some. If a pet licks it off, no harm is done. It may be applied many times to skin lesions with no harm to the pet. The 1:1,000 strength usually proves practicable. Its one great disadvantage is its color. Few people want great purple patches on their pets.

TANNIC ACID is an astringent—an agent that causes shrinking and stops discharges. Considerable difference of opinion exists among veterinarians as to whether it is preferable to apply an astringent and dry up an area affected with dermatitis, or to inflame it with some substance like turpentine and, with the aid of the inflammation, to cure it with other drugs.

In a 5 or 10 percent solution tannic acid is effective over raw areas, such as those eroded by disease organisms or sore from constant scratching, since it causes a film protective protein to form. But there is a question whether, except in the case of burns, this is always desirable. Dogs may bite and scratch the film off as fast as it forms.

IODINE, the old standby of a generation ago, is slowly being replaced as a skin remedy, as it is as an antiseptic. For the fungus infection called ringworm in animals, iodine is used in the proportion of 50 percent of the tincture with an equal amount of glycerine. Iodine surgical scrub is useful not only to the surgeon prior to surgery but for its antiseptic qualities in superficial skin infections in dogs. Unlike the tincture, it should be applied three times daily to have much effect. Although better than most antiseptics in killing bacteria, there are some it will not destroy.

Burn Remedies. When an animal is burned by fire, scalding, corrosion, acids, caustics, or other chemicals, the capillaries of the skin become dilated all over the burned area. You will remember that any skin burn produces moisture. This seepage goes on and on until, in cases of large burned areas, so much plasma escapes that the animal's blood-volume loss is extremely serious. That is point one to remember. The second point is that all of this area affords an excellent growing medium for bacteria, whose toxic by-products may cause death to the burned victim. The third is that supportive treatment for the animal is essential because you often find a temporary improvement followed by prostration, due to shock. What drugs can you use for burns?

It should be emphasized that only a surprisingly small percentage of a dog's body needs to be burned before a life-threatening situation develops. The pain and anguish is obvious initially, then the hair falls away and simultaneously with the exuded serum disastrous infections set in. With some of the newer antibiotics the infections can be controlled until healing begins. If infections can be minimized there will be less scarring. The resulting scars from healed burns will not grow hair, but this is a small price.

For even minor burns remember your veterinarian is as close as your phone and he or she will tell you the proper prescription to use or may determine that the dog should be brought in.

Drugs for Cuts and Scratches. This may sound unprofessional, but any ordinary cut or scratch or scraped area that the pet can reach to lick is just as well off left untreated. If the wound is so small or unimportant that it does not need suturing, it does not need medication—if your dog can reach it. As we have said, the scales on dogs' tongues can clean a wound beautifully, and clean wounds heal well. There are, however, many wounds in places our pets cannot reach, such as those on the head, neck, and shoulders, abscess formations under the skin, and wounds under long hair. These should be treated. The variety of drugs available for treatment is wide, and the list is growing. Here we need discuss only the most important ones.

Disinfectants, germicides, antiseptics, bacteriostatics, fungicides, bactericides—what are these things? Disinfectants free areas of infection by destroying bacteria, fungus organisms, viruses—all kinds of infective organisms. Antiseptics inhibit the growth of bacteria or other infecting agents but do not necessarily kill them. Germicides and bactericides are agents that kill germs. Contrary to what you may have thought, there are not very many that will kill germs and not injure tissues too. Bacteriostatics arrest the growth of bacteria. A virucide is an agent which kills viruses. Fungicides are agents which destroy fungi.

IODINE was one of the mainstays of veterinarians of a few years ago, as it was of the average household. And tincture of iodine still has its uses. It is germicidal for most bacteria and many fungi and viruses, regardless of what type they are. It is twice as potent as phenol as a germ killer. Since a number of applications to the same area may result in burning, when several treatments are indicated it is better to use the tincture diluted by an equal amount of water. Iodine discolors, and animal hair once discolored with it may retain the stain for months. This, plus the fact that the treated area burns and smarts when it is applied, makes its use of limited value for pets.

TAMED IODINE, unlike tincture of iodine that burns and stains, is gentle on tissues, does not stain, and is just as effective. Prior to donning gloves for surgery the surgeon scrubs for many minutes with a "tamed" iodine soap solution. It destroys most bacteria on the hands and can be used effectively on cuts and abrasions. A solution without soap is also useful and both are available at pharmacies without a prescription.

HYDROGEN PEROXIDE, when applied to raw tissue, produces a fizzing and a white foam appears. This means that the peroxide is decomposing into water and oxygen. And only while this decomposition is occurring is the treated area being disinfected. But this fizzing helps wonderfully at times to loosen debris in wounds. As a germ killer, hydrogen peroxide is less efficient than many others. Phenol is about one hundred times as potent. In external treatment hydrogen peroxide is best employed to cleanse wounds and to flush out the sheaths of male dogs when they become infected. The drugstore strength is 3 percent, which has been found best for all such tasks.

MERCURIC COMPOUNDS come in many useful forms. What household does not have Mercurochrome or Merthiolate? Recently much publicity has been given to the failure of these mercury compounds to kill germs. The inference is that they are worthless. Actually, at the "drugstore" dilutions, they are bacteriostatic and, to some extent, bactericidal. To our knowledge, that is all the manufacturers ever claimed for them. If bacteria or their spores cannot grow in the presence of these drugs, then they serve a useful purpose. The red dye they are in shows where the product has been used. As an application to sutured incisions, mercuric compounds prevent infection, but used under bandages, they may cause irritation.

SILVER has few uses in veterinary medicine, but one compound may be mentioned that is effective in a minor emergency. That is silver nitrate, available in styptic pencils, which is used to reduce bleeding in a broken nail or one cut too short.

SULFA DRUGS

The person who did not own pets B.S.D. (before sulfa drugs) cannot possibly appreciate what their discovery has meant to pet owners. True, most sulfa drugs are outdated and most are being replaced for some purposes by the antibiotics, but veterinary medicine is now a far happier profession because of them.

The first to be discovered was sulfanilamide. Shortly thereafter unfounded claims were made for it as a cure-all; it was said to be a specific for coccidiosis, viruses, including distemper in dogs, and all kinds of bacteria. But further research showed that its field was very narrow—that it killed only a limited number of bacteria and was ineffectual against viruses, coccidiosis, warts, bad disposition, or ingrowing toenails! Moreover, it killed some patients.

One sulfa drug after another appeared for many years until so many shortcomings were observed that most have quietly faded away. However, a few remain and are lifesavers. Others are returning to be used with other drugs much more effectively than by themselves.

Powdered sulfa drugs are often sifted into surgical incisions and wounds, where they are of great help. Now they are being used in solutions, such as in propylene glycol, and poured into inaccessible wounds where they often prove to be true miracle drugs.

ANTIBIOTICS

When researchers learned that some bacteria and molds give off substances toxic to others, a new branch of bacteriology was born. When further research demonstrated that these substances would kill or inhibit bacteria and not poison animals, a blessing of inestimable value was bestowed upon both us and our pets. And as wonderful as penicillin, streptomycin, and tetracycline are, they were but heralds of far more wonderful drugs. As yet none has been found effective for viruses.

There are several points that should be kept in mind when your dog is given medication such as an antibiotic. First, we are rather treating the animal than the disease. We are attempting to tip the scales in favor of the animal and not actually destroy all the disease organisms. Each antibiotic must develop levels of concentration adequate to either hinder the reproduction of the organism(s) or to destroy some of them. When the disease ceases to flourish in the host, your dog is able to overcome it by building immune bodies to it.

Some of the antibiotics are called broad spectrum, meaning that they affect a great variety of microorganisms, whereas some zero in on a few infections and have no effect on others. When a dog has an infection, veterinarians have a choice. If the animal has responded to a particular treatment 90 percent of the time, the decision may be to treat it with the usually successful treatment. If that is ineffective, the patient may be put under a more detailed investigation. It seems to us this is a logical approach from the economic point of view. The more detailed investigation consists of culturing the microorganism, inoculating the disease organisms in material they are expected to grow well in, and exposing these organisms to small disks saturated with different agents that may be effective in preventing their growth.

This is not an inexpensive procedure and does not result in a black or white answer. First, it may be difficult to obtain a sample that contains only the organisms causing the problem, since many organisms may grow together. If several organisms are cultured, it may be difficult to determine which is causing the disease. Furthermore, some innocuous organisms may grow luxuriously and some dangerous ones slowly. It requires a bacteriologist with experience to interpret the results.

It is not rare for a veterinarian to send a sample to a bacteriologist and start a treatment, hoping it is helpful until the laboratory results come in. When they arrive, often many days later, we may learn that our prescribed medication would not have eliminated the disease. Then, on contacting the owner to change the prescription, we may be told the dog has responded to the original treatment! A top bacteriologist once told me that bacteriology is half black magic. It is of fantastic help in many cases and misleading in others.

It is not rare to find a canine patient that cannot tolerate a given medication. If the effect of the antibiotic or other medication is worse than the disease, we must obviously withdraw it. However, the dog may need a given drug and only *that* drug to combat an infection, in which case by persisting it may become tolerable.

We are fortunate to have a vast number of antibiotics, many of which are used for similar disease conditions but others specifically for one or two diseases. Some are effective but toxic to some animals. Some are abused, some are employed where less expensive members of the family are as effective. One reason we have such an imposing list of antibiotics is that some bacteria learn to live in the presence of a specific one, a condition called resistance. But there is conjecture that one day all bacteria will be resistant to all antibiotics.

Antibiotics, like sulfas, are prescription drugs. At first they were given in quickly absorbed doses, mostly intramuscularly and at very frequent intervals. Later a way was found of combining them in vehicles from which they are slowly absorbed, so that in some cases injections given once every twenty-four hours suffice to furnish a high enough concentration in the blood to effectively destroy or inhibit the germs against which they are being used. Today a majority are given orally.

EMETICS

Hydrogen Peroxide, used at half the ordinary drugstore strength, which is 3 percent, probably is the best emetic yet discovered for dogs.

Mix equal amounts of peroxide and water and either make the animal swallow it or administer it with a stomach tube. Vomiting occurs in about two minutes and is repeated at intervals of about thirty seconds for several minutes thereafter.

Apomorphine is a prescription drug. It can be injected, or it can be given by dropping a small tablet under an eyelid, from which it is absorbed. Your veterinarian usually uses a solution and gives about one milligram to a forty-pound dog. The animal becomes restless and may shake. Sometimes a severe depression follows its use.

Mustard is difficult to administer orally and is better given via stomach tube. One teaspoonful of ordinary household mustard from a jar will cause vomiting fairly effectively for a forty-pound dog. Larger doses may continue the vomiting for too long a time.

Ipecac, although many laymen try to use it to make pets vomit, is about the slowest-acting emetic of any and therefore of small use in emergencies. Drugstores carry syrup of ipecac. The dose is generally half a teaspoonful for a forty-pound dog.

Salt, common table salt, may be used, but it is difficult to administer. A strong solution should be administered so that the animal—a forty-pound dog—receives a teaspoonful of salt.

CATHARTICS AND LAXATIVES

Drugs that promote defecation may be classified in a variety of ways according to their severity (mild, medium, violent); their natures (oils, salines, glandular stimulants, and so forth); their action (lubricants, bile-flow stimulants); and so on. We shall list simply the most easily available cathartics and a few of those prescription drugs that your veterinarian uses or prescribes, and tell you why. The order of their listing is no indication of their comparative value.

Castor oil is a fairly quick-acting cathartic. Dogs defecate about two hours after dosing. The stool is not fluid but only slightly softer than normal, unless overdoses are administered. Castor oil should be given on an empty stomach for the best results. The dose for a forty-pound dog is one half to one teaspoonful. Remember that in giving castor oil you are not trying to lubricate the intestinal tract, but that an irritant acid is causing a speedup of evacuation. Racinic acid does the physicking; the oil is partly digested.

Mineral oil, in contrast to castor oil, when given orally is almost all deposited with the feces. It is a lubricant. Larger doses may be given, but overdoses are inadvisable because they run out, and dogs sometimes will lick themselves and thus take feces into their stomachs. Overdosing is common. We have known clients to give a puppy a tablespoonful, which would be equivalent to the owner taking more than a glassful.

The chief danger in using oils is that inadvertently some—even a little—may be poured into the windpipe and cause pneumonia. However, some dogs will often lap mineral oil out of a dish. They may not refuse it if it is thoroughly mixed with their food. There is little difference in the cathartic effect of the light and heavy mineral oils. Two teaspoonfuls is the dose for a forty-pound dog.

Long-continued use of oil is not advantageous, since it dissolves the fat-soluble vitamins out of the food, preventing their absorption.

Milk of magnesia is magnesium hydroxide, one of the mildest of the cathartics. Less than 10 percent of milk of magnesia is hydroxide. It is therefore a moderate laxative. Doses of a teaspoonful produce laxation in a forty-pound dog in about six hours. Overdoses do little harm but do retard digestion because of their reduction of stomach acidity. In pets, the pill form is seldom satisfactory.

Epsom Salts would be an excellent cathartic for dogs were they not so intensely disliked, even in solution, because of the bitter taste. Several theories have been advanced as to how the salts accomplish their results. Probably they do it by drawing large amounts of water from the intestine (osmosis) and, by thus filling the intestine, soften the contents and mechanically stimulate its action.

The dose for a forty-pound dog is a teaspoonful, usually partially dissolved in water. Its action is fairly rapid, with evacuation occurring in two to four hours after dosing.

BIOLOGICS

Serum is the liquid part of the blood of an animal. There are several different types of serum, depending on their source. *Convalescent* serum comes from the blood of an animal just recovered from a disease. *Immune* serum is that which has been produced from an animal immune to the disease in question. *Hyperimmune* serum is made from animals that have been hyperimmunized against the disease, that is, by subjecting an already immune animal to massive doses of the virus. All these types are in use in veterinary medicine.

Since it is made from the blood of recovered animals, serum is full of antibodies. When we inject it we simply add these antibodies against the disease to the blood of the animal we want to protect or try to cure. This addition does not in any way cause the body to produce more antibodies, and after a few days they are lost and the body is no longer protected. When serum is used as protection against disease it must be given repeatedly at not more than two-week intervals.

Vaccines are biologics for preventive inoculation. They may be bacterial or virus and induce the body to produce antibodies against the disease-producing agents.

Vaccine may consist of several different materials. It may be bacteria, live or dead; virus, live, dead, or attenuated. If we are vaccinating against a bacterial disease, we sometimes use live bacteria of some strain that does not produce a disease of much intensity. This is done to vaccinate against undulant fever. The animal is given the real disease, but of a strain that has proved from long study to produce mild symptoms. The animal actually becomes sick, recovers, and is henceforth immune. *Autogenous* vaccine is made from cultures of the very organism affecting an animal and then used against the disease.

Dead bacteria in suspension form a common type of vaccine which is used for several diseases of pets—always as a preventive. Sometimes several species of bacteria are mixed in one vaccine in order to immunize our pets at one time against all the diseases these bacteria cause.

Vaccines may be of *live virus*, so the animal actually is given the disease. *Attenuated virus* vaccines are those that have been either attenuated (weakened) by passage through a different species, grown in cells, or by chemicals. Everybody has heard how smallpox if given to a calf produces cowpox, and how if we are given that disease it immunizes us

Applying gauze bandage prior to adhesive tape for an injured foot or as a "boxing glove" to prevent scratching.

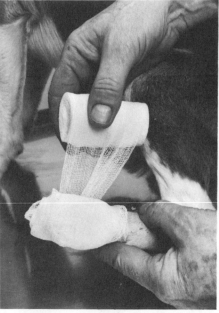

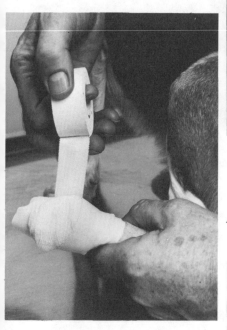

Applying tape over the gauze.

The finished bandage—the adhesive tape is applied to hair an inch above the gauze.

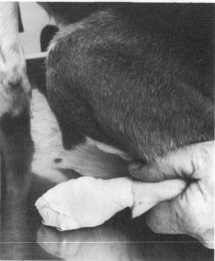

The lip-pouch method of administering a fluid.

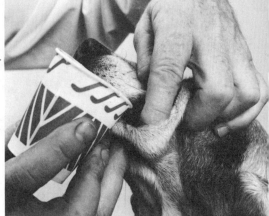

Then fluid is poured into the pouch for the dog to swallow.

Opening the mouth in preparation to administer a tablet or capsule.

Be sure to push the lower lip in over the teeth.

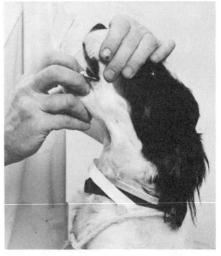

Push the medication over the curvature of the tongue.

Examining gums and teeth.

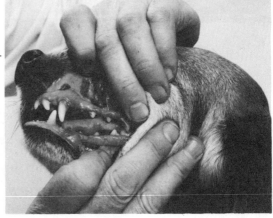

Muzzling a dog with gauze bandage keeping hands at a safe distance. A simple overhand tie above the nose.

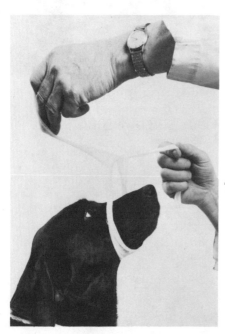

The tie is drawn tight.

Then the tie is knotted securely.

Another overhand tie under the nose.

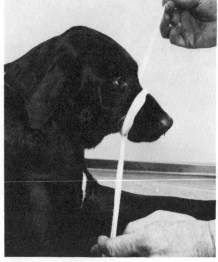

The ends drawn under and behind the ears and tied with a bowknot for easy release.

The pedicure.

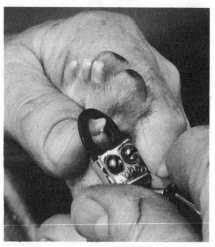

The proper finger positions for expressing the anal glands.

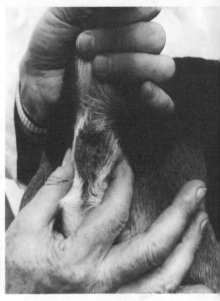

Cover with cotton and express the glands.

The results.

Taking the rectal temperature using a lubri-
ated rectal thermometer.

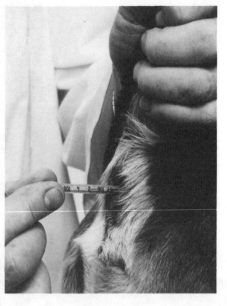

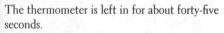

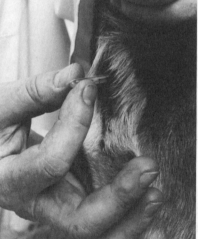

The thermometer is left in for about forty-five
seconds.

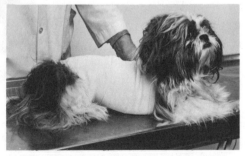

A body bandage using stockinette.

Restraining a dog with a commercial restraining pole

Two may safely restrain an aggressively mean dog with two leashes.

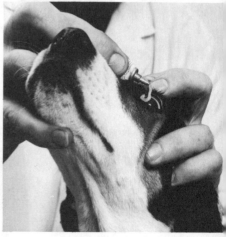

Applying an ophthalmic ointment.

against cowpox *and* smallpox. When attenuated vaccine is injected under the skin of dogs it is absorbed into the bloodstream and the dog's body goes to work building up immunity by destroying the attenuated or dead virus by stimulating the production of antibodies. The dog is henceforth immune, as though it had actually had the disease. Some individuals may lose immunity in a year or so.

Although it is illegal to ship distemper vaccine into many states to nonveterinarians, the law is unenforceable as far as mail-order companies are concerned. A word of warning if you contemplate vaccinating your own dog. We have known litters of puppies to die of distemper after such products have been used. The savings are not worth the chance of obtaining bad vaccine.

An intramuscular rabies vaccination in an adult animal lasts for over three years, and other vaccinations last for varying lengths of time. In the early days of vaccines it was thought that in order to establish a high antibody content of the blood and cells (titer) it was necessary to give several small doses of vaccine. Newer research indicates that best results may be attained by the injection of one large jarring dose which shocks the body into building up huge antibody content. Moreover, the practice of giving the same amount of vaccine to all animals regardless of size is slowly being replaced by the grading of the dose to the size of the animal. Surely it has been wrong to give the same dose to a Pomeranian as to a St. Bernard, about thirty times as large, yet for years this has been the accepted procedure with the result that so many dogs of large breeds may not have been properly protected.

STEROIDS

There are dozens of members of the steroid group of which cortisone is one. Steroids are powerful agents which reduce inflammation but also reduce the immune mechanism of animals. They do not cure inflammatory disease conditions but in a myriad of problems remove the signs of the problem. If your dog has an itching sensation which makes it bite and scratch, an injection or a few tablets and the itch is gone. If the inflammation is in an arthritic joint, the pain leaves as the inflammation disappears.

However, it should be obvious that an inflamed condition may have to be abided because maintaining a healthy immune system may mean life rather than death. Steroids are used in patients, usually human, with transplants to prevent the immune system's rejection of the strange new tissue. We have all heard how human heart transplant patients die of pneumonia, not from the transplant.

So steroids at best are a mixed blessing. When used to control the itching which accompanies skin irritations, there is no way to evaluate the effectiveness of a medication. If the medication is not helpful the itching returns as the effects of the steroids wear off. If steroids are administered to a patient with an infection, it is necessary to give the correct medication, antibiotic or other, to control the infection or the body's defenses will be reduced, permitting and perhaps stimulating the infection to flourish.

Many experts suggest that long-acting steroids not be given by injection since unfavorable results cannot be stopped as they might be by withdrawing oral medication.

Some steroids have inconvenient side effects. The desire for food and water is exaggerated, resulting in a dog's inability to go through the night without having to urinate. In many cases, however, this inconvenience is a small price to pay if in the long run the animal benefits. In cases of autoimmune disease in which the dog rejects part of its own anatomy—red blood cells or the lining of the intestine, for example—lowering the immune response over a period of weeks may reverse the condition.

Another example of remarkable effectiveness of steroids is in old dogs with severe arthritis. We have had many elderly animals brought in for euthanasia whose arthritis was so advanced they could no longer walk. One example was a male Standard Poodle that was twelve years old and had to be carried into the examining room. We asked the owners if they would try steroids for a few days before we made the final decision. They were delighted to postpone the act and even more delighted to see such improvement that in five days the dog climbed stairs he hadn't climbed in five years.

That Poodle lived for two years until at age fourteen he developed an inoperable cancer and euthanasia was performed. We suspect the steroids reduced the immune system, permitting the cancer to proliferate, but he had two beautiful years he would not otherwise have enjoyed.

There is no doubt that in many animals excess steroids cause a hormone imbalance that results in the loss of hair and other side effects, which are examples of how steroids are indeed a mixed blessing.

Some years ago a chemist working for a paper company and studying some of the by-products of wood noticed that on touching a compound he had extracted he almost immediately noticed a strange taste in his mouth. Others in the laboratory touched it and had a similar experience. DMSO was discovered. This compound, able to penetrate the unbroken skin, holds promise as a vehicle to carry other chemicals through the skin. At present it is used in riding horses to transport steroids to inflamed tendons, which in many cases removes the cause of the lameness.

TRANQUILIZERS

The first tranquilizer, reserpine, was discovered by a veterinarian. Since that time dozens have been used for canines as well as for humans. But tranquilizers do not have as predictable results in dogs as they apparently have in humans. We usually start with a small dose and increase it daily until the dose is established for a certain animal. These tranquilizers are prescription drugs and those that give the best mileage are usually the most expensive. They are a great help with pets that can't stand noises, such as fireworks, and for nervous dogs that don't like to travel.

Tranquilizers are also effective to prevent motion sickness but we prefer homatropine, which dries the secretions that are the indications of the first stage of car sickness. Sometimes small doses of phenobarbital are given with the homatropine. These are prescription preparations and your veterinarian will make helpful suggestions on a choice for your dog.

13

How to Give Medicines and Apply Accessories

All dog owners should know how to administer the common drugs used with animals, how to give their pets medicine in liquid, capsule, tablet, or pill form, how to apply the standard bandages, how to take the temperatures of animals—in short, how to handle all the little problems of caring for a sick or injured pet.

Your veterinarian will diagnose your dog's condition, prescribe the proper medication, and tell you the kind of care and attention your pet needs. That alone is not enough to restore the animal to health. In most cases you will treat your pet at home, and it is your responsibility to carry out the veterinarian's instructions. The most effective drug ever prescribed will not help your pet if you cannot manage to get more than 5 percent of the dose down its throat. If you allow the animal to remove the bandage the veterinarian has applied and permit it to expose an open wound to infection simply because you don't know how to reapply it, you can hardly expect a quick and satisfactory recovery.

Your veterinarian will outline a course of treatment for your sick pet, but the way you carry out his or her instructions and the care you give the animal will usually determine how effective the treatment will be. If you can give the kind of intelligent cooperation that your veterinarian has a right to expect, your pet's chances for recovery will be greatly increased.

Here let us stress the importance of reading the directions for any medication (and that the prescribing veterinarian should make those directions clear should be obvious). Five days after we had written a prescription for a pet, the client phoned to ask a strange question. She didn't mind the 2 P.M. dose but for the 2 A.M. one—did she really have to set the alarm and get up? The directions on the container seemed clear to us: "2 tablets A.M. and P.M." She had overlooked the word, "tablets" and had been giving the dog one tablet at 2 A.M. and one at 2 P.M.

Another client had taken the last pill in a container herself and as they appeared to be helping her, she studied the label for information to refill the prescription. To her horror she discovered that the pill was the last of 250 we had given her to treat worms in several litters of puppies. She phoned in distress and we were happy to tell her that the medication would not harm her but that we presumed she had the cleanest gastrointestinal tract in the state of Connecticut. The pills had been dispensed in a container identical to one her pharmacist used to fill her M.D.'s prescription. Always read the directions.

METHODS FOR GIVING MEDICINE TO ANIMALS

Liquids. Whenever liquids are to be given, you should always remember that if certain of them enter the lungs they can be very dangerous. The first question you should ask yourself is, "What would happen if the animal inhaled some?"

Pure water solutions of quickly soluble drugs are least dangerous. Hydrogen peroxide turns to water and oxygen when it decomposes in the fizzing effect known to everyone. On the other hand, milk, which is sometimes used as a base or vehicle for drugs, contains solids. Fat is one of them, and fat in the lungs is especially dangerous. If the drug used is harmless if it gets into the lungs—that is, if it is a water solution—it is fairly safe to fill the animal's mouth and throat and force swallowing. If some of the medicine trickles down the windpipe, the only unfortunate thing that can happen is a blast of the medicine in your face or on your coat sleeve when the patient coughs. But when a solution dangerous to the lungs is to be administered, it's best to give a little at a time.

In either event there are two practical ways of giving a liquid medicine: the lip-pocket method and by stomach tube. Let's see how and when each of these is used.

THE LIP-POCKET METHOD: Although an experienced person can accomplish this alone, you will probably find that two people are necessary for satisfactory results. Place the animal on a table broadside to you. Make it sit. Tilt its head back so that it is looking at the ceiling. With your right hand hold the chin in this position. Slide the fingers of your left hand under its lip, push back, and catch hold of the angle where the lower and upper lips join. Pull this out and upward. Now you have a cup or pocket which will hold a considerable amount. While you hold the patient thus, your assistant pours the medicine or liquid food in. As it runs between the teeth and onto the back of the tongue, the animal will swallow it. When this is gone, pour more in until the whole dose is given. A word of caution: the assistant should stand out of the line of fire, for if the animal coughs, he or she is liable to be thoroughly sprayed.

If an especially resistant pup is being dosed, the assistant has another duty. With one hand he or she holds both front paws firmly so that the dog can't pull them loose and with the other hand pours the medicine into the lip pocket.

THE STOMACH-TUBE METHOD: What seems a great task is in reality a simple and safe method if two people cooperate to dose an animal. A piece of rubber tubing, one eighth inch inside diameter and twelve to eighteen inches long, depending upon the size of the animal, is large enough for a dog. You can get both the tube and a bulb syringe—either glass or rubber will do—at your pharmacy. The syringe should be filled with the medicine and left within reach. When you are ready to insert the tube, hold the animal as described above with the head straight up. As the tube is pushed over the back of the tongue into the throat, the patient will gulp and swallow it down. If it has been moistened, it will slide down the esophagus with reasonable ease.

There is one danger to guard against. You must be extremely careful not to get the tube into the windpipe, for if fluids are administered down the tube into the lungs by mistake, the results may be tragic. By holding the upper end of the tube close to your ear, you can tell whether the other end is in the windpipe by the sound of air rushing in and out of the tube with each respiration. If the tube has entered the esophagus properly, you will not hear any sound at all. Feeling the throat is another method of being sure where the tube is. The windpipe is in front and closest to the skin, and in animals that are not too fat you should have no difficulty in feeling the tube in the esophagus behind it.

When you are certain that the tube is where it should be, have your assistant—who needs both hands for the job—connect the syringe to the tube and administer the medicine or liquid food down the tube. In mature animals the stomach tube may be left in for several minutes without causing discomfort; the animal goes right on breathing normally.

This stomach-tube method is particularly useful in feeding tiny puppies that are too cold or too weak to nurse. We have saved countless dozens this way and have taught many assistants to do it, using a premature human infant stomach tube. It is a quick way of feeding and one that is most useful in supplementing an inadequate maternal milk supply. To be sure, you must always be certain that the tube is in the esophagus, but that is not hard to determine once you have done it a few times. When you consider that we have reared hundreds of litters of puppies experimentally in this fashion, it is easy to see that one person who passes a tube on a litter of eight, 5 times a day, or a total of 280 times a week, must not experience too much difficulty.

It is very unsuccessful to squirt a drug into your dog's mouth, snap it shut, and expect the animal to swallow it. Most of the solution runs out. The animal shakes its head and the administration is a failure. You can sometimes overcome your pet's dislike for some drugs by disguising them in sweet syrups thinned down. Glucose (dextrose) is often administered to advantage to sick animals, but if given in the form of corn syrup or honey it is difficult to pour. It must be thinned. If any sweet substance is given carefully and without a struggle, the subsequent dosages will be simpler and dogs in particular can often be trained to open their mouths and take it without a fuss. We have seen many that soon were willing to lick the syrup from a spoon.

Pills and Capsules. It doesn't require sleight of hand to get a pill or capsule down the throat of a dog, even when the pet resists. It's all in knowing how. Opening the animal's mouth, dropping in the medicine, closing its mouth, and rubbing the throat may work now and again, but it's not a sure enough method to rely on.

With the left hand (if you're right-handed) grasp the top of the animal's muzzle and pull its head upward. Squeeze the thumb on one side and the fingers on the other, thereby pushing the lips over the teeth and partly opening the mouth. The dog won't close its mouth because to do so it will have to bite its lips. With your right hand pick up the pill or capsule between the thumb and first or second finger and with the little finger pull down the lower jaw. Hold it open with the side of the little finger and drop the pill as far back on the tongue as possible. With your forefinger, or with the forefinger and second finger, push the pill gently but quickly as far back into the throat as you can. Then withdraw your hand quickly, let the mouth close and hold it together until the dog sticks out its tongue in the act of swallowing. Several pills and capsules may be poked down in this way at one time.

Some capsules contain bitter or irritating drugs. If a dog bites them they may cause fright, suffocation, and a taste so obnoxious that the animal will try for many minutes to cough or scratch it out. If you are giving your pet medicine of this sort, you will want to be certain that no capsules are dropped between the teeth or insufficiently pushed down the throat.

Short-nosed breeds, such as Boston Terriers, Boxers, English Bulldogs, and Bullmastiffs, have such fat tongues and restricted throats that laymen frequently have difficulty in properly medicating them. When wet, the pills or capsules become slippery and slide around sideways over the back of the broad tongue. It is wise never to try to give wet pills, especially wet capsules. If you are unsuccessful in the first attempt to give the medicine, take the capsule out and dry it. It will often stick to your finger just enough to enable you to pilot it into the back of the throat properly. Sometimes two fingers can keep it from sliding sideways, and on large dogs even three fingers may work well.

There are other effective methods you may prefer in the administration of pills, tablets, and capsules. Some may appeal to you. You may have noticed how when offered a tidbit of food dogs smell it, pick it up gingerly, chew, and swallow it. If it is to their liking, most gulp the second and subsequent morsels. With this in mind, prepare three units of, say, peanut butter, cheese, or liverwurst on crackers. Place the capsule or tablet under the chosen goodie on the second cracker. Give the dog cracker number one, which will be checked out thoroughly, then give the second cracker with the medication and immediately show the third tidbit. The dog will often gulp the second to get the third.

The advantage of using crackers with goodies lies in the fact that while crunching a cracker a dog is not apt to notice the pill if it is crunched at the same time.

The next method concerns candy and this brings to mind the fact that many pet owners tell us their dogs have never tasted candy. Although many people eat candy themselves they believe it is somehow unhealthy for dogs. We fed 20 percent corn syrup to puppies from weaning until they were two years old to try to produce cavities. We produced no cavities and that litter of six were as healthy as any puppies could be. Sweets in moderation cannot harm a dog.

Hiding a pill or capsule or tablet in a soft-centered chocolate candy is a simple and good way to administer it. Once again, use three candies; the second one offered should have the medication. There is another method using candy wherein the dog must be "pre-fooled" before it starts taking the medication. As a treat, toss the dog broken pieces of Life Savers every now and then. When the time comes that the dog needs medication, toss the pill or tablet along with a few pieces of Life Savers on the floor. Most dogs will pick up the pill or tablet along with the sweets.

Another client found that with the spherical capsules we had prescribed he could put one in a "pea shooter," open the pup's mouth, and blow it into its throat, close the mouth and rub its throat: "No problem, Doc."

One of my clients solved the problem by sewing chicken skin around each capsule and placing them in the refrigerator to give to her dog as directed.

One of our favorite methods of administering solid medications is in marshmallows. Leave a few exposed to the air for a few hours until they become tough on the outside, then insert the medication in one of three. Once again, give one without the medication first. Gumdrops, raw hamburger, meatballs, and soft cheese are other ways favored by pet owners.

Liquid medicine when not given by the lip-pouch method presents perhaps a greater challenge. It may work to combine it with honey or corn or maple syrup and pour the mixture on a piece of bread, and some find an ice-cream sundae—with the liquid medicine as the topping—poured over it as a sauce works, too.

With a little knowledge of your pet's likes and dislikes and a little ingenuity you should be able to outwit it. You still have the more forceful methods previously described.

BANDAGES AND THEIR USES

Of the many kinds of bandages used by physicians and nurses, only a few are very useful in veterinary work. Rolls of muslin and gauze, many-tailed bandages, and adhesive are those needed. Anyone can rip an old sheet into three-inch-wide strips to make a bandage in a pinch. But those strips should be rolled tightly before applying. Two three- or four-inch bandages, six feet long, will usually be sufficient to bandage any dog.

Many-tails are simply strips of cloth as wide as the area to be bandaged on the patient and torn in the same number of parallel strips from each end toward the central area.

Adhesive tape one inch wide should serve almost any purpose. To cover a wide area it may be lapped, and if a narrower strip is desired, it may easily be ripped.

Most bandages applied at home will be for minor cuts and blemishes or used as stopgap measures before taking the pet to the veterinarian. After this, if bandaging is necessary, the veterinarian will instruct the owner how he or she wants the bandage applied in the future.

The most common use of bandages in pets is to prevent self-injury. Suppose a dog has been caught in a steel trap. It is found before the part of the leg below the trap bit has lost its blood supply. The skin has been cleaned and the veterinarian has sutured it. If not prevented from licking it, the dog will remove the stitches and open the wound. Moreover, after the bandage is applied, there will be considerable weeping from the wound and, despite antiseptics, an odd odor will develop. This is not a bad sign but rather a good one. The dog smells it and becomes frantic to lick it, since there is something about the odor that animals either enjoy or that excites them to lick. At any rate, they may rip bandages off, necessitating application of new ones fairly often.

In covering this kind of wound, several things must be kept in mind. The bandage cannot be wound too tightly or circulation will be restricted and the area below it will swell with blood and lymph. It must be wound tightly enough not to slip. If swelling occurs, the bandage may be cut but not necessarily removed. New adhesive must then be wound around it.

First some surgical dressing, powder, solution, or salve is applied, and usually several thicknesses of gauze put over it. The bandage is unrolled around the wound firmly until several thicknesses have been applied.

When the bandage fails to go on smoothly, or when it is necessary to go from a thin place on the leg to a thicker section, if the roll is twisted occasionally, as shown in the illustration, it will go on with professional smoothness. If one layer of adhesive tape is then applied, making sure that at least one half inch sticks to the hair above the bandage, it will hold the bandage material in place and be sufficient protection against most of the animal's efforts to remove it.

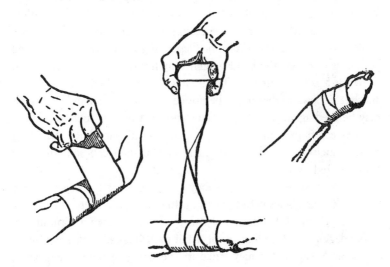

How to apply a bandage. A smooth job can be done if you reserve the roll occasionally. Right, pressure bandage to stop blood flow. Usually these bandages are applied too loosely.

One of the most frequent uses made of bandages is to stop hemorrhage. In this case we call them pressure bandages. Dogs often cut their feet on glass, tin cans, or other sharp objects. Since the feet are extremely vascular, even a small cut may bleed enough to leave large blood spots everywhere the dog steps. Cuts higher on the foot can cause sufficient hemorrhage to make a dog anemic, but we have never seen one bleed to death from such a gash.

To stop the flow of blood, apply a small cloth sponge directly to the cut and quickly wind a bandage tightly about the foot many times. It may become red from blood soaking through it, but it will slowly stop bleeding.

Tourniquets are so often recommended to stop bleeding in human beings that pet owners sometimes resort to them injudiciously. With a pet, a strong elastic band can suffice or even thumb pressure over the cut artery. If a tourniquet of any sort is applied to a whole limb, it is important that it be released every ten minutes to let blood in and out of the part below the tourniquet.

Many-tailed bandages are usually used wrapped around the body. When dogs scratch and chew holes in themselves because of skin infections, there is often no better accessory treatment. Skin remedies are applied and the bandage put on. Depending upon how much of the body it is to cover, the bandage generally has two or four holes cut to allow the legs to go through. Then a row of knots is tied along the back and left in bows so that it can be untied to remove the bandage, which may be used again. Head operations and ear troubles, such as splits or sutured ear flaps, can best be protected with many-tails. Also long surgical incisions on the sides, back, or abdomen can sometimes be kept covered by many-tails.

A man's vest makes a handy body covering. Place the dog's forelegs through the armholes with the vest buttons along the back. Take a tuck in the fabric on the underside if it is too loose to make it form-fitting.

Bandaging the bleeding tip of a tail in a long-tailed dog is often a problem. A happy dog may strike its ever-wagging tail on door jams, walls, or furniture, causing repeated bleeding spells. A bandage on the tail presents several problems. The dog seems to resent this dressing more than most bandages and unfortunately it is readily removed when the animal pulls it with its front teeth, or worse, bites through the bandage, further injuring the tail. To prevent the bandage removal and self-mutilation, an Elizabethan collar, which we will describe shortly, is a great help. However, you may prefer to use tranquilizers or sedatives prescribed by your veterinarian. In any event, the bandage must be covered with adhesive tape extended up the tail perhaps four to six inches on the hair. Furthermore, healing is slow, necessitating re-bandaging perhaps twice weekly for several months.

Don't hesitate to consult your veterinarian or one of his or her assistants about which is the best bandage for your dog's particular situation.

USING THERMOMETERS

Ordinary rectal thermometers, which you can purchase in a drugstore, are adequate for taking the temperature of a dog. It is a simple matter to shake one down, then dip it in Vaseline or mineral oil and insert it three quarters of its length into the rectum. It should be left in for more than sixty seconds, removed, wiped clean with a piece of cotton, and read. Don't wash it in hot water. Anyone can read this kind of thermometer by turning it slowly until the wide silver or red stripe appears and seeing which figure opposite the top of the column it has got to. Most thermometers are graduated in fifths, and since each fifth equals two tenths, the reading is usually expressed in tenths, that is, 102 1/5° F is 102.2° F. An adult dog's normal temperature is 101° F.

DEVICES TO PREVENT SELF-INJURY

After any pet's operation, or even to prevent it from chewing or scratching at an area of skin infection, it may be necessary to apply one of several devices designed to permit healing without interference.

Boxing Gloves. After a surgical procedure of the head or neck, a dog may scratch the area with the nails of a rear foot. This scratching is common during the healing period when there is an itching sensation. At that time many dogs will tear open a surgical site. A simple precaution is to pad the foot with cotton and cover the area with adhesive tape, which must extend well above the padding to the hair of the foot to anchor it. The end result is a bandage that looks like a boxing glove and will prevent damage from scratching. For face wounds, the dewclaw on a foreleg may require a strip of one-inch tape applied around the foot. Pad the dewclaw with cotton to prevent chafing before applying the tape.

A spray can of automotive starting fluid is handy to remove tape from hair without discomfort to the dog. These sprays are available from automobile accessory departments and service stations. Wipe the dissolved adhesive tape from the hair before the solution dries.

Tying the Legs. When a dog refuses to let its face alone and insists on scratching with its front paws, and if only a day or two of prevention is required, the front legs may be crossed and taped together at the wrists. The tape is, of course, removed while the owner takes the dog on a leash for its outdoor duties.

Elizabethan Collars. There are several kinds of Elizabethan collars. They may be purchased as inflatable rubber collars to be slipped over the neck and then blown up. They may also be made, easily enough, by using two pieces of thin plywood, heavy stiff cardboard or plastic, which are put together and held with shoelace or cord ties.

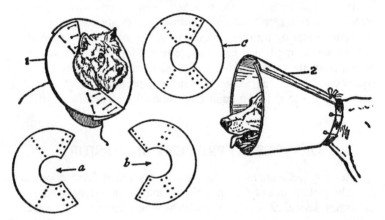

Devices to prevent self-injury. (1) An Elizabethan collar, improvised from thin plywood or extra strong cardboard, is helpful in preventing an animal from chewing cuts or sores or removing bandages. A, b, and c show how collar is made and put together. (2) Head funnel of plastic or heavy cardboard prevents an animal from scratching sores or irritations on its head and ears.

Head Funnels. Also called a cone collar, a head funnel is made by cutting a piece of flat, flexible plastic to make a partial cone. The edges are punched and the device is brought together around the head. The small end of the cone may either be fastened to the collar or left free; the larger end of the cone (the base) should be a little beyond the dog's nose. (See the illustration.) Cone collars can be obtained as well from vets, animal hospitals, and pet stores, in various sizes.

In the same spirit as a cone collar, if the correct size plastic bucket or trash container is handy, cut a hole in the bottom just large enough to slide over your dog's head. After punching holes around the opening, slip it over the head and thread twine through the holes and around the collar. A dog with its head in such a bucket cannot reach back to abuse itself.

14

Hereditary and Congenital Defects

Although the principles of dog genetics have been written about in countless volumes, there has been little mentioned in respect to the problems of implementing them. It seems to us a sad commentary that we have such a host of inherited defects in our dogs.

The average breeder proclaims improvement of the breed as perhaps the most important part of a breeding program and yet we see a continued perpetuation, if not an increase, of recognized defects. The problem is at least twofold. First, most genetic problems are not observed until after the puppies are sold. Some are not obvious until the dogs are adults. The second problem is the difficulty of a program to eliminate defects once they are discovered.

HIP DYSPLASIA

When first described twenty years ago, hip dysplasia was thought to be a dominant trait genetically. Another study a few years later indicated it to be a recessive trait.

First found in a few breeds, hip dysplasia was soon described to be in almost all breeds. Whole, healthy, active litters would show signs of weakness in their rear quarters at as young an age as four months and by eight months they were so crippled with pain they had to be destroyed. Why the dog world assumed this to be a genetic problem we find difficult to understand. On talking with old kennel owners from this country and from England, none, with a lifetime of breeding and raising the same breeds that are heavily afflicted now, had experienced this problem. One breed we raised that is high on the list of affected breeds today was the Bloodhound. Our White Isle Kennel was the largest Bloodhound kennel in the world in the 1930s and 1940s, and although we lost dogs because of other reasons we had none with weak hind quarters that vaguely resembled the problems we have since seen. Although the use of X rays was not commonly used to detect hip dysplasia in those days, the signs of it could not have been missed were they present.

Then how did a genetic condition arise suddenly in virtually all breeds of dogs over a span of a few years? We believe there is an environmental influence and that there may be a genetic resistance some animals lack that predisposes them to hip dysplasia.

We feel the problem with hip dysplasia was the assumption that hip dysplasia was a genetic defect in the first place. It is obviously imperative that we separate inherited from acquired defects.

We would like to speculate as to the cause. One environmental factor may be that the insecticide DDT had just become widely used when the problem arose. We also had a new type of distemper inoculation which became widespread at that time. Also, all sorts of pollutants in the environment were becoming prevalent. Vitamins with a longer "shelf life" were added to commercial dog foods about that time.

We think also that overvitaminizing and overfeeding nutritious foods seem to predispose growing puppies to hip dysplasia. If any puppies of a litter are destined to develop this malady, the largest seems to be most often affected. It is obvious that there is merit in keeping growing puppies thin, especially during the four- to ten-month growing period.

We are believers in using anti-inflammatory medications during the growing period of any puppy showing the telltale signs of early hip dysplasia—the bunny-hopping gait, the pain on arising, and the stiffness following resting after exercise. The medication plus little exercise and a rough surface to walk on may prevent the potential crippling of dysplasia.

At one time and to a lesser extent now, the removal of part of a muscle, the pectineous, was dramatic in the relief observed following surgery. However, many dogs will show the same problem a year or so later.

Another approach to the surgical correction of hip dysplasia is the removal of the head of the femur. The hip is called a ball-and-socket joint and this surgery removes the ball. Reconstruction during healing follows with a mushrooming at the surgical site and a flattening of the socket area, forming an amazing new joint.

HARELIPS AND CLEFT PALATES

There are other defects that appear to be inherited, such as harelips and cleft palates; but we know that a bitch fed a borderline vitamin-A-deficient diet will produce one or more such puppies and, if fed a diet with little or no vitamin A, most, if not all, will be so afflicted.

RETAINED TESTICLES

On the other hand, a problem such as retained testicles appears to be a true genetic defect. But this is a difficult defect to eliminate from a strain since it skips generations and may require genetic material from both parents to produce it. If a litter is produced with even one such puppy, we would not repeat the mating.

PERSONALITY PROBLEMS

There can be little argument that personality traits are inherited as are coat, eye color, and scenting either with the nose close to the ground, as with hounds, or with head high, as with bird dogs. To breed dogs with good dispositions is one of the easier challenges for the breeder and yet there are perhaps ten casual matings for each well-studied mating. With such odds it is no wonder we see personality traits that are unacceptable. Strains of some breeds are bred by design to be attack and guard animals. Unfortunately many of these puppies find their way into households where there is no one to train them and they grow up to be dangerous animals.

Because of the unfortunate but necessary experience of destroying unwanted dogs in pounds it is obvious that fully half of them are personality misfits; in other words, they are untrustworthy and will bite. This destruction of unwanted unfit animals is tragic but it does destroy genetic material that should not be reproduced.

We think for every breeding there should be an unbiased committee of three people, one of whom might be a veterinarian, to approve the male and female before a mating. Most dogs with personality problems can be spotted by strangers who can examine the animals in the absence of the owners.

PROGRESSIVE RETINAL ATROPHY (PRA)

Retinal problems are usually hereditary and are found very commonly in our purebred as well as mongrel dogs. Retinal dysplasia is any retinal developmental defect.

Although excellent screening of young animals has been done by breed clubs with the help of veterinary ophthalmologists, the problem is all too frequent. This is because there are a lot of people who can't be bothered with such testing and, since PRA appears to be a recessive trait, a normal female when bred to even a normal male carrying the trait will produce puppies with the problem.

Usually PRA is diagnosed in a dog anywhere from six months to five years old when it is brought in to a veterinarian because of progressive loss of sight. There is no treatment and no preventive for this problem other than the use of proper breeding practices.

Years ago a Collie male won best-of-breed at the Westminster Kennel Club dog show. He was a beautiful specimen—but had a problem. He was blind when he won that show and only the handler and the owner knew it. Being in great demand at stud, he sired many litters before the truth was out. No doubt he was not the only dog to perpetuate this inherited eye disorder, which often leads to blindness, but he was part of the problem that responsible breeders have fought quite effectively at a great expense in recent years—not to let this happen.

MONSTERS

As examples of excess susceptibility or congenital defects, we will list those we have seen in a single breed (without naming the breed). Many other breeds would have as long a list.

Cataracts
Esophageal dilatation

  Epilepsy
  Renal cortical hyperplasia
  Hemophilia
  Persistent right aortic arch
  Subaortic stenosis
  Sprue
  Hip dysplasia
  Retained testicles
  Panus
  Personality problems
  Panosteitis
  Pituitary dwarfism

To this we might add all sorts of "monster" puppies which are found in all breeds from time to time: puppies with one eye in the middle of the forehead or those with crooked tails, extra toes, deformed jaws, and cleft lips and palates, to name a few.

With such an imposing list, the problems with trying to improve a breed seem insurmountable for all but the breeder with large numbers of animals who works diligently at it for a lifetime. Moreover, this kind of breeder must either keep the progeny until they are old enough so the problems can be identified or the puppies must be farmed out and not bred until they are obviously free of one or more genetic defects.

About the best contribution most breeders can make is to breed sound animals and either destroy defective animals or sterilize them to prevent defective genetic specimens from perpetuating the problem.

HEMOPHILIA

Of the many inherited defects, bleeding disorders are extremely common. There is a reason and it is the all too frequent practice of inbreeding without eliminating the defective offspring. Inbreeding, as previously mentioned, is effective in intensifying desirable traits but it also perpetuates such undesirable disorders as hemophilia.

The most common blood disease is one found in humans also, hemophilia A or Factor VIII deficiency. Reported in almost all the breeds of purebred dogs, it has also been found in many mongrels. As is true of the human disease, it is usually carried by a normal mother and spread to her male offspring.

Hemophilia B is also known as Christmas disease or Factor IX deficiency. It is inherited from normal mothers by their male puppies, the same as is hemophilia A. It has been identified in only six breeds. Von Willebrand's disease is a rare form of hemophilia and found also in the bloodlines of only six breeds, none of which have had hemophilia A, but dogs of other breeds have been diagnosed as having this. There are many other bleeding problems too rare to discuss here.

Platelets are microscopic objects in the blood that are necessary in clotting, and platelet defects are responsible for several other bleeding disorders.

Their symptoms often are joint hemorrhages with swelling or unusual swellings from blood clots anywhere in the body. Or there may be unexplained prolonged bleeding from the nose, mouth, or any normal opening as well as from surgery. The proper diagnosis may not be able to be made without special laboratory procedures and verification may require inquiry into the breeding program to determine the mode of inheritance.

Blood transfusions are necessary to save dogs that have lost excessive blood usually from surgery or injury. Do dogs have different types of blood? Yes, there are eight major blood groups. But fortunately about 40 percent of dogs have A-negative blood and are universal donors. These dogs, however, must receive A-negative blood when they are recipients of whole blood. The other 60 percent as recipients can be given any canine blood. Many veterinarians keep A-negative donors on hand to supply blood for any dog without matching.

15

Diseases and How Your Dog Catches Them

If your dog contracts pneumonia you will know that it is sick. But unless you know more than that, there is little that you can do for the animal. On the other hand, when you know something about the types of diseases and their causes and your pet becomes ill, you can handle the situation much more intelligently. You may be able to recognize the symptoms well enough to diagnose the condition and often treat it yourself. If you do not recognize the symptoms, or if it is a serious disease which you cannot treat, you will realize the importance of having the pet properly cared for by a veterinarian. You will also be much better able to give the veterinarian the specific, accurate information he or she needs to treat the animal quickly and effectively.

A knowledge of the causes of the diseases to which our dogs are subject and of the ways they contract them is even more important from the standpoint of prevention. Many diseases can be avoided by observing a few simple precautions. Some of these maladies, once contracted, are difficult or impossible to cure. To the pet owner and to veterinary medicine, the prevention of disease in animals is as important as it is in humans. A dog that is kept well is a good pet—a lively, active companion.

A simple understanding of the basic facts about disease is sufficient for pet owners. You don't need to learn and remember a series of medical names or technical terms. You should know the broad general classifications into which all diseases are divided, be familiar with the common characteristics of each, and have a general knowledge of the way each affects animals. This is hardly too much to expect of any person who is really concerned with his or her dog's welfare.

To most pet owners all animal diseases are more or less alike—the result, they think, of some vague thing called "germs." Actually, of course, there are a number of distinct types of diseases, and they are classified according to their causes. Some are caused by bacteria, some by viruses, and others by fungi, or parasites, or deficiencies. To understand the diseases themselves it is necessary to know something about these causative agents.

BACTERIA

Bacteria are single-celled organisms; those that cause disease are called *pathogenic*. There are many forms causing disease, and all are in some way transmissible from one animal to another.

Since bacteria are too small to be seen without magnification, they must be studied through the microscope. There they appear as different from each other as the various farm animals. Some are spirals, some are little balls, some have whiplike attachments, and some look like baseball bats.

(1) Streptococci (grow in strings). (2) Staphylococci (grow in bunches). (3) Bacteria. (4) Bacteria.

Coccal bacteria are round. *Streptococci* (pronounced strep-toe-cox'-eye) are round bacteria that grow in strings. They produce such diseases as pneumonia and abscesses. *Staphylococci* are round forms that grow in groups like bunches of grapes. They are notorious pus producers and abscess formers.

Bacilli are rod-shaped bacteria, which sometimes complicate other diseases. These rod-shaped forms, of which there are many, cause bubonic plague, tularemia, and some poultry diseases. *Salmonella* organisms cause food poisoning in man and other diseases in animals. *Shigel-*

lae cause dysentery in puppies; *Clostridia* cause lockjaw, food poisoning (botulism), and gas gangrene; *Mycobacteria* cause tuberculosis.

Spirochetes are corkscrew-shaped organisms that cause diseases such as trench mouth and leptospirosis.

Since these are all comparatively large forms, too large to enter the

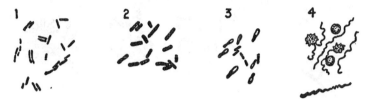

(1) Bacilli (rod-shaped). (2) Bacilli (rod-shaped). (3) Clostridia (form spores). (4) Spirochetes (among blood cells).

cells of the body, bacteria float or propel themselves about in body fluids or remain stationary. Some invade the blood; some are specific for certain tissue, such as pneumococcus types for lungs; others are found confined to the stomach and intestines.

RICKETTSIAE

Rickettsiae are different from bacteria. They are smaller—so small that they have been found inside cells. They are responsible for such diseases as Rocky Mountain spotted fever, which is spread by the parasites of rodents, dogs, and humans. Rickettsiae also cause salmon poisoning in the Northwest.

FUNGI

A third class of infecting organisms most interesting to the veterinarian and to the pet owner is the fungus (pl. fungi or funguses). Fungi are plants of a low order; they produce spores which are like seeds. Spores resist drought, heat, cold, and other environmental factors. When conditions of moisture and temperature are right, they grow into mature forms.

Many skin diseases in dogs are of fungus origin. Ringworm that grows in individual cells is a fungus. Molds are fungi. There are a great many kinds of fungi—good, bad, and neutral types. Penicillin, one of the most extraordinarily effective drugs ever discovered, is made from a mold.

(1) Mold. (2) Rickettsia (greatly magnified). (3) Fungi (grow by budding). (4) Fungi (grow in threads).

VIRUSES

Viruses live *in* the cells. They are so small that they are invisible through an ordinary microscope. Photographs of them made through the electron microscope indicate that, like bacteria, they grow in various forms. Their exact nature is not understood, nor has a cure for the diseases they cause been discovered. If your veterinarian diagnoses your dog's disease as a virus disease and tells you that he or she has no medicine that can cure it, believe it. If he or she does effect a cure with drugs, your pet did not have a virus disease. At least, this seems to be true on the basis of what we now know about viruses.

Viruses, even more than bacteria, have affinities for certain tissues in the body. Rabies, for instance, is neurotropic, which means that it attacks nerve tissue. Distemper has an affinity for the epithelial tissue (skin and mucous membranes). Some viruses attack the lining of the nose and throat, and others attack lung tissue.

One of the tragic facts about viruses is that they so weaken tissue that bacterial diseases can get a start and develop. Certain bacteria are such constant companions of viruses that we once believed that bacteria caused a number of virus diseases because bacteria were constantly present. This was true, for example, of distemper, which we thought was caused by a bacterium called *B. bronchisepticus.* Of course veterinarians should and do try to cure any part of the disease they can. If penicillin or sulfa drugs will destroy bacteria that complicate virus diseases, they should be used, *but not to treat the virus,* because they are worthless against it.

PARASITES

Cestodes are the flat worms, such as the tapeworm, and are common in dogs. The flea is the intermediate host of the most common member of this group, followed by the rabbit tapeworm. Fish, pork, and beef all may infect dogs with tapeworms common to each. The telltale segments of the worms may be observed on stools or clinging to the hair around the anus.

Protozoa are one-celled organisms that, among other diseases, cause amoebic dysentery in humans and dogs and in other animals. Amoebas are passed around to other animals in stools. Coccidia and giardia are additional examples.

Nematodes include parasites such as roundworms, hookworms, and whipworms. Nematodes, too, are spread through stool—a dog ingests eggs found in the feces of another infected dog.

Arthropods are minute parasites spread by close surface contact. An example is sarcoptic mange, which can affect the pet owner as well as the pet. Arthropods are microscopic and are diagnosed by identifying the parasite under the microscope from a skin scraping.

DISEASE TRANSMISSION

Before animals can contract a disease, they must in some manner be exposed to the infecting organism. Exposure can come about in many ways.

Bacterial diseases may be contracted by an animal eating infected food, by inhaling the bacteria, or by bacteria entering cuts or puncture wounds. If a dog is bitten by another dog, the wounds may fester by the multiplication of bacteria inserted by the tooth. Bacteria may be drawn into the system or they may be present in air passages, waiting for a virus or general loss of resistance to weaken tissue and set up conditions favorable to their growth.

Some virus diseases can be passed from one animal to another by inhaling one brief sniff of a sick animal's breath, or even by inhaling air in a room in which a sick animal has sneezed and left minute droplets floating about carrying the virus. Other virus diseases can be transmitted by bites, as is what happens in rabies.

Fungus diseases are spread in several ways: by contact, by wind, by water. Suppose your Collie develops a concentric bare spot on its nose. How did it get there? The dog may have pushed its nose against a spot on your infected cat, or it may have rested in a couch where the cat had been lying previously, or a breeze may have blown spores on it. Somehow they settled on the nose and grew. Some of the worst skin diseases a dog can get are contracted by its lying on a lawn or rubbing against another dog, or from dust blown on it that contains spores that find a way into the skin through fleabites.

IMMUNITY

Some knowledge of the body's defense against diseases and of immunity is necessary in understanding methods of prevention and cure.

When a dog that has been bitten develops an abscess, its body builds a dam around the area and walls it off from the rest of the body. The next time the dog is bitten other infections may develop from the same bacteria. But if, instead of developing a localized abscess, the bacteria invade the bloodstream, a different condition develops. *If the dog survives by its own bodily mechanism or chemistry,* it will be immune to that species of bacteria for a long time afterward. But if the dog is treated with medicine such as penicillin, which destroys every bacterium of that type in the body within a few days, then solid immunity may not be developed. Why?

Because the body builds up defenses to overcome infections in several ways: white cells may engulf them, or the body may develop antitoxins which counteract the toxins elaborated by the bacteria. All animal bodies have the power to develop specific counterchemicals that will act to destroy invading bacteria. We call these defense chemicals antibodies. It is amazing how specific they can be. The antibodies against one disease organism are seldom of value against another. Recovering from one species of coccidiosis, a dog can still contract another form. But if the dog is to develop immunity, it may have to recover without medication. If the recovery from a bacterial disease is due to chemicals added to the blood, the animal does not always develop antibodies which will solidly protect it against that form of disease in the future.

There are different kinds of immunity. *Passive immunity* is conferred by additions of biologics to the blood that ensure temporary protection. *Inherent* or *inherited immunity* is transmitted from parent to offspring. *Acquired immunity* is acquired after birth. *Active immunity* is produced by an animal's own tissues or fluids. It may be produced by (1) having a disease and recovering; (2) constant mild exposure to the disease-producing organism; (3) injection of dead organisms or products of dead organisms; or (4) injection of attenuated or dead viruses. The viruses are attenuated in several ways: by the addition of chemicals to live virus; by passing the disease through another species; and by growing it in cell or tissue cultures.

16

Problems of the Reproductive and Urinary Systems

FEMALE REPRODUCTIVE PROBLEMS

The female organs of reproduction are, from the outside in, the vulva, clitoris, vagina, cervix, uterus, Fallopian tubes, ovaries; and, on the lower abdomen, the udder, which includes the mammary glands with their accessories. The udder is actually a group of skin glands, and its ailments are considered here only because they are so closely tied in with the reproductive processes.

The reproductive system is subject to many ills, but those most obvious to the layperson are growths, unnatural discharges, irregular heat periods, infertility, and insufficient milk production. In addition there are many disorders and infections which, though not evident from the outside, can cause infertility and even death.

Ovarian Problems. A bitch's ovaries are about as large as pea beans and are surrounded by capsules on the outside of which the fallopian tubes twist along and end in spongy-looking edges called fimbriae. The ovaries have most commonly one problem.

CYSTS. Not found in young bitches (up to six or eight months old, let us say), cysts in older animals are the most frequent ovarian problem in our experience. We have removed at least ten thousand pairs of ovaries and uteri in spaying operations.

Cysts do not grow out of the ovaries proper but from the tissue connected with them. They may be as large as pigeon eggs but more often are half an inch across or smaller. Many exploratory operations to determine the cause of sterility have been performed, and when cysts were discovered, it was found that merely rupturing them resulted in a bitch's coming in heat promptly and producing sizable litters.

Cysts around the ovaries do not always produce complete sterility, and they usually affect the general health very little. For example, there is the case of Mary, the most prolific bitch we have ever heard of. She produced an average of sixteen puppies per litter for eight litters. Then came three litters of five, four, and five puppies, respectively. Her drop in fecundity was found to be due to cysts on both ovaries. She had shown no signs of ill health, and if an exploratory operation had not been performed we never would have known that she had cysts.

Tumors of bitches' ovaries are rare. For example, in a study we did of approximately seven hundred cases of neoplasms we found no ovarian tumors.

Uterine Problems. Most of the troubles of the reproductive tract are centered in the uterus, and usually these conditions are not apparent unless one is watching carefully for them. Three principal types of problems occur: those connected with the process of birth; those due to infection not associated with pregnancy; and tumors.

PERITONITIS AND RETAINED PLACENTAE. Bitches may die of peritonitis a few days after whelping a litter, frequently because of failure to expel a dead puppy. Often puppies die in the uterus, decompose, and infect the mother, who cannot give birth to them. For example, the mother may have received a blow that killed one or more of the unborn litter. A disease she may have contracted can kill her puppies. Or occasionally one huge puppy will block the birth canal and cause complications of this type.

As frequent a cause of death as any to bitches in this general category is the retained placentae. These large lumps of decaying tissue may cause the uterus around them to die too. When that happens the uterus ruptures and the putrescent material enters the abdomen; peritonitis develops and without prompt treatment the bitch dies.

There is doubtless some dietary connection with the inability to pass the puppies and placentae properly. Bitches on inadequate diets have such complications much more frequently than those on complete, wholesome diets. Our own nutritional studies indicate that when a known complete and balanced diet was fed, retention of placentae was extremely rare. But years ago among the dogs owned by our clients it was a common difficulty. Many of the animals had been fed the old meat-and-dog-biscuit or kibble diet; others had been given inadequate assortments of table scraps.

Following birth it is important to see that all of the afterbirths are passed. A wise dog owner will sit with the bitch and, as each puppy is born, catch the cord and hold it, exerting a slight pull until the placenta comes out. The bitch may be allowed to eat it without any harm being done and perhaps with some benefit to her. She always will do this if she is left alone. If there are not as many placentae passed as there are puppies, the veterinarian can inject one of several drugs that will help speed up the muscular contractions in the uterus and help force out any afterbirths that remain. Sometimes high douches will remove a placenta, and quite often, as the uterus shrinks and shortens, a veterinarian can feel a retained placenta in the uterus through the abdominal walls, insert a pair of long forceps into the uterus, and remove it.

If retained placentae become infected, the condition interferes with milk secretion, produces an elevated temperature, and results in a foul smell and a long, continued discharge from the uterus. It also interferes with future pregnancies and, because of the general debilitating effect on the mother, prevents the proper development of the puppies. When bitches that have retained placentae recover, it is not unusual to find blackened areas in the uterine wall. It has been observed that those that do recover are generally the ones that have a healthy thirst even though they do not eat during their illnesses. Antibiotics must be given, and judiciously, since the puppies will receive some in their mother's milk.

PRODUCTION OF MONSTERS. Monsters—puppies of odd forms or immensely oversized—frequently cause death or require cesarean sections to be performed. Among the monsters are great headless lumps covered with hair, two-headed puppies, and greatly oversized abnormal pups. Sometimes a puppy will die before birth, become contaminated with bacteria, possibly of blood origin, and blow up with gas to many times its normal size so that the mother cannot possibly pass it. Others become distended with fluid, as happens in dropsy. All such dystocias, or interferences with normal birth, require prompt veterinary care.

RESTRICTED PELVIS. Bitches whose pelvises have been broken and in healing have become constricted cannot have normal births. They should not be bred except in some very unusual cases.

TWISTED UTERUS. Occasionally the uterus becomes twisted. Once in a while a puppy manages to get down one horn of the uterus and up the other, so that it is part way in each and its back is toward the body of the uterus. Manipulation can generally effect a normal delivery, but by herself the mother may not be able to expel a live puppy.

DELIVERING GIANT PUPPIES. It has been observed that matings of large males with small females may produce puppies so large that they cannot be delivered normally. A good deal more research on this subject is needed. It may be that the dam has more effect on birth size than we yet know. However, we have mated, artificially, a 120-pound St. Bernard and a 30-pound French Bulldog bitch; a 55-pound German Shepherd with a 22-pound Poodle; a 90-pound Bloodhound with a 33-pound Basset Hound; and many other such crosses. In all cases the puppies were whelped without difficulty.

GROWTHS OF THE UTERUS. There are a number of growths that develop in the uterus. Some of these are relatively harmless, but there are others that seem to predispose the organ to infection. Some types develop rapidly, and with these it is often impossible to save the bitch. Growths, especially those in the pelvis, have been known to cause difficult birthing.

INFECTIONS OF THE UTERUS. There are three infections of the uterus we'd like to discuss briefly: *metritis*, inflammation of the whole uterus; *endometritis*, inflammation of the lining of the uterus; and *pyometra*, pus in the uterus.

The first two, metritis and endometritis, are evidenced by a swelling throughout the whole reproductive tract. Even the vulva is swollen. These conditions are more or less tied up with the aftermath of birth but also occur following an accident such as gunshot wound or some other type of injury, as well as unknown causes that can occasion the uterus to become inflamed.

Pyometra is different. It occurs in between mating cycles. The small, resting uterus—normally no larger in diameter than a soda straw, but with thicker walls—fills with bacteria that proliferate in enormous numbers, causing pus formation until the uterus is distended to seemingly incredible proportions. We have removed from a German Shepherd a uterus that was two and a quarter inches in diameter with each horn being three and a half feet long. It was amazing that an animal could carry this amount of pus and live. The kidneys, which have tried to handle the wastes of such a problem, may be seriously damaged by it.

With infections of this sort the abdomen becomes distended, the temperature is generally fairly high, and the bitch often has a great thirst. A yellowish discharge from the vulva with a fetid, sickish-sweet odor is an obvious symptom, often being sufficiently copious to wet the tail and hind legs and attract flies in warm weather. Some species of flies will lay eggs in the moist hair, and maggots develop. The vulva is somewhat larger than normal. The bitch loses her appetite, becomes thin and somewhat potbellied, is weak with a tottery gait, and has a general unhealthy appearance.

When this condition develops it is best to have the uterus and ovaries removed. Intravenous fluids during and after the operation greatly increase the chances of success, and few bitches die when the whole uterus is removed, unless it is ruptured and the pus has escaped into the abdomen. It is important to seek help promptly.

A few veterinarians tell us they have corrected pyometria in one or two bitches without surgery, but most agree that surgery is the only accepted corrective measure. With the use of an experimental drug called Malucidin some years ago, a few cases were cured but the demand did not justify the time and inconvenience of producing the product. The drug was also used to abort pregnant bitches.

Vaginal Problems. Compared with the uterus, the vagina gives little trouble. Most of its problems are those connected with the mating cycle. There are a host of vaginal infections that bitches live with that have no obvious ill effects on them but are ones that their puppies are exposed to during the birth process. Herpes virus, for one, can be disastrous, resulting in rapid failing and death five days after birth. Other diseases, bacterial in nature, affect the gastrointestinal tract. Within the vagina are the cervix—actually a part of the uterus—the hymen, and the external urethral opening and clitoris.

PERSISTENT HYMEN. Before copulation can be started, it is sometimes necessary to insert an instrument to break the hymen. This is not often present in bitches, but in certain strains of most breeds it is a constant feature. If a male cannot insert his penis far enough to become tied, an examination should be made. About two inches inside the vagina a vertical web of tissue across the opening can be felt and ruptured by cutting. We have seen these strips so tough that they would have prevented a bitch from ever mating unless they were corrected surgically.

CLITORIS ENLARGEMENT. The clitoris increases greatly during the mating cycle. In some bitches it becomes so huge that a male's penis cannot push it out of the way. It may stick out of the vulva and show as a red knob. It may lead to a prolapse of the vagina, so that a red bunch as large as an average-sized tomato protrudes from the vulva. In a few instances we have seen clitorises as large as a small grapefruit.

Swelling becomes evident early in the heat period gradually enlarging until about ovulation time when the clitoris shrinks back to normal. However, if untreated it may become irritated from sitting, with infection invading the damaged tissue. We advise surgery when such a swelling first becomes obvious. A wedge-shaped area is cut away and the remaining edges are sutured.

INFLAMMATION AND INJURIES. Inflammation of the vagina (vaginitis) is usually accompanied by similar inflammation of the vulva, which becomes unduly red, much as it does when the bitch is in heat. In ordinary vaginitis there is a discharge of a whitish nature. A good deal of licking is done by the bitch and she strains to urinate because the inflammation partially closes the urethral orifice. Urination probably causes a burning sensation, so that only small amounts are voided.

Vaginal infection may be caused by injuries to the vulva. Curious children have been known to insert sharp objects into the vaginas of bitches. Bullet wounds cause trouble. Bird shot sometimes penetrates the skin and lodges in the vaginal lining, where it sets up severe irritation until it is removed. The vulva is also subject to neoplasms. Barbed-wire cuts are not uncommon. There may be damage from biting wounds when bitches fight with other dogs or from automobile accidents.

With adequate surgery these injuries may be repaired quite easily.

Mammary Gland Problems. In our experience there are three general classifications of problems that affect the mammary glands of bitches: growths, injuries, and the ailments associated with reproduction.

GROWTHS OF THE MAMMARY GLANDS. There are two common tumors of the mammary glands and others are rarely found. Of these two, adenocarcinoma is life-threatening, whereas the other, a mixed tumor, is not, but it is more inconvenient to the animal.

It is often said that cancer of the mammary gland is caused by the production of milk and the "drying off" process. It is true that when a bitch has ceased to give milk after weaning puppies a lump can sometimes be felt in the udder. Possibly there is activity in the breast tissue that encourages development of a tumor. And after a tumor is removed from a bitch, more may grow in new areas of the mammary glands. But if she is spayed, new ones are not apt to develop. If your veterinarian advises spaying your bitch, even though she is not young, you will be wise to trust his or her judgment.

Other types of tumors also grow on and in breasts, but they are rare and you are not likely to see one. Needless to say, a growth anywhere should have prompt attention, and this is especially important in the case of growths in the mammary area.

INJURIES. The mammary gland area is especially vulnerable to injury, particularly during lactation, when it is enlarged. Next to the feet, it is the most likely part of the dog to be torn or cut. Bitches frequently rip their udders on barbed-wire fences as they crawl between the strands or cut their udders on glass or other sharp objects when they crawl under fences.

Such injuries must be sutured carefully after the tissue has been cleaned. Active udders become infected easily. If the blood supply to this organ is cut, it may die and slough out. In that case it is better to leave a wound open and allow the bitch to lick it until she has removed all the dead tissue, after which it may be sutured to promote quicker healing and result in a smaller scar.

A bad bruise of a mammary gland may cause outpouring of blood into a section of the udder. Bacteria may creep up through the teat and cause infection. Abscesses may form, and they must be opened and flushed with medication, which is a job for the veterinarian.

Udder infection enters through nipples, or it may be in the breast before weaning. Such infection is called *mastitis,* whether it occurs before or after weaning. Udder infection is one of the chief causes of puppy death. Puppies die of infection which can be contracted from infected milk.

When an udder is infected for some time, sections involving several nipples may become inactive. At subsequent lactation periods, only part of the udder will be useful to the puppies. But even with fewer teats, the mother will produce almost as much milk as if she had them all functioning.

PSEUDOPREGNANCY. The question most often asked the veterinarian about any phase of udder trouble is, "Doctor, my dog's breasts are all swollen. What can be the matter?" Usually nothing is the matter. She was in heat two months ago and wasn't mated. All bitches that ovulate develop so-called phantom or pseudopregnancies. If they do not, they failed to ovulate. So this condition is a normal one. If your bitch comes in season and fails to develop swelling of the breasts later, then you should consult your veterinarian.

If a bitch has a false pregnancy with well-developed mammary glands, we believe it is an indication she will be a good nurturing mother when she is bred.

We remember a late-night call from a frantic owner whose whelping female had delivered eight fine puppies and was still heavy with pups. "How can we shut her off?" he asked. An hour later she had a total of twelve and finally she stopped with sixteen beautiful offspring. When that female had been in season, her mother, who was in the same house, had been in season at the same time but was not bred. The mother was experiencing a false pregnancy, which was fortunate for such a large litter, for she climbed into the nest box and nursed half the litter as if they were her own.

CAKED BREASTS. Swollen breasts after weaning result in congestion, which is nothing to be alarmed about. That is nature's way of shutting off the milk flow. Rubbing with softening remedies actually accomplishes nothing. It is probably best to leave the breasts alone; eventually they will soften. This advice applies, of course, only when there is no infection; if that occurs, your veterinarian should be consulted.

If inflammation is obvious along with very firm breasts, ice packs or cold compresses for ten minutes three times daily will reduce the blood supply and offer temporary relief, but in a few days the problem will solve itself. Sometimes the care of a lively litter of partially weaned pups is such a burden, the owners sell them or give them away. If the bitch has been supplying most of the puppies' food, she will be in unnecessary anguish with huge caked breasts in twenty-four hours. Instead of subjecting her to this condition it is far better to keep one or two puppies to nurse for a week or two. They will take enough milk to prevent caking and the mother will dry up as nature intended her to.

MALE REPRODUCTIVE PROBLEMS

It has been our experience that more male dogs are sterile than are unspayed females. That is not surprising when we consider the delicate mechanism of the reproductive tract (see Chapter 2). Neoplasms of the testicles are common. The pathway traveled by the sperm offers many chances for infection, and the accessory organs along the way may also cause trouble.

Testicular Problems.

GROWTHS. In a study once made of neoplasms in dogs, about 8 percent were in the testicles. This occurs in a high percentage of old dogs. When a growth occurs in one testicle, the other generally atrophies. When the testicle with the growth is removed, the shrunken testicle usually increases to normal size again, and there may be a return to normal production of sperm.

Some tumors growing in the testicles may cause the dog to take on female characteristics. He develops enlarged nipples, does not lift his hind leg when urinating, and has no interest in mating with bitches.

INJURIES. The testicles are frequently damaged by accidents and fights. The sheath may be torn away and require extensive suturing. We have known even of cases in which the scrotum was frozen to a rock: the dog may sit on a very cold surface until numbness sets in, and when he stands up the outside layers of the skin can literally be torn off. The sheath often thickens from injuries and infections, but it is fairly easily treated with medication.

INFLAMMATION. *Orchitis* means inflammation of one or both of the testicles. You can often tell that a dog feels pain in the testicles by the way he moves about. He walks with his hind legs spread slightly, giving a stiffness to his gait. If an infection sets in, the testicle may have to be opened and drained. The scrotum may also be infected. All injuries and abscesses in this area are extremely painful to the dog, and any pain-deadening agent is a humane adjunct to treatment. Your veterinarian can give you effective drugs, but in the absence of something better, aspirin will ease the pain.

CRYPTORCHIDISM. In cryptorchidism a testicle is retained in the abdomen or in the abdominal ring between the layers of muscle through which it normally descends. In adult dogs surgery is recommended as the best treatment. Retained testicles may cause undependable dispositions in dogs and a significant percentage become cancerous. The operation for testicles retained in the abdomen is equivalent in risk to the ordinary spaying operation.

Prostate Problems.

ENLARGEMENT AND INFECTION. As dogs grow older their prostate glands tend to enlarge. This may be caused by infection, by a hormonal action, or by growths. Prostatic enlargement causes such a lump in the pelvis that it may give the dog a sensation of stool in the colon and cause him to strain a great deal in an attempt to relieve himself. As we have seen, this enlargement of the prostate is often related to perineal hernias. It is also a cause of constipation, because it blocks the passage of large, firm stools, permitting only very soft stools to pass over it.

An infection produces pus along the tube that conducts the sperm. Each emission of semen shows myriad pus cells mixed with the sperm, and such semen generally is incapable of effective fertilization of eggs. This is one of the most common causes of male infertility.

In stud dogs the use of antibiotics helps substantially. We have restored fertility to many studs in this way. In the case of dogs whose germ plasm is of no great value, two methods of reducing the prostate are useful: castration, and feeding of the synthetic female sex hormone, stilbestrol. Either method effects a cure but also causes sterility. Stilbestrol has not been incriminated in causing cancer in dogs as it has in humans.

MALE STERILITY. In treating sterility in the male the cause should be determined if possible, but unfortunately it is not always possible. The spermatic fluid may be cultured to find a microorganism capable of causing sterility. Since the nature of some infections preclude simple treatments, combinations of medications are frequently used. If medications are unsuccessful a needle biopsy may be helpful. A pathologist may study the tissue and determine that there is so much damage that treatment cannot succeed or that medication may be helpful. At least one sterility-causing disease, *brucellosis*, may be diagnosed by a blood test. Brucellosis will be considered further in Chapter 26.

ABSCESSES AND GROWTHS. Abscesses are not infrequently found in dogs' prostate glands. A veterinarian can drain them through an abdominal incision and biopsy them to determine the nature of the lesion. Malignant growths have been reported in dogs' prostates. If caught in time, they can be removed surgically.

Penis Problems. The most frequent problem of the penis is injury from tears, gunshot, and dog bites. Neoplasms also cause considerable trouble. When the penis is injured it takes a considerable time to heal because the tissue is spongy and because the sheath prevents air from reaching the wound. Clotting does not occur easily, and the blood may continue to trickle out for some time. The bulb at the back of the penis, when injured by a dog bite, can cause considerable blood loss.

We have seen a dog whose penis was pierced by a .22-caliber bullet bleed to such an extent that he was too weak to walk. An injury of this type should be left to the veterinarian, who may suture to check the blood flow.

GROWTHS. There is one form of tumor, probably mistakenly called lymphosarcoma, that may be contracted by copulation. It grows on the penis, and mere contact will infect a bitch, which in turn can infect other males. It transplants readily and we have made four transplants to study it. In addition, we have removed several types of malignant growths from the sheaths of dogs but none from the penis except the one mentioned above. When this growth has to be removed the dog is practically valueless as a stud thereafter, unless only a very small area is initially affected.

DISCHARGES AND INFLAMMATION. All dogs constantly drip smegma, a greenish yellow or creamy yellowish discharge from their sheaths which they themselves customarily clean. This drip comes from the space, a deep pocket, between the sheath and penis. There is nothing abnormal about it. However, some dogs that fail to keep themselves clean become objectionable because of it.

Douching this pocket with a mild antiseptic under fairly strong pressure will do a lot to reduce the amount of drip. If there is inflammation, the condition is known as *balanitis*.

PHIMOSIS, PARAPHIMOSIS, AND SWELLING. *Phimosis* is a condition in which the opening of the sheath is too small for the penis to pass through at the time of copulation which renders the male incapable of copulating. It can be corrected by a simple operation.

Paraphimosis occurs often in puppies about the time of adolescence. The penis protrudes through the sheath, swells, and then cannot be withdrawn to its natural cover.

An irritation in the penis sometimes causes it to swell within the sheath, which cannot stretch to the full size of the distended penis. This creates great pressure and attending pain. The dog evidences his discomfort by running around and frequently sitting and licking his penis.

The best treatment for either of these two conditions is to get the dog's interest turned in some other direction. Taking him for a walk, soaking him in cold water, brushing him with a stiff brush, mentioning a ride in the car if he has learned to like it, or even saying, "Where's kitty?" to a dog that knows what it means may effect an almost instant reduction in the size of the penis. Even then, however, the pain from the distention diminishes only gradually.

DISEASES OF THE URINARY TRACT

The blood-filtering mechanism of the kidneys, with their complex system of tubules, is subject to a number of problems. The whole system may be thrown out of balance or there may be a failure of one or more of the parts—in the ureters, the bladder, or the urethra. In addition to the damage done by these primary failures, infections or defects in these organs directly affect the functioning of other parts of the body and sometimes are instrumental in causing other diseases.

The awareness of a problem in its early stage is a real challenge to even an observant pet owner—a dog cannot specify that it is out of sorts with a dull backache as humans can. But spotting an early-stage kidney disease can prevent disaster.

You will be able to have your dog treated while the disease is in the early stage. The final, definite diagnosis of the specific problem will usually be made by your veterinarian. A urinalysis is generally necessary, for only an examination with a microscope will reveal that kidney tubules have shed their lining, that the urine contains crystals or bacteria, or that a number of other difficult-to-detect conditions indicative of a particular disease are present. Nevertheless, early recognition of the common symptoms discussed in this chapter is important, for these outward signs are usually first indications of trouble and as such are the basis for further examination. These indications may be one or a combination of the following: a desire for fluids in excess of the usual amount drunk; either excess or more frequent urination than is usual; a slight loss of pep or enthusiasm. As a condition progresses, these signs become more pronounced, more obvious.

KIDNEY PROBLEMS

Inflammation. The scientific name for kidney inflammation is nephritis. Pronounced inflammation of the kidneys may be recognized by excessive thirst, some fever, and sometimes by pain indicated when pressure is applied over the kidney area. If the thirst is great, the urine may be very diluted. Protein may be present in the urine, and this can be determined only by testing. There may be nausea occasioned by a rise in the uric-acid and waste-product content of the blood; a weak and rapid pulse; blurring of the eyes; lessened appetite; and a stiff gait.

During the onset of nephritis the dog loses its appetite and thirst. Its urine will then be more concentrated than normal urine and highly colored, perhaps orange or red from blood. It may even appear opaque from pus. When a dog suffers pain from this trouble it frequently passes only a small amount of urine at a time, even though there may be a considerable amount in the bladder. In a severe case the dog may be dizzy, stagger, have convulsions, and eventually lapse into a coma.

In some cases these acute symptoms terminate not in death but in a chronic state of affliction. Often dogs cured by proper medication can be kept in good condition by proper diet. One fact is strongly in the dog's favor: the kidneys normally do not use their entire filtering mechanism all the time. Consequently only a comparatively small part may be damaged and, when the condition is corrected, the balance of the organ may still be able to function.

In its most severe form nephritis may cause the kidneys to enlarge—even to double their size—or it may cause them to shrink until the organs are only half their normal size.

Nephritis is caused by bacterial infection of the kidneys, by food toxins, or by poisons. It may also be brought on by blows over these organs. Bacteria carried in the blood become lodged in the tiny tubules and grow, causing destruction of all or part of one or both kidneys. The tiny, delicate tubules are especially vulnerable to poisons and often become useless after an attempt to filter out an overload of these toxic substances. In many instances all organs of a dog except the kidneys may recover from an excess dose of poison.

Kidney inflammation often follows an attack of some disease elsewhere in the body and apparently is due to the stress placed upon the kidneys in trying to eliminate the toxins caused by the bacteria producing the disease. A bitch whose uterus is infected very often suffers severely damaged kidneys. After a serious attack of septicemia or peritonitis, a dog may be affected in the same way.

The symptoms which we have listed could, of course, be indicative of other diseases. One easy test which anyone can make will help to establish a fairly accurate diagnosis. Catch some of the dog's urine and ask your veterinarian for an analysis. When the kidneys are damaged they are unable to handle the albumin as they should and the excess will be found in a soluble form in the urine. In this form it is colorless. The proper evaluation of the condition should be left to your veterinarian, as should the treatment.

Obviously if a dog can't handle albumin properly, large amounts should not be fed. The dog with chronic kidney disease needs a small amount of high-grade protein in order to live. This it can get in whole milk and specially prepared home-cooked foods like the diet described on p. 270.

Since permanently damaged kidneys cannot adequately filter the wastes out of the blood, one often finds weak hearts associated with kidney failure. With these two organs functioning improperly, fluids naturally accumulate in the body. The heart loses the strength it once had to force the blood through the circulatory system and back again, so some stagnates along the way. The abdomen is the easiest place for it to filter out, so we frequently find large amounts of fluid accumulating in that cavity. We have tapped (taken out) as much as a gallon out of a twenty-pound Boston Terrier. The legs often swell, as does the skin and tissue under the chest and abdomen. If you pinch this tissue it causes the dog no pain but leaves a pit, indicating edema.

If water is withheld, the dog may be forced to absorb much of this fluid back into its circulation. The treatment is rigorous and not desirable. The dog's great thirst drives it to beg for water or milk, and its owner often gives in. The animal is then ready for tapping again, and even that may be useless. We have seen a number of young dogs with severe dropsy that recovered without additional treatment after a few tappings, but in old dogs it usually brings only temporary relief. However, this is an indication for a medication referred to by many as water pills. It is amazing how often pet owners will remark that they or other family members take the same medication for the same problem.

The debate over high- versus low-protein diets for dogs with damaged kidneys has gone on for years and continues to this day. It seems to us that, since the kidneys must eliminate nitrogenous wastes among other things, a diet low in the production of such wastes is desirable. There are prescription diets available to accomplish this result about which a veterinarian can tell you. We suggest a trial diet of one third by volume of cooked inexpensive hamburger, one third boiled rice or noodles, and one third of stewed tomatoes. If several urinalyses indicate a reduction in protein eliminated on this diet, we add a vitamin mineral supplement. Many dogs can exist for years on this diet or on prescription diets.

Kidney Stones. When a dog occasionally passes small amounts of blood in the urine, there is a rare chance it may have stones in a kidney, especially if its bladder and urethra are found to be clear. Even though kidney stones are detected much less frequently than bladder stones, postmortem examinations show them more often than most people suppose. In the majority of cases the dogs' owners had no suspicion of their presence.

In acute cases, affected dogs may show great pain, walk with arched backs, cry, or whine. These are not diagnostic symptoms, however, because they can indicate many other disabilities. X rays are necessary to show the stone(s).

Of all the cases with which we have dealt, most were brought to us by owners after the dogs had been exercising heartily—jumping, swimming, retrieving. It appeared that the exercise had altered the position of the stone and produced the spasm of pain and/or blood in the urine. Unless the attacks are severe or frequent, an operation is not advisable. One of our own hounds lived to be eleven years old and always had a kidney stone. It suffered mild attacks and passed blood only after it had been hunting.

If one kidney appears to be normal and the other is diseased, the diseased kidney may be removed to eliminate a stone or serious disease condition. An animal that has this done will be healthy as long as the remaining kidney functions normally.

Uremia. Many an old dog dies because its kidneys fail to function as they should. Eventually the whole chemistry of the body is disturbed by an excess amount of uric acid in the blood. This condition is called uremia. It is a kind of blood poisoning, but not the bacterial sort, since it is a toxic condition. (Younger dogs may die from this condition as well—possibly due to other causes, such as long retention of urine because of stones in the bladder or a ruptured bladder.)

The poisoning or toxemia associated with uremia produces nausea. After a few days the dog will vomit anything it consumes, including water, and it may evince a great thirst or none at all. Some dogs act dizzy; some become blind; some have convulsions, and some end in comas. Often an old dog exhibits all these conditions.

The odor of stale urine is obvious upon smelling the dog's breath, and if there is a doubt in your mind your veterinarian will recognize it.

When the point of obvious uremia is reached treatment is usually unsuccessful. In humans hemodialysis or peritoneal dialysis is used, but hemodialysis is not available for dogs. Peritoneal dialysis may prove helpful but cannot be repeated for thirty-six hours weekly for the remainder of a dog's life as it can be in humans.

BLADDER PROBLEMS

When fully distended, a dog's bladder occupies a considerable area in the abdomen. It has a capacity far greater than that of many other species. Perhaps because of its size, a dog's bladder seems particularly vulnerable to injury. Dogs that are struck by automobiles—especially those that have just been let out of the house to relieve themselves—often have their bladders ruptured. The bladder is frequently punctured by gunshots, ruptured by kicks or blows, and sometimes even by falls.

A normal bladder shrinks to a very small size after urination. Its walls are thin and pliable. When it is inflamed, however, it feels thick and hard. This fact sometimes leads to errors in diagnosing problems. For example, a bladder filled with stones also has greatly inflamed walls and is likely to give one the impression that the stones within are larger than they actually are.

Ruptured Bladder. A dog with a ruptured bladder soon exhales the odor of urine on its breath; its temperature falls; it collapses and, unless quickly and effectively treated, dies in a short time. If an injured dog is brought to the veterinarian in time, surgery may be able to save it. We have sutured a number of ruptured bladders. After flushing out the abdomen, we leave a catheter in the urethra so that the urine will drain away as fast as it enters. Intravenous fluids are helpful and antibacterial medications are a must.

Bladder Infection. Common in dogs, especially in bitches, is bladder infection. They may go about urinating far more frequently than normal, and as if they felt a burning sensation, they may even cry as they urinate. The condition is called cystitis. Occasionally a little blood may follow the urine; the temperature may rise a degree or two. When a dog has been affected for several days, the urine may appear stringy or cloudy from pus and blood. Males show similar symptoms and may stand for long periods with a hind leg lifted and only produce drops of urine.

It is not safe, however, to assume that because you see these symptoms your pet is necessarily affected with cystitis; it may have stones called calculi. It is best to consult your veterinarian in such cases and have him or her make the necessary diagnosis.

Twisted Bladder. In a perineal or an inguinal hernia, the bladder sometimes twists about and protrudes into the hernia under the skin. It fills with urine and, unless it is tapped and replaced, the dog dies. This is also a matter for your veterinarian.

Bladder and Urethral Stones. A great deal can be told about the bladder by the palpation of a skillful and experienced practitioner. The layperson ordinarily cannot diagnose ailments by this method, although occasionally one does—for example, the dog owner who brought us his pet, saying that he had felt bladder stones "like gravel that crunches together." As it happened, the stones were a variety that were not visible by X ray, but they could be felt and they were surgically removed.

When a dog owner sees some of the stones that a veterinarian has removed from a pet's bladder, he or she often can scarcely believe it. "How did they ever get there?" Or, "I never knew my dog to eat stones." A stone that was eaten couldn't possibly get into the bladder. It would pass through the alimentary canal. Urinary stones are gradual accumulations of mineral matter in the urine around initial crystals that formed and in some way failed to pass out with the urine. Not all bladder stones are of the same composition. Some, as we have indicated, fail to show on X rays, whereas most types appear as distinct as do bones.

Stones are found in all sizes, from tiny crystals to huge accretions as large as hen's eggs. Often a bladder is filled with assorted sizes, from fine gravel up to huge stones. The surfaces of the stones vary too. Most are smooth from constant rubbing, but occasionally a stone may be as rough as coarse sandpaper and more or less adherent to the bladder wall, the inner surface of which has become pitted to correspond with the irregularities of the stone.

Weight alone can make a load of stones uncomfortable and probably somewhat painful. More serious, of course, is the fact that they irritate the bladder, causing it to bleed. They afford a perfect environment for bacteria to multiply among them. But the worst feature is the tendency of the small stones to work into the urethra. At the point where the urethra joins the bladder, a small stone can easily form an obstruction. In the male the most common place for a stoppage is just behind the bone in the penis. There the urethra runs through the bone. And although a stone could pass down the elastic urethra, it cannot pass through this rigid bone, and so it lodges behind it.

The only way to remove large stones is by surgery followed by bladder antiseptics. When the operation is performed by a skillful surgeon, mortality is low. If the dog is nursed at home, close supervision and faithful medication are essential. If your veterinarian gives you drugs to administer and the dog vomits them, report that promptly. If you can't make your pet swallow the prescribed medicine, let the vet know. Don't take your dog home to be treated unless you are able to follow unequivocally the veterinarian's directions.

In females, as well as in males, bladder stones become lodged in the urethra, but females may pass them upon occasion, which is painful. It is sometimes possible to massage them out by inserting the finger in the vagina. In some cases your veterinarian will be able to dilate the urethra while the dog is anesthetized and catch hold of the stones with the tip of long slender forceps and remove them. If this doesn't work, the vet can operate.

After being removed, stones are analyzed to determine by their composition how best to prevent the problem from returning. One theory suggests infection is necessary for the development of stones, so it behooves us to check and recheck a dog that has undergone surgery to treat any infection promptly if it arises.

Urinary Incontinence. Incontinence is usually called "dribbling." While it is a common complaint with older spayed bitches, this disagreeable condition occurs at all ages and in both sexes. It should not be confused with the reaction so common in some dogs of squatting and wetting, or wetting without squatting, from the joy of seeing a familiar person or from fear or excitement. These are nervous reactions based largely on heredity. Here we are discussing disease or disability. Some male dogs, some unspayed females, and many that have been spayed are unable to retain a full bladder of urine. The sphincter muscle is weak, and as soon as the bladder begins to stretch, urine leaks from the urethra.

Bladder irritations as well as weak sphincters may be the cause. Stones, infections, and adhesions can also produce the same result. One of our patients, a female Miniature Schnauzer, has passed a pea-size or larger stone about once every two weeks for years. The owners have two teacupfuls on their mantel piece as proof.

Another patient, a St. Bernard male, had every indication of a stone obstructing the urethra at the bladder. If he strained to urinate, it appeared he was forcing a stone into the urethra, effectively blocking the passage of urine. When he ceased straining urine dribbled out as he walked along. A catheter relieved the bladder of urine and no stone could be found. Apparently a flap of sorts was present which acted as a valve preventing the voluntary passage of urine. The solution was simple. If the dog urinated frequently he had no problem, but holding it for ten hours as he had with the owner at work produced the problem. We suggested the dog be kept outside where he could urinate at will while the owner was away for long periods. The condition was thus corrected. After a few weeks he was able to retain his urine for twelve hours with no problem. The condition was corrected but the cause remains a mystery.

To effect a cure, one must be certain of the cause first. Drugs are used for infections; surgery for stones; and a simple expedient is helpful for spayed bitches—administering female sex hormones as a substitute for the natural secretion of the missing ovaries.

Bladder Tumors. The formation of tumors in the bladder is extremely rare in dogs and is a matter for surgery after diagnosis has been established.

Bladder Worms. There are also bladder worms of two sorts, *Capillaria plica* and *Dioctophyme renalis*. Both are such curiosities in dogs they warrant no more than a mention.

17

Problems of the Digestive System

In this chapter we shall include all the problems that occur anywhere in the digestive tract, from a dog's lips to its anus.

THE TEETH

There is no doubt that in many cases good and bad teeth are genetic. Some kinds of dogs, particularly the small breeds, lose many teeth by the time they are two years old. Others have healthy teeth all their lives. Frequently the owners of a two-year-old show dog with loose teeth that need to be extracted will not permit the procedure to be done until the dog has finished its show championship.

Tartar. The principal problem with teeth is the tartar, or plaque, that builds up on them. It is theorized that some dogs have saliva that encourages this tartar buildup. It is not unusual to find thick crusts of tartar larger than the teeth. In some dogs this may be removed in the veterinarian's office without an anesthetic. Other dogs will not permit such treatment and must be given a short-acting anesthetic in order to have their teeth cleaned. In any event the insides of the teeth may be cleaned only after anesthesia has been administered.

Some biscuits do help to clean a dog's teeth but only minimally so. Better is a raw beef rib bone into which the teeth sink—but bones may not be for your dog. Chewing the tags of meat and cartilage from a beef soup bone will also help, but many dogs eat mushy food all their lives and have beautiful teeth with no tartar or gum disease.

Problems in Puppy Teeth. If a puppy has a prolonged fever before the permanent teeth erupt, the permanent teeth may have pits or eroded-appearing areas of the enamel which remain for life. These teeth used to be called "distemper teeth" as so many puppies had that disease with its prolonged fever.

When any one of the tetracyclines, which are antibiotics, is administered to a puppy under three months of age, the drug affects the developing permanent teeth, which are stained yellow when they appear. Such teeth appear to fluoresce when exposed to a black light. The yellow stain remains for the life of the dog and is of no consequence except for the unsightliness of jaundiced-looking teeth.

We see puppies that do not lose their puppy teeth on schedule. Most common is the failure of the sharp canines to fall out when the permanent canines come in. If uncorrected, the front upper teeth may slowly change their positions—to their detriment later in life—and the permanent canines are not only displaced but tend to develop gum problems. We had noticed that when puppies break their deciduous teeth before the permanent ones come in, the broken root appears to dissolve and drop out or be absorbed. We tried breaking off these persistent canines and they had the same fate. We have broken hundreds of these persistent canines with no resulting problem, and we do not use anesthesia in these cases.

Broken and Loose Teeth. Broken teeth do not appear to trouble dogs but they should be removed to prevent infection. Some dogs carry stones around in play and may wear their front teeth off and even their gums. Worn teeth are usually no problem. A gray tooth is one that has lost its blood supply from injury and as long as the gum around it is healthy it should not be removed.

When teeth are loose they should be extracted. This brings up the question, "How will the dog eat?" The answer is that dogs don't need teeth to eat the commercial foods we feed them, and any dog with a loose tooth doesn't use that tooth for chewing anyway. A loose tooth is painful to use.

After the extraction of all of his dog's teeth, one of our clients brought in his toothless pet and fed it hard dog biscuits in our presence. The dog crunched the biscuits with its gums and ate the pieces. And we once fed a group of dogs dry pelleted dog food, then gave them an emetic. The vomited pellets other than being moistened appeared as they had before ingestion. Chewing was unnecessary.

Abscessed Roots. From middle age on, dogs can have root abscesses, most of which drain into the mouth, but two teeth present problems that may seem unrelated. When an upper canine tooth has an abscessed root, the abscess may open into the nasal passage. This usually causes excess sneezing with blood at times.

The other problem tooth is the upper fourth premolar, which, when one root is abscessed, commonly necroses the bone over it and forms a swelling under the eye on the same side. Untreated, the abscess ruptures, drains, and heals only to repeat the performance until the tooth is extracted.

Anesthesia. All too often owners of very old dogs decline dental work requiring anesthesia, believing the old dog will die under anesthesia. As we have said, perhaps too often, an old dog can and does take anesthesia well and certainly a mouth full of abscessed teeth will not prolong a dog's life. Nor with its horrible breath will it endear itself to members of the family.

THE GUMS

The tartar buildup forms an ideal space between itself and the gums in which food lodges and bacteria develops, which cause a receding of the gum in that area. As the gum area recedes and more of the tooth is exposed, the tartar builds up on it and infection works around the tooth, and even follows it to the tip of its root.

Some dogs develop tartar that is necessary to remove every three or four months to prevent gum disease.

If your dog has this problem and will permit it, a simple method of removing tartar while it is soft is to dip a moistened wad of cotton in baking soda or powdered pumice stone and rub the discolored teeth. If done on a regular basis it prevents trips to the doctor.

THE TONGUE

The base of the tongue and surrounding areas are subject to infection from foreign bodies such as needles, splinters, and vegetation such as foxtail which penetrate the surface of the area and migrate as porcupine quills do. The seed fronds of some grasses when eaten penetrate the mucosa often at the junction of the two jaws. As the foreign body migrates, it may lodge in the area of a nerve, causing great pain and the inability to open the jaws wide. Some of these objects migrate upward, producing an abscess over an eye, or downward, producing an abscess under the jaw that resembles human mumps before it ruptures. If the foreign object does not slough out in the discharge the abscess heals and reforms.

The tongue can be lacerated from a dog's licking sharp objects. If it so happens that the tongue becomes impaled by the sharp edges of an open can's lid that's been pushed into the open can, an anesthetic is sometimes necessary in order to remove it if the dog is difficult. The dog should be seen immediately by a veterinarian, as should any dog whose laceration continues to bleed for more than twenty minutes.

Tumors of dogs' tongues are rare.

PROBLEMS OF THE THROAT

When it was once popular to remove tonsils from children, we veterinarians also removed many enlarged or inflamed tonsils. Today this surgery is virtually never performed on either humans or animals. Tonsillitis responds to many medications.

Pharyngitis and Laryngitis. The general terms used to designate inflammation of the pharynx and larynx are pharyngitis and laryngitis and they are applied to a number of conditions. Virus diseases and bacterial agents, such as streptococcal diseases, will all inflame the throat including the tonsils and the surrounding glands. The small lymph nodes and the salivary glands may also become inflamed. When these glands are felt between the finger and thumb, they may appear to be round instead of flat, as they normally are.

Coughing induced by any of these conditions tends to irritate these areas just as it does in humans. The tonsils and epiglottis take a great deal of strain. Tonsils may be found so greatly enlarged that they look like little roosters' combs protruding from their clefts and almost touching across the back of the throat. It is no wonder that dogs with chronically enlarged tonsils vomit frequently, even though they may not run fevers. They must feel as we would if we were to tickle our own throats with a feather.

But merely finding redness instead of the proper pink color, or small deep red areas perhaps only as large as pinheads, or enlarged tonsils is not a diagnosis. These conditions do not tell you *why* there is such inflammation or enlargement. To determine the basic cause, one must also have a complete knowledge of temperature, history, and other symptoms. The treatment depends on the disease that is causing the symptoms in evidence. Chronically enlarged tonsils can be removed safely; tonsils enlarged from upper respiratory diseases may not be removed as safely, since the surgery may provide access to the bloodstream for viruses and bacteria, which are ordinarily confined to the mucous layer of tissue. Once in the blood they may do further and more serious damage.

Your veterinarian will prescribe drugs if he or she is sure that the condition is of bacterial origin or if it is necessary to prevent bacteria from developing in the tissue damaged by viruses. But virtually no known drug can *cure* true virus diseases. Don't expect it anymore than you would expect your doctor to cure your cold or influenza. In both cases, however, some alleviation or easing is possible.

SALIVARY GLAND DISORDERS

Salivary Gland Infection. The salivary glands sometimes become infected with various kinds of organisms. Mumps in the parotid glands occasionally occurs, but with antibiotics the dog is soon cured. The parotid glands may also swell from collars that are too tight and squeeze them. Kicks, shot wounds, and traffic accidents may damage them, but such traumas are rare.

Obstructed Salivary Ducts. Three sets of salivary glands empty into the mouth of the dog through little tubes called ducts. We have considered the functions of these glands in Chapter 2.

The ducts may become obstructed by bacteria and sometimes even by foreign bodies such as stones, with the result that the saliva can't get out. The sight or smell of food causes the production of saliva and the gland becomes distended. If it is squeezed, the pressure will sometimes push the obstruction into the mouth. If this does not work, an incision through the skin must be made by the veterinarian and the thick, viscous, syrupy fluid drained out. Don't ever attempt to do this yourself, a puncture in the wrong place might sever the large jugular vein. After proper medication, the duct is freed, the incision heals, and the gland functions normally. In some cases the gland must be removed surgically.

FOREIGN OBJECTS

Every veterinarian has an imposing list of objects eaten by dogs that caused trouble, if not death. First, let us clear the air about ground glass, which over the years has been thought to be a cruel method of killing dogs. Just as ground glass will not kill dogs, so too a myriad of unusual objects pass through the digestive system unobserved. Most rocks, wood splinters, pins, needles, and safety pins seldom create serious problems. However, all of the above have been reported to cause obstruction or harm on occasion. A needle with a piece of thread is not as dangerous as one without, since the thread tends to leave the stomach first and pull the eye end of the needle on through the system without problem.

Foreign Bodies in the Mouth. Dogs frequently get bones or sticks wedged across the top of the mouth so tightly that proper forceps and considerable strength are necessary to dislodge them. Bone chips forced between the teeth sometimes cause gum ulceration. It is not uncommon to find a dog unable to close its mouth and, upon examination, discover that a tooth has been driven through the center of a short ham bone in such a way that the bone has become a long cap protruding above the tooth. The bone is often so firmly lodged that it is difficult to remove.

One of the more bizarre cases occurred at the University of Pennsylvania Emergency Clinic when a dog was brought in that, on a radiograph, showed in its stomach a long wooden-handled butcher's knife. It was removed without complication.

Any object that can expand after ingestion is more dangerous than ones that can't. Also, rubber objects such as balls, nursing nipples, and sponges may create a problem. We have removed peach pits and pieces of corncob many times. Most objects are trapped in the small intestine, and removal by surgery is the solution. Fever, loss of appetite, and vomiting are common indications that a foreign body is in the intestine; however, if the dog is given antibiotics any infection may be brought under control with the temperature returning to a normal 101° F. The vomiting will stop but the dog will not eat. When the antibiotics run out, the signs all return. In time the intestine may rupture, producing peritonitis and death.

One of our patients, an adult Newfoundland, ate a twelve-foot leather leash. The owner observed a foot of it hanging out and phoned for advice. We suggested, since the dog appeared normal, he gently pull the leash and cut off all he could extract. Later we learned the dog passed about two feet at a time, which was cut off until the twelve-foot leash was removed.

Another Newfoundland brought in was emaciated, had been unable to eat for months, and was obviously dying. We found that the dog had eaten the cord used to bind a roast of beef and had caught a loop under its tongue. After remaining there for months, the cord had cut the underpart of the tongue almost in half, which had healed afterward. The dog's death was due to peritonitis: the two ends of the cord dangling into the small intestine had cut through the lining of the gut.

Some foreign bodies, for example, a needle or an undigested bone chip, may pass through the intestine and turn sideways at the rectal area. Strain as it will, the dog cannot pass them and veterinary attention is required.

Bones. The question often arises, "Is it all right to feed my dog bones?" Since bones can cause obstruction problems, we see no advantage and many disadvantages to feeding dogs bones. It should be pointed out that a normal dog has hydrochloric acid in its stomach as we have, but it is almost twice as concentrated. The stomach fluids soften bones and blunt their sharp points quickly, so that they become harmless. The acids, coupled with a protein-digesting enzyme, do a very thorough job on most bones. A bone in a normal dog's stomach dissolves in a few hours. And there is little chemical action on the calcium in bones once they have left the stomach. However, if a dog has digestive upset and does not secrete enough acid, bone chips can be a disaster. Some dogs have too little acid and vomit bone chips, and these dogs, above all, should never be exposed to the problem.

When bones are eaten and digested they form a light-colored hard bowel movement that is usually difficult to pass, which is a good reason for not feeding bones. Some dogs become so constipated that literally gallons of water are required to be administered in enemas to remove the solid mass. It is not uncommon to find bones in the stools of dogs, or sharp bone chips in the rectum. All these are simply evidence of indigestion. However, if whole bones are found instead of the calcareous (containing lime) feces, it is an indication of stomach trouble.

ESOPHAGEAL INJURIES

The esophagus—the gullet, as it is often called—is the tube that leaves the pharynx parallel with the windpipe and down which—and sometimes up which—food passes.

The esophagus is subject to a number of ills, all of which cause the dog difficulty in swallowing and often in retaining food. Vomiting after eating may be a symptom of such difficulty, as well as of a number of other maladies. When the esophagus has been burned by an acid or caustic, or cut and scratched by any sharp object, the treatment that it needs is rest, so that it can heal. Many laypeople, not realizing how long a dog can go without food, try to force it to eat. This is a great mistake. Milk, broth, and foods that trickle down the gullet with as little irritation as possible are best.

STOMACH PROBLEMS

The stomach is susceptible to many of the same injuries as is the gullet. After all, it is in a sense only an enlargement of the gullet and a connection to the intestinal tract. It has a valve on each end and certain specialized functions.

Poisons, corrosives, and acids which might pass so rapidly down the esophagus they damage it little or not at all can lie in the stomach for long enough to do the damage there. Sharp objects can penetrate the stomach's walls easily; gas formation, if the gas is unable to escape, can balloon it so that its walls are stretched sometimes permanently. Parasites live in it. Hot or cold foods affect it. Grass, straw, hay, pine needles, hair, cloth waste, coarse shavings—all kinds of foreign bodies may irritate its delicate lining or form impactions. Stomach ulcers may occur on its inner surface. Infectious diseases may inflame it and retard its functions. Accidents may rupture it, especially if it is full of food; it may be punctured by bullets or sharp objects. Abnormal growths may appear on either of its surfaces. Adhesions may cause the intestines to cling to it. How can a layperson recognize any of these conditions? What can he or she do to alleviate them? Should a veterinarian be consulted?

We have considered the question of recognition and treatment of poisons in Chapter 10. Now let us consider the causes and care of some of the other common difficulties.

Penetration by Sharp Objects. When a dog shows pain and vomits blood you should consider the possibility of stomach punctures by sharp objects. If you have reason to suspect that the animal has swallowed any such object, prompt veterinary treatment—usually surgery—is necessary. X rays show some objects very clearly.

Foreign Material Causing Impactions. Mature dogs with impactions—masses of material that cannot be assimilated—generally show considerable pain, sometimes vomit, and lie around without showing much interest in what goes on about them. The condition is not always easy to detect. One more or less constant symptom is the tenseness of the abdominal muscles. This is a symptom of nearly all pain in and about the stomach. Occasionally dogs will assume a position of standing on their hind legs with their chests resting on the floor.

Puppies with foreign bodies in the stomach react similarly. They may be altogether so tense that one cannot feel the abdominal contents properly. When an emetic is given, the stomach empties and the abdominal muscles relax with the disappearance of the pain.

X rays may be helpful in revealing foreign bodies in the stomach, though they often fail to show such things as wood, glass, grass, or cigar butts.

When dogs eat pieces of meat or bones while lying on straw or bedding, very often the bedding sticks to the food and is swallowed. But dogs also eat such matter all by itself and apparently from choice. It is more or less to be expected that a dog will nibble at grass and sometimes vomit within an hour after eating it—or even within a few minutes. But there are dogs that eat great quantities of grass—they eat and eat until the mass in their stomachs cannot move one way or the other. Dogs sometimes develop a passion for pine needles—we have known them to stand up on their hind legs to eat needles off the trees. Dogs eating garbage, especially from restaurant pails or barrels, often consume quantities of bologna cellophane wrappings, paper, and other indigestible residue. Material of this sort forms a large lump in the stomach. In the Whitney Veterinary Clinic we have seen impactions containing twigs, cinders, hay, leaves all intertwined and causing great distress to the dogs. It is not uncommon for dogs to swallow women's stockings and other material of the sort.

But puppies take the prize for the oddities they will swallow. We have removed a ten-inch knitting needle from a ten-week-old Cocker Spaniel's throat; spark plugs from a puppy's stomach; metal jacks; golf balls partly chewed; rubber balls; a child's watch; dice, stones, cinders, coal of all sizes; steel wool; cigar butts; and glass, to mention only a few.

The treatment of such impactions is better left to your veterinarian. Occasionally, when long objects have been swallowed, one end will still be in sight and the object can be pulled out. Emptying an impaction of vegetable matter can frequently be accomplished with repeated large doses of mineral oil. If a tablespoonful is given twice a day it not only helps the mass to untangle but lubricates the irritating material as it passes through the intestines. We have recovered as much as two quarts of pine needles from a large dog, wads and wads of hay and straw, as well as rope, cloth, and quantities of sticks and bones.

There are impactions that only surgery can remove, foreign bodies that cannot be extracted in any other way. Needles and wire may penetrate the stomach, work through the liver and diaphragm, scratch the heart, and kill the dog unless removed in time. X rays are, of course, invaluable in such cases.

INTESTINAL PROBLEMS

The same kinds of troubles may occur in a dog's intestines as those we find afflicting the esophagus and stomach. The intestinal lining, however, is so delicate, studded as it is with microscopic villi, that it requires less irritation to damage it. A dog's intestine is approximately five times as long as the dog, and in that ten or fifteen feet a great many things can happen.

Evidence of pain, excretion of foul feces, vomiting, and fever are all symptoms of enteritis—inflammation of the intestinal lining—but it is not always easy to determine the exact diagnosis or cause.

From a study of the feces, however, one can tell a number of things about the condition of the intestine. Feces may be residues of undigested food. If they are, then one can tell whether the food is being properly digested. Feces may also be only wastes from the intestines and stomach. Or feces may be—and usually are—a mixture of the two as well as billions of helpful bacteria.

If we find undigested bones, pieces of meat, or food ingredients in their original form, we know something is wrong. If by using a microscope, we find worm eggs, then we know the dog has worms. Or if tapeworm segments appear on the feces, we know tapeworms are present. If a microscopic examination shows pieces of intestinal lining, some part of the intestine has been injured or eroded and has sloughed off. This is, needless to say, an indication of serious trouble.

If we find brown, partly digested blood, we know an injury exists well up in the intestine; whereas if the blood is bright red, it obviously comes from down in the lower part, probably from the colon. If the stool is especially evil-smelling, gray, and sticky, we can suspect insufficient bile is being secreted by the liver or that the bile duct is plugged, and we look for the trouble outside of the intestines. If the stool is fatty we may consider a pancreatic problem.

Occasionally, but rarely, the intestines of dogs twist and knot and preclude the passage of food. Sometimes a dog will have a hernia and a loop of intestine will pass into it, become filled with stool, and become useless.

In one four-month-old puppy a peculiar lump developed just beside the loin and a fetid odor rose from the ooze which seeped from the opening in the lump. The tip of a wire could be felt at this point. When pulled out, it turned out to be an eight-inch piece of wire used to seal freight cars. The pup had eaten the wire and passed it into the intestines, where it had made a fistula through the skin. Yet the dog had never missed a meal. The intestines become more amazing as one understands them better.

Foods taken after there has been intestinal damage must be soft; do not feed the dog bone or bran, which can scratch the soft intestinal lining. Bone chips also irritate it. Meat, cheese, and milk are largely digested and have little residue. Boiled milk, hard-boiled eggs, and soda crackers all tend to be constipating; they can be given when there is diarrhea but should be avoided if the stools are firm. Glucose, in the form of corn syrup or as dextrose powder dissolved in water or milk, makes excellent food and is quickly assimilated. It is an incomplete diet to be sure but is valuable both as a form of energy and because of its tendency to prevent dehydration. Dogs often can retain it when they vomit any other food.

Intussusception. Another cause of bleeding is a telescoping of the bowel called intussusception. A fold of intestines slides inside the adjacent intestine and is gradually forced farther and farther along until perhaps ten or twelve inches has become invaginated. This really means that three times that much of the intestine is involved, as can be easily understood. A ten-inch intussusception involves thirty inches of intestine. The invaginated part dies from pressure and because its blood supply is compromised. Food cannot move through it, nor moisture.

Once suspicion points to this condition, detection is not difficult, because a long, swollen section with an abrupt beginning can generally be felt quite easily through the abdominal wall. Usually the dog so affected vomits everything it eats. It becomes dehydrated, its temperature rises, its expression and attitude show pain. A day or two after the condition has become established, the fecal material begins to appear watery and to have an acrid odor. Usually this watery secretion turns reddish from the blood exuded by the entombed intestine, whose lower end is free.

The causes are not well understood. We reported a case in which a mother dog and six puppies all developed the ailment and died. No one had the faintest suspicion that they were so affected until the third had died. The mother was operated on, but three more intussusceptions developed. It has been said that giving strong purgatives tends to produce intussusceptions, but these particular dogs had received no medication. Foreign bodies that stick to the intestinal lining are often implicated. And growths, like large polyps, sometimes move downward, dragging the intestine after them in a fold.

Surgery is the one treatment for this condition. A piece of intestine has to be removed together with the blood supply to the section. It is true, however, that there have been cases in which intussusceptions have just started and been detected by feeling, and surgery has been averted by manipulation, which has worked the fold out and prevented its further development.

Intestinal Parasites. Intestinal parasites may cause bloody stools and diarrhea. Probably because of their toxins, even roundworms cause profuse diarrhea in puppies. Hookworms, which are like little leeches, draw large amounts of blood, living on the serum and letting the red cells loose in the intestine. They are the worst kind of worm when it comes to the production of bloody stools. Coccidia are protozoa which, because of their great numbers and consequent damage to the intestinal wall, produce bloody diarrhea. These conditions are easy to cure by the simple procedures of eliminating worms and waiting for the body to build up its immunity against coccidia. (See Chapter 23.)

Constipation. Difficult evacuation, constipation, is difficult usually because the fecal mass is too large or too hard to pass through the anus, because its consistency is such that it causes pain, or because of ineffectual peristalsis, weakness in the muscles that effect evacuation. Unless the dog is greatly overweight, an impacted mass in the rectum may easily be felt through the abdominal walls.

One of the most common victims of constipation is the overfat, underexercised city dog. For this condition there is little excuse. It is caused more frequently than not by feeding an unbalanced mixture of dog biscuits, meat, and bones. Biscuits are usually made principally of second-grade white flour. Meat has very little residue. Bones have a dry mineral residue. When the three are fed together without other material, the stools resemble a kind of modified concrete.

Enlargement of the prostate gland frequently causes constipation when the diet is not regulated accordingly. The prostate, being just below the rectum in front of the pelvis, when enlarged will present a formidable obstruction which leaves a very small space for the passage of the feces through the rectum.

A dog whose pelvis has been broken and has healed in a partially collapsed position is likely to be constipated again and again. The dog may have no more than half the natural pelvic orifice through which the stool can pass. Special attention must be given to its diet.

As a matter of fact, diet is related to all forms of constipation. If owners would simply feed their dogs properly, the bowels could be easily regulated, unless actually affected by a tumor. Too often, however, owners are willing to resort to drugs rather than take the trouble to regulate the dog's diet to relieve constipation. The addition of an item of food or the elimination of one is usually all that is needed. Certain types of food cause increased laxation: the coarse, raw fibers in bran or alfalfa meal; milk sugar in skim milk, buttermilk, or whey; raw egg white; and fruits such as pears, apples, and peaches. Other foods are constipating: bones; muscle meat; hard-boiled eggs; boiled white rice; barley water; and dog biscuits. If a dog's diet is regulated to include the proper amounts of the right types of food, constipation can easily be prevented or relieved.

Cure for the temporary condition is to give enemas, and if they do not enable the dog to expel the mass, the veterinarian will have to crush it with the aid of instruments until it is small enough to pass out —a disagreeable experience for any dog.

Accidents. The intestines are less often affected by accidents than are the other organs. It is not often that crushed or ruptured intestines are found in a postmortem examination of even an animal that has been run over by a vehicle. The liver and spleen may be split open and mashed, and the pelvis broken in many places, but unless the intestines are filled with a constipated mass they are usually unharmed.

It is true, however, that they can be punctured by bullets or bird shot, but sharp objects that penetrate the abdomen generally push the intestines aside. It is amazing how resistant they are. We once had the job of replacing a yard of intestine in the intestinal cavity of a dog that had received a four-inch tear in the abdomen. The intestine had worked out and had been dragged through dirt and hemlock needles in the woods. The owner brought in his pet wrapped in a blanket, with little hope that anything could be done. The dog was anesthetized, the intestines were washed, and the soil and needles flushed out of the abdomen. After the intestine was replaced, the wall was sutured and the dog recovered.

RECTAL AND ANAL PROBLEMS

Accumulation in the Anal Glands. Ailments of the anal glands, also called pouches (see photographs), are among the most common troubles with dogs. The normal secretion of these small glands is a yellowish or brownish liquid that is expressed by muscles when the dog is frightened. If too much secretion accumulates in the glands, the dog often sits down and drags itself along in order to force the liquid out. This puts pressure on the glands, and the fluid oozes out and is wiped on the ground, the rug, or elsewhere.

If the dog is unable to squeeze the fluid out, the glands swell with the accumulation and then become thick with bacterial growth. It may be thick, black, and sticky, or thin, yellow, and filled with curds, or gray and dry, or brown and thick, almost like feces. The glands, instead of being of any use as secretory organs, become pouches causing trouble. We have expressed more than a tablespoonful of vile-smelling, thickish fluid from a Newfoundland dog and more than a teaspoonful from a Cocker Spaniel.

It is difficult to say how much harm is done by the accumulation that develops in anal pouches. It hardly seems possible, however, that such vile material could be retained in these glands without some of their toxins becoming absorbed to the detriment of the dog.

Expressing the gland contents is so simple that anyone can do it if he or she is not too squeamish. First locate the glands. They feel like small or large lumps in the skin, one on each side and below the anus. Spread a piece of absorbent cotton over the hand that will cover the anus. Squeezing with the thumb and index finger behind and slightly below the glands forces the liquid or gummy contents out of the ducts through the opening of the anus onto the cotton.

But be sure that the cotton is held over the anus. If you neglect this, the stuff may spurt and soil you badly. The odor is *extremely obnoxious* and stays in cloth for a long while.

Fat dogs are difficult to treat because it is so hard to feel the glands; in these cases a veterinarian should be employed to do the job. In some cases he may have to insert one finger inside the anus and squeeze from both sides.

Once thoroughly cleaned out, and kept cleaned out, the glands shrink considerably, so that the dog no longer drags its rear along the ground—an activity which, incidentally, is your best indication that his glands need expressing.

Abscesses in the Anal Glands. There are occasions when the accumulation of debris in an anal gland becomes infected and an abscess forms. First evidence is the dog's constant licking of the spot. It becomes red, distended, and smooth with a soft center. It is too sore for the dog to sit and drag himself. Some dogs run about uneasily, as if unable to have a comfortable moment.

If the abscess is untreated and ruptures of its own accord, a large, slow-healing opening is left which discharges for days and occasions incessant licking. The dog is likely to leave a spot everywhere he sits. But when the abscess is opened surgically and flushed out deeply every day, it will usually heal rapidly and leave no scar.

There are cases where the anal glands become so troublesome they should be removed surgically by your veterinarian, who can do it with one of several ingenious methods. This ends the nuisance permanently.

LIVER PROBLEMS

A dog's liver is less affected by disease and injury than are other organs of its body. In the first place, though it is larger in proportion than the livers of many other species, it is quite well protected by its location. Moreover, it repairs itself after many abuses. Few dogs actually die of liver trouble, but there are a few liver problems of some importance that a layperson can frequently recognize. Along with liver disorders we include those of the gallbladder, that little balloon in which bile is stored as it is manufactured by the liver.

One of the most obvious signs that all is not well with the liver is the yellow pigment seen in the whites of a dog's eyes, in its skin, gums, and mucous membranes. When these turn yellow the dog does not have a *disease* called jaundice; he has a *condition* called jaundice. The disease that causes the condition is not always apparent. It might be toxemia, or an occlusion of the bile duct, or a tumor.

Jaundice, with or without a pasty gray stool, is a warning sign. It should give all dog owners cause for concern and send them hurrying to the veterinarian.

Hepatitis. When the liver is enlarged, some of it pushes behind the protection of the ribs and can be felt easily. Liver damage from any cause which produces enlargement may be permanent but is usually only temporary. Even though the liver does reduce in size to normal, it still may not be able to function normally.

Obstructive Jaundice. Any condition that prevents bile from escaping into the intestine may be said to be responsible for its becoming absorbed in the blood and turning the tissues of the body yellow. The urine, too, becomes yellow or orange. The stools, without bile mixed with them, become gray and sticky.

Obstructive jaundice is caused in dogs by roundworms which get into the bile duct and plug it, by inflammation of the duct, by stones in the gallbladder which block the exit, or by cancer or growths which press against the duct or gallbladder.

Your veterinarian should be consulted. When the difficulty is caused by a simple blocking of the gallbladder, two household substances will cause it to discharge its contents—fat and any magnesium salt (Epsom salts, milk of magnesia). And a teaspoonful of Epsom salts sometimes brings good results.

Gallstones. Though gallstones have been reported, they occur rarely in dogs. If the diagnosis is gallstones, feeding fat or giving magnesium salts may be unwise. Your veterinarian should provide the treatment or surgery.

Infections. Another cause of jaundice, not of liver origin, is the breaking down of red blood cells, as in bacterial disease (see page 398), which also damages the liver. Still another is *infectious hepatitis* (see page 396).

Toxins. Poisoning often injures the liver and indirectly causes jaundice. Poisoning with such metals as mercury, arsenic, phosphorus, or thallium may in time cause a reduction from normal in the size of the liver. In such cases the symptoms may be grayish stools, general debility, and occasional vomiting.

Growths. Tumors are often found in dogs' livers at a postmortem. Livers are found greatly enlarged (hypertrophied) and occasionally are filled with connective tissue (cirrhosis). Abscesses may form when bacteria invade the liver and multiply.

Fatty Livers. These occur in enormously overweight house dogs. Fat cells become interspersed among the liver cells, but how much this interferes with their function is not known. It is impossible to feel the liver or any of the organs in an overweight dog because of the surplus fat all over and inside of the abdomen. Weight reduction removes fat from the liver as it does elsewhere about the body.

Injuries. The liver may be pierced or cut by sharp objects that work through the stomach wall. Being run over, falling from heights, receiving blows may cause the liver to rupture.

Again let us urge you to consult your veterinarian if you have any reason to believe that liver trouble is present. Watch for the telltale symptoms—jaundice and gray, sticky stools accompanied by debility.

VOMITING

Although vomiting has been considered as a symptom to specific problems, it may be helpful to review some of its ramifications.

There are two forms of vomiting. Projectile vomiting is involuntary vomiting, where a sudden contraction of the stomach causes fluids to spurt out of the pet's mouth. It may occur during play or excitement and is usually not an indication of a serious condition.

The second form is voluntary, where there are active contractions of the abdomen and the animal lowers its head with each contraction. This is repeated until contents of the stomach and/or the esophagus are discharged.

Acute Vomiting. When a dog ingests toxic material, the lining of the stomach may be irritated or the toxin, absorbed into the blood, may affect nerve centers in the brain. Both conditions can cause vomiting. Moreover, inflammation of the brain or toxic substances from tissue destruction which are blood-borne to the brain also may cause vomiting.

A sensitivity to food must be considered, with perhaps the most common item causing vomiting being pork. But the amount of the food causing vomiting is important. Many dogs eat a strip of cooked bacon or a bite or two of pork roast and have no problem, but any more than that brings on the problem.

It appears to us there are dogs that eat the same diet day after day and because of a particular ingredient or ingredients vomit perhaps once every week or two. Some of these dogs eat grass before vomiting, suggesting that they eat it to vomit.

The percentages of the various ingredients of commercial dog foods change from time to time. In such a competitive business the ingredients are the result of a computer's printout. The computer is programmed with information indicating a balanced and nutritionally complete ration. Then the costs of all the possible ingredients available are fed into it, and the resulting formula is the least expensive possible. So if fish meal is less expensive than another source of protein, there may be more in a certain batch than has been in previous batches. If your dog has a problem with fish meal, for example, vomiting may result.

The dog with occasional vomiting is one of the more difficult to diagnose. However, one simple method of treatment is to feed the animal a simple diet with few ingredients, such as one of one third cooked hamburger, one third cooked rice, and one third canned stewed tomatoes. The diet must be given exclusively over a period of time long enough to demonstrate no vomiting occurs. If one commercial food is a problem, change to another and, if none can be found, compound one of your own.

A chronic vomiting dog that promptly eats the vomitus may not secrete sufficient acid in its stomach. The second time down stimulates enough hydrochloric acid for digestion. Salting the diet helps a percentage of these dogs and adding diluted hydrochloric acid during the preparation of food often helps.

It is normal for the nursing bitch at weaning time to eat a meal and vomit it for her puppies to eat. This is their first solid food when she follows nature's dictates. In the wild her mate does the same.

Dogs can and do live with intestinal parasites. They may not live as well but they do live. When the parasite load is too great, especially with tapeworms, toxins released by the worms cause vomiting.

When the body cannot rid itself of many substances, not only ingested substances but also wastes of normal metabolism, vomiting results. A good example is the geriatric dog whose kidneys no longer filter wastes from the blood properly. Uremia develops with vomiting. In the case of uremia a urinelike odor may be detected on the dog's breath.

Acalasia is a defect thought to be an inherited one, but environmental problems may also cause it. It is a pouchlike area involving the esophagus anterior to the diaphragm. When inherited, it is usually observed soon after the weaning puppy eats its first few meals. Some dogs show signs of this problem at three or four months. When the puppy eats a meal, a percentage does not enter the stomach but rather gathers in this pouch. After a while the uncomfortable puppy vomits the contents of the pouch. Surgery is difficult in this area and fortunately is often unnecessary.

Some years ago a beautiful but emaciated Irish Setter pup with a history of vomiting after eating was brought in to us. After a few swallows of barium, acalasia was diagnosed by X rays. We explained the difficulty, danger, and expense of surgery, but the owner was convinced that the choice of surgery over euthanasia was the better choice. Since surgery could not be scheduled for three days, we suggested the puppy be fed from a table so that gravity might help the food gain entrance to the stomach. The day the surgery was to happen the owner phoned to say the puppy had not vomited since being fed in that manner. He had put the food in a dish on a windowsill on which the puppy placed its front feet, and by the puppy's eating in that almost vertical position the problem was corrected. In two months that setter had gained twenty pounds and looked beautiful.

Another genetic cause of vomiting, which we presume can also be caused by injury, is a stricture of the outlet of the stomach, which prevents food from entering the small intestine when it's ready to go there. This vomiting of very acid and sometimes foul-smelling vomitus occurs many hours after eating. The dog will not reingest this material. Special diets may not help here, in which case surgery is suggested.

There is a long list of infective agents that may cause vomiting. Hemorrhagic gastroenteritis is a catchall term for any disease causing bleeding in the stomach and intestine. Several viruses discussed in Chapter 24 and a host of bacterial diseases can cause such bleeding.

Blood accompanying vomiting does not always indicate a disaster since it may be the result of such vigorous vomiting that small blood vessels rupture and produce small streaks or even clots of blood. A surprisingly small amount of blood mixed with a large amount of other fluid appears to be all blood.

Vomiting does give us an indication of the area of the intestines that are affected in cases of diarrhea. There is usually no vomiting if only the lower bowel, the colon, is affected, but if after a few days of diarrhea the dog begins to vomit it suggests the infection has ascended to the small intestine. In such cases there may be a regurgitation of bile from the small intestine into the stomach, resulting in bile-tinged gastric juice and saliva.

DIARRHEA

The causes of loose bowel movements are as many and as varied as are those in vomiting. Some overlap, having common sources. Toxic substances ingested may irritate the full length of the gastrointestinal tract, resulting in loose bowel movements sometimes with blood.

When food enters the intestine it is in a semisolid form with ample fluid secreted by the stomach wall, even if the food was a dry kibble when ingested. As the semisolid material enters the large intestine, called the colon, or the lower bowel, it is still of moist consistency, but as it descends the colon it is dehydrated, resulting in an acceptably formed fecal mass.

Anything that interferes with this dehydration or anything that reverses the process causing fluid to be secreted into the colon results in diarrhea.

A sensitivity to food is high on the list of causes. A sudden change of diet apparently will produce a reversal of the dehydration process so that a bowl of milk to a dog that has not had milk in some time acts as a laxative or worse. Pet shops rarely offer puppies milk and instruct new puppy owners to withhold milk for that reason. After giving milk for a few days or making other changes of diet, if you are persistent, the condition is self-corrected.

It is, therefore, obvious that changes of diet be gradual when possible. A tablespoon of milk to a twenty-pound dog has no ill effect and if the amount is increased gradually over a period of four or five days no problem develops. Incidentally, a cup of skim milk to a dog is a good natural laxative.

One of the more common causes of loose stools is whipworm infestation. These parasites live in a blind pouch called the cecum and on down through the colon to the anus. In a dog with a serious case of whipworms, diarrhea with bright blood and mucus will precede death. The whipworm-infected dog is unhealthy, tires easily, and is not quite as responsive as it was before the infestation. This is a matter of degree, however, since dogs through the ages have adapted to life with a few of many types of parasites. The problem arises when the worm infestation exceeds the dog's natural resistance.

Late one night we received a frantic phone call from a gentleman who insisted his dog had been poisoned. It was passing bright blood and mucus, which is in effect part of the lining of the tract. We asked that the dog be rushed in. It was dead on arrival and the necropsy revealed the surface of the lower bowel to be so covered with parasites that the dog appeared to have a fur coat from the cecum to the anus. For more on this subject refer to Chapter 23.

Hookworms, too, can cause loose bowel movements along with a host of protozoan organisms, a good example of which is coccidial, also discussed in Chapter 23.

Just as "tourists' " disease, a bacterial infection, affects people, there is a small army of bacterial diseases that can affect our dogs. Most of these diseases, perhaps more than 75 percent, fortunately are easily overcome by the dogs, but in the case of some, help is required from you. If you can visualize a bright red rash over the lining of the intestines and then consider a rough stool mass passing over and further irritating it, we think you will better appreciate that the type of food fed to an infected dog is of great importance. In the first place, a food that may enhance the undesirable bacterial flora does not make sense.

Fighting fire with fire seems to work in this situation in that the introduction of helpful bacteria can theoretically outgrow the disease-producing ones to the advantage of the dog. Yogurt (lactobacillis acidophilus) helps some dogs with bacterial infections. We prefer a bland diet, such as well-cooked meat and cooked vegetables well blended into a creamy consistency. Many commercial dog foods have undigestible roughage and bonemeal, which can further irritate the already irritated intestinal mucosa.

If the diarrhea is not too severe, a diet of one third cooked hamburger, boiled rice, and stewed tomatoes is remarkably effective. The importance of the tomatoes is that they have pectin, a jellylike indigestible material that surrounds each seed and acts as a lubricant. A further advantage is the high percentage of digestibility of this diet, resulting in good nourishment with a small volume of waste. Because it is so digestible, the food mass does not distend the irritated intestines, a further advantage.

But when diet alone may not be enough to inhibit the bacterial growth, antibiotics are useful. Some of the coating agents, although more effective for stomach-wall coating when given in large amounts, will coat the intestines, which is a plus. Don't permit diarrhea to become too well-entrenched before asking for veterinary help.

Virus diarrhea may be more common than suspected in the past. We have all heard of outbreaks of virus diarrhea in newborn baby wards in our human hospitals. When such a condition exists all the babies who are well enough are sent home and no new babies are permitted near the infected ward. Eventually everything is sterilized and the wards are repainted before they can be used again.

Since we can readily identify bacteria in diarrhea and only with special techniques identify viruses, most diarrhea is diagnosed as bacterial in nature. There is more and more evidence that many of the so-called bacterial diarrheas are essentially viral with bacterial secondary invaders. It is entirely possible that certain bacteria work with certain viruses to cause disease that one alone could not cause. Parvovirus and coronavirus infections apparently do cause diarrhea and are considered in Chapter 24.

When persistent diarrhea without vomiting is present we can assume that only the large intestine is affected. If the cause ascends into the small intestine, vomiting may accompany the problem, and if the gastric area is invaded, vomiting is common.

Dehydration can be a complication of diarrhea with or without vomiting. Dogs have gone without any food for months and survived, so a few days or a week is not as tragic as some pet owners believe. To maintain hydration, however, a clear broth such as chicken broth, bouillion, or consommé should be given to the dog. If diarrhea is permitted to progress it will contribute to the demise of an animal that could recover if proper hydration were maintained. In extreme cases, a consultation with your veterinarian often results in your dog's being hospitalized and given intravenous fluids—and in your dog surviving.

18

Problems of the Respiratory System and the Circulatory System

THE RESPIRATORY SYSTEM

The respiratory system is composed of the nose, the windpipe, or trachea, the bronchial tubes into which the trachea divides, and the lungs. Like other parts of the body, each of these is subject to disease.

The primary function of the lungs is to absorb oxygen from the air and to eliminate carbon dioxide. However, there are many other functions, such as warming cold air and cooling hot air and carrying scents to the olfactory area in smelling. We should not overlook vocalizing. In the process of inhaling and exhaling, the particles that are not trapped by the moist nasal membranes may be trapped by the lungs. If the dog lives in an industrial area its lungs will become black as human lungs do.

The Nose. When an animal's nose is moist with a clean, watery dampness, it is a sign of good health. This moisture is one means of temperature regulation. The moisture of the nose is evaporated by the air passing through it, and thus the nose is kept cold. On very cold days a dog's nose is dry. When it curls up it puts its nose down between its legs. A dog that has just uncurled from resting or sleeping in this position has a warm nose.

The noses of trailing breeds sometimes crack deeply; often they become worn and the lips irritated until they are raw. Medication is impossible because the dog licks medicine off as soon as it is applied. A dog heals itself, and medication is unnecessary except in deep cracks, where the tongue does not reach.

Noses that change color with the seasons are not abnormal and seem to be characteristic of certain breeds. Irish Setters, for example, may have black noses in one season and liver-colored noses at another. The reasons for color changes in noses have not been definitely established. Some people believe that the sun darkens noses; others hold the contrary view that the sun bleaches them.

The purulent nasal discharge following diseases such as distemper may last for several weeks but is usually either self-limiting or corrected with the help of antibiotics and other drugs.

COLDS. Although dogs do have disease conditions with many signs similar to human colds, they do not have colds—only humans and chimpanzees have colds. But we still get people who tell us their dog has a cold in its back, which is preposterous. A cold is a respiratory disease. When some of the flu viruses affect humans in a household it is not unusual for owners to observe some of the same signs in the house dog, but the symptoms are so mild it is hardly worth mentioning.

SNEEZING AND NOSEBLEED. There are many reasons why dogs sneeze: allergies; inhalation of fumes, or caustic or acid dust; nasal parasites; foreign bodies such as from the weed, foxtail, or a bit of grass; and tumors.

Among nasal parasites a dog may contract is one called the nasal mite *(pneumonesis caninum)*. The first one we observed came from a dog that had traveled widely with his Army officer owner, who told us he had observed small insects on his sneezing dog's nose from time to time. We thought he had seen some insect from vegetation but, rather than telling him we doubted that they came from his dog's nose, we gave him a vial with alcohol and requested he send us one if he saw one in the future. In a week we received the vial in the mail with three specks in the fluid. Under the microscope they were unmistakably mites of some sort so we sent them to an expert at Yale for identification. We chuckled when they were returned to us along with a note suggesting we send them to an expert at Harvard. That expert suggested we send them to an expert at the University of Maryland, who did indeed identify them.

The texts mentioned nasal and lung mites but there was no suggestion as to the treatment, so we asked the Maryland expert about the insect's life cycle, hoping to arrive at a treatment, and his answer was surprising. He wrote that the mite had been found in whales off the coast of Alaska, in lions in Africa, and in a dog in Orange, Connecticut, and he didn't have any idea what the life cycle might be.

Since then we have seen many cases and we believe we have cured the more recent ones. One client had observed one of her two German Shepherds with this parasite. We suggested she place a dichlorvis bar in a large plastic bag and place the bag over the dog's head. Dichlorvis is a gas which impregnates the plastic strips used to kill flying insects and is available from hardware and even grocery stores. In preparation she placed the plastic bar on a chair. Both dogs approached and smelled it —and hundreds of insects crawled out of their noses. The dogs were cured by placing them in a small room with the exposed insecticide plastic strip every night for two weeks.

Nosebleed can be both the cause and effect of sneezing. It is frequently produced by long, continuous, and violent sneezing. Many dogs sneeze so violently that they bump their noses on the floor or ground sharply enough to cause bleeding from the injury. Nosebleed may also be due to tumors.

In mild cases of sneezing or nosebleed, administration of a sedative will allow the dog to rest and promote healing. Stopping the sneezing permits clots to form. The use of ice packs is helpful. Injecting ice water or drugs directly into the nasal passages, however, is likely to cause worse sneezing. If nosebleed cannot be controlled by any of these methods, your veterinarian may examine the area with special instruments with the dog under anesthesia.

COUGHING. There is a discussion of kennel cough in Chapter 24. This is the most common cause of persistent coughing in dogs. In the early stages it occurs only after considerable exercise, but as the problem progresses it becomes more pronounced so that even moderate exercise and excitement bring on a coughing spell. In the older dog the most common cause of coughing is congestive heart disease, which will be discussed later in this chapter.

The dog with certain heart problems coughs because the weak heart cannot profuse the lungs with blood adequately, resulting in an excess of carbon dioxide. The excess carbon dioxide in the blood affects the cough reflex center in the brain, causing the cough. When the cough stops or is markedly reduced, this is in one sense helpful to the veterinarian who had prescribed drugs to strengthen the heart: the cough becomes a barometer of the heart's condition. There is also commonly a fluid buildup in the lungs of dogs with some heart problems and coughing helps clear some of it.

As with humans, coughing dislodges phlegm when necessary, which dogs usually swallow. Persistent coughing is a good reason to seek veterinary help.

THE TRACHEA

Tracheitis and Bronchitis. Tracheitis, or inflammation of the windpipe, and bronchitis, inflammation of the bronchial tubes, often occur at the same time. Their general symptom is coughing. This may be a dry cough, a phlegmy cough, or a mild, annoying cough such as humans often have during the resolution stage of coryza, or cold. In some cases the coughing may be so paroxysmal that it causes vomiting, and it is not unusual for a constant irritating cough to cause bleeding from the lining of the windpipe.

When inflammation is intense, shortness of breath is another symptom; the air spaces may become so constricted that the normal flow of air is retarded. Moreover, a considerable amount of mucus is discharged and this further interferes with normal breathing. Coughing is partly an attempt to rid the system of this phlegm.

The inflammation is symptomatic of disease, since tracheitis and bronchitis are seldom disease entities in themselves. Treatment of the cough in such cases usually involves elimination of the underlying disease of which this inflammation is a part. Consequently, the first step must be an exact determination of the cause of the inflammation, as this will in turn determine the most effective treatment. There are several viruses that inflame these tissues; certain biologics may be helpful in combating bacteria which enter the tissue weakened by a virus infection.

If the inflammation is due to inhaling irritating smoke, gas, or dust, it may be advisable to prevent coughing to allow healing. Often there is the problem of deciding whether the cough produces the irritation or vice versa. If the cough is productive, that is, if it raises phlegm, it would seem inadvisable to administer drugs that help stop the coughing. But if a nagging cough merely irritates the membranes without serving a useful purpose, a drug like codeine may be used for relief. A dog's coughing sometimes troubles the owner more than the dog, and in these cases stopping the cough is almost essential. A mixture of drugs, sold in every drugstore, is frequently prescribed by veterinarians. Some coughs are cured by the simple expedient of using sedatives to give the involved tissues as much rest as possible.

PROBLEMS OF THE LUNGS

Pneumonia. Dogs may contract many types of pneumonia: bronchopneumonia, lobar pneumonia, verminous pneumonia, traumatic pneumonia, and inhalation pneumonia. Owners, however, need not concern themselves with learning to distinguish among these types. It is sufficient if they are able to recognize the symptoms common to all kinds of pneumonia—fever, shallow breathing, the loss of appetite. Mucus may be discharged from the dog's nose, but this does not always occur. The chief distinguishing feature is the vibrating, grating sound in the dog's chest. If these symptoms are observed, the dog should be taken to the veterinarian.

Treatment consists of killing or inhibiting the germs that cause the disease and maintaining the animal in a comfortable environment. Pneumonia germs are almost always present in a dog; pneumonia is an opportunistic disease which develops when the system is run down or when the guards against disease are off duty. It is not necessarily contagious. Therefore it is apparent that the dog must be restored to good health principally by improving its general physical condition. It should be encouraged to eat by being fed the foods it likes best. If it is cold, place the dog in a warm environment.

As mentioned in Chapter 25, there are many viruses that predispose a dog to pneumonia; some cause virus pneumonia.

Treatment is started as early as possible. Since the dog's body is no longer called upon to do all the work of combating the invading pneumonocci or other germs that cause the disease, it is not necessary to wait for the crisis, which was once a crucial time in pneumonia medication. In an advanced case, in which the lungs are badly congested, the use of an oxygen tent may be necessary to save the dog's life. Your veterinarian will decide if such treatment is needed.

VERMINOUS PNEUMONIA. Verminous pneumonia is common in puppies. A puppy has it in some degree when the larvae of roundworms and hookworms are tunneling in the lungs. This type of pneumonia disappears with the elimination of the larval invasion. However, as there is always the possibility of bacterial pneumonia getting a foothold in the injured tissue, a few days' dosage of an antibiotic may be advisable.

INHALATION PNEUMONIA. Inhalation pneumonia is due to contamination of the lungs with dust, gases, smoke, and oily vapors which injure the delicate membranes. Treatment can do little more than prevent bacterial invasion. Drugs keep these organisms from taking hold and allow the injured tissue time to regenerate.

Another form of inhalation pneumonia is that caused by improper medication. When an owner pours mineral oil, castor oil, or drugs in an oily base indiscriminately into the back of a pet's mouth, the dog can easily inhale some of the liquid into the windpipe. When oil or other material difficult to expel stays in the lungs, tissue death may result and putrefactive bacteria multiply, causing death.

City dogs inhale so much dust that their lungs on postmortem examination show black mottling effects from it. Dogs kept about dusty factories and plants where stone dust fills the air may be victims of *anthricosis;* the lungs become impregnated with the fine powder, which stays in the tissue for life.

Edema of the Lungs. When the body has fluid retention the lungs may also fill up and develop edema. Shortness of breath is a symptom of this condition. Besides the pressure from abdominal distension, the fluid in the lungs puts a burden on the respiratory system and demands drastic withdrawal of fluids from the body with drugs.

Emphysema. As an aftermath of diseases of the lungs—and from other unknown causes—sections of the honeycomb lung tissue break down, allowing large pockets to form. These pockets often collect mucus. When many of these pockets are present, a great deal of the lung tissue is useless and the dog has to breathe faster and deeper to oxygenate the blood. This is the disease which in horses is commonly known as heaves. The symptoms are similar in both species. There is no cure, but temporary alleviation of symptoms is possible. Treatment, however, should never be considered more than temporary relief.

Pleurisy. After pneumonia, when bacteria may have worked through the pleura or coating of the lungs, there may be infection across the chest cavity to the pleura on the rib side. In such cases the two surfaces may adhere to each other in spots when healing is completed. While the inflammation is present, an exceedingly painful pleurisy can result. Areas of the chest cavity may become filled with fluid, which the veterinarian may have to tap and draw off. There may be areas of fluid that prevent heart and lung sounds from passing clearly. When these areas are tapped with the fingers, a dull thud is heard instead of a hollow, healthy resonance. In "dry" pleurisy a sharp, sandpapery, grating sound is produced with every inspiration and expiration. Treatment for pleurisy is the same as for pneumonia.

Hydrothorax and Pyothorax. Hydrothorax, or fluid in the chest cavity, and pyothorax, or pus in the chest cavity, may follow lung infections, growths, or accidents. Treating these is a task for your veterinarian. The symptoms are shallowness in the dog's breathing and, frequently, bluing of the tongue and gums, resulting from the dog's inability to obtain sufficient oxygen. Your veterinarian may draw the fluid off by tapping or by inserting a drain for several days.

Tumors. Tumors in the chest cavity are not uncommon. They are difficult to diagnose but may be suspected when the dog loses weight too rapidly, has shortness of breath, and develops an abnormal expansion of the rib cage. Tumors sometimes occur in the lungs themselves. This type often sends out buds (metastases) which grow in other parts of the body. Colonies from one type often appear in the skin. Conscientious owners will ask their veterinarian to have every surgically removed growth examined in a competent laboratory. Radiology is the prime diagnostic procedure for lung problems.

THE CIRCULATORY SYSTEM

The Heart. The heart has many diseases and problems. The dog owner will learn to recognize some of the more common conditions; others he or she will not be able to diagnose or treat. To diagnose heart problems the veterinarian uses a stethoscope, X rays, and an electrocardiograph. Valve dysfunction, due to several causes, is of one general class. Inflammation of the pericardium is another. The pericardium, you will remember, is a kind of unattached skin or bag about the heart which is formed by the pleura. The area between the heart and the pericardium may become infected and distended with fluid. The heart muscle itself may become infected (myocarditis) or dilated. Its walls can stretch until the heart becomes two or three times as large as normal. Occasionally a heart is damaged as a result of an accident.

LEAKY VALVES. The hissing sound characteristic of leaky valves can be clearly heard if you listen with your ear against a dog's chest, close to the heart. A person with a keen sense of touch may even feel leaky valves through his or her fingertips when picking up a dog, if the hand supports the dog under the heart. Leaky valves may sometimes produce such potent vibrations that no one can fail to feel them.

You should learn to listen to the heartbeat and interpret what you hear. If you hear the heartbeat skip every fifth or sixth beat, it is not necessarily abnormal. An abnormal heart beats steadily without skipping. The rate of the heartbeat varies with the state of excitement, physical condition, outside temperature, physical exertion, and the size of the dog. When the dog is at rest and fully composed there will be a normal pulse rate of a hundred or more in a small dog and perhaps seventy-five or eighty in a large dog. There is no standard pulse, as in a human, whose normal pulse rate is about seventy-two.

For all their inefficiency, leaky valves seem not to shorten a dog's life appreciably. There is no known treatment or cure, nor has the cause been definitely established. A generalized bacterial disease which produces "vegetative growths" on the valves is often blamed and is one problem that lends itself to treatment.

Years ago a newly purchased eight-week-old Cocker Spaniel puppy was presented for an examination and inoculations. We checked under the rib cage and felt something unusual going on in the little chest. The stethoscope verified that this puppy had a major problem with a series of squishing sounds and no typical, normal lub-dub. We predicted the puppy would not live beyond six months of age and that it should be returned to the seller. The owners decided to keep the puppy and give it a few months of tender loving care and have it destroyed when the predictable problems arose.

The owners, outdoor people who spent all their spare time mountain climbing and backpacking took the dog with them on their expeditions. For fourteen years that dog was brought in for inoculations and minor problems and for fourteen years the owners reminded us of our prediction. The dog never did have a normal heartbeat and had to be destroyed at age fourteen—not from heart failure but because of a hopeless cancer.

CONGESTIVE HEART DISEASE. Congestive heart disease can often be recognized by the dog's sluggishness, shortness of breath, loss of vigor, inability to sustain exertion, blueness of tongue and gums after exertion, and a weak, thready, feeble pulse which can be felt on the inside of the dog's hind legs close to the crotch. Dropsy is sometimes present. Fainting spells may even occur. A dog that has always bounded up the stairs ahead of you may be so seriously affected that it will wait for you to carry it up.

Stimulants like caffeine and digitalis, or some derivative such as digoxin, can be used. Once digitalis is started under your veterinarian's direction, the dog must have the dosage for the remainder of its life. And since digitalis is eliminated by the kidneys, it may be necessary to reduce the dose as a dog's kidneys become less efficient with age.

ENLARGEMENT. A dog with enlarged heart may seem perfectly healthy when at rest around the house, but it cannot endure continued exertion. The condition seems to develop in young dogs that are overworked. If the strain is too great for the heart muscle, it stretches and stays stretched. Its elasticity is lost. Naturally if it occupies a larger space in the chest, it can be heard with the ear over this large area. There is a very noticeable contrast between the sound of a normal heart and that of an enlarged one. Enlarged heart conditions may be found in sled dogs broken in too early and used for heavy loads, in field-trial coon and fox hounds, and even in setters and pointers. Since the heart cannot be reduced to normal, it will never become strong enough to allow the dog to indulge in what would have been its normal activities.

The presence of large numbers of heartworms displaces so much blood that the heart enlarges just in order to have a normal volume of blood to circulate. A radiograph shows a typical enlargement in these cases.

RUPTURE OF THE HEART. A ruptured heart is usually associated with accidents. Not infrequently the heart is ruptured by a broken rib which punctures it. The dog does not always die quickly. If the pericardium is not broken, the blood fills the space between the heart and the pericardium and expands that membrane. If the pericardium is broken, the blood runs out into the chest cavity. It may take several apparently healthy hours before death comes. When it does occur, the dog may die very suddenly. Usually the owner has no idea of the cause of death unless a postmortem examination is made. There is no treatment.

A tumor at the top of the heart called a heart base tumor may cause many signs similar to other heart problems and must be diagnosed by chest X rays.

The Blood Vessels. Dogs have many of the same blood vessel diseases found in man. Of these the pet owner usually is able to recognize only hemorrhages (which we discuss in Chapter 10) and a few others. Yet there are two common conditions that anyone can easily learn to recognize: embolisms and strokes.

Following surgical operations, blood clots have been known to loosen, be carried through the circulatory system until they reach a junction in an artery, and then occlude this junction. The entire area fed by that artery will then be without a blood supply unless other collateral arteries can supply it. If there is no blood supply, degeneration sets in. When the area is near the surface, infection may work out through the skin, but when it is in a muscle it may cause great pain and eventually death.

A stroke is caused by the rupture of a blood vessel in the brain. The effect depends on the size of the area of the brain involved. Fortunately strokes are not common in dogs.

Paralysis rarely occurs in dogs with strokes but a dog with paralysis will be unsure of its footing, will hold its head to one side, may have one pupil larger than the other, and may have a condition of the eyes called nystagmus, which means they twitch from side to side.

The Blood. Some blood ailments may be recognized by pet owners. Others, such as anemia, excess urea, excess sugar, and excess bile, can be easily determined. Various larvae and microorganisms can also be detected with a microscope. These are discussed in Chapter 23.

ANEMIA. Anemia is a blood condition caused by too little blood, too few red cells, or insufficient hemoglobin to enable the blood to take up its normal load of oxygen from the lungs. The dog's gums and tongue are pale, its endurance poor. Depression is marked in severe anemia. The dog's eyes become sunken, the appetite feeble, and emaciation progressive. Frequently the first sign of anemia observed by an owner will be spells comparable to our blacking out. When this happens, a dog may stagger for a few moments or it may actually faint for a few seconds.

In case of hemorrhage, the dog may lose enough blood to die or be close to death. The blood may be lost externally or it may flow into the abdomen or chest cavity. After the blood clots in any cavities, the fluid component returns to circulation and may save the dog's life. The clot eventually hemolyzes and is picked up by the blood and passed out in the urine. When the danger of hemorrhage has passed, a transfusion may save the dog's life. Transfusions have also saved the lives of many dogs made anemic by lice, hookworms, and whipworms.

To determine the cause of anemia often requires detective work. Is it from blood loss? Are red cells being produced and destroyed or are the blood-forming tissues such as the bone marrow somehow being depressed? Once we know which category the anemia falls into we then have to identify the cause to determine the treatment.

Treating anemia is usually a matter of finding the cause, removing it, and supplying the food to stimulate blood building. Iron is essential. (See Table I for good sources of iron.) Liver, dried or fresh, will help greatly. Curiously enough, diets especially planned to cure anemia sometimes do not have sufficient salt. All dog food should contain at least 1 percent salt, and a little more can be fed to good advantage to anemic dogs.

HEMOPHILIA. There are an unfortunate number of types of hemophilia in dogs as there are in man. One case in a fine, sturdy, ten-week-old St. Bernard puppy was perhaps typical of one type. The puppy was brought in with a swollen leg with no pain or obvious discomfort, so our suggestion was to do nothing but observe the leg from day to day. A week later the puppy was brought in with a large swelling over the top of the head; we presumed it was an abscess and lanced it. The puppy bled for two weeks and was given repeated blood transfusions to save it. With transfusions and intravenous fluids the puppy recovered from the bleeding episode and was taken to a research facility where with tender loving care he made valuable contributions to science and lived out a full life span. The disease was identified as Christmas disease, which is inherited from a grandfather through his granddaughter by his grandsons. Females carry it but only males have the bleeding problem. The three male pups in the St. Bernard's litter were all afflicted.

Different kinds of hemophilia are mentioned in Chapter 14 concerning inherited defects.

AUTOIMMUNE BLOOD PROBLEMS. When discussing anemia we mentioned red blood cell destruction as one cause. The destruction may be due to the system rejecting the cells by an immune process perhaps similar to the body's rejection of some infections. The condition has the name of autoimmune hemolytic anemia. Fortunately this process is usually corrected with the help of medications, and there is evidence that the condition is spontaneously reversible in many cases.

SCLEROSIS. Hardening of the arteries, or sclerosis, is a curse of old age in dogs. The vessel walls lose some of their elasticity which results in a poorer diffusion of blood through the vascular system. The telltale sign is observed in most old dogs' eyes: the pupil, once black, has become cloudy or grayish as a result of the small vessels of the lenses becoming "hard" or thick-walled. That its blood does not circulate as it did in the past is one of the reasons an old dog slows down.

BLOOD PARASITES. Parasites of the blood cells and those free in the blood such as heartworms are discussed in Chapter 23.

19

Problems of
the Nervous System

What we think of as the nervous system consists of the brain and the spinal cord together with all the larger and smaller nerves emanating from and leading to them, down to the tiniest terminal branches. The system is affected by various troubles, ranging from injury to the terminal branches to the involvement of the brain itself by viruses, bacteria, protozoan organisms, toxins, and mechanical injuries.

To appreciate all the chances for nerve injury to which a pet is liable one need only consider for a moment the innumerable ramifications of nerves about an animal's body. Aside from the possibilities of mechanical injury, the nerves are governed by secretions of the ductless glands and manifest odd and abnormal behavior when the glands fail to function properly. If the pancreas, for example, fails to secrete insulin, the blood fails to store sugar in the liver; if the blood becomes overwhelmed with sugar, a nervous manifestation—a convulsion—occurs. If there is too much thyroid secretion, the animal becomes nervous and overactive; too little, and it is sluggish. Interfere with the function of the parathyroids and a different kind of convulsion occurs. And when the pituitary is disturbed, a whole host of abnormalities in behavior develops. These manifestations are all nervous and all are controlled by or due to chemical secretions.

Drugs taken through the mouth may affect the nerves. A dog poisoned with strychnine trembles violently, then rests a moment and trembles again. Put its nervous system out of commission with an injectable hypnotic and the trembling stops, indicating that the nerves were directly affected by the poison.

In other sections of this book we consider many of the common nervous complications in connection with the functions of other parts of the body. We see the effects of poisons on the nerves. And we discuss the relationship between the glands and the nerves. We have seen that nerves can regenerate and animate tissue to which the nerve trunk has been severed.

PROBLEMS CAUSING CONVULSIONS

Running Fits. From about 1920 or a little earlier until comparatively recently, an epizootic of running fits was prevalent in the United States and to some extent in other countries, notably England. Dogs had violent fits for which no cause could be assigned—no parasites, fever, or sickness of any kind. The dog would run about yelping or crawl cowering and quivering under some protected place and finally stretch out stiff while its jaws clamped together and froth whipped up in its mouth. It usually urinated and defecated uncontrollably. The general conception was that these running fits were due to some deficiency in diet. Minerals, vitamins, proteins, orange juice, and dozens of other things were tried.

A change of diet often cured it—provided the change was away from dog biscuits and kibbled food. Because of this, we were convinced that there was something *in* dog biscuits that was to blame. In our experience no case developed when dogs were taken off biscuits and fed a different food that furnished a balanced diet. Working on this premise, we set out to find what there was in the biscuits. We studied molds in kibbled biscuits and found no harmful ones. No harmful bacteria were found. But everyone who asked our advice was told to give up kibbled biscuits. Invariably the fits stopped in their pets.

The substance in the kibbles was not found then, but in 1947 Sir Edwin Mellanby, the same English scientist who discovered vitamin D, found that nitrogen trichloride, the bleach used to whiten flour, was the causative agent of these running fits. The old method of bleaching flour has since been discontinued, and thus one major cause of running fits in dogs has been removed. It would be interesting to know how many humans had medical problems from eating such flour.

Epilepsy. The diagnosis of epilepsy consists of eliminating all other causes of seizures. There is no test and even the electroencephalogram, which is not available to most veterinarians, is of little help. Epilepsy is considered an inherited defect and veterinarians recognize its presence in strains of many breeds. Most cases develop in dogs six to eighteen months of age but it is not unusual for older dogs to be brought in after a convulsion which may be the first of a long series of seizures. It is unusual to find a disease of such magnitude in man about which so little is known. We do not know what triggers it or what happens in the brain just before and during an attack. It is indeed frustrating to know so little about it. In its mild form it is not a violent condition but mild cases all too often progress gradually into major seizures.

It appears to act as a chain reaction of excited cells in the brain that pass that excitement along a neural pathway that becomes more (extensive) with each seizure. If the condition is observed before many attacks have occurred, antiepileptic drugs may prevent the tract's memory from being retained and in a few months or years the memory may disappear and subsequently the medication may be withdrawn.

Occasionally an animal is brought in for some other reason, at which time the owner describes what appears to be the forerunner of seizures. The dog suddenly stops playing and stares into space for ten or so seconds and then resumes playing as if nothing had happened. Some animals are described as appearing to follow an imaginary flying insect also for a few seconds. This behavior suggests a condition similar to petit mal seizures in humans. But in dogs these infrequent mild changes develop into brief seizures wherein the animal may *not* lose its footing and may *not* lose contact with the environment. We suspect this is a more common picture than reported by owners. There are usually long periods of time during which most dogs are not observed by their owners, such as when they're asleep or when their owners are away from home.

Many owners have observed seizures once or twice a year, and these usually are not medicated as three times daily medication to prevent such rare convulsions does not seem practical.

When not treated, some epileptic animals have a convulsion once or so a month initially and as months go by the seizures become more and more frequent until the poor animal finally develops a convulsion from which it cannot recover. This condition is called *status epilepticus* and demands intensive veterinary care for any chance of recovery.

The problem varies so with individual animals that it is impossible to predict the future, even with the best of medications. One form of the disease apparently causes only one severe convulsion and is never experienced again.

Of the four most common drugs to control epilepsy, we prefer and have more success with the proper dose of phenobarbital, which is determined by administering an initial loading dose. A loading dose is one in excess of the eventual dose which is determined by the loading dose's effect on the animal. The dog acts drunk when more than the necessary amount is administered. The eventual object is to administer the maximum dose without the patient showing any effects of it.

The object of the treatment is to prevent future convulsions but usually there will be a patient that still has less severe and less frequent seizures for the remainder of its life. Other drugs such as primidone may be the drug of choice or combinations may prove most effective. It will be necessary to work closely with your veterinarian for any hope of stabilizing the dog.

One dog was brought in that had a seizure only on the full of the moon for two full moons. We explained that we see coincidences regularly in veterinary medicine and the owner appeared to be satisfied. We started medication and for three more full moons the dog had seizures. Each time the owner came in with his pet he asked all sorts of questions about the effect of a full moon on dogs. We had no explanation except coincidence, but during the next two years, during which time the convulsions became less and less severe, not one happened to occur during a full moon.

Encephalitis. Encephalitis is not in itself a disease but a term for inflammation of the brain. There are many causes. High on the list are infections which are caused by viruses, bacteria, fungi, and other agents. After epilepsy, infection is the most common cause of seizures and of the infections, distemper virus stands as number one.

Encephalitis fits are of a different nature. There is less tendency for a dog to run. It is more likely to stand, sit, or lie in one spot until the fit is over. Also, as with epilepsy, the convulsions come at closer and closer intervals until the dog may die in a long, almost continuous convulsion. Or the convulsions may stop and a twitch may develop, depending on what part of the brain or spinal cord is affected. Rabies is a primary cause of encephalitis. Meningitis too produces fits and sometimes pain in the back. Some cases may be cured with antimicrobial drugs. Heartworm, microfilaria in vessels of the brain, and migrating young roundworms can cause encephalitis.

Hydrocephalus, or water on the brain, is a rare congenital defect and is more common than brain tumors; both of these may but not necessarily do cause seizures.

CEREBELLAR HYPOPLASIA

A developmental defect, cerebellar hypoplasia is second only to hydrocephalus among the developmental defects that cause seizures or other neurological problems in dogs. With this problem the cerebellum does not develop normally, resulting in such poor coordination that the animal does not make a satisfactory pet.

In cats it is caused by a parvovirus infection in the mother before the kittens are born. The discovery of a parvovirus that affects dogs is relatively new but it has not been incriminated as a cause in dogs of cerebellar hypoplasia. There is good evidence that this appears to be an inherited genetic susceptibility.

Injury. Injury is the most common cause of hemorrhage in the brain but also spontaneously ruptured blood vessels have been noted to be a cause. Signs similar to those indicating stroke or brain hemmorhage may be observed if blood is prevented from entering parts of the brain.

With all brain lesions the area or areas affected determine the signs the patient displays. It has been observed that a dog sick with distemper virus may eat ravenously a day before nervous symptoms occur, perhaps because the appetite nerve center is stimulated by the virus as it invades other areas of the brain. Sorting out the cause among as many possibilities is often a difficult problem, even for the veterinarian.

Worm Seizures. In puppies, any form of worms in large numbers may produce convulsions. Elimination of the worms stops the seizures. In older dogs severe roundworm infestations are so rare they can be disregarded as a cause of fits. But hookworms, both from the anemia they cause and from their toxins, can and often do cause fits.

Whipworms too may be a cause of fits, especially in dogs which are exercised. When infested dogs are taken hunting, no matter what their ages, they may have half a dozen fits in a single outing. Fear of the fits has caused many a fine hunting dog to lose its enjoyment of hunting. To experience something as terrifying as a convulsion just as it becomes excited over the chase is sufficient to spoil its pleasure in hunting. Tapeworms in appreciable numbers are debilitating and secrete toxins that produce fits. Elimination of any of these parasites may end the spells within twenty-four hours.

Fever Seizures. Fever seizures occur in the initial phases of infectious diseases which elevate the temperature. In distemper the visible symptoms may be ushered in by a few days of seizures. Such seizures occur only with the diseases accompanied by high fevers. Diseases in which the temperature runs 103° F (101° F is normal) seldom produce a fit. When canine influenza was rampant in the 1940s it was marked by fits that lasted a few days and then disappeared.

Eclampsia. What may give the impression of a fit to the uninitiated is a malady common to all species during the lactating period—eclampsia, also called milk fever. The bitch, whose blood calcium has been partially exhausted by her nursing puppies draining it away in milk, starts to quiver, develops a wild, startled expression, and then shakes violently. Bitches with eclampsia do not froth at the mouth. Sometimes they develop quite high temperatures, their muscles remain rigid, and the whole picture is alarming.

This condition is easily and quickly relieved by the injection of calcium gluconate into the vein. Although this condition is thought to be due to calcium depletion, injections of steroids and also magnesium, both intravenously, will reverse the convulsivelike condition.

Food Poisoning and Chemical Poisoning. Poisoning from food and chemicals also affect the nervous system. For treatment see pages 178–80.

Tetanus (Lockjaw). More commonly known as lockjaw, tetanus produces convulsions, but they are not accompanied by frothing. The lips are pulled downward by the muscles so that there is the appearance of a sickly grin. The gait is stiff, the head stretched out in front, and the tail held stiffly behind. The third eyelid (nictitating membrane) nearly always becomes especially prominent. Intensive veterinary treatment if started in time is lifesaving.

Diabetes and Uremia. Convulsions occur from too much sugar in the blood, caused by sugar diabetes (diabetes mellitus), and also from uremia, caused by acute or chronic kidney disease. In the latter case the temperature is usually subnormal.

Hypoglycemia. Hypoglycemia, or low blood sugar, is a metabolic problem due to a host of causes. One is stress, which is so often associated with shipping young puppies, especially of toy breeds. They apparently burn up their blood sugar and may convulse as a result. Corn syrup or honey given orally three times daily for a few days usually corrects this problem if it is not complicated by disease.

The tradition with owners of hunting dogs is to take them into the field with empty stomachs so that the dogs will return to the hunter at the end of the session to be fed. The problem with this plan is the occasional dog with borderline low blood sugar that burns up too much from the exercise then convulses. Dogs like this may be given a candy bar or a doughnut prior to the hunt, which adds enough blood sugar to see it through.

Heatstroke. Heatstroke can produce what appears to the layperson to be a convulsion. The dog is trying so desperately to breathe and its breath is coming in such rapid gasps that the owner may believe it is having a fit and not recognize the cause of the trouble. With heatstroke the temperature is very high, sometimes 109° F; the dog exhales and inhales rapidly, and the tongue and gums may be purple or blue. A deficiency of salt in the diet may be the predisposing cause. Although the majority of such cases are caused by leaving a dog in a car in the sun, others are caused by overexercising a dog in hot weather. The dogs with short faces are more vulnerable since they cannot cool the air before it enters the lungs as well as dogs with longer faces.

If a dog has heatstroke, turn the hose on it or let it lie in a stream or tub of cold water. Cold-water enemas using gallons of water may be lifesaving and intravenous fluids and steroids help after the temperature is reduced.

Foreign Bodies. Some dogs will have convulsions from foreign bodies in their stomachs. We have seen puppies have fits after meals of dog biscuits that they did not chew into small enough pieces. Stones, lumps of coal, bones, and other hard objects that have been swallowed may produce fits. An emetic soon brings relief.

Bones or sticks that wedge across the roof of the mouth, between the teeth, may cause such misery and fright that the dog gives every indication of having a fit. We have known dogs to roll down flights of stairs, run about pawing at their faces, froth at the mouth, and exhibit symptoms that would frighten anyone.

Salmon Poisoning. Salmon poisoning, a highly fatal parasitic disease, found in the Pacific Northwest, affects the brain. It is caused by a fluke (a parasitic worm) and is contracted by ingesting raw salmon.

Tick Paralysis. The tick is an insect that can release a nerve toxin that affects the brain, causing a paralysis. Another parasite producing a nerve toxin that may cause convulsions is any of many species of tapeworm.

Other Causes of Convulsions. Diets that are deficient in vitamins A, E, and B, including biotin, have been described as causing problems of the central nervous system as well as an excess of vitamin A, which well-meaning owners add to the diet in spite of the adequate amounts found in dog foods.

Insecticides are well known for their toxic effects when mishandled or when a particularly sensitive dog is exposed. These include flea and tick preparations as well as agricultural insecticides.

Nature has protected many creatures with toxins that are dangerous to dogs when ingested. After ingestion, many lizards, toads, and frogs cause convulsive seizures followed by death. Even the beautiful red eft, the land phase of the red-spotted newt, contains a powerful toxin.

Diseases of the liver and kidneys may prevent either the breakdown or elimination of toxins from the body, resulting in toxic encephalitis with convulsions or other brain-related complications.

PROBLEMS OF THE SPINAL CORD

Of course, the spinal cord is a continuation of the brain and as such has many of the problems associated with the brain as well as many unique to itself.

Compression. The most common problem with the spinal cord is compression. The suddenness of the onset is all important since gradual compression can be compensated for, whereas sudden compression, although no worse, may produce paralysis. This is due to the inflammation associated with a problem severe enough to suddenly compress the spinal cord.

In the Dachshund, perhaps because of the elongated spinal bones, there is a predisposition to ruptured intervertebral disks with paresis, paralysis, or paraplegia. In this situation the compression of the spinal cord must be treated promptly with either medication and rest or with surgery and rest. There are several surgical procedures but time is important since excess pressure on the spinal cord will produce necrosis after a few days. Radiography is imperative for diagnosis in such cases.

Congenital Spinal Cord Problems. Not unusual are congenital spinal cord problems, but they are rarely diagnosed until the puppy is eight weeks of age or older. Some conditions, such as one found in German Shepherds called degenerative myelopathy, are not observed in dogs under six years of age and usually in those over ten. These conditions do not lend themselves to either surgical or medical treatment.

Tumors. Spinal cord tumors are not a rare finding and treatment is usually unsuccessful. Tumors produce insidious signs as they develop and may be difficult to prove in their early stages even with X rays. Even a minute lesion causes signs depending on its location. In time as the lesion grows, radiographs prove its presence and delicate surgery is the only possible way to deal with it.

Traumatic Injury. Of the traumatic causes of injury to the spinal cord, automobile accidents head the list. The tragedy of the dog lying on its side on the road with front legs in full extension is all too common. The rigid extension of the forelegs usually indicates a spinal cord injured beyond repair. X rays reveal the fracture with displacement indicating a severed spinal cord. However, the cord may be sheared off with the fracture, returning to an almost normal position. Animals in this condition should be humanely put to sleep. Surgery to relieve pressure in less severe cases is well worth the chance in a loved pet.

Chastek Paralysis. We consider Chastek paralysis separately because it is a distinct form of paralysis with a known cause. It is produced by the consumption of raw fish in quantity. In raw fish there is a vitamin B_1 (thiamin) inactivator; therefore the disease is really a thiamin deficiency. It is relieved by adding the vitamin to the diet and by feeding the animal only cooked fish, since cooking destroys the inactivator.

Other Possible Causes of Paralysis. Several other factors are known to produce paralysis. Mineral deficiency and inadequate protein may be involved with central nervous problems including paralysis. Moreover, we know that blows to the spine, autointoxication from long spells of constipation, great accumulations in the anal glands, and damage from many other diseases may cause nerve problems.

If you find your dog suddenly paralyzed, gently put it on a flat surface and take it to the veterinarian. The veterinarian may be able to operate on a broken back or a ruptured intervertebral disk, and if the spinal cord has not been too severely injured, your pet may be well again in time.

If your dog has developed paralysis slowly, your veterinarian is apt to suggest treatment. And here more devoted nursing is needed than in any other ailment your dog may have. Start with the possibility in mind that recovery to normal may never occur. Be grateful for every bit of improvement shown. You may have to build a carriage for your pet's rear quarters. The animal will have to be kept on some soft absorbent material that must be changed frequently or the urine passed may burn the skin. Bedsores develop easily. Feces must be removed. There may be just enough innervation in the back legs to hold its weight. This simplifies matters greatly, because a dog can be taken outside and taught to urinate and defecate when pressure of your fingers is applied over its bladder on each side of the abdomen. A dog whose legs can support its weight is a good patient and remains housebroken, but a completely paralyzed dog requires great care and only a loving master will have the patience to see such an illness through.

Definite nerve destruction on a large scale cannot be repaired, and the posterior paralysis following distemper unfortunately is often hopeless. Your veterinarian will be able to give you some idea of the extent and progress of the disease.

COLLAPSE

Nervous collapse following an accident or serious surgical operation is called shock. With it, the dog is debilitated, its pulse is weak, the color in its gums is pale, as is the case with anemia. Some dogs lie as if they were dead; others may show signs of nervousness and tend to bite if touched. Treatment of shock is discussed in Chapter 10.

PROBLEMS OF THE PERIPHERAL NERVES AND MUSCLES

All the nervous tissue other than the brain and spinal cord are called the peripheral nerves. These nerves carry information from the rest of the body to and from the spinal cord and brain. Since the nerves control the muscles, the muscles will be mentioned here as well as in Chapter 20. If a problem exists that interferes with the electrical signal passing to or from the central nervous system, there is an impairment of function.

The most common cause of problems of these nerves is injury, and it follows that the larger the nerve and the closer its proximity to the brain or spinal cord, the severer will be the functional deficit.

Radial Nerve Paralysis. Radial paralysis is an injury that often appears to be a dislocation or a fracture. In one sense it is this, because the whole shoulder droops yet all the joints remain intact. This condition is due to the injury of the radial nerve plexis. A heavy blow against it may cause a permanent break or bruise which may cause either temporary or permanent paralysis.

Because this nerve controls the motion of the front of the foreleg, lack of its influence, plus the activity of the nerves on the back of the foreleg, causes the foot to pull backward. This bending backward, plus the dropping of the shoulder, makes the front leg, from the wrist, or carpal joint downward, drag on the ground; and if it is unprotected, the skin will in time wear away. In the case of hopeless radial paralysis the affected leg is often amputated to prevent the sores from becoming infected in the useless limb.

A few physiologists are equipped with electrical devices and a precise knowledge of the location of nerves, which enables them to determine the exact extent of the injury. If the nerve is not too badly impaired, the dog's leg should be placed in a splint to prevent the tendons from becoming contracted, so that when normal motion has been restored, the dog may walk normally again. You can see that when a nerve is injured the muscles to and from which the nerve travels will be non-functional. When muscles are nonfunctional they shrink or become atrophied. Fortunately if nerves heal—even though the healing may be slow—the shriveled muscles quickly redevelop with exercise. We have seen dogs recover use of a leg even six months after the injury but only if the leg is constantly exercised to prevent tendon contraction with the resulting inability to straighten the carpal joint (wrist).

Muscle Spasms. With irritation of nerves the muscles may develop spasms that are one of the most painful experiences a dog can have. The dog moves in "boat" fashion with a stiff neck and walks as if it were on broken glass. Touch the dog's skin anywhere and it may scream in pain. Ascending stairs or jumping on a favorite chair becomes too painful to attempt. We know disk problems, particularly those in the neck, will cause such spasms but there appear to be neuromuscular spasms produced by unknown causes, perhaps a virus. Dogs with this kind of problem are sometimes called "screamers."

It appears that muscle atrophy may occur without obvious nerve involvement. Myositis or inflammation of a muscle with its subsequent myopathy or atrophy is bewildering since usually no cause can be demonstrated. An example is the atrophy of one or both temporal muscles. These muscles are involved with chewing or mastication and are located on top of the head on either side of the bump of knowledge, or occipital protuberance. Many old dogs have an atrophy of both muscles, which adds to their old appearance. Some dogs develop a rather sudden atrophy of one of these muscles, leaving them with the strange appearance of a one-sided sunken head. This condition usually persists for the lifetime of a dog but sometimes a spontaneous reversal results and the muscles return to normal.

Heat may be of great help in many causes of nerve irritation and muscle spasms. After suffering through the cool damp weather of springtime, some dogs will become animated and happy, apparently pain-free on hot bright summer days. When a cool damp spell comes, the trouble is evident again.

In some cases vitamin-B-complex injections seem to afford relief but if the condition is not too severe old tried-and-true aspirin may bring relief. Give one five-grain tablet for each twenty pounds of the animal every three hours before trying more effective anti-inflammatory drugs.

There is concern that the latter, which incidentally are more expensive, are not without possible side effects. When giving aspirin always wrap it in some food so that the tablet does not rest on one area of the stomach lining while it dissolves or it will irritate the stomach mucosa. If your dog vomits after being given aspirin the dose should be reduced or discontinued.

20

Problems of the Bones, Joints, and Muscles

THE BONES

Puppies are stepped on, dropped from people's arms, fall down stairs, and are otherwise stressed, usually with no skeletal damage done, but bones *can* fracture and joints can be sprained. Injury is the number one cause of bone problems. Fortunately, growing puppies' bones heal rapidly and since their bones are not brittle as those of adult dogs they may bend and straighten rather than snap. The greenstick fracture (see page 327) often heals without human intervention.

There is no doubt in our minds that the majority of bone problems in growing puppies other than those due to injury are caused by their owners feeding them improperly. This of course is because of an innocence or lack of knowledge, even indulgence, on the owners' part. They are not aware of the proper nutrition puppies require or whether or not the commercially available foods have the necessary ingredients for adequate nutrition.

For the healthy development of the skeleton, the ratio of calcium to phosphorus is critical. The National Academy of Science recommends .6 percent calcium and 0.4 percent phosphorus in the diet. And the presence of the proper amounts of vitamins A and D are necessary for the bones to develop properly. So when owners want "big bones" in their dogs and add a handful of bonemeal to the daily ration the results may be more unfortunate than the constipation it causes. It is better to put the bonemeal around the roses in your garden.

By the same token, excess phosphorus is dangerous, but fortunately growing puppies can exist on improper diets and still do fairly well. But why not feed them properly from the start?

Of the problems described next we do not know that nutrition is responsible for all but it must play a contributing role.

One problem in rapidly growing larger breeds is called panosteitis, which is the inflammation of every part of a bone. Changes in the shafts of the long bones of the forelegs cause lameness, which may move from one leg to another. For a few days or weeks one foreleg will be lame and suddenly the puppy favors the other one. Perhaps this is similar to the condition in children called growing pains. X-ray diagnosis and rest is advised for this self-limiting problem. The X-ray diagnosis is important to rule out joint problems or injuries that may need agressive treatment.

An excess of meat in a diet can affect the parathyroid glands, stimulating them into overactivity, perhaps from the low calcium to phosphorus ratio. The result is a demineralization of the bones, the exact opposite of the normal process. If this condition is extreme, a puppy can fracture a leg just playing with a littermate.

We remember an ocelot, one of the medium-sized wild cats, that was brought in with a fracture of the midshaft of a femur. After anesthetizing the animal and before X rays were taken we gently bent the "normal" femur and accidentally broke it between the fingers. We had to set both fractures. The same can happen to dogs. The poor ocelet was a victim of malnutrition from its hamburger diet. Changing the diet to whole chickens, feathers and all, corrected the problem.

Dwarfism has been reported and is due to a pituitary defect. One German Shepherd Puppy with it reached a top weight of sixteen pounds and died at five years of age.

Other endocrine gland problems cause skeletal defects, for example, excess estrogen results in stunted adults. Among the damage that cortisone and other steroids can cause, such as Cushing's disease (discussed in Chapter 25), they can and do inhibit the absorption of calcium from the intestines. The result is osteoporosis (a condition that causes weakened, brittle bones) observed in the long bones and spine.

At the points where the ribs and the cartilaginous extensions of the breastbone meet, one sometimes finds enlargements that may persist throughout an animal's life. These enlargements may be normal, or an indication of disease, or evidence that the pet was inadequately fed or was sick for a considerable part of its growing period. In conjunction with these one generally finds abnormal enlargements on the lower end of the radius, a large bone of the forearm, where it joins the wrist (carpal) joint. The spongy end may be so abnormal that it turns the leg, making it crooked (bandy leg) or weak, so that the leg from the wrist down bends out sideways. Some dogs are born with hereditary "bench" legs, which are characterized by the front feet turning out sideways, a condition not due to rickets or other dietary deficiencies.

Fractures and Dislocations. The causes of both breaks and dislocations are so varied that it would be of little use to list them; they range from being kicked by a horse to catching a toenail in a crack between boards to being hit by an automobile.

Before discussing specific types, let us consider the general categories of fractures. Three different kinds are most often found.

In a *greenstick fracture* the bone breaks but stays in its natural position. Usually one side is broken but the other only bent.

A *simple fracture* is a clean break in which the tissue surrounding the bone is left intact.

A *compound fracture* is one in which there is an opening connecting the site of fracture to the outside of the body. This opening may be due to a wound inflicted from without or to a hole punched outward by the end of the bone being driven through the surrounding tissue and skin.

In addition there are other descriptive classifications. There are complete fractures where bones are broken clear across; comminuted fractures where bones are splintered; linear fractures in which the break is lengthwise of the bone; neoplastic fractures where the bone breaks from a growth in its substance; and sprain fractures in which a tendon tears away a piece of bone to which it is attached, and numerous other variations.

Virtually every veterinary establishment has access to X-ray equipment, which is a necessity in dealing with many skeletal problems. Even the experienced veterinarian cannot tell the nature of fractures by mere observation and it is foolhearty to operate without the evidence of radiographs to illustrate the complexity of the injury. Ask to see the films, and your veterinarian will show you the problem. Frequently he or she will need another X ray after the fracture is repaired to be sure the bones are aligned properly.

You should know how to treat your dog for shock, which may de-

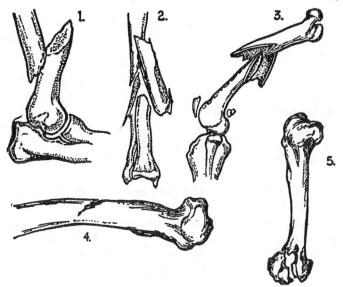

Common fractures. (1) Simple. (2) Compound, when some of the bones penetrate the skin. (3) Comminuted. (4) "Greenstick." (5) Condylar.

velop when it suffers broken bones (see Chapter 10). If a veterinarian is near, you should call him or her immediately. The animal should be kept warm while being transported to the veterinarian for the necessary treatment.

Dislocations must be "reduced"—slipped back into place—and this, too, is better left to the veterinarian. Breaks of almost any bone can be set. Some, like broken jaws, may need wiring; some may require complicated pins, plates, or joining by grafting. The methods require considerable study and a great deal of experience. So does the decision whether to use intramedulary pins, wire, plates screwed in position, splints—and what kind of splint, Stader or Thomas—or plaster casts interspersed with cloth, with or without windows, and so forth if the fracture is compound. The dog's character must also be considered. Some dogs will try to chew almost anything off; others will cooperate as good patients should.

Every fracture case should be monitored by your veterinarian once a week or as often as recommended, so that the apposition, the healing, the straightness can be observed, and so the splint or cast or other devices may be removed at the right time. In growing puppies it is often safe to remove a splint three weeks after the break; in mature dogs a month is the usual time.

PELVIC FRACTURES. Probably the greatest number of broken bones are caused by automobile accidents and, in our experience, of these, pelvic fractures lead all others in frequency.

It is not difficult to tell when the pelvis is fractured. Usually the dog will not be able to stand, or if it does, the hind legs spread apart and it either collapses in pain or waddles with difficulty. The tail may hang inert.

When the veterinarian dons a glove and inserts an index finger into the rectum, he or she may feel the break or breaks clearly. By this method it can be ascertained whether a bone edge has cut through the rectum or the vet can push a collapsed pelvis back into place by digital pressure and thereby relieve the dog considerably. He or she may feel a break in the spine where the first tail vertebra joins the last sacral one, which accounts for the "dead" tail. If the dog can wag its tail, it is good evidence that the backbone is not broken. Of course, X rays are necessary for a definitive diagnosis.

A fractured pelvis may involve any of the six bones that make it up (three pairs of bones) and sometimes, as we have said, the spinal column is involved. The bones of the pelvis are the ilium, ischium, and pubis. Look at the illustration of a dog's skeleton (page 15). Now imagine it is covered with flesh and skin and is your dog. Imagine you can see that skeleton through the flesh and skin. The bones of the pelvic girdle are these six (13 to 15) plus the sacrum, that section of the spinal column consisting of five or six vertebrae ending where the tail vertebrae start. When the pelvis is fractured, any of the six pelvic bones may be broken, or the injury may be to the backbone, to the joints where the sacrum and the ilium join, one on each side, to make the sacroiliac joint, or to the muscles and ligaments that hold this whole box together.

FRACTURED FEMUR. An examination may find that nothing is wrong in the pelvis, that no bones feel as though they were broken, and yet the dog appears lopsided when viewed from behind. This may be an indication that the head of the femur—the head of the thigh bone—is broken off. It may also mean that the hipbone is dislocated, a condition which we will discuss on page 330.

In our experience, fracture of the femur is the second most common fracture. This fracture is frequently surrounded by a pocket of blood because, as the dog trots home on three legs, the bone edges rub on the muscles and cut arterioles or venules—sometimes even a large artery or vein. An animal with such a break should be hustled to a veterinarian, who will have to anesthetize the patient to set the break. Anesthetics not only render the dog insensible but also relax the muscles and so make the job easier for the veterinarian.

Many a well-set bone separates and slips so that it sets in a side-to-side position instead of end to end. If this should happen, the healing process will take longer and the broken leg will be shorter than normal. Even so, the dog will manage to get about with less limping than one would expect.

FRACTURES OF THE TAILS AND TOES. Dislocations occur in the tails and the toes of dogs of all breeds. Puppies born with tails that bend backward actually have dislocated vertebrae (an uncorrectable condition). Bending the tail to straighten it usually results in breaking it or damaging it so severely that the end below the break dies and must be removed.

Toes that are broken at the joints usually are easily repaired by applying casts to the feet after reduction or setting. But when a ligament of the toes is cut or broken, it seldom regenerates and the nail bends upward. This is a familiar sight to veterinarians, who see so many steel-trap wounds. We have repaired feet where these little ligaments were cut on three of the four toes. Thereafter the nails, which no longer touch the ground and wear away naturally, have to be cut at frequent intervals.

HEAD FRACTURES. Head fractures result from a variety of accidents—from the head being struck by a baseball to being hit by a truck. If the skull is cracked above the brain case, the dog may live, but generally so much brain concussion occurs that the prognosis is unfavorable. If the skull over the brain case is not fractured, very often some other part of the skull is. A spot often fractured is the bone covering the sinus in the forehead. The sinus itself may be penetrated and infected. Your veterinarian may have to pick pieces of bone out, flush the sinus, and cover the hole with skin.

The arch of bone over the eye, which has a fixed joint through it, often breaks and presses inward, causing the eye to bulge. This necessitates pulling the arch back into shape, where it usually stays because the dog lets it alone after learning that pressure against it occasions pain. The eye generally becomes inflamed and may even be damaged so that it has to be removed.

Jaw injuries are common. In our practice we have more frequently seen breaks in the center of the jawbone than breaks involving either of the bones (mandibles) which together make the jaw. The mandibles are joined by a cartilaginous attachment while the dog is young. With age they fuse together. When the break occurs here, it is obvious, because the jaw loses its firmness. If it is permitted to heal without medical attention, it often sets crooked. A veterinarian will wire it together so neatly that it will heal like new. Nursing on the owner's part is of primary importance. The saliva seems to prevent infection, so that no medication is required unless the wire is placed from below after the skin has been parted. Antiseptic agents should be used on the suture. The diet must be of a nature requiring no chewing—milk and mushy food.

HIP JOINT DISLOCATIONS. A dog's hip joint comes apart (is dislocated) more often than do any other joints. This ball-and-socket joint, like most others, is surrounded by a capsule. Ligaments and muscles, too, hold it in place. In spite of the fact that it is held very strongly in place, falls and blows such as those inflicted by automobiles somehow force the ball on the femur out of the socket (acetabulum).

This dislocation may be such that the ball is above, below, or in front of the rim of the socket. Even the rim itself may be damaged so that it is extremely difficult to get the joint to stay together. Often the capsule, ligaments, and muscles which hold the joint together are so mutilated that the femur can be put back with ease, only to slip out again just as easily.

We have seen some dislocations of this type in large dogs difficult to reduce and others that were snapped back by merely bending the leg and giving it just the right kind of twist. You may say, if you watch your veterinarian set one, "It's all in knowing how." But no expert can get all hip joints together easily.

SHOULDER DISLOCATIONS. Shoulder dislocations can be observed by comparing the feel of the two shoulders. Generally a quick forward pull while someone holds the dog firmly will snap a dislocated shoulder into place, with very little resulting pain. But a difficult dislocation should not be pulled more than once. There may be tissue between the two parts. Your veterinarian can locate the trouble quickly and, by anesthetizing the dog and then twisting the leg, will be able to replace it quite simply.

WRIST AND HOCK DISLOCATIONS. When dislocated, the wrist (carpal) and hock joints are usually said to be broken. The many little bones of which the joints are composed are held together by ligaments which may be ruptured. The leg may hang sideways with skin and ligaments on one side torn away, and yet when it is straightened and held immobile, the joint heals and in time the animal will be able to walk as well as before the dislocation.

Injuries to joints may require many weeks of careful nursing. Ligaments do regenerate and skin does grow across, but the spot will be bald. That is why the veterinarian tries to draw the skin as closely together as he or she can—that and because the skin makes the best and the natural covering.

Bone Healing. The process of bone healing is most interesting, and it is worthwhile to understand it in case you have to manage a pet with one or more fractured bones.

Let us suppose that a fairly simple break occurs in the bones of the foreleg of a dog. When the dog returns home after an accident, the broken leg is obviously shorter than the others. The dog holds it up, crying with pain. The veterinarian waits until the dog has recovered from shock then sets the leg. The ends of the bone are brought together, *"in apposition,"* as the veterinarian calls it. Then the ends of the bone must "knit." Here is where it is worthwhile for the owner to know exactly what happens so that he or she can give the pet all the attention and care required.

For several days the body decalcifies, or withdraws calcium and other minerals from the bone ends. Gradually they become soft, like cartilage. At this stage it doesn't make much difference if the bones are not perfectly matched at the break. The second step, after the softening process, is the growth from each end of connective fibers that join the bone ends together. These shrink, pulling the ends closer. This process is completed in fourteen or fifteen days. During this period it isn't as important how straight the bone is kept, as long as the ends are in apposition. At any time during this interval it is possible, but not desirable, to bend it at the break.

Next comes a stage when the junction, or callus, becomes impregnated with mineral salts of calcium and phosphorus; in other words, it hardens. At this point it is essential that the bone be kept straight, and meticulous care must be given to seeing that it is. If there is any change in the position of the bones your veterinarian will want to see the dog at once. Remember that a leg set crookedly is a poor advertisement for the vet, but more important is its effect on your dog's future, with which both you and the veterinarian are concerned. You owe both your pet and your veterinarian the cooperation of careful attention at this point. Once the callus is strong enough so that the bone will not bend, the device holding the bone ends together can be removed if it is an external device.

The last period involves the shrinking of the callus. Some bones will set with what appears to be a disfiguring bulge about the break, but in time this largely disappears leaving a bone that is even stronger at the fracture point than in the adjacent unbroken parts.

Many injured bones can't be set properly. Some are so badly shattered and infected that chips must be removed and nature trusted to do her best. The pelvis, that girdle of bones forming a framework for the rear part of the abdomen, can be broken into many pieces; it often, without any attention, heals itself without too much constriction of the pelvic passage.

Bone Cancer. There are two major types of cancer involving bones. One affects the covering of the bones and the other the bones themselves. These are discussed in Chapter 27, as is the bone-lung disease, pulmonary osteoarthropathy.

THE JOINTS

Arthritis. As in humans, arthritis is the major problem of the joints in dogs and usually just as mystifying and difficult to treat. A diagnosis is made by an animal's history, laboratory tests, and X rays. In rheumatoid arthritis, lameness, pain, and swelling in the joints, with an elevated temperature, are all present. There is no satisfactory treatment, although aspirin and cortisone and other steroids are helpful in many cases, but the dry, painful joints will develop relentlessly in the end.

LUPUS ERYTHEMATOSUS. Lupus erythematosus is another common problem often affecting joints. Here again the laboratory tests and X rays are necessary for diagnosis. In many cases corticosteroids and aspirin have kept this disease in remission for years.

OSTEOARTHRITIS. A degenerative joint disease, osteoarthritis, is common in older dogs and medications are of great help in relieving pain. More properly the name should be osteoarthosis since "-itis" means inflammation and in this condition there is a minimum of inflammation. In any event, bony growths accompany a degeneration of the cartilage at the ends of bones making up the joint. Frequently bone spurs form which may limit the joint's function but are not necessarily painful in themselves. There is discomfort in bearing weight and overweight animals are at a disadvantage. Aspirin is a great help in such cases at a dose of one tablet for each twenty pounds as often as every three hours. If aspirin does not help, steroids may be prescribed, often with excellent results.

Problems of Specific Joints. Some joint diseases have an affinity for specific joints and are of unknown cause. One of these, *osteochondritis dessicans*, is always located in a shoulder joint where a pocket of cartilage erodes away, leaving a small craterlike area. This area is the glistening cartilaginous surface of the humerus. When the dog attempts to bend the joint and put weight on it, as in walking, there is great pain. Sometimes the area heals on its own as strangely as it has formed, but more often surgery is necessary to correct it. X rays must be used to make a diagnosis.

THE ELBOW JOINT. We often see degenerative changes in the elbow joint with a condition called an ununited anconeal process. We are not sure whether this condition exists from birth or results from injury, but it is a real problem in young adult animals which is diagnosed by X rays. There are several operations that can correct it.

THE KNEE JOINT. Perhaps the most complicated joint in a dog's body, the knee joint, or stifle, is subject to more problems than any other joint. Most common is the luxating patella. Many small breeds have anatomical configurations that predispose the animals to these kneecap dislocations. In some breeds dislocations occur when the puppy is a few months old and these animals compensate for the problem as they grow, living out their lives with it but without discomfort from it.

On the other hand, an adult dog may tear the lateral ligament of the patella, allowing the bone to slip to the inside, and this is a painful development. A dog in this situation limps when the kneecap is out of place and may stretch its leg, allowing the bone to return to its normal position. When due to abnormal anatomical alignment, this condition can be surgically corrected. We have had poor results with splints and casts in an attempt to correct it.

More rarely the patella luxates laterally and we are faced with a surgical procedure to correct that problem too. In many cases anti-inflammatory drugs, rest, and time will help dogs to live with the problem. In time no signs of lameness or discomfort are observed in some fortunate animals.

RUPTURED CRUCIATE LIGAMENTS. Your dog may run happily out to play, turn suddenly, give a yelp of pain, and return on three legs, holding a rear leg up. You examine the leg from the foot to the hip, flex and extend it with no discomfort registered on the part of your pet, but the injured dog will not put any weight on it. This is a story veterinarians hear regularly and more often than not the cause of this problem is the rupture of a ligament on the inside of the knee or stifle joint. We compare the problem to that of a football player whose knee is hit from the side. We might be able to correct "football knee" with a pressure bandage if the area were shaped like the human knee, but as it is cone-shaped, bandages slip down and just don't work. There are a host of surgical procedures to correct it.

When an anatomical defect is present in one leg, it is apt to be present in the opposite leg also, so an injury to one results in the dog having to carry its weight on the good leg. This may precipitate the same injury as in the affected leg, resulting in two painful limbs.

The Hip Joint. The hip joint is a close second to the stifle joint in the number of problems found. The one most serious problem, because of the large numbers of dogs affected, is hip dysplasia. This is a joint instability or incongruity which may result in changes so severe that the dog becomes a cripple. This condition is discussed in more detail in Chapter 14.

ASEPTIC NECROSIS. A condition caused either by an inherited defect or by an injury to the hip is called aseptic necrosis, in which the head of the femur degenerates in the absence of infection. This is a painful condition and requires the same femural head resection as is done for hip dysplasia.

Joint infections in young puppies and penetrating injuries to joints as from dog bites present difficult therapeutic problems. Untreated, an infected joint degenerates and a fusion may occur preventing movement for the life of the animal.

There are times when fusion is the only solution to a constant pain in a joint. It is the surgeon's last resort and the lesser of two evils.

Most joint injuries with cracks and chips and infections are so varied they must be treated on an individual basis, but common to all of the joint problems is the need for detailed radiographs or X rays and where there is any question the radiographs may be examined by a board-certified veterinary radiologist. Their charges are one of the best buys in the veterinary diagnostic field.

Chapter 10 discusses first aid for fractures in more detail.

Spinal Joints. The bones of the spinal column are vulnerable to both injury and degenerative problems. In normal-appearing old dogs it is common to find many vertebrae fused together. But the joints between the bones have many of the problems that affect man. The ruptured intervertebral disk usually represents a degenerative process of long duration with a sudden onset at the moment the disk ruptures. The disk protrudes to exert pressure on the spinal cord with results commensurate with the amount of pressure. This pressure may be sufficient to cause an irreversible necrosis of the spinal cord if untreated, with a permanent paralysis of the hind legs.

Radiographs alone may not pinpoint the exact site of the problem unless a dye is introduced around the spinal cord. The dye ascends until it reaches the obstructed area and then the radiographs will indicate the exact area of involvement. If the protrusion is not too extensive, anti-inflammatory drugs and rest may be adequate and many veterinarians choose that alternative. In many cases surgery is the only hope for recovery, and once the space involved is identified the surgeon operates to relieve the pressure. If this happens in time the dog will make a complete recovery.

Fractures of the spinal bones may be repaired with bone plates with good success as long as the all important spinal cord is not irreparably damaged.

MUSCLES

When nerves leading to muscles are injured those muscles shrink from lack of use. They can't function until the damage is repaired, at which time the shriveled muscles develop normally and become useful once again. If, however, the nerve does not heal the muscles will not develop again. Refer to pages 14–15 for a description of muscles.

21

Problems of the Eyes, Ears, and Nose

There is an interesting relationship among these three organs that may not seem obvious. There are tear ducts called lacrymal ducts that conduct excess tears into the nasal cavity and there are Eustachian tubes connecting the throat to the inner ear. So an infection in an eye can spread through the tears to the nose as can an infection from an ear infect the throat.

It is difficult to explain why an outer ear infection is so commonly reflected by a tearing eye on the same side. When you see an eye with excess tearing, examine the ear on the same side for a problem.

THE EYES

The Eyelids. In a discussion of eye problems the lids must be considered since there are problems of the lids that irritate or otherwise involve the globes of the eyes.

The most common problems of the eyelids that affect the eyes are tumors. Usually benign, they grow on the edges and often irritate the corneas by the constant blinking of the lids. Some tumors protrude away from the eyes and are only unsightly but those that irritate corneas should be removed surgically or blindness may result.

Small hairs growing in from the edges of the lids may also irritate the corneas, and this condition also necessitates surgery.

Some animals of the brachycephalic (short-headed) breeds have folds of skin protruding so that hair constantly touches the corneas and this may be corrected by surgery or by matting the hair with Vaseline at least once daily.

An abnormal drooping of either eyelid or a turning in or out of a lid predisposes the eye to problems and should be surgically corrected.

The Conjunctiva. Under the eyelids and around the globes of the eyes is pink tissue called the conjunctiva. Normally, in spite of dust, pollens, and other debris entering the eyes, this area is sterile. Cultures of tears from normal eyes have no microorganisms that grow. So when we see sudden excess tearing with mucus in the corners we then first suspect foreign bodies, such as a bit of bark or sand, which can cause the discharge by irritation but in a sterile environment. Anesthesia and a careful examination may be necessary, but more often the foreign material will work its way out in a day or two. A few drops of mineral or vegetable oil in the eye may facilitate the removal of foreign material.

Even when infection is present we also see mucus and inflammation, which is evidenced by the rosy appearance of the whites of the eyes, the sclera. Raise the upper lid and the sclera, instead of china white, will be pink or red due to the inflammation. When infection is present most dogs respond to a variety of drops and ointments, but those that do not should have cultures and sensitivities run to determine the proper medicinal agent to use.

We once worked on one dog for two years with fair results but were unable to correct what we thought was an infection in spite of finding no bacteria on culturing. A comment in a textbook suggested a yeast may cause such a problem so we sent a culture out for a yeast culture and prescribed an antifungal agent. Before the laboratory results were back the eyes appeared normal and finally a yeast infection was verified. Two years is a long time to treat an animal without good results. We tell our clients, as we would urge for any human or an animal problem, to speak out if not satisfied and ask for another consultation. We veterinarians are interested in one primary objective and that is to cure your dog. A fresh look at a difficult case may lead to a solution.

As do many animals, dogs have a third eyelid that lies across the lower inner part of each eye. Sometimes the edge of one has pigment and the other is white or pink, suggesting that the eye with the nonpigmented membrane is a weak eye—not so. It is as normal as two pigmented or two nonpigmented third eyelids.

When irritated these membranes rise up over perhaps half of each eye, suggesting that the dog's eyes are "rolling back in its head." It may look that way, but dogs' eyes don't roll back in their heads. The raising of this membrane indicates irritation, and irritation may be caused by anything from chemicals, such as fertilizers, to pollens and dust to which the dog is sensitive. Of course, infection is high on the list of causes.

DRY EYES. Another cause of irritation is the lack of tears or dry eyes. The reason for tear glands ceasing to produce the tears that are necessary for lubrication are not well understood but this is a serious problem that needs professional attention. Sometimes antibiotics help, as does medication, to stimulate tear production but sometimes nothing helps but drops applied every half hour. An interesting surgical solution is to transpose to the eye a duct that normally leads from a salivary gland to the mouth. The saliva discharged into a dry eye works about as well as tears. One warning, however, when the family sits down to eat: a dog that has had this surgery on smelling the food will tend to salivate and then tears may run down its cheek. This, though, is preferable to having to medicate an eye for the remainder of a pet's life.

"CHERRY" EYE. Cherry eye is the name given to a bright pink object about the size of a pencil eraser that suddenly forms in the inner corner of an eye. It is really the prolapse of glandular tissue from the inside of that third eyelid discussed previously. If treated promptly, the "cherries" may be replaced without surgery by your veterinarian and a medication dispensed to correct the problem. Some of the replaced "cherries" will reappear almost as soon as you leave the vet's office. Surgery is simple and effective but if it is necessary in one eye it is common to see one appear at a later date in the other eye.

The Cornea. The surface of the globe of the eye through which we see the pupil and the colored or pigmented area, the iris, is called the cornea. Injury, from cat scratches to any penetrating objects, is the most common problem with corneas. When damage is superficial and before infection has set in, antibiotics with steroids are often spectacular in their results. When there is an infected injury to the cornea, steroids must not be used.

There are surgical procedures and even corneal transplants to deal with lacerated corneas with or without infection.

Ulcers of the corneas may lead to blindness and should be treated immediately.

One case of a corneal ulcer we treated for two years and with two operations. The human ophthalmology department of Yale was the ultimate in cooperation but we could not correct that nagging small ulcer. At one point the client applied drops every twenty minutes for two days. She set her alarm clock and didn't miss a dose. A year and a half after the onset, on examination under an operating microscope it was decided to use steroids for the first time and in twenty-four hours the ulcer had almost penetrated through the cornea. It was worse than when first examined. Emergency surgery saved the eye but the ulcer persisted. The problem was corrected by use of a soft contact lens within one week of its application.

One problem with treating corneal ulcers is the defoliating effect of the blinking eyelids. As delicate new cells form in an attempt to heal, the blinking lids literally wipe them away. The solution may be suturing the lids together of the affected eye or other surgery to protect the healing ulcer.

"BLUE EYE." Among the diseases recognized by veterinary ophthalmologists is infectious canine hepatitis, "blue eye," in which a bluish cast to one or both corneas develops. It does not require a specialist to make the diagnosis of this virus disease with its "blue" color, but other diseases must be considered.

Though the obvious corneal opacity of infectious canine hepatitis is easy for anyone to observe, when the signs are subtle it usually takes an ophthalmologist to make the diagnosis.

Some of the other diseases in this category are leptospirosis, toxoplasmosis, lipodysproteinemia, and mycotic infections such as cryptococcosis, and coccidioidomycosis. Parasitic diseases such as erlichiosis and visceral larva migrans are rare findings.

PIGMENTARY KERATITIS. Another unfortunate corneal problem is an inflammation accompanied by the deposition of pigment called pigmentary keratitis. The condition starts at the junction of the sclera, or the white of the eye, and the cornea and spreads slowly but surely across the eye. It may be compared to a black window shade being drawn across the eye. If the condition is discovered in time ointments applied four or five times daily usually cause the pigment to recede. When the eye is covered with pigment surgery may restore sight.

Other Eye Conditions and Diseases. The automobile is the cause of many eye injuries and if you have the misfortune of finding a dog with an eye protruding out of its lids you may save both the dog's eye and sight by gently pushing the eye back in its socket. Otherwise the optic nerve will be stretched for too long a period if it requires very long to locate a veterinarian.

The eyes must be kept moist, and in the case of a prolapsed eyeball wet cotton should be held on it until you find help.

A good ophthalmologist can make many diagnoses of eye problems with an ophthalmoscope. There are board-certified veterinary ophthalmologists in many areas to help with difficult problems.

Progressive retinal atrophy is discussed in Chapter 14.

GLAUCOMA. Glaucoma is the condition where too much pressure develops within the eyeball itself resulting in an enlargement, pain, and destruction of tissues in the eye. Early medication is helpful in some cases but in others early surgery may be needed to save sight.

CATARACT. The lens of the eye is translucent and is located behind the pupil. In the young animal it cannot be seen, but as a dog ages the lens develops hardening of the microscopic arteries resulting in a faint gray appearance at first. With extreme age the pupils look blue. This lenticular sclerosis is not to be confused with cataract formation, which is denser and sometimes white in appearance. With old-age blue pupils, the dog can still see a fly on the wall but with advanced cataracts blindness results.

Cataract surgery should be done on young dogs with ripe cataracts but when cataracts develop in a dog eight years or older usually degenerative changes in the retinas accompany this lens problem. Surgery in this condition will not help.

Another problem of the lens is luxation, which means the lens loses its attachments and gravitates down in the front of the eye.

PROBLEMS OF THE EARS

Ear Canker. For years we have referred to a condition of dogs' ears as canker. As time and research progress, we realize canker is a catchall word for many problems of the ear. The rapidity of onset of some ear problems is spectacular, with a normal ear canal progressing in twelve hours to become a brightly inflamed area and an ear full of a tacky, often foul-smelling pus. When this happens, the animal holds its head with the infected ear down and shakes gingerly—scratching brings forth a yelp of pain.

Perhaps more often the onset is insidious and progresses over a week or two before the animal is obviously in trouble. If you suspect a problem, don't be above smelling the ear and if you find a foul odor you may be sure there are bacteria that will soon cause a more serious problem if not treated.

There are many over-the-counter preparations for ear canker, none of which are very effective and most of which may delay a trip to the veterinarian. If you want to try a home remedy purchase propylene glycol from a pharmacist. (Propylene glycol appears to be oily but is water soluble; it is not to be confused with ethylene glycol, which is antifreeze for car radiators and poisonous when ingested.) In most states you can purchase antibiotic capsules without a prescription from any pet shop that sells aquarium supplies. Five capsules of 250-mg tetracycline in each ounce of propylene glycol will cure a large percent of ear canker cases, but if you do not see a good improvement in twenty-four hours make haste to your veterinarian.

All too often ear mites, which will be discussed later in this chapter, open the way for bacterial infection and, when properly applied, mineral oil will destroy them. However, if the bacterial infection is a particularly difficult infection to destroy, as is the case with one called pseudomonas, the mineral oil will enable the infection to flourish instead of curing it.

If you permit an ear infection to remain untreated there is a danger of erosion of the tympanic membrane, or eardrum. This opens the way for the infection to enter the middle ear with its delicate and vulnerable tissues and presents a challenging problem to a veterinarian to correct.

One of the ways of diagnosing ear canker in order to provide the correct and best treatment consists of removing some of the causative infective agent on a sterile swab and performing a bacterial culture and sensitivity of it. There are times when all efforts to treat an ear infection are unsuccessful and the veterinarian properly will suggest surgery to open the canal to expose it to air and to facilitate the application of medication to the infected area.

Tumors of the ears are relatively common and may become the focal point of infection. They should be removed.

Ear Mites. Ear mites are small insects that live in the external ear canal. A few of these insects cause great distress in dogs, unlike in cats where hundreds of mites cause little apparent discomfort. If your dog suddenly begins to shake its head and scratch violently and there is no moisture and debris in the ear, you should suspect ear mites. After many days of discomfort a mahogany-colored crumbly wax develops. When placed on a black surface, this may be observed to have minute light-colored objects moving on and around it. A magnifying glass makes the diagnosis easier.

How does a dog contract ear mites? Since our feline friends are predisposed to ear mites and since many cats live with little attention from people, they appear to be the principal reservoir of infection. An infested cat wanders through shrubbery around a house and shakes its head, shedding a few insects on the leaves of the shrubs. Your dog, interested in the cat scent, gives the area an olfactory going-over and while poking its head through the shrubbery picks up a pregnant female mite.

Dogs commonly have ear mites in one ear only and why this is so is a curiosity of nature. In studies done on bats, ear mites are common but are never in both ears. When mites are removed from an infected ear and placed in the unaffected ear, they leave that ear and travel back to the infected one. Interestingly, when an unaffected bat has mites placed in both ears, the mites thrive in one ear and those placed in the other leave. The idea of selective tissue immunity may be recognized as important as curiosities of nature are solved through continued research.

Hematoma. An injury to a blood vessel in the ear flap may cause a blood clot, or hematoma, to form. The ear appears to be slowly inflating over many days until the ear resembles a small football. We think nine out of ten such hematomas are caused by the dog scratching a new infection of ear mites. In any event, one has a choice of surgery to correct it or leaving the swelling alone. If not corrected the swelling recedes, leaving scar tissue contractions and an ear resembling a potato chip in configuration. Surgery is preferable.

A laceration on an ear tip is more of an inconvenience than an emergency. Dogs will shake their heads, causing blood to be forced out of minor vessels at the site. The tip of the ear may strike the top of the head and under the neck, leaving bloody areas there. If the laceration is small, sit with the dog and hold cotton with pressure against the area until the bleeding stops. This may require an hour or more. The vessels will eventually retract if the cut is not too deep. Remove the dog's collar(s) since with continued shaking the tags and buckle will reopen the lacerations. If you cannot control the bleeding in a reasonable time, call your veterinarian.

PROBLEMS OF THE NOSE

Stenotic Nares. Stenotic nares is a term given to the nose when there is a partial obstruction due to the anatomy of the animal. If this is not corrected, the animal may strain to inhale through the nose, causing a partial vacuum in the throat and even the trachea. This vacuum causes tissues to swell and further obstruct the respiratory tract and may even cause a partial collapse of the trachea. Stenotic nares should be bred out of the lines of the affected breeds but for an individual animal with the condition, surgery can correct it.

In these same breeds the lacrimal ducts are often obstructed and cannot conduct excess tears into the nasal passages properly. This results in the chronic overflow of tears that keeps the skin and hair of the inner corners of the eyes moist. This is a good situation for infection and is at best unsightly.

These brachycephalic breeds frequently develop an elongated soft palate, further aggravating breathing. This situation may best be corrected by surgery.

Nosebleed. Nosebleed, or epistaxis, is usually caused by injuries as is the case with humans, but vigorous sneezing may cause a dog to strike its nose on a hard surface causing bleeding.

Infections of the nasal cavity should be treated promptly, since the invasion of the sinuses with long-standing infection presents a difficult problem to combat. When the infection is in one nasal cavity only there is a good chance some foreign material such as a blade of grass or a twig may be present. Special instruments and lights are used under anesthesia to remove the cause.

Besides infection and foreign objects, tumors do cause nasal discharge of purulent material with or without bleeding. There is little one can do at home with these problems and veterinary attention should be sought promptly.

Snorting. The reverse cough, or snorting, is a problem that causes many dog owners to rush for professional help. This is usually not a serious condition. When the onset is sudden a dog owner may describe it as an "asthma attack," which it isn't. When snorting occurs a dog will stand with its legs spaced apart and its head down drawing air through the nose and expelling it out the mouth. This results in the repeated snorting sounds that all who have been around many dogs have heard. Some dogs have these paroxysms when they pull on a leash. Some seem to have them seasonally and others snort off and on all their lives. When we receive a call in the middle of the night from a frantic owner whose dog has this problem, we suggest one of many human cold medicines containing an antihistamine. The children's dose is to be given to medium and small dogs and the adult human dose to larger dogs. Although antihistamines are not as helpful for dogs as for humans, they do hold this problem in check.

We suspect particles in the air such as pollens and house dust may be contributory causes of snorting. One of our house pets has attacks if it is exposed to hair spray.

Nasal Discharges. Nasal discharges are common when the immune system is suppressed, permitting usually nonpathogenic bacteria to thrive. A good example of this problem is canine distemper with its mucopurulent nasal discharge. Since the nasal passages have direct contact with the sinuses, these pockets may become involved, making a more difficult problem. When sinus infection becomes entrenched, surgery to drain the sinuses is a last but often successful resort.

Sense of Smell. It is rare to find even an old dog with hardening of the arteries that loses its sense of smell. This ability to smell extremely diluted odors and aromas means that our dogs live in an environment we cannot comprehend. In a recent study with Labrador Retrievers, an odor was diluted until people could no longer recognize it; when further diluted twenty thousand times it was still recognized by the dogs. A Bloodhound trailed and located a criminal 105 hours after the crime. A bird dog can scent a bird 100 yards upwind and run with head high until close enough to point it.

Science has contributed so much to sound and sight exploration but virtually nothing to the exploration of odor detection and identification.

When deaf and blind, most old dogs can locate food and water with little effort. Only rarely do we find an animal that loses all three senses and when we do it is obvious that its life is not worth living.

Other miscellaneous problems of the nasal area are cleft palates, eroded palates from burns from chewing electric cords, and infection from diseased roots of teeth. Extractions and antibacterial drugs usually correct the infection but plastic surgery is necessary to mend palate defects.

22

Problems of the Skin

It is accurate to say that canine dermatology is not an exact science. Even when we are aware of a cause of a problem it is not always possible to effect a cure. We can divide skin problems into three general categories: external, internal, and externally caused internal problems, such as inhalant or food allergies.

One of the first observations made by veterinarians in the evaluation of skin disorders is to note the locations of lesions and whether or not they are symmetrical. If the lesions are equal on both sides of the dog the condition is suspect of being of internal origin. If asymmetrical, it is thought to be of external origin.

Many skin problems are self-limiting in that even after extended periods of severe dermatitis the problem disappears permanently without treatment. An example is red mange, which is discussed in Chapter 23. Many, perhaps most, young dogs develop this problem, which usually—but not always—disappears with maturity. The question is asked of veterinarians, why, if the problem is contagious, doesn't the second dog in the house have it too? The answer is that some dogs have an immunity to a particular disease to which another may be susceptible.

Pruritis or Itching. One of the more perplexing dermatologic problems in dogs is pruritis, or itching, which is usually seasonal in the late summertime and into the fall. Dermatitis and eczema are catchall words, but since we like labels, many in the profession call the condition "summer eczema."

Once a name is given to a problem we veterinarians are as human as anyone and we assign a cause. Years ago we called summer eczema a grass allergy. Dogs are exposed to grass to which they are allergic by contact. They develop a typical itchiness accompanied by hair loss starting around the base of the tail and extending up the back.

After grass allergy came the term "grass fungus"; a fungus that was also found on grass could be cultured from the skin of affected dogs. More recently many veterinarians have decided flea bite dermatitis is the cause, the theory being that affected dogs are allergic to the saliva of fleas and, theoretically, even one flea can bring on the condition and when are most dogs without one flea in the summertime? There is little doubt that some dogs are allergic to flea saliva, but this should not be sweepingly considered the cause of all summer itching.

We would like to offer quite a different opinion. We think affected dogs are sensitive to some unidentified substance given off in the moisture secreted by the skin. Of course dogs don't sweat as we do because they have few sweat glands in their skin, but moisture is given off normally. We contend more moisture forms in hot weather and dogs susceptible to this irritant in the moisture suffer.

There is no doubt that baths give temporary relief to the itching of summer eczema but often for only twelve or so hours. Medicated soaps are effective but an oily solution which we call "yellow oil lotion" seems to be better. Perhaps the oil prevents the contact of the irritating unknown substance with the skin. The formula of one third each by volume fine sulphur powder, corn oil, and kerosene has been a great help to relieve the itching but has the disadvantage of messiness.

Pursuant to our belief that moisture is the cause of itching, we have asked owners of dogs with early-stage summer eczema to dust their pets with an antiperspirant powder—human antiperspirant *not* a deodorant —daily. Many believe it has brought great relief and prevented the problem of previous years.

Only in desperation should steroids be given to stop itching, as steroids depress the immune system. It is suggested the route of administration should be through the mouth and not by injection; once injected steroids cannot be withdrawn.

Lip-fold Pyoderma. Some breeds have folds of skin along the lower jaw that are subject to an infection that usually produces a foul odor. Many owners think the problem is halitosis perhaps caused by bad teeth or gums, but touching the area with a fingertip and smelling it reveals the odor. Antibiotics and even tamed iodine will correct this problem. An occasional dog experiences this problem even without having the deep lip folds.

Moist Eczema or "Hot Spot." Moist eczema begins as a spot the size of your little fingernail one day, grows to the size of a silver dollar the next, and is the size of your palm on the third day. The hair falls out; the area is yellow, glistening, and painful. One of our colleagues said he thought that seven days in the hospital with treatment three times a day cures this disease; if treated otherwise it takes a week. We think the yellow oil lotion described previously is the best treatment we have used on dogs with this problem. It must be applied liberally twice daily until the scab that forms works off. The hair grows back with no aftereffects. This treatment usually reduces the discomfort and corrects the problem in less than a week.

Shedding. It is perfectly normal for a dog to shed. The denser the coat, the more obvious the condition. Even what may appear to a pet owner to be excess shedding is a sign of good health. Dogs maintained outside tend to shed twice a year, in spring and fall, but pets living in the house and exposed to the outside a few times a day tend to shed 365 days a year. Breeders refer to a dog "blowing its coat" when shedding is at its peak. It is not normal for shedding to leave nude areas and if this happens you take the animal to the vet.

That hormonal problems are reflected in problems of the skin is well established and many are mentioned in Chapter 25. One good example is the loss of the coat in a female a month or so after whelping a litter of puppies. Many females in the wild lose a good deal of their coats to line their nests prior to whelping, but perhaps in domestication we have altered the dog's physiology.

Allergies. Allergies may be caused by inhalation or ingestion of allergens. Once the cause is established some dogs may be desensitized by injections.

One city dog had been treated for recurrent attacks of itching, scratching, localized hair loss, and open lesions off and on for a year. We thought we were helping when the owner phoned to ask if we thought a month in the country at a lake would be harmful to the family pet. We told him to try it. After two weeks' vacation the dog's skin was normal. One day it was driven into the city for the day. In the car the dog began scratching and biting itself mercilessly. Back in the country it was normal again. The dog was allergic to wool and the family car had a wool blanket over the seat. To double-check our assumption we had the owner massage lanolin, which is wool fat, into the skin of the abdomen as a test. The area was red and swollen in hours. Allergy problems due to ingestion are in effect year-round. One of our canine patients cannot tolerate meat but can eat eggs with no ill effects. Remember, commerical dog foods have meat and fish in dehydrated form. Food allergies can often be diagnosed by the owner who selectively withholds a particular food from the diet over a two-week period. Milk and eggs must be high on any list of allergic foods and, since these foods are commonly used in baking, all foods with any combination of these should be withheld.

One of the more dramatic allergy reactions to food manifests itself by large hivelike lesions that expand as you watch them. Some reach two inches in diameter and rise over half an inch above the normal skin. A dog with such a reaction usually shows no discomfort from this "hob-nail" pattern of swellings all over the body. This dog may be rushed to a veterinarian as an emergency and the veterinarian may watch the swellings recede before his or her eyes. If this condition is persistent, steroids are helpful. One problem lies in the difficulty in the determination of the cause. It may be food ingested twelve or more hours prior to the reaction. The instance of a dog on a commercial food that has received a specific food in addition may give us the clue necessary, but as so many dogs either forage outside or are fed a variety of leftovers it may be difficult to pinpoint the causative agent.

Food and Skin Disease. It is often said that certain foods are too "heatening to the blood," that they cause skin disease. There is very little truth in that idea. We used to be advised too often (and still, alas, are) that we must never feed fat or starches in hot weather because they cause eczema.

But let's put the old clichés aside and recognize that whatever the cause and effects there are some foods that affect some dogs adversely. We are inclined to think the cases are rare but some are so dramatic they should be mentioned. One handsome German Shepherd male was brought in as a last resort, the owner commented. The dog had been treated without results by two of the most prestigious veterinary institutions in the country. With the exception of a few times when he had received a cortisone-type medication, he had been biting and scratching for two years. We learned he had been skin-tested four different times for allergies and had had repeated blood tests. Not being dermatologists we decided to try to find areas not investigated by the experts. After a good deal of conversation one obvious fact emerged. Although many diet changes had been advised, including one week when only raw hamburger was fed, there was always the common denominator: meat. Of course dry commercial dog foods contain meat in a dehydrated form. We suggested we make a vegetarian of the dog and in three days the itching and biting ceased and the open lesions were healing nicely.

The vegetarian diet consisted of a mixture of one half soybean meal cooked in a pressure cooker with one quarter of either boiled rice or oatmeal and one quarter crushed cooked mixed vegetables. We added a vitamin mineral mixture and two tablespoons of corn oil.

The dog has been normal since that time except for one twenty-four hour period after a cookout, when someone fed the dog half a hamburger.

Since the meat-sensitive German Shepherd we have found another dog that can eat only small amounts of meat without breaking out with an itchy rash. However, many of our vegetarian clients' owners are feeding our vegetarian formula out of choice, and we suspect some eat it themselves.

Many dogs have a violent reaction to pork—not small amounts but on that rare occasion when they are fed a meal of leftover smoked or fresh pork. The results are usually vomiting and diarrhea for part of a day.

Lick Granulomas. Chronic thickened skin on the surface of a foreleg and occasionally on a rear leg where it is convenient for a dog to lick may be a lick granuloma. The hair falls out and the skin appears to be tough and leatherlike. When medication is applied without a bandage, the dog promptly licks it off. At one time these lesions were treated by injecting them with snake venom. Cobra venom was the choice and did help many such cases, but steroid injections seem to be more effective with topical antibiotics. Bandaging may help but often the dog licks the edges of the bandage, resulting in a new lick granuloma. Surgery helps some cases but not infrequently the dog licks the healing wound and produces another area of involvement where the affected tissue had been removed. There is good evidence that if the dog stops licking the lesion heals. And one wonders if the saliva contains an agent capable of causing a lick granuloma.

Interdigital Pyoderma. Pyoderma means pus in the skin, and some breeds appear particularly susceptible to this disagreeable problem. Abscesses develop between the toes, swell and rupture, then drain and heal. In a few weeks the swelling returns and the same sequence of events happens. Some dogs develop these abscesses between all the toes on all four feet but more often there will be only one or two at any one time. The cause is not understood but experience indicates small doses of the antibiotic tetracycline in the food daily does control but not cure the problem. Surgery helps to correct some of these lesions.

Fly Strike. In some areas of the country a blood-sucking fly will attack the ear tips of erect-eared dogs, causing bleeding and scabbing there. These flies attack only animals that are kept outdoors. It helps to keep the flies away by mixing a fly repellent, such as tolumide, with Vaseline and applying it to the ear tips three times daily. Your veterinarian can tell you whether these flies are a danger in your area.

Dandruff. The outer surface of the skin is shed constantly and even when this shedding is normal it appears excessive in three- to four-month-old puppies. Many dogs have a coat texture that permits the dandruff to fall out unnoticed, but other coats seem to hold it, suggesting a problem. Any good shampoo and even dish-washing detergent will remove it with a bath. But excess dandruff shedding can be abnormal and caused by many problems. A lack of fat in the diet predisposes many dogs to have dandruff. Both allergy and the common types of mange can cause it. Irritants such as too strong a soap used in a bath may create large flakes of dandruff some days later.

Persistent excess dandruff may indicate the early stages of one of several hormonal problems and a veterinarian should be consulted.

Coat Color Changes. Some dogs with dark coats may grow lighter-colored hair after a skin infection. Others with light-colored coats may grow dark hair. Usually this color change returns to normal after shedding.

Ringworm. The term "ringworm" has nothing to do with worms but is a fungal infection that may be contracted from humans or vice versa. It is discussed in Chapter 26.

Mange. Both demodectic and sarcoptic mange are skin problems caused by mites, and they are discussed in Chapter 23.

Cheyletiella Dermatitis. Another less common mite-related dermatitis is cheyletiella dermatitis. It is easily destroyed by flea sprays, powders, and rinses.

Alopecia. There are more inherited skin problems affecting several breeds than space permits describing. One of these inherited problems, alopecia, may affect all breeds. The word refers to abnormal loss of hair with no recognized infection or hormonal imbalance. There is no inflammation and no itching involved, but unfortunately we know of no reliable treatment.

Nasal Solar Dermatitis. Although also called "Collie nose," nasal solar dermatitis is not confined to that breed. The problem is a sensitivity to the sun that causes a dermatitis on the surface of the nose. The condition sometimes eventually extends up to the eyes. When the problem is advanced, the nose becomes disfigured and erodes away. When the dog is kept out of the sun, the condition improves. Tattooing, covering the nose with black ink from felt marking pens has controlled many cases, but the tissue may be so damaged that tattoos may not "take." Perhaps making the dog a nocturnal animal is most effective. Steroids and antibiotics also help minimize solar dermatitis.

Canine Pemphigus. Superficial ulcers of the lips, eyes, anus, vulva, and penis that progress to deep ulcers which then spread to other areas is a condition called pemphigus. When present this autoimmune disease is not correctible with antibiotics and antiseptics but steroids and other medications do help to control it. Pemphigus is considered incurable.

Acanthosis Nigricans. With acanthosis nigricans a few breeds and dogs of mixed breeds develop a dark pigmentation, usually under the forelegs, that progresses slowly to other areas of the body. The skin becomes thickened and is sometimes referred to as elephant skin. We know of no external treatment to cure this nuisance disease but palliative salves and lotions help to minimize it. It is found in dogs with a decrease of thyroid activity.

Seborrhea. Seborrhea is a result of overactive glands of the skin called sebaceous glands exuding a waxy substance often with a rancid odor in excessive amounts. When this occurs, the dog is miserable with some itching and thickening and scaling of the skin. Although there is no known cause, seborrhea can be controlled by bathing at weekly or less intervals for the life of the dog. Special medicated soaps are necessary, which your veterinarian may prescribe.

Atopic Dermatitis. Skin inflammation from inhaling airborne particles that produce an allergic reaction is called canine atopy. The agents most commonly responsible are pollens, dander, dust, and wool. The tendency to get this dermatitis, which starts between one and four years of age, is thought to be inherited. Saliva-stained extremities and itching are common signs, but many dry itchy conditions may be atopy. Skin testing is usually helpful in a diagnosis.

Contact Dermatitis. Many substances applied to the skin either intentionally or accidentally, such as acids, caustics, strong soaps and detergents, may cause irritations. Synthetic fabrics including carpeting and wool have been found to cause this as have chemically impregnated plastic collars. Some people claim poison ivy causes contact dermatitis but our research, which involved massaging the leaves into our own Beagles' lower abdominal skin twice weekly for two months, produced no reaction, although one of us developed the typical poisoning. Even eating from plastic dishes may cause dermatitis of the lips and nose in sensitive dogs.

Frostbite and Burns. It requires prolonged low temperatures to cause frostbite in dogs and virtually never occurs if a dog is free to find shelter. If an animal is chained or otherwise confined where there is inadequate shelter, however, the ear tips and scrotum are the most vulnerable areas to be affected by frostbite. Systemic antibiotics and antibiotic ointments are the treatments that should be used. They are obtained from a veterinarian.

Perhaps the most common cause of burns is hot fluids, such as coffee or tea, being spilled from a stove. You should apply an ice pack for fifteen minutes and take the animal to your veterinarian. He or she will give you an antibiotic with a steroid to be applied frequently. More serious burn cases should be hospitalized.

23

Parasites

Parasitic diseases from which our pets suffer are real diseases, often tragic in their consequences. Have you ever thought of lice infestation as a disease, or hookworms, or mange? Fortunately these are the easiest diseases to manage, as long as we remember that the cure is only half of the job; the important part is to prevent reinfestation. For this reason every pet owner should know, in a general way, the life history of all of the common parasites.

There are so many misconceptions about parasites—the damage they do and the symptoms indicating their presence—that it is perhaps best to begin by pointing out a few of the things they do *not* cause. The facts should make you suspicious of the suggestions of uninformed neighbors and friends who will almost invariably insist that your dog, if it is out of sorts for any reason whatever, needs deworming—or "worming," as they usually put it. Perhaps it does. And then again, perhaps it doesn't. A well-meaning neighbor's diagnosis is rarely conclusive. A simple test will shed light on the question. Intestinal worms, external parasites, or heartworms do not cause the temperature to rise. Don't deworm your dog simply because it shows signs of not feeling well, especially if it has a fever. Find out first what is wrong. It will only complicate matters to dose your dog with something it doesn't need just because a friend's dog benefited by deworming.

If your dog rides around on its hind quarters, pulling its body with the front legs, don't accept some volunteer adviser's word that this is a sure sign of worms. It is not. The chances are good that your dog is trying to express the accumulation in the anal glands or that that area itches.

When your dog has a cough, that in itself is not necessarily a sign that there are worms. Nor when it scratches, or becomes bald, or eats odd foods, even sticks and stones, or has a bad disposition, or whines, or deposits loose stools, or vomits, or has fits, or likes garbage. Any of these symptoms *might* be an indication of worms but probably is not.

INTERNAL PARASITES

Roundworms. Roundworms include all worms under the classification of nematodes, such as hookworms, whipworms, esophageal worms, heartworms, lungworms, and kidney worms, as well as the large round worms that most pet owners recognize. But as we use the term "roundworms" in this section, we shall limit it to the whitish or yellowish worm that grows up to five inches long in the stomach and intestines of pets, is pointed at both ends, and inclined, while alive, to curl up like a spring. When dead, it straightens out so that it may appear to be simply bowed at the ends.

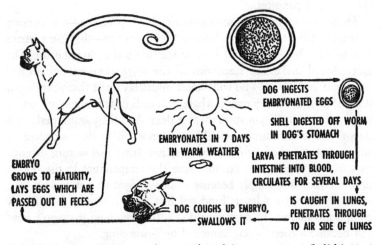

EMBRYONATES IN 7 DAYS IN WARM WEATHER

DOG INGESTS EMBRYONATED EGGS

SHELL DIGESTED OFF WORM IN DOG'S STOMACH

LARVA PENETRATES THROUGH INTESTINE INTO BLOOD, CIRCULATES FOR SEVERAL DAYS

EMBRYO GROWS TO MATURITY, LAYS EGGS WHICH ARE PASSED OUT IN FECES

DOG COUGHS UP EMBRYO, SWALLOWS IT

IS CAUGHT IN LUNGS, PENETRATES THROUGH TO AIR SIDE OF LUNGS

Life history of a common roundworm. Above left, mature worm (half life size). Above right, egg, magnified four hundred times.

Although there are several kinds of intestinal roundworms, their life histories are much the same. The eggs pass out of the animal with every bowel movement. In less than a week, if the temperature and moisture are propitious, a little worm forms in the egg. In other words, it has to incubate before it can hatch. Now this egg is in the infective stage and, as such, it will live for years, waiting to be picked up by a suitable host. It may enter the host in any one of dozens of ways. A dog may walk in a spot where feces have entirely disintegrated but where the eggs remain. They stick to its feet; it licks itself and becomes infested. A puppy may find the eggs on its mother's breasts, or a dog may drag a moist bone through an infested area.

The egg enters the stomach, and the shell, or coat, is digested, liberating the embryo. If it happens to be an egg of *Toxascaris leonina*, the larva moves along into the intestine, where it penetrates the lining, remains there for ten days, and grows. Finally it returns into the lumen, or hollow part of the intestine, and continues to grow to maturity, feeding on the animal's partially digested food.

If the roundworms are of the *Toxascaris canis* or *T. cati* variety, they are much more harmful to their host. In the intestine the little larvae bore through the intestinal lining and enter the bloodstream where they grow. Many may be found in the liver and spleen while on their way to the lungs. In the lungs they penetrate through from the blood vessels into the air spaces and are moved on to the windpipe. Up this they move in mucous secretions until the irritation causes the animal to cough and gag as if clearing its throat. The small amount of mucus with the worms in it is swallowed. Down the gullet go the parasites, which from then on until old age overtakes them, or worm medicine kills them, live in the intestine, migrating up and down at will, copulating and laying thousands of eggs.

Not only do roundworms give off a toxin, but the migrations of the larvae in the body, especially in the lungs, frequently cause death.

In puppies these worms cause potbellies, lethargy, diarrhea, anemia, often subnormal temperatures, and dull coats. When only a few worms are harbored, the symptoms are, of course, less noticeable and may consist only of a general lethargy, in spite of a fair appetite. In older dogs the worms' ravages are much less severe. Perhaps the most serious injury done by roundworms is to the lungs. Dogs develop verminous pneumonia as a result of the damage inflicted by large numbers of larvae boring from the blood vessels to the air sacs, causing irritation as they work up the bronchi and trachea to the throat.

PREVENTION: Prevention consists in deworming a bitch before breeding and keeping her off soil and out of quarters that are contaminated with roundworm eggs. If there is any chance that she has been where roundworm eggs are present, wash her teats before the newborn puppies nurse. When the puppies are walking, they too must be kept out of infected quarters. Bones and food that can be dragged around in filth are common sources of infestation.

TREATMENT: With puppies, a fecal examination should always be made before treatment. If worms are present, the puppies should be treated with Piperazine, which may be obtained from pet accessory establishments. It is the one over-the-counter drug that is safe, efficacious, and inexpensive. Veterinarians have medication that destroys several types of worms at one time.

One owner rushed in with a sick six-week-old Beagle puppy that was dead on arrival. It was one of six in a litter of seemingly healthy pups that became suddenly ill. Necropsy determined that the one-and-three-quarter-pound puppy had 179 roundworms. As the worms matured in the pup, overwhelming toxins were released. The other five littermates were treated successfully.

If tremendous numbers of roundworms are suspected, it is wise to follow the Piperazine in an hour with half a teaspoon of milk of magnesia to move the dead worms along. It is best to reworm parasitized puppies in three weeks.

Some owners ask at how young an age puppies can have roundworms and at what age can they safely be dewormed. We have kept a careful record of the age of infested dogs and have found a high percentage of three-week-old puppies with worms. These, of course, had been contracted before birth. It proved safe to deworm the youngest infested puppy. In our opinion it is safer to deworm them at the first sign of worms rather than to wait until they are two or three weeks older and sicker; they will tolerate it at the earlier age much better.

Hookworms. Hookworms are minute leeches living on blood that they suck from the intestine, to which they cling with a set of hooks or teeth about the mouth.

The animal hookworm is not the same worm that causes so much hookworm anemia in humans. Female animal hookworms are over five eighths of an inch long and males are slightly shorter. Three types are found distributed in different sections. *Ancylostomum caninum* has a very wide distribution, while *A. braziliense* is more or less confined to the South and tropical regions. *Uncinaria stenocephala* is a northern hookworm found in wild foxes and dogs kept in northerly climates.

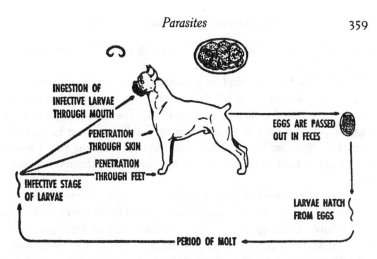

Life history of the hookworm. In the body the larvae behave much like the roundworm larvae, spending their early days in the dog's blood and lungs. They are coughed up and swallowed. They then attach themselves to the small intestine by their hooks. Above left, mature worm (life size). Above right, egg, magnified four hundred times.

The life history of the hookworm is interesting. The eggs, passed out of the host in the feces, need warmth to develop. Therefore the warm months are the hookworm months in the North, whereas the whole year is hookworm time in the deep South. After the eggs have incubated from three to six days, larvae emerge. These are called the first-stage larvae. Three days later the larvae molt and become the second-stage larvae. Eight days later they molt again to become third-stage or infective larvae and then lie waiting for a host. Hookworms can bore through the skin to reach the bloodstream. More often they are ingested through the mouth and are sometimes inhaled with dust kicked up in a place where stools have disintegrated and become mixed with soil.

If the larvae have reached the bloodstream by boring through the skin or internal tissues, they eventually reach the lungs, bore into the air sacs, are finally coughed up, swallowed, reach the intestine, and molt two more times. By three weeks after they first entered the body as larvae, hookworms are large enough to lay eggs. Sometimes hundreds cling to an animal's intestinal lining. They are very debilitating. A hookworm can suck half a teaspoonful of blood in a week. A thousand can suck one and a half drinking glasses *in a day.* No wonder hook-worms cause anemia!

With these facts in mind, two questions can now be answered:

How can mother animals lick their offspring clean of feces without becoming infested with intestinal parasites? The answer is that all the eggs of parasites have to undergo several days' incubation to be infective. The eggs that the mother cleans from her offspring pass through her digestive tract and lie in her feces, unharmed, to become infective later.

How can two-week-old puppies be passing eggs of hookworms, for instance, when about three weeks are required for the eggs to develop into worms old enough to lay eggs? The answer is that the puppies were infected while they were embryos. Since several species of parasites spend some time in the blood, these larvae manage to penetrate through the placenta and into the blood of the embryos, whence they find the intestinal tract.

The principal damage done by hookworms is the anemia they produce in young dogs and puppies. As dogs grow older and are subjected to repeated infestations, they develop partial immunity.

Infested puppies first suffer from lung damage similar to that caused by roundworms. The next result is anemia. One glance at the gums will reveal the puppy's condition. There are many other variable symptoms. The puppy may have seizures; diarrhea may become persistent and the appetite picky; sometimes the legs will swell. It may moan; usually it remains lying down, as if even standing up were an effort. It will lose weight, breathe more rapidly than a normal pup, and there is usually an acrid odor due to the discharge from diarrhea that coats its anus and the surrounding hair together with part of its tail.

Older dogs often have fits when first heavily infested. They, too, lose their appetites, develop anemia, become sluggish, have a hangdog appearance, and develop a generally unthrifty look. If proper food is not provided, even older dogs may die—because the best efforts of their red-blood-cell-building mechanism is insufficient to make up for the loss caused by the hookworm infestation.

PREVENTION: Prevention is the same as that indicated for round-worms, but in the case of hookworms, diet is more important. Iron and copper are essential and the protein fed to the animal must be of good quality.

TREATMENT: There are several excellent treatments for hookworms and a preventive drug, all of which veterinarians keep on hand. But supportive treatment is advisable. Food of high quality helps the dog to recover quickly. Transfusions often work wonders, once the worms are gone, or even before, in very anemic dogs.

Dog breeders often say it is better to build up an infested dog before it is dewormed. This seems to us to be a great mistake, because we have always found that a dog can't be built up as fast as its blood is being thinned by the worms, except by transfusion. The promptest possible action in getting rid of the worms is best if the dog is to be saved.

Having rid the dog of its pests, a diet rich in iron and copper should be provided. Some liver is excellent. Meat has iron. Good-quality dog foods all have sufficient amounts for ordinary requirements, but if a small pinch of ferrous sulphate or ferric and ammonium citrate is added to the diet daily, the redness will come back into the gums and the dog's energy returns more rapidly.

One treatment is not sufficient to completely rid a dog of hookworms anymore than it is enough to eliminate all roundworms. A second treatment two weeks after the first will kill the worms which were blood-living larvae when the first treatment was given. If the dog picks up another infestation, it will go much less severely than the first, and each subsequent infestation will build up a degree of immunity.

Whipworms. Considering their small size, whipworms are one of the most debilitating parasites that pets harbor. The whip handle, or body of the worm, is approximately half an inch long, but the whip part is about one and a half inches. This part is "sewed" into the lining of the intestine, but the pest can withdraw it to move. The worm is very thin; even the body is no thicker than the diameter of coarse sewing thread. Whipworms are usually found in the intestine, but in dogs they are found in large numbers in the cecum—a blind gut—where so many can sometimes be seen on postmortem that the lining of that organ appears to be covered with white hair, especially at its upper end.

The females lay yellowish eggs of a lemon shape. Incubation in the soil requires about three weeks at a fairly high temperature before the embryos are infective. So far as is known, upon being ingested, the larvae are liberated and at once seek the protection of the dog's cecum or fasten themselves along the intestine in the large bowel or colon.

A mild infestation of whipworms produces no more indication of

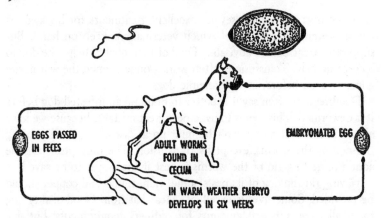

Life history of the whipworm. Above left, mature worm (life size). Above right, egg, magnified four hundred times.

their presence than alternating soft and firm stools. Severe infestations may produce seizures even in old dogs. Though the worms do not suck blood as do hookworms, they elaborate toxins which cause anemia. Loss of appetite, unthrifty coat, some eye discharge are all symptoms.

PREVENTION: As an important measure of prevention, all feces should be removed promptly and the sand in the kennel runs changed. If a house dog has the habit of defecating in any one small area, the top two inches of dirt should be dug up and replaced with uncontaminated sand.

Some of the worst cases of repeated whipworm infestation have been in dogs that used a part of a cellar to defecate in. Even though the feces are removed, there is bound to be a soft residue that sticks to the concrete floor. The furnace heat incubates the eggs. Then the dog drags a bone or dog biscuit about, manages to contaminate it with whipworm eggs, and thus becomes infested by eating the biscuit or lapping and chewing on the bone.

Even scrubbing concrete with soap and water will not remove all the eggs. No better means of disinfecting it has been found than the use of a flame torch. It is possible to obtain one that will burn the residue and heat the surface sufficiently to destroy all worm eggs in a few minutes. Around a kennel where fairly large areas of concrete require disinfection a flame torch is practically indispensable. If you do not have access to one, and your cellar floor is infected, a plumber's blowtorch may be used, though it takes longer. However, the time and effort spent will be amply repaid, as it will prevent your dog from continually harboring whipworms.

Viable whipworm eggs have been found in abandoned dog runs ten years after the dogs were removed. The eggs are practically indestructible except by heat and chemicals too dangerous to use. Rock salt and lime are not effective but powdered borax may be spread over a surface with fair results. However, the borax will also kill every living plant it touches and even trees if their roots extend under the treated surface.

TREATMENT: Years ago the usual method in treating dogs for whipworms was the removal of the cecum—an expensive surgical procedure. Today we have several effective means which are much less drastic.

All whipworm medications must be used with care. Some veterinarians insist on hospitalizing a dog for these treatments and all explain the problems and the necessary followup fecal examinations in three or so weeks to their clients. Whipworms may present a diagnostic problem since a dog can harbor many of the parasites without passing worm eggs in the stool.

If your dog has had a problem with whipworms there is a sign to look for that indicates reinfestation. In the early stages a dog will be seen to pass a normal stool but will keep trying, then pass soft stool at the end of the movement. As the condition progresses each day a little more of the stool will be loose until bouts of fluid stool with or without blood may be observed.

Tapeworms. Tapeworm infestation, also called taeniasis, is a disease just as is any one of the ailments caused by bacteria, though its effects need not be serious.

In small numbers tapeworms produce few ill effects, but when large numbers infest a dog they can make it a sick animal showing symptoms of nervousness, restlessness, and sometimes irritability. Because human beings are thought to have an increased appetite when they harbor tapeworms (it is doubtful if they really do), dogs also are generally expected to be hungrier. But they are not. Actually dogs usually lose their desire for food to some extent when they are infested with many tapeworms. Owners constantly bring their pets to veterinarians and tell us that the dogs must have tapeworms because their appetites are so enormous. Usually these prove to be healthy puppies, not sick dogs.

Tapeworms can cause such loss of condition that the dog has convulsions; its coat may become thin, its digestion be disturbed. There is often a marked tendency to vomit small amounts—enough to be a source of worry as well as a nuisance in a house dog. Occasionally segments of the worms lodge in the anal glands and cause irritation, so that the dog pulls itself along on its rear quarters.

Detection of segments of tapeworms on the dog's stool is the most certain method of determining the presence of the pest. A fecal examination may be made, but in the case of the flea-host worm it is not conclusive even when done by a thoroughly competent technician. They tend to retain their eggs, and the examination of any particular stool may not show evidence of infestation even when the worms are present in the dog.

There are two general kinds of tapeworms—the armed and the unarmed. The armed have suckers and hooks with which they cling, while the unarmed are equipped with only a pair of grooves which hold to the intestinal lining. A large armed tapeworm has powerful devices that enable the worm to hold fast despite all of the pull exerted on it by the passing food. It seems almost impossible that the little head can hold all of the worm, yet that is what it does. Besides the host in which they spend most of their existence, all tapeworms require an intermediate host and, in some cases, two such hosts. All are composed of a head to which are added a series of flat segments, joined one to another.

THE FLEA-HOST TAPEWORM (DIPYLIDIUM CANINUM): The most common tapeworm of our pets, the flea-host tapeworm occurs in dogs, foxes, and cats. It is about a foot long. The head is smaller than a small pinhead and the segments close to the head are stretched to the thinness of a thread. This section is called the neck. As the worm grows, the segments become wider and shorter. The last few segments are again longer and contain eggs. When ripe, these segments are shed and passed out with the stool. If no stool is present, the segment is moved downward and out of the anus, where it may cling until it dries into a small, brownish, seedlike grain that drops from the pet.

The eggs are not extruded without considerable pressure to the segment; then they appear in capsules and look, under a microscope, like bunches of grapes. When your veterinarian makes a fecal examination and tells you that your dog is free of worms, do not blame him or her for not detecting the presence of tapeworms. After you have seen a

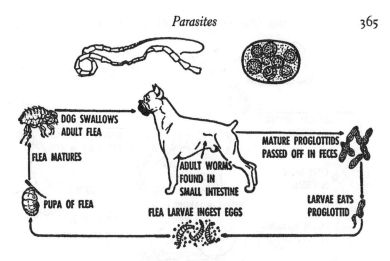

Life history of the flea-host tapeworm. Above left, mature worm (life size); it often grows to be eighteen inches long. Above right, capsule with eggs, magnified one hundred and fifty times.

dozen segments, you may have an examination made and receive a negative report. Your veterinarian studies the stool for eggs, and if the tapeworm has lost no segment in the specimen being examined, he or she won't find any. Finding segments is the only effective way to determine the presence of this worm.

Fleas and biting lice are the intermediate hosts of the common tapeworm. When fleas are in their larval stage, they feed on tapeworm segments among other foods. The eggs from these segments develop into tapeworm larvae as the flea matures. If an animal ingests the flea, the tapeworm larva is released and attaches itself to the intestinal wall, where it remains and grows.

THE RABBIT-HOST TAPEWORM (TAENIA PISIFORMIS): The rabbit-host tapeworm is a coarser worm than the flea-host tapeworm. Sometimes five to six feet long, its segments are larger and more active. The intermediate host is the rabbit or hare. This tapeworm lays many eggs that pass out of the dog in the stool and cling to vegetation. Rabbits eating the vegetation become infested. The larvae work into the liver of the rabbits to develop, and from there into the abdominal cavity, where they attach themselves to intestines in small cysts. When a dog eats an infested rabbit, it too soon becomes infested.

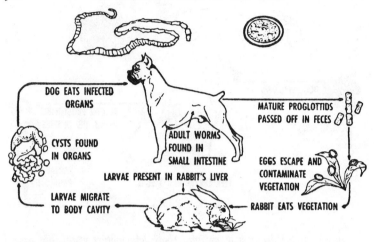

Life history of the rabbit-host tapeworm. Above left, mature worm (life size); it often grows to be two or three feet long. Above right, egg, magnified four hundred times.

THE PORK, BEEF, AND SHEEP TAPEWORMS (TAENIA SOLEUM, T. SAGINATA, T. MARGINATA, T. OVIS): It is rare to find the pork, beef, and sheep tapeworms in city pets. These tapeworms have been reported as long as fifteen feet. In country animals, which may feast on carcasses of dead animals, infestations may occur. Hogs, cattle, or sheep that have fed in pastures where human excreta has been deposited can eat grass to which tapeworm eggs cling. The dog eats flesh from these animals and becomes infested from the cysts containing the tapeworm heads. In the North a tapeworm, *Taenia krabbei*, infests dogs that eat infested reindeer muscle.

THE RODENT-HOST TAPEWORM (TAENIA TAENIAFORMIS): Widely distributed, the rodent-host tapeworm probably does its worst damage to cats. Rats, mice, squirrels, muskrats, and other rodents may act as intermediate hosts. The heads in the cysts develop in their livers and remain dormant until eaten by an animal. Cats are the most likely pets to suffer from this parasite and indirectly spread it to dogs.

THE HYDATID TAPEWORM (ECHINOCOCCUS GRANULOSIS): This unique parasite, the hydatid tapeworm, is dangerous because it does damage to so many species of animals. It infests many pets that eat meat. As intermediate hosts, most animals, including man, can be infested if by any chance the eggs are ingested.

The embryos bore through the intestines to the bloodstream and are transported to various organs where they become cysts which may measure three inches in diameter. The lining of the cyst produces numerous brood capsules in which heads are formed. A brood capsule may contain as many as forty heads six months after infestation. If a dog eats an organ infested with the hydatid he eats many heads, and in less than two months the worms that develop from the heads are laying more eggs to infest other animals which inadvertently consume them.

There are three unarmed tapeworms that are important to dog owners.

THE FISH-HOST TAPEWORM (DIPHYLLOBOTHRIUM LATUM) occurs in pets fed on freshwater fish, generally within a few hundred miles of the Great Lakes in the United States. *D. mansoni* affects cats and dogs in Puerto Rico. *D. mansonides* has been reported in New York and Louisiana.

A human harboring the tapeworm passes the eggs in feces which are dumped via sewers into a lake. Small crustaceans eat the eggs. In the first type, fish eat the crustaceans; in the latter two types, amphibians, such as frogs, or mammals that swallow the crustaceans can be the second host. Of course dogs that eat the fish or frogs or infested mammals become infested in turn. Raw whitefish, trout, salmon, pike, and perch have all been responsible for passing the cysts of these huge worms to pets.

Some of these worms have three to four thousand segments and at their widest may be half an inch or even more across.

TAENIA SERIALIS: Between two and three feet long, the *taenia serialis* is an intermediate worm which dogs and foxes frequently carry in their intestines, and which they contract by eating cysts and their inhabitants—the heads which may number a dozen or more—when they eat hares, rabbits, or squirrels. Some cysts may be an inch in diameter and cause the intermediate host great discomfort. The rabbits or squirrels become infested from eating grass, nuts, or other vegetation to which eggs of the worm are sticking.

It should be noted that many pets that are only intermediate hosts can be made very sick by the cysts of tapeworms developing within their organs and muscles as well as in their intestines. Rabbits are notorious in this respect.

PREVENTION: While it is obviously impossible to avoid all contact between a dog and any potential tapeworm host, the owner should try to reduce the contact to a minimum. The animal should never be fed any raw rabbit and whenever possible should be prevented from catching and eating them. It is also wise to see that all beef, pork, and fish fed to the dog is well cooked. Both the dog and the dog's quarters should be dusted with flea powder in order to reduce to a minimum its chances of catching and swallowing this insect host. If a dog has been infested, the kennel and the rugs and furniture in rooms it has been in should be thoroughly gone over with an efficient vacuum cleaner to remove all dried worm segments. It is also necessary to burn or bury the feces for a time to eliminate the chance of reinfestation.

TREATMENT: No worm treatment is always effective so even the medications veterinarians have at their disposal are not 100 percent effective but they are the best available. Over-the-counter drugs are of little use for eliminating tapeworms. Once eliminated, reinfestation is common.

TRICHINAE (TRICHINOSIS)

Trichinae are carried in the flesh of infested animals. Since an infestation is difficult to diagnose in a live animal, not many cases have been reported that could definitely be identified as trichinosis. Most of those that have been detected occurred when both the dog and its owner had a meal from the same undercooked pork. In a number of cases both had eaten undercooked bear meat. In these instances the owner has reported that a dog apparently experienced the same symptoms. Usually a domestic pet is not known to have had trichinosis until a postmortem reveals it. It is amazing, however, what a large proportion of both dogs and cats are found to have had an undetected infestation. One study showed that 8 percent of those examined were infested.

When the cysts are forming in the muscles of the dog, there is pain and stiffness, depending in severity upon how many trichinae there are present. The animal may have a fever, loose stools, loss of appetite, some grunting when it has to move. It is difficult to get it to show the reactions of a normal dog in play or in any activity in which exertion is required. Since there is no remedy for trichinosis, don't feed pets raw or undercooked pork. Hunters should not feed raw bear meat, raw raccoon, or the raw flesh of any other meat-eating animal. Never allow a dog to eat dead rats or mice which have been living on garbage. Garbage-fed hogs that die should be buried deeply, after first being covered with quicklime, to prevent dogs or wild animals from eating them.

ESOPHAGEAL WORMS

Here, again, is a parasitic disease that is not always easily diagnosed. Dogs infested with esophageal worms exhibit the symptoms of coughing and vomiting. The tumorlike pockets or pouches in the gullet, with many worms protruding, cause irritation. Sometimes one or more such tumors may be felt in the gullet behind the windpipe. Considerable damage to blood vessels is believed to result from the migration of the larvae in reaching their resting and living place in the esophagus. Dogs often lose weight, and their frequent gagging and coughing is racking to the dogs and a source of worry to their owners.

The intermediate host for esophageal worms is the dung beetle. Therefore, keeping dogs clean and removing stools frequently will do much to prevent infestation.

FLUKES

When dogs eat raw fish in which the cysts of flukes are present, they become infected, and in a week the flukes are mature and are laying eggs. Salmon poisoning, one of the fluke diseases, is serious in the Pacific Northwest and southwestern Canada.

The symptoms of fluke disease are somewhat like those of distemper, except that the temperature is much higher—106° to 107°. The dog shows great thirst, refuses food, and has an eye discharge. In some dogs it causes a swelling of the face. After a day of high fever the temperature drops and the stools become liquid and bloody. This and the effects on the organs cause emaciation and dehydration. In six to eight days the temperature falls below normal, and the dog soon dies. The mortality is high—75 percent of untreated dogs die. Study has convinced researchers that the presence of the flukes themselves is not the cause of the disease, but rather that a bacterium associated with flukes is the actual agent of infection.

Other fluke diseases, such as heart disease and lung disease, are serious in their localities, but these are prevalent chiefly in Asia and the Philippine Islands. The invasion of the lungs produces coughing and pneumonia symptoms, while the heart is weakened to the point of inefficiency and even death by the presence of the parasites in large numbers.

With one or two exceptions, the avoidance of feeding uncooked fish is the important precaution in the prevention of flukes of most varieties. If dogs can't get raw salmon they are spared salmon poisoning. If they are not fed raw fish of any sort, they will not contract fluke diseases generally. Among the fluke diseases, only salmon poisoning in dogs can be treated.

PROTOZOA

Besides these already mentioned, there is a different kind of organism that produces diseases of a very serious nature in pets. This organism is the protozoa, thought to be the lowest form of animal life. There are several forms, of which the sporozoite named *coccidia* is the most important. These one-celled minute organisms live among the cells of the intestinal lining. Their life history is exceedingly complicated, and the damage they do is accounted for by the enormous numbers that develop before the body eventually overcomes them. Two other types, babesia and toxoplasma, cause considerable damage as parasites of pets.

Coccidia. Each species of animal and bird is infested by specific types of coccidia, but some have more than one. Dogs and cats have three principal forms affecting both species. Rabbits, poultry, and even reptiles are afflicted. All types of coccidia are extremely prevalent, the year round in warm climates and in the summer in the cooler climates.

This disease, coccidiosis (pronounced cock-sid-e-ósis), affects dogs of all ages. It is self-limiting and usually passes with no treatment just about as quickly as with any treatment devised to date. Any dog, once recovered, will never again have the disease caused by that particular

Coccidia. Three common types as they appear when enlarged through a microscope. Left, Isospora rivolta; right, Isospora felis.

species of coccidium but can be infested by one of the other species. However, once immune, a dog is a carrier all the rest of its life, as indicated by eggs (oocysts) that can occasionally be found in fecal examinations.

Puppies are usually quite severely affected, while mature dogs may show no symptoms other than impairment of appetite and loose stools. Symptoms to be watched for are loose stools, often with bloody color, maturating eyes, elevated temperature (about 103°), loss of appetite, general unthriftiness. In severe cases, weakness and depression are apparent as well as emaciation, dehydration, and death.

In size, coccidia are microscopic. The form found in the feces, the egg, or oocyst, is roundish with a nucleus inside. Some oocysts show divided nuclei. The forms infesting dogs and cats are *Isospora rivolta, I. bigemina,* and *I. felis.* We are fortunate our dogs have only three principal forms. Birds may be host to at least a dozen species.

After it has been outside of the host for several days, the coccidium egg form develops into the infestive stage, provided conditions are favorable. Flies carry it to feeding pans or animals pick it up by licking their feet or by getting feces into their mouths. Inside the animal the coating of the egg form is digested and the infestive forms that have developed in the egg are released. These bore into the cells lining the intestine and develop until they divide into other bodies.

This division and growth damages or destroys the cells, but these new forms now enter other cells and repeat the cycle. This goes on through several divisions and attacking of new cells, until at length male and female forms are produced. The males fertilize the females and thus produce the egg form that is passed out with the feces and deposited with the loose stool to infest other animals.

Coccidiosis is a disease not easily differentiated by external symptoms from some other diseases. Microscopic investigation is necessary to establish the diagnosis. Puppies affected during the teething period (from three and a half to five months) may be left with pitted teeth, as they may be from distemper and other febrile diseases.

When nursing puppies are infected they seem to have mild cases. It affects them much more severely after they have been weaned. Whether this is the result of changing from a diet rich in fat to one with a very low level of fat, as is so often done, or whether the mother's milk possesses some antibody, or the puppies possess some maternal immunity, we cannot say. It is known, however, that puppies weaned on a high-fat diet survive the disease with less loss of physical condition and weight than those on a low-fat diet.

Puppies can contract the disease from their mothers' breasts. They also pick it up from infected quarters. Coccidiosis has been called the "pet shop disease," because where puppies are placed together indiscriminately there is likely to be one or more infected. Not being housebroken, they drop stools into which other pups are bound to walk, and infection is a certainty in that case. When direct contact is not responsible for infection, flies are usually the cause. Even in kennels where the environment is immaculate, where puppies are raised in wire-bottom cages, we find coccidiosis occurring regularly as long as other dogs in the kennel are carriers.

PREVENTION: By thoroughly screening pens and cages and by thoroughly cleaning one's own hands and feet, it is possible to raise pups in kennels and to keep them free from the disease. But it is difficult to realize that what we can't see may be present, and here we are dealing with organisms only a few sizes larger than bacteria.

Do we want to raise puppies free from the disease? Most parents are not greatly disturbed when their children contract one of the so-called children's diseases. They feel that it is best that the children be immunized early rather than be subject to these diseases later, when they may be more difficult to deal with. We are not unhappy when our kennel dogs have coccidiosis and recover. They will, in all probability, have it anyway, so perhaps we should not complain of the loose stools indicative of the disease. The danger is that the puppies might have more than coccidiosis. When several diseases strike at once, puppies may not recover. If they have to have it, it is better for them to have passed the young-puppy stage, for when they are a little older they will recover from coccidiosis quite easily.

From the life history of the infecting organism, it becomes obvious to us that for a puppy or a dog to have the lightest case it is essential that it get as few reinfestations, one heaped on the other, as possible. The first is bad enough, but if every day it is exposed to new eggs in large numbers it has far less chance of recovery.

The wire-bottom pen is the best possible insurance against heavy reinfestation. If it is screened on the outside down to the ground, flies cannot continue to carry eggs from feces to food dishes or lips.

TREATMENT: Almost all cases of coccidiosis that are treated are already on the way to recovery, since the whole duration of the disease is only about three weeks. Let's assume your puppy shows definite signs of sickness. Its eyes maturate; it has a fever of 103° F; its stools are watery. You may reasonably think it has coccidiosis. Your veterinarian makes a fecal examination and finds thousands of coccidia eggs. By that time the pup is at the height of the disease. If you give it brick dust, cobwebs, sulfa drugs, vinegar, and molasses, or any other remedy, the puppy will probably recover—but not because of the treatment. The puppy is getting well anyway. As one scientist has said, "Coccidiosis is the disease about which more foolish cures have been reported than any other disease of animals." Every so often a study reports a new cure, but usually the investigation has been made without untreated controls for comparison. However, some promising treatments are now under scientific investigation and your veterinarian will tell you about them if they prove satisfactory.

Feeding wholesome food with rich milk and fat constituting up to 25 percent of the diet is a good treatment. Here again a diet of one third each of cooked hamburger, boiled rice, and stewed tomatoes is helpful supportive treatment. We suggest antibiotics, not to treat this protozoan, but to treat or prevent secondary invaders which may set up housekeeping in the damaged intestinal lining. The addition of a heaping teaspoonful of bone ash mixed with the food, for a puppy the size of a five-week-old Cocker Spaniel is helpful. A tablespoonful a day is the dose for a large breed puppy. Remember that bone ash is not bonemeal or steamed bone. It is an entirely different product obtainable through your veterinarian or druggist.

Immaculate cleanliness is as important as anything. If the pup uses paper for defecating purposes, destroy the stool before it can walk in it. If you prevent reinfection, the chance of recovery is better than 90 percent.

There is a scientific question of the possibility of one type of coccidia being the same protozoa as toxoplasma.

TOXOPLASMAS

Toxoplasmosis, the widespread disease caused by toxoplasmas, has been found in many species of mammals and birds. It has received a good deal of attention, particularly in the sensational press, since it is communicable to people. As is not true of felines, the organism does not appear to be spread by canines, so our dogs, although capable of contracting it, do not threaten us with it. For dogs the logical sources for ingestion are infected cat feces or poorly cooked meat, which contain the parasites.

The signs displayed by dogs with toxoplasmosis are so varied they defy any but a presumptive diagnosis without laboratory help. Central nervous system signs, eye damage, lung, and gastrointestinal problems may all be due to this protozoan parasite. It can cause abortions in bitches and mortality in newborn puppies.

Laboratory tests can confirm a diagnosis but only after a series of tests has been performed. A combination of drugs is necessary for treatment, but the disease must be treated promptly before the parasite becomes overwhelming. A majority of adult humans have had and recovered from this disease.

EHRLICHIA CANIS

Ehrlichiosis, also called tropical pancytopenia, is a rickettsial disease caused by the organism called Ehrlichia canis and transmitted by ticks. It appears to develop in two stages, the first lasting two to four weeks wherein the animal has depression, loss of appetite, fever, nasal and eye discharges, and a dramatic loss of weight. When the disease is diagnosed in the early stages antibiotics are effective.

The more protracted stage, with blood changes, hemorrhages including nose bleeding, and edema or swelling of the limbs and elsewhere, is usually fatal. Concurrent infection with another disease, babesiosis (which is discussed next), is not unusual. The same tick spreads both. With the increase of ticks in many areas, Ehrlichiosis may be more serious than we realize. Studies in Maryland indicated 45 percent of the wild raccoons were infected and in Connecticut 100 percent of adult raccoons in a small sampling was discovered to be infected. This disease has historical significance. In 1890 veterinarians investigating the high mortality of cattle along the route of the great cattle drives from Texas to the Northeast made an important contribution to science. The names Daniel E. Salmon, Frederick Kilborne, and Theobald Smith made history when they proved that ticks transmitted the disease known as Texas fever. It was an outrageous suggestion to medical people the world over to think an insect could spread disease and the three veterinary scientists were ridiculed mercilessly. However, it was their work that suggested to Walter Reed that perhaps mosquitoes transmitted yellow fever and with that knowledge the yellow fever-carrying mosquito was controlled and the Panama Canal completed. It was through their efforts this and all insect-transmitted diseases have been recognized and therefore controlled.

BABESIAS

Four species of babesia have been identified with the tick-borne protozoan disease, babesiosis: *Babesia canis, B. gibsoni, B. vogeli,* and *B. felis.* The first three affect dogs and the fourth, cats. These organisms are so tiny that they live in the red blood cells. From one dog to the next the transfer is made by ticks, especially the brown dog tick.

Babesiosis is more prevalent in some sections than in others. There are places where dog owners have never heard of it because it apparently doesn't exist in that locality. There are other areas where it is present, though rare, and still dog owners have never heard of it. In the southern part of the United States—especially in Florida—it is a serious disease. The British Isles have been virtually free of it. Some sections of South America report it. Wherever ticks are prevalent, the protozoan organism causing babesiosis may be present.

Babesiosis can be very serious when it is acute. When it is chronic it may simply keep a dog feeling miserable for a long while and afford a splendid opportunity for ticks to replenish their supply of the infecting organism and spread it further. In other words, the chronic cases are carriers.

In the acute form it may be difficult to distinguish the outward symptoms from those of other diseases. The dog's temperature rises; the third eyelid looks redder than usual; the pulse and respiration both increase; the appetite diminishes; the urine may be reddish brown. But *unlike* dogs with distemper, and *like* dogs with leptospirosis, about half the dogs afflicted with babesiosis develop jaundice. In the acute form, even with adequate treatment, mortality is high.

In chronic cases the mucous membranes, such as the third eyelid, gums, and lips, all become pale instead of a healthy pink; the temperature rises and falls intermittently; the dog's appetite is poor and picky. The animal refuses to play, preferring to lie about. And as mentioned, it may develop a mild jaundice in a protracted case.

How can you be sure that your pet has this particular infection? First, your veterinarian, becoming suspicious because of the reddish brown urine, can detect the organism in the red cells from a small sample of blood.

Diagnosing the chronic form is not too easy, so in kennels the veterinarian draws a little blood from a suspected dog and injects it into one or two puppies known not to have been exposed previously to the disease. If the dog has the disease, the organism will show up in the blood of the puppies in from four to seven days. Then the veterinarian can cure both the adult dog and the puppies.

PREVENTION: The best prevention is to keep the dog free of ticks.

TREATMENT: A series of injections of various drugs is used to treat babesiosis. Your veterinarian knows and will tell you what needs to be done and how you can cooperate. Even with blood transfusions and good supportive treatment mortality is high.

EXTERNAL PARASITES

Fleas. Those little elusive insects that jump so far and those big, brown, long-bodied insects that crawl about on our pets are fleas. The big ones are always females; the little jumpers may be either males or young females. Fleas are a serious threat to the health of animals. They carry and spread tapeworms and bubonic plague. They also cause summer skin diseases, loss of weight, and poor coats on their hosts.

Of about sixteen thousand species of fleas on earth and about two hundred and fifty in North America, there are four common types of fleas important to dogs: the human flea, dog flea, cat flea, and sticktight flea. The human flea may breed on dogs and cats as well as on humans. The dog flea and the cat flea infest either dogs or cats, but prefer their specific hosts. When they bite humans it is only because they lack a dog or cat to feed on. The sticktight flea is most often found infesting the rims of the eyes of animals but may also be found attached to other parts of the body.

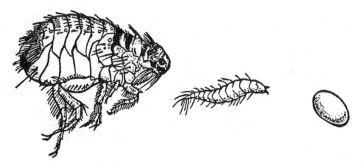

Stages of the flea, magnified fifty times. Left, adult; center, newly hatched larva; right, egg.

Fleas produce large numbers of eggs which drop off the host. The eggs sometimes get into cracks in the floor, into a sandbox, or into the furniture where the pet sleeps, and they may lie there in a dormant state for many months before conditions become right for their development. Some hatch very soon after they are dropped. Moisture and heat are essential for hatching. The egg is deliquescent, absorbing water from the air, so that whenever the weather becomes warm and humid, flea eggs soon hatch. In excessively dry climates fleas are almost unknown.

Out of the egg comes a worm, the larva. The worm feeds on organic matter such as scales from dog skin. It grows quickly. When it reaches the size of a very small maggot, it spins a cocoon and pupates like the caterpillar. Out of these cocoons come males and females, and at this stage they look very much alike. They are able to jump prodigious distances and are remarkably well protected against pressure. If you roll one tightly between your fingers and let it go, it will jump about as well as it did before.

After they hatch, fleas crawl up anything vertical and wait there, about a foot from the ground or floor, for a host to pass. If your pet is removed from your house during the summer, you may find after a few weeks that the fleas are attacking you instead. The fleas you find in the house have developed from eggs that were dropped from your pet, and since the original host has been removed, they use you as a substitute. Nor are the fleas confined to the house or kennel. You may easily be flea-bitten in the garden if your pet had the run of the grounds and eggs were dropped there.

Sticktight fleas do not move about or jump but cling to the skin, often in large clusters. The female burrows into the skin and lays her eggs in the ulcers she produces. After the eggs hatch the larvae fall to the ground, where they complete their development in about four weeks, when conditions are right. This flea is more prevalent in warm climates than in cold. Not only dogs, cats, and other four-legged pets are infested by sticktight fleas, but birds as well. This is a good fact to know where sticktight fleas are a problem; it may help you keep your dog free of them.

In some sections ticks are called sticktights. This is a colloquialism. Actually they are not the same thing.

Lice. The louse lives all its life—embryonic and adult—on an animal or bird. All species of pets may be infested, and it is believed that no type of louse can live for more than three or four days off the animal or bird on whose body it depends for sustenance. There are two kinds of lice—sucking and biting—and each type is subclassified into several species. Some are red, some gray, some bluish, but in spite of obvious differences their life histories are very similar.

A louse hatches from its egg, called a nit, which the female has fastened to a hair. The little louse, if it is a sucking type, crawls onto the body of the animal, fastens its mouth in the skin, and sucks blood. A large number can suck so much blood and give off such a toxin that the host often becomes anemic and dies. The biting louse, on the other hand, feeds on skin scales and organic matter as well as on blood. The males and females copulate; the female's body fills with eggs, she crawls up the hair shafts, and she attaches to them tiny silvery eggs that are large enough to be seen. The eggs of the biting louse hatch in five to eight days; those of the sucking louse in ten to twelve days. The young mature two or three weeks after hatching. Lice do not drop off their hosts spontaneously. In general, infestation is spread by contact and by close association. Apparently lice move from one host to another of a different species quite easily. For example, dogs and cats kept in close proximity are usually infested equally.

Lice may be a cause of death for whole litters of puppies. When a bitch is infested with lice, the fact may be unknown to her owner; but, when she has puppies, the lice tend to leave her and gravitate to the puppies—apparently the latter are more tender morsels. Before the owner knows it, the pups have developed dry skin that has lost resiliency, fail to thrive, and die. Every litter of puppies should be watched constantly for the presence of lice.

Scratching by dogs is one of the means by which lice are spread. Naturally the dog itches when infested, and scratching the itch can't

Lice and nits, enlarged twenty-five times. Left, blood-sucking louse; center, biting louse; right, nit glued to hairs.

help but remove a small number of the parasites. It is believed that this is one of the chief means of transferring lice from one dog to another, provided, of course, that the new dog comes along before three days have passed. The same occurs in the case of hairs which the dog breaks off in scratching. If nits are attached to those hairs, they may lie around for a considerable period before hatching.

One type of human louse, *Pediculus capitis*, can live on dogs. In many cases pets that have been treated for lice have become reinfested by lice from human beings. Fortunately most types of human lice are not able to infest dogs.

Ticks. Ticks have become a very great problem to dog owners even in areas where they were unknown a few years ago. They are often a nuisance in the house, even in a house where no pet is kept. Ticks feed on many species of domestic animals as well as on wild ones, and some are found on birds. One characteristic of the most common ticks found on pets and man is the necessity for each to feed on blood at some stage of its life.

Dog ticks, wood ticks, spotted-fever ticks, Pacific Coast ticks, brown dog ticks, lone-star ticks, Gulf Coast ticks, black-legged ticks—all are common names for the several kinds of ticks. Some kinds are known by several names. All of them are very much alike and all have similar life histories.

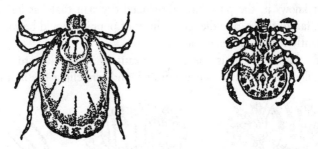

Dog ticks, enlarged six times. Left shows adult female before feeding; right, adult male.

Ticks pass through four stages: egg, seed tick, nymph, and adult. The female lays enormous numbers of eggs in a mass on the ground or in a clump of grass. There may be as many as three to six thousand eggs in one mass. When the American dog tick hatches from the egg as a seed tick, it has six legs. It attaches itself to a rodent which carries it about from two to twelve days and loses it after it has become engorged with blood. By this time the tick has eight legs, has molted, and is called a nymph. It again attaches itself to a rodent and for three to ten days stays on the rodent and engorges blood, then drops off and molts again. It is now mature and, in order to attach itself to a larger animal, gravitates close to a path through the woods and climbs a bush, where it is rubbed off onto its new host. It is an interesting if unexpected fact that studies made of these pests show greater concentrations along paths than in the pathless woods.

After the female has attached herself to a host, the male crawls under her and mating occurs while the female is filling with blood. If you look under the big beanlike body of female ticks on an infested animal, you will almost invariably find a male—a small creature which does not grow nearly as large as its mate. The female engorges on the host from five to thirteen days, then drops off, falls to the ground, and, being enormous and practically helpless, lays her eggs and dies.

Some ticks are not quite as discriminating as the American dog tick. Some spend their seed tick and nymph stages on birds and even reptiles, and one, the Gulf Coast tick, spends its immature stages on birds that live on the ground, such as quail, turkeys, and pheasants. Still others feed on birds their whole lives, notably *Argas reflexus,* whose host is the pigeon.

The brown dog tick, which is becoming the most widely distributed tick in the North, prefers to pass its early life inside dwellings. It is often found under picture moldings, behind baseboards, and in furniture. Even adult ticks can be found in such hideaways. Fortunately they do not suck human blood as some other species do.

Two varieties of ticks may cause a flacid quadriplegia (paralysis) in dogs. This paralysis is thought to be caused by a nerve toxin in the saliva of the female tick, and its first sign is a weakness in the hind quarters. This develops into a complete posterior paralysis that ascends to the brain, causing death. The removal of the offending tick and all other ticks results in a cure in hours.

Mites. There are many kinds of mites. Mange on pets is caused by *mange mites,* which are so small that they cannot be identified without a microscope.

The *red mange mite (Demodex canis)* is also known as the demodectic mange mite and follicular mange mite. When a dog shows a baldish area under an eye, on the cheeks, on the forehead, or on the front legs, it may have red mange. If it is not checked early, mange may soon have serious consequences. One of these is the bacterial infection that often develops, causing pustules and intense reddening of the skin, which is exacerbated by the violent scratching from the irritation.

The young mites, as they hatch from the eggs, appear to be elongated globs, but they mature very quickly to look like minute eight-legged worms. They live in sebaceous glands and in hair follicles, so that when an animal has been infected the hair soon drops off the area. They reproduce prodigiously. In eight days 1,000 female mites might increase to 12,000. In eight more days these might become 132,000.

Sarcoptic mange mites (Sarcopters scabeii) produce a disease called scabies. This is the disease most commonly transmitted from dogs to man. These mites are round, with four pairs of short legs. The female

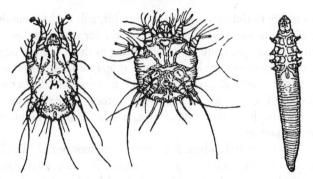

Mites that attack mammalian pets, all greatly enlarged. Left, ear mange mite; center, sarcoptic mange mite; right, demodectic mange mite, also called red and follicular mange mite.

tunnels into the skin and lays from twenty to forty eggs which hatch in three to seven days. One female can easily produce one and a half million descendants in three months. The newly hatched larvae have three pairs of legs, but they molt to become nymphs which molt still again before they become adults. This process requires two to three weeks for completion. Only the adult female burrows beneath the outside layers of skin; males and immature forms live on the surface under scabs or skin scales.

Because humans as well as dogs can become infested with scabies, a person who develops spots that itch persistently should consult a physician. Many veterinarians who have discovered sarcoptic mites on pets have also found that the pets' owners were infested. Human diagnosis is often difficult because it is necessary to scrape the skin quite deeply in order to uncover the burrowing females.

Ear mange mites (Otodectes cynotis) are round and have somewhat longer legs than the sarcoptic mites. They live in the ear canal, causing a crumbly wax which is quite distinctive from normal wax. Actually the substance found in the ear is composed more of scabs than wax, because the mites pierce the skin to suck plasma. The irritation causes animals to shake their heads sharply, which helps distribute the mites to other animals. Some dogs scratch their ears so vigorously that blood tumors develop between the layers of the ear flaps.

The life history of the ear mite is believed to be similar to that of the sarcoptic mite.

The *sand flea (Leptus irritans)* is also called a chigger, harvest mite, chigga, chigre, jigger, red bug. Adult red bugs, which are quite large, do not bother humans or pets. Nor does the second, or nymph, stage. The larvae alone attack animals, and then only shortly after they have hatched. Like ticks, they suck blood and drop off to molt. After this molt the nymphs may feed on plants, but not on mammals. The tiny larvae annoy pets a great deal. They often cause severe scratching and sometimes loss of weight, without the owner's understanding the cause. Birds are also troubled by this pest to such an extent that they have been known to die from the attacks. Red bugs are native to the southern United States and semitropical countries.

HEARTWORMS

There was a time when the disease called heartworm, caused by heartworms, was recognized only in a small area of the southeastern United States but it soon spread to the Ohio River Valley and more recently has been found in most, if not all, states. Part of the problem is no doubt our increased mobility, with pets accompanying us on vacations, and with dogs being taken to field trials and dog shows all over the country.

Japan and the Philippine Islands hold the dubious distinction of having the highest incidence of heartworm in the world. Since many species of mosquitoes transmit the disease, and since it is virtually impossible to keep mosquitoes from feeding on dogs, it is small wonder the disease is so prevalent.

The female worms are fourteen inches long and the males are ten inches long, and they live in the blood in the right side of the heart. When there are fifty or more of these worms in the heart there is insufficient room for blood and the heart enlarges. The worms reproduce at a rate of one female producing ten thousand young, called microfilaria, every twenty-four hours. These microfilaria cause a lot of damage in the miles of capillaries of the body, and it is from the capillaries that the mosquito draws infected blood to transmit to another dog when it needs another blood meal.

A dog with enough of these worms to show signs of illness usually tires easily on exercising, often has a soft cough, and is generally unthrifty. There are a host of other problems seen from time to time but

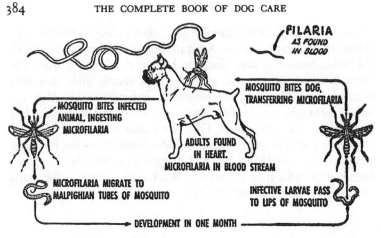

Life history of the heartworm. Above left, one half life size; above right, microfilaria, magnified four hundred times.

with more and more knowledgeable owners most dogs are tested and diagnosed before the disease becomes too debilitating.

The test for heartworms consists of your veterinarian drawing blood and concentrating the microfilaria, or wigglers, and identifying them under the microscope. Unfortunately a certain percentage of dogs, between 10 and 20 percent, have only the adults without any circulating wigglers. Other tests and X rays are necessary to make a diagnosis in these cases.

PREVENTION: Concerned pet owners have blood tests done on their dogs yearly and give preventive medication, diethyl carbamazine, to all the canine pets in the household or kennel. Since it takes five to six months after exposure to an infected mosquito for veterinarians to diagnose heartworms in dogs, they should be tested every spring or anytime in warm climates and given preventive medication without fail. The same drug is taken in the tropics by humans to prevent human filarial diseases. It must be given daily and comes as a powder, tablet, or liquid.

One of our clients with an ungroomed Old English Sheepdog had chosen not to give the preventive medication but did request a heartworm test. As we drew the blood he remarked that no mosquito could get through the mat of hair on his dog. The dog was positive and had to be treated. Some people say long-haired dogs have less heartworm infection than shorthaired types, but in our experience the length of the coat does not matter. The mosquitoes can always find skin, if only around the eyes and lips.

There is a constant discussion about the undesirable side effects from the preventive medication. Breeders claim bitches miss when bred and stud dogs are not as potent. We have seen nothing to verify these things. One experience was interesting. We dispensed a gallon of the preventive solution to a kennel owner with the instructions to give one cubic centimeter for each twenty pounds of weight to each dog daily. He misunderstood, did not read the label on the gallon jug, and gave one teaspoon instead of one cubic centimeter. That was five times the suggested dose. After six weeks he mentioned that he had used over half of the gallon, and the mistake was corrected. During the six weeks he had given five times the normal dose to pregnant females, females that were being bred, stud dogs, and puppies, with no ill effects.

Although many dogs detest the taste of the preventive medication, it is a rare dog that is allergic to it. We are great believers in the less medicine the better. Still, we think in the case of heartworm preventive medication is by far the lesser of two evils, as compared to the treatment.

TREATMENT consists of first testing the dog to be sure all its organs are functioning within normal limits and, if so, an arsenical drug is administered intravenously four times over a two-day period. Optimally the dog should be monitored twenty-four hours a day by someone who can recognize a problem if one develops. If a problem develops, the treatment is discontinued and intravenous fluids, antibiotics, steroids, and other measures as necessary are taken.

In our area where we rarely see a heavily infected dog we seldom lose a dog to this disease, but in a case where there are an overwhelming number of worms we doubt a dog can be cured. The surgical procedure for removing the worms is considered by most to be less successful than the medicinal approach.

It is thought the adults live for about four years and the microfilaria for no more than two and perhaps only one. It has been suggested that the adults stop reproducing after two or three years.

When we consider that a small blood clot will kill a person, it seems incomprehensible that fifty dead adult heartworms in the bloodstream may not kill a dog. After the arsenical treatment these adults die and white blood cells in the blood destroy the dead worms cell by cell until they are no more. If, however, there is a large mass of dead worms in the heart after the treatment and the dog suddenly exerts a lot of energy, the heart may force the mass into the lungs suddenly and obstruct the pulmonary artery, which conducts the blood from the heart to the lungs. The dog may drop dead. That is why, after the heartworm treatment, the dog should be kept quiet and on a leash when taken outside for at least three weeks after the treatment.

But killing the adults is only half the solution to this disease as the wigglers in the blood are a potential for spreading it. There is an interesting debate as to a preference for killing these microfilaria before or after killing the adults. We have used both methods and suggest you follow your veterinarian's recommendation.

In any event the wigglers must be destroyed and tablets, which are given according to your dog's weight, are available for this purpose.

People can contract heartworm from infected mosquitoes and there is little doubt in our minds that it is more common than the human medical profession indicates. Man is called an end host for heartworms. In other words, the heartworms do not mature and reproduce but, rather, finding themselves in a poor environment in the human heart, they migrate to the lungs. There the body encapsulates the young worms or walls them off so that they are destroyed. That doesn't seem too serious—except when chest X rays indicate this kind of area in a lobe of one of our lungs, it may appear to be cancer. If a doctor decides to split the chest and remove the lobe containing the lesion, the surgery is much more dangerous than the incysted parasite, which does little harm.

A new product called "covermecton" appears to be one that when given to a dog will destroy virtually all external and internal parasites. Though it is not officially approved, members of the veterinary profession are using it even now.

24

Contagious Diseases

Our love for our dogs and their unquestioning loyalty and devotion to us are so much a part of our lives that we all have moments when we think with dread of the time when old age, or accident, or disease may take them from us. Age we cannot control; an accident may strike the pet of the most careful owner; but we *can* do something about diseases. With sufficient knowledge of prevention and cure, we can both reduce the incidence of a disease and limit the injury it does.

The early recognition of disease symptoms is, of course, closely linked with intelligent day-by-day care, the general principles of which we have considered in the earlier sections of this book. If you know the normal behavior of your dog—how it should and does act when it is in good health—you will be able to judge more easily when it is suffering from one of the many maladies it may develop. To care for your pet intelligently you must know something about the most frequent ailments—their specific symptoms, cause, complications, and treatment. By *contagious* we refer to diseases passed from dog to dog and not necessarily those passed to people, which are considered in Chapter 26.

There are two types of general classifications of diseases to which dogs are most subject: those of virus origin and those resulting from bacterial infection. In this chapter we will consider the virus group first.

VIRUS DISEASES

Virus diseases are among the most dangerous to our dogs because we have no medication to treat them with. Viruses are so small the only technique for positive diagnosis may be the electron microscope, which is expensive to use. These minute organisms live inside cells, unlike bacteria which live outside cells.

Distemper. The name "distemper" is a misnomer but evolved in days gone by from many maladies that were called "a distemper." Benjamin Franklin writes in his autobiography that he had "a distemper" for many months.

There is no doubt that this one disease was responsible for dog population control in days prior to preventive inoculations.

So feared by dog owners and once the scourge of dogs, distemper is now rapidly dwindling in incidence. Although still a menace in some areas, in others it has been practically eliminated and is approaching the status of human poliomyelitis in its infrequency. The control of distemper is an eloquent demonstration of the excellent results of cooperation between researchers, veterinarians, and dog owners.

Distemper is a disease of the epithelial tissue, which covers the body inside and out. All of the mucous membranes, such as the lining of the nose, the mouth, the tissue around the eyes, the intestinal lining, the internal genital organs, and the bladder lining, are attacked, as are the glands and those cells that secrete substances.

Although the incubation period is five to seven days, we do find animals that appear to develop signs of distemper many weeks after a known exposure. Puppies taken from shelters that cannot afford to give inoculations may be normal until five days from exposure, at which time they have a sudden elevation of temperature to perhaps 104° F. At this time vomiting and listlessness are evident, as well as photophobia, or a fear of light, in many cases. In a few days the temperature returns to normal and the dog acts better, but for only a day or two, and then the temperature rises again to 104° F or higher. It is thought by many that the initial viral attack weakens the dog so that opportunist bacteria, which are always present, can flourish in the damaged tissue. In any event, a dry cough, purulent eye and nose discharges, diarrhea, and vomiting may all be present.

Throughout the course of the disease the coat appears rough and unkempt. In some cases pustules may be found on the skin of the abdomen. As the disease progresses with the secondary diseases that complicate it, dehydration often occurs. The skin can be pulled up in folds and does not snap back into place as healthy skin does but remains in ridges that return to normal very slowly. The tongue usually is coated and sometimes ulcerated.

Distemper generally lasts a full four weeks. When complicated with certain diseases, it may be a three-month disease.

These are the symptoms that are obvious to the dog owner. Your veterinarian can find others of more certain diagnostic value.

If this were the total extent of the problem most cases of distemper would recover, but serious complications do occur, the worst of which is encephalitis, or inflammation of the brain. This is the result of the virus attacking the brain and inflaming it, not the result of a secondary disease.

Some dogs are left deaf, blind, or with an impaired sense of smell. Of those that survive encephalitis, many are left with a chorea jerk in one or more muscles; some have complete reversals of personality, and some develop epileptiform seizures.

METHOD OF INFECTION: From infection with the virus until the appearance of the earliest symptoms, the incubation period is five to seven days. During that time the disease is extremely contagious. It requires no more than the merest sniff of a sick dog's breath to infect a healthy dog.

Infection probably occurs chiefly through the nose, eyes, and mouth. It is believed flies and other insects can spread it. Even earthworms may become infected from excreta, keep the virus alive in their bodies, and spread it when they crawl up out of the ground. Distemper is not confined to any one season of the year, nor does it exempt any age, sex, breed, or color of dog. One possible exception is the remarkable resistance of the pregnant bitch, who in some way is protected by her pregnancy to such an extent that one often hardly realizes she has the disease. If she does contract it toward the end of pregnancy, she may whelp her puppies and, at this time, lose her protection and be as severely affected as any other dog.

It has often been suggested that dogs in fine physical condition are able to throw off the disease. This is doubtful. Whole kennels of dogs in top condition have been known to contract distemper.

How long will the infection last in an area after a dog has died with the disease? Outside the body the virus is generally short-lived. It may live for several days in insects, and dogs that eat them will be infected. We don't know whether the virus can be transmitted by fleas, but in all probability it can be. In extreme cold the virus may not die for a number of years. Heat kills it quickly. In moist stools it may live longer in cool weather than in hot. But the old idea that a new dog may not be brought into a house for six months after the previous dog has died finds no support in modern research. In summer the safe period is probably nearer to a week.

IMMUNIZATION: Since distemper is such a loathsome disease, it behooves all dog owners to have their dogs properly protected against it. Even though in some sections the disease is dying out, immunization still remains the humane, sensible, sporting, and economical thing to do. It is easy to accomplish.

Whereas the disease ran rampant in pet shops years ago, it is virtually never found in pet shop puppies today since breeders inoculate their puppies prior to shipment and pet shops reinoculate them upon receipt. The reservoir of infection today is in shelters that keep animals for adoption. With animals collected from one area and housed often in crowded quarters, the disease is transmitted freely. The operators of these kinds of shelters usually cannot afford to pay for inoculations for unwanted animals.

TREATMENT: The history of the treatment of this disease is interesting. With the advent of sulfa drugs we were told we had the cure for the disease. The same was said when antibiotics came along, but in fact we know now we have no medication for such viral diseases.

Some people claim that forcing a dog to inhale ether on a regular basis improves the chances of recovery, but of all the reasonable and unreasonable treatments we will mention one that we believe has saved many lives.

This treatment came about by clinical observation and the consideration of some seemingly unrelated facts. First, we know that anticancer preparations are thought to deplete the system of folic acid, necessary for certain types of cancer to flourish. Second, we were told by the then chairman of the United Nations Committee on Jaundice that people with the disease, infectious hepatitis, have a higher mortality if they take vitamins. But perhaps most important was the observation that frequently a puppy or two treated by some "uninformed" person would survive the disease whereas the remainder of the litter would succumb with our treatment. After hearing of survivors all too often, we swallowed our pride and phoned people who had saved sick puppies to ask what they had done. There were many treatments involved, such as aspirin, mustard plaster, and herbal teas, but in every case two items were mentioned which at first seemed to us to be medicine from the Dark Ages. All the puppies that survived had been fed raw eggs and whiskey. Now as ridiculous as this appears on the surface, when considered more carefully it becomes obvious that these two substances have something interesting in common. Raw egg white is indigestible in dogs and it also robs the system of biotin which is necessary for life. Alcohol also has the effect of robbing the system of part of the vitamin B complex. We thought that perhaps the virus needed the nutrition that these two substances depleted the system of, just as the antifolic acid drugs do in cancer therapy.

The first dog we tried the treatment on was an Old English Sheepdog puppy that was in the encephalitis stage, having started convulsing. It was brought in as a consultation since euthanasia had been suggested. With two raw egg whites and a tablespoonful of whiskey three times daily and a diet devoid of fresh meat or milk for two months, the dog made a miraculous recovery. Apparently the dog could outlast the virus on a deficient diet. This treatment has worked on many dogs since, but the disease has been so rare that we have not been able to mass test it to reinforce the treatment's effectiveness.

Presently accepted treatments vary with veterinarians but antibiotics are useful in keeping secondary infections under control and fluid therapy will maintain hydration.

Hardpad. Toward the end of the distemper era a condition called hardpad appeared which still bewilders many researchers. Dogs that appeared to have all the signs of distemper also developed a foot pad condition wherein the pads of the feet became hard and, in those that recovered, dropped off. We have a collection of pads which are a vivid memory of that disease. The disease perplexed researchers because it resembled distemper in so many ways and was eventually called a variation of that disease.

When affected dogs walked across a hard surface their pads were so hard a clicking sound was heard with each step. This variation is prevented by proper distemper inoculations but a large percent of those not properly protected develop the same type of encephalitis that terminal distemper cases develop.

Rabies. Because of the many popular misconceptions concerning rabies, it seems advisable to consider a few general facts about the disease and its spread before taking up the specific symptoms.

Rabies is a virus disease transmissible to almost all kinds of warm-blooded animals.

Not all dogs bitten by a rabid dog develop rabies. Of dogs bitten by rabid dogs, 40 percent die; with horses, the percentage is also 40; hogs, 30 percent, and cattle, 30 percent. Only about 15 percent of the humans in one study who took no treatments to protect themselves after being bitten developed the disease. In the past, when rabid wolves bit humans, a higher percentage died.

It is the saliva of the rabid animal that is dangerous. The bite drives the virus in the saliva deep into the victim's tissues, where, being a neurotropic virus, it attaches itself to nerves and grows. (If the virus is able to attach itself to a nerve after the dog has been bitten, the dog has rabies. If the dog's body is capable of destroying the virus, the dog does not have rabies.) It is not dangerous on the unbroken skin. When an animal is bitten, there is no certainty about how long the virus will take to grow up the nerves until it reaches the huge mass of nerve tissue called the brain. The position of the bite has some effect. If a dog is bitten on a back foot, the virus will have quite a distance to travel before it reaches the brain; whereas with a bite in the jaw the elapsed time would be much less. From 15 to 285 days are the extremes found in a study to determine how long it takes.

What we think of as rabies is merely the manifestation of brain inflammation—encephalitis—and the dog may exhibit any of several typical forms of that malady. Thus present-day students of rabies have come to hold concepts of the disease completely different from those of our forefathers. Even the old name, hydrophobia, is no longer used. The conceptions of dumb and furious rabies have been dropped because the symptoms these terms describe are only two manifestations of encephalitis. In rabies, dogs do not have fits and then recover, as they may with other diseases. Once the symptoms appear, it is a downhill drag until death ensues.

SYMPTOMS: The earliest sign of rabies may be what seems to be a perverted appetite, but this may be due to hunger coupled with such a dimming of the sense of taste that anything will be chewed and swallowed. Another sign may be restlessness, excitability, a desire to move which becomes accentuated as the virus grows in the brain. Complete character reversals are frequent. Some ugly dogs become docile, while some lovable, kindly dogs may become ferocious. As the disease progresses we find a whole range of symptoms from drowsiness to such violent reactions to exciting disturbances that the dog appears wild. A startled look haunts the eyes. Some dogs may be paralyzed and stupid and quiet, giving rise to the idea of "dumb rabies." Other dogs may become fearless and run about, head down, biting anything that moves. Since its peripheral nerves are partially or completely paralyzed, the dog has little sense of feeling when bitten. In fights with dogs that refuse to run, the rabid dog can stand terrific punishment. When confined to a cage, it may break its teeth on the bars without apparent pain.

Probably the paralysis of the throat causes panic because the helpless feeling of not being able to swallow drives the animal wild. Rabid dogs do not have a phobia, or fear, of water; they simply cannot manage to swallow it, try as they may, and after many attempts to drink naturally they behave queerly toward it.

In the paralytic form, the lower jaw may hang; it is not held open by muscle power but rather from want of it. The frothing from the mouth in some cases is well known to all who have heard about mad dogs. Indeed, the common conception of a mad dog is of an animal running about with froth drooling from its mouth. This misconception should be corrected. That type of behavior is far from being the typical form of rabies, and because this fact is not generally recognized, many people have died.

In all forms of rabies, once the severe encephalitis symptoms appear, death generally ensues in less than a week, sometimes in three days. The dog's bite can be infectious three days before anyone knows it is sick. One dog was found to have infected saliva eight days before it showed the typical symptoms.

Diagnosis beyond the suspicion created by the symptoms is possible only by microscopic and biologic means. In order to do this, the suspected dog must be destroyed and a portion of the brain examined for inclusion bodies by a test called a fluorescent antibody test.

We wish we had space to tell of the many cases we have seen of the encephalitis following virus diseases and how exactly some followed the course of rabies encephalitis. Thousands of dogs that died of other virus diseases have been suspected of having rabies. We have suspected at least a dozen to such an extent that we had the brains examined. One dog bent heavy wire in its cage front, snatched a one-inch-square stick out of someone's hand, chewed and swallowed some of it, ate the metal of a feed pan, ate the equivalent of a newspaper that was on the floor of its cage, and died with legs in rigid extension. Its brain was sectioned but the tests were negative for rabies. The next step in diagnosis was to inject some of the tissue into mice, and they, too, showed that the dog was not infected with rabies. If a dog dies in the early stages of rabies, no inclusion bodies have developed, so mouse tests are used as standard procedure in diagnosis.

PREVENTION AND CONTROL: Suppose you think your dog may be rabid. What should you do? Confine it in a veterinary hospital or dog pound. Give it time to develop characteristic symptoms. If it does have rabies, have it destroyed, have the brain examined, and put yourself in the hands of your veterinarian.

These questions are often asked. Why don't veterinarians try to cure dogs affected with rabies? If dogs can't drink, why aren't they given water by vein? Isn't there any serum for rabies? The answer to all these questions is that human beings don't want to handle rabid dogs, so practically nothing has been done in the way of treatment.

Prevention is the keynote in rabies control. It can be made more effective by keeping all dogs under supervision and by rigid enforcement of the regulations requiring dog wardens to pick up all strays. Prevention consists of animal vaccination. These are made very inexpensive in some states by subsidies and veterinary volunteers.

If there is a possibility that infected saliva or other excretion from a rabid dog has entered a cut or abrasion, a person can be given treatment, which, if taken in time, causes the human body to develop immunity in the blood, and the immune bodies in turn attack the virus growing on the nerves and destroy it.

What chance have you of owning a rabid dog? Since we have set down in some detail the dangers of this disease to man and his pets, and warned dog owners of the precautions to be taken, a more cheerful note may well be struck. Table XII shows the relative prevalence of the disease by states in the United States. It is accurate to state more people die of infected hangnails in the United States each year than die of rabies. This would not be the case if vaccination programs were discontinued.

As of this writing the outbreaks of epizootics in raccoons seems the most serious reservoir of the disease but rabid house cats also are increasing in numbers. House cats should all be inoculated.

Table XII
TYPICAL NUMBER OF LAB-CONFIRMED
RABID ANIMALS IN THE
U.S. AND CANADA

TYPE OF ANIMAL	NUMBER OF SPECIMENS POSITIVE IN U.S.	NUMBER OF SPECIMENS POSITIVE IN CANADA
Skunks	1,631	431
Dogs	120	73
Cats	108	85
Cattle	186	244
Horses and mules	18	32
Sheep and goats	10	25
Swine	3	10
Bobcats	4	0
Coyotes	12	1
Foxes	122	593
Raccoons	281	3
Bats	637	38
Other wildlife	48	1
Rodents and lagomorphs	1	1
Humans	0–1	0

Parvoviral Gastroenteritis. This virus disease, parvoviral gastroenteritis, was recognized by Texas researchers in 1977. Most older dogs have little problem recovering when given medication to relax the gastrointestinal motility and antibiotics to prevent secondary bacterial infections. Vomiting lasts a few days and diarrhea, often bloody, continues for the best part of a week. It is more severe in puppies than in adults, and young dogs may have a bluish cast to their eyes similar to that found with infectious hepatitis.

Pathologists consider this disease to be similar to cat distemper but susceptible kittens cannot be infected with canine parvovirus. There is always the conjecture that in attenuating (weakening) feline distemper virus, a mutant may have been produced that when given to cats protected them but at the same time caused them to be carriers of parvo to dogs. If that is the case, it could account for the disease appearing all over the United States and in Canada within one year's time.

In severe cases with vomiting and diarrhea, hospitalization with fluid therapy to combat dehydration, which accompanies the disease, seems to save the affected animal. However, even with this treatment there is a high mortality rate in young puppies. Apparently healthy, plump puppies may be found dead with no previous symptoms, while others have the typical vomiting followed by diarrhea, which progresses to a bloody diarrhea. Their temperatures may reach 104–107° F. These puppies may die in a day or two after a good deal of crying, refusal of food, and dehydration.

Many questions come to mind concerning this disease. First, how long has it been around before it was identified by electron microscopy? We're inclined to think we have seen it for years and called it garbage poisoning, snow poisoning, and bacterial enteritis, among other names.

It is so highly contagious one wonders why it does not run rampant in all boarding kennels and veterinary institutions. Still another question is why it appears to be so sporadic, with many dogs apparently immune to it.

It is thought feline distemper inoculations will protect dogs for some months but a verifiable track record has not been established thus far.

Infectious Canine Hepatitis. Recognized in 1928 but not studied and named until 1947 in Sweden, infectious canine hepatitis is one of many diseases that was common for a few years and resulted in a high mortality in puppies. Puppies may die so suddenly there is little time to get them to a veterinarian. When a litter is affected the puppies involved show sudden pain evidenced by constant crying. Death often comes in a few hours. In a large litter it is common to have half the puppies affected and die while the other half show no signs at all.

This was a major disease in England and the United States from 1948 to about 1952 after which it became rare. If it affects adult dogs it is not serious and pathologists virtually never find it as a cause of death in adults.

Canine hepatitis is classified as an adenovirus and called canine adenovirus (CAV-1). For years a percentage of dogs inoculated for this disease developed a bluish cast to one or both eyes seven to ten days after the inoculation. With present-day vaccines this eye discoloration no longer occurs.

Kennel Cough. There is some evidence that even in sufficiently inoculated dogs an aerosol exposure can produce a kennel cough. More properly called tracheobronchitis, kennel cough is more than a simple virus disease. Rather, it is one of several viruses perhaps with bacterial secondary invaders. When the virus, canine parainfluenza (CPI), is accompanied by mycoplasma and a bacterium called Bordetella bronchiseptia the condition is much more severe and protracted than when the virus is present by itself.

In any situation where many dogs are brought together and where ventilation is not adequate, the disease travels rapidly to all the dogs in the area. Five to seven days after exposure, the susceptible dogs start a dry-sounding nonproductive cough that is persistent off and on day and night usually for weeks. Early in the 1970s it could be predicted that infected animals would cough for six weeks, but from the late 1970s on the length of coughing in animals is rarely over three weeks. Kennel cough is not life-threatening, but it is a nuisance. Medications are helpful to control the cough but the virus must run a course until the dog builds an immunity. Unfortunately the immunity lasts only for six months or so and preventive inoculations are only partially effective for less than a year.

Canine Adenovirus Infection. Adenovirus (CAV-2) also causes a tracheobronchitis usually more severe than CPI. It is listed as one of the kennel-cough-causing agents. The incubation period for this virus disease may be two or three days. As with CAV-1, the disease is much more severe when the bacterium Bordetella and mycoplasma are also involved. In a small percentage of cases, life-threatening lung problems develop so many veterinarians utilize antibacterial preparations to prevent secondary complications.

Coronaviral Gastroenteritis. Coronaviral gastroenteritis disease was first described by veterinarians working with military dogs in Germany in 1971. In 1978 it was recognized in most states of the union as a disease with a very sudden onset—after only a day or a day and a half after exposure. Often the first sign is vomiting followed in a few hours by diarrhea that persists until blood is obvious in the stool. It is an alarming condition, with a dog showing depression and loss of all enthusiasm. Although most dogs recover after four or five days without help, some must have intravenous and supportive treatment. The mortality is very low if they are taken to the veterinarian promptly.

Canine Herpesvirus. Here again in canine herpesvirus we find a virus that has been recovered from normal as well as diseased dogs. This disease is thought to be present in the vaginal canal, where it infects puppies as they are born and can kill newborn puppies up to two weeks after birth. After two weeks it appears to be unimportant. When isolated from cases of kennel cough it is not life-threatening.

Canine Reovirus Infection. Canine reovirus is yet another group of viruses that can produce respiratory problems in dogs.

It becomes obvious that kennel cough is truly a catchall phrase and as such, without an inoculation for all the agents which cause the tracheobronchitis symptoms it is difficult to produce an effective vaccine. Research has brought us a long way and the inoculations we have are a great help. We can anticipate more effective vaccines in the future for the many virus diseases we recognize and for those to be discovered.

BACTERIAL DISEASES

There are a few bacterial diseases that have a wide distribution throughout the body rather than affecting only one or two of the organs. These are known as generalized diseases.

Leptospirosis. Of spirochetal origin, the bacterial agent that produces leptospirosis is spread to dogs most frequently by dog urine. It is a common disease of dogs in many areas of the world. Since dogs can pass it to humans, it is important for us to discuss it here. In humans it is called Weils disease or Canicola disease which may cause jaundice. The symptoms are similar in all species. The disease appears in two forms, the *canicola* and the *icterohemorrhagic* (jaundice hemorrhages). The former is often inaccurately diagnosed since it presents particularly difficult diagnostic problems.

Both types produce a number of common symptoms—unsteady elevation of temperature, nausea, lassitude, loss of weight, loose stools, and stiffness—that can be traced to the impairment of certain organs by the spirochetes. An almost constant symptom in both forms is the congestion of the tiny blood vessels in the whites of the eyes, which may be a coppery red. The canicola form shows a few additional symptoms. The dog generally dies quite emaciated, and the urine may range in color from orange to chocolate brown and may at times contain blood.

The second type (icterohemorrhagic) differs in the symptoms it produces in the manner implied by the name. There is bleeding in the intestines and gums, and sometimes tiny hemorrhages scattered throughout the body. The vomitus may show blood; the stools appear bloody.

A further diagnostic symptom is one that a disease of the liver would be expected to exhibit: jaundice. The mucous membranes, skin, and whites of the eyes appear a more and more intense yellow as the disease progresses, until, at death, some tissues may be almost a canary yellow or orange. By the time the yellow has appeared, however, the disease has progressed so far that serious damage may have been done to the kidneys and liver. The difficulty of identifying the disease at an early stage makes it difficult to cure the first dog in an area to contract leptospirosis. By the time the diagnosis has been definitely established there is usually little hope. Even if the dog should survive, the damage that was done before the treatment was started will often make it an invalid for the remainder of its life.

Leptospirosis in a kennel or in a pair of dogs is a different matter. If one dog dies, diagnosis by postmortem and bacterial examination is possible. Then, after the disease has been identified, treatment may be started immediately with those pets that have been infected a shorter time. When the disease is detected at an earlier stage, the dogs may—and usually do—recover if proper treatment is given. Urinalysis can be a helpful indication. Every dog not entirely well, particularly those that show indications of a fever, can be treated. If the temperature fluctuates markedly from very high to almost normal, it may add to one's suspicions, for leptospirosis does not cause a uniformly high fever even initially.

The disease is most frequently spread by rat urine. Almost all recorded cases—and they are sporadic—can be traced to garbage or bones that were left where rats had access to them. Inoculations are not very effective since the immunity is of short duration.

Tuberculosis. We do not know how many dogs are tubercular. Certainly the number varies in different parts of the world. There are three types of the disease: human, bovine (cattle), and avian (bird). Dogs may contract all three types, but the human type is three times as prevalent as the bovine type and the avian type is rare.

Doubtlessly dogs with lung tuberculosis cough TB germs. Yet, as far as we have been able to find out, no human being—man, woman, or child—has been reported as having contracted the disease from a dog. Still the possibility does exist, and it hardly seems sensible to allow children to fondle tubercular animals. That dogs have contracted the disease from humans can hardly be doubted.

Tuberculosis in a dog is seldom recognized. The symptoms are not distinctive. Coughing may be characteristic of many diseases, and so may loss of weight because of only a fair appetite. Very few dogs that on postmortem showed tubercular lesions were known by their owners to have had the disease, and many passed for healthy if not flourishing dogs. The postmortem examinations that revealed lesions showed them principally in the lungs.

Canine Brucellosis. Canine brucellosis has been reported in a few humans and so is of public health interest. It is a common bacterial disease causing abortions in females and sterility in males. It is one of the few venereal diseases in dogs and is spread by contact with genital discharges and saliva. It is not a debilitating disease and usually is not suspected until a female aborts, usually between the forty-fifth and fifty-fifth days of pregnancy. The puppies may be dead or weak and few survive.

An infected male may have sired many litters but after infection, although he mates normally, he no longer sires litters. The diagnosis is made by a blood test. It is strongly recommended that an infected animal be isolated for the years necessary for a blood test to become negative. If this is impractical, euthanasia may be the last resort.

Tetanus (lockjaw). Few known poisons are so deadly as that produced by lockjaw germs. Before discussing the peculiarities of the bacterium which causes tetanus, let us consider some of the symptoms.

SYMPTOMS: Growing in a sealed-over wound, forming a minute pocket, yet giving off their deadly toxin, these bacteria produce a stiffness in the dog, due to muscle contraction, which is generally diagnostic. The gait is stiff, the head tends to be extended too far in front, the tail is held out stiffly behind, the ears are hard and cocked, not hanging pendulously as they should in the case of a lop-eared dog.

All the reflexes are sharpened. Any noise causes a quicker response than is normal. The facial expression shows anxiety. Occasionally dog owners may suspect their dogs of being rabid. Locking of the jaw muscles is not a universal feature. In fact, some dogs have only parts of their bodies affected and their jaws not at all. But once the jaw muscles have contracted so that the dog can neither eat nor drink, he is helpless without radical treatment.

METHOD OF INFECTION: When a dog becomes infected with spores of the bacterium *Clostridium tetani,* it does not necessarily mean it will have lockjaw. In fact, the germs are exceedingly common over the earth's surface and often grow outside of animal bodies. They are found in soil, around manure piles, and also in many unsuspected places as well. An interesting fact about them is that they grow when oxygen is excluded from their environment. They do not grow in an open wound to which air has access. But with other bacteria in a deep wound they thrive. The other types of bacteria exhaust the oxygen supply and render the environment propitious.

PREVENTION AND TREATMENT: Prevention consists in having every dog with a puncture or bullet wound given antitoxin and the wound cleaned. In treatment very large doses of antitoxin are injected and the source of infection is thoroughly disinfected. Antitoxin is a chemical antidote for the toxin. When used in large enough amounts, it "knocks out" the toxin, as bacteriologists say.

Supportive treatment of relaxing the muscles by drugs that the veterinarian can give is helpful. Then, too, if the dog's jaws are affected, it must be fed by vein or rectum until the jaw muscles are sufficiently relaxed to allow it to eat.

The treatment of tetanus requires extreme patience, but it is often rewarded by the joy which comes in watching a dog recover when there had appeared to be little hope.

Anthrax. Anthrax is a rare disease in dogs but is worldwide in incidence. It is usually contracted by ingesting remains from the carcass of an animal that has died of the disease. Penicillin and other antibiotics are effective in treating an infected dog but since man is also susceptible care should be exercised in handling the animal.

Hemobartonella. *Hemobartonella canis,* once considered a protozoan disease, has been identified as bacterial in nature. The bacterium is a parasite of the red blood cells. Though common in man and dog it is rarely diagnosed since most recover from an attack without showing any symptoms. Hemobartonella is thought to be contracted from ticks or by eating undercooked meat, and it can cause an anemia. It is diagnosed at times in dogs that have had their spleens removed. For these animals, blood transfusions and broad spectrum antibiotics can be used effectively.

Canine Ehrlichiosis. First described in dogs in Algeria, Canine Ehrlichiosis, a recently recognized disease, has been called tropical canine pancytopenia. It results in a fatal hermorrhagic disease in dogs. Some dogs that have recovered from this disease have been found to be carriers for over two years later.

Lime Fever. First identified as a tick-borne human disease in the area of the town of Lime, Connecticut, researchers found dogs as well as many other animals also contract the disease. It is caused by a spirochete and has been identified in many states. The arthritis caused by this disease is self-limiting but treatment shortens the course.

25

Noncontagious Diseases

Two questions are often asked, "What caused the infection, Doctor?" and "My dog is kept in a fenced-in area, has regular inoculations and checkups, and yet why is it sick? There are dogs running loose all over the neighborhood and nothing seems to happen to them."

In answer to the second query, those dogs loose in the neighborhood have many more problems than the protected dog—dog fights, poisoning, lacerations, and injuries from automobiles, to name a few.

As far as why many infections arise, we just don't know. The dog may have an infected area in an ear, for example, and we explain that if a human had such a condition there would be no explanation either. And of the many theories we have for problems are just that—theories that change with new knowledge.

We do know there are microorganisms capable of causing diseases around us all the time in amazingly large numbers. If enough of one of them gain entry to the system in a location in which they can grow and if the dog is susceptible they may cause disease.

We are sure there are changes in the immune systems of all animals from time to time from unknown causes. This is a theory that explains why, in mid-summertime, a well-nourished, emotionally well-adjusted dog in a household with other dogs develops pneumonia.

Diabetes Mellitus. One disease fairly common in the dog world is *diabetes mellitus,* or sugar diabetes. An excess of sugar in the blood produces sugar in the urine and subsequently the body strives to rid the system of the excess. We believe the excess blood sugar is present because of a lack of insulin and we know that insulin is produced by cells in the pancreas.

The earliest sign of this problem is usually great thirst followed by unthriftiness and some loss of pep. Eventually there will be a loss of weight, and with prolonged elevated blood sugar extreme depression precedes coma and death.

Insulin must be injected into a dog with diabetes and the problem for the veterinarian is to determine how much insulin is needed. Given too much insulin, the dog's blood sugar will drop too precipitously, producing convulsions, coma, and death. The veterinarian suggests a diet that must remain constant for the rest of the dog's life and the food must be eaten at specified times. Since exercise burns up blood sugar it is very important to control and standardize it.

To determine the amount of insulin necessary, a given amount is injected, followed by a blood sugar test sometime later. If the insulin dose is excessive, sugar may have to be administered to the animal. Finally, when the correct dose is established, you, the owner, are instructed in the simple technique of injecting your pet at regular intervals.

We do not know why a dog on a given dose of insulin has a fluctuation of blood sugar even after months of successful treatment. But it does happen, and that is why test kits are available for blood and urine sugar. We do know that an unspayed female often has a great fluctuation in sugar during her heat periods. We have not observed a genetic pattern in diabetes as there is in epilepsy, for example, but it is unwise to breed a diabetic because of the difficulties involved with maintaining normal sugar levels during pregnancy and whelping. We suggest spaying diabetic females.

Sugar diabetes is caused by a shortage or complete absence of the secretion of the islets of Langerhans in the pancreas. Affected dogs are unable to store sugar in the liver and become sick if they eat large quantities of carbohydrates or sugar. They need proteins and fat, with a minimum of carbohydrates. This, as you will remember, is the opposite of the diet needed by dogs with kidney disease.

One of our patients had been stabilized on sixteen units of insulin for two and a half years when the owner phoned to say that the urine sugar test had suddenly become normal. Since we like to find a trace of sugar in the urine, it was suggested the dose be reduced by two units. The test remained normal. A blood test indicated a dangerously low blood sugar and we reduced the insulin again. After ten days and many tests, the dog returned to a normal blood sugar and remained normal for three more years, when it met an untimely death from an automobile accident.

Diabetes Insipidus. This rare disease, diabetes insipidus, is a problem caused by injury, inflammation of the brain, cancer, or unknown factors, almost invariably involving the pituitary gland, which is located at the base of the brain. It is usually caused by a tumor. A hormone that controls the kidneys' ability to concentrate urine is reduced, resulting in a tremendous thirst and urination. A small dog may drink a gallon of water a day. A hormone is available and when injected into an affected dog its thirst intake and urine output return temporarily to normal. These injections are usually given at home every forty-eight hours. When this diabetes is caused by a tumor the animal usually dies but when caused by injury, complete recovery is not unusual.

Table XIII DISEASES EXHIBITING DIABETES-LIKE SYMPTOMS

	ORGAN AFFECTED	SPECIFIC GRAVITY	SUGAR TEST	APPETITE	INDICATED DIET
Diabetes mellitus (sugar diabetes)	Pancreas	Higher than water	Positive	Normal	Low sugar and starch
Diabetes insipidus (incipient diabetes)	Pituitary gland	Like water	Negative	Ravenous	Normal
Nephritis (kidney disease)	Kidneys	Normal	Negative	Normal or depressed	Low protein

Pneumonia. There are several types of pneumonia caused by one or more of a host of microorganisms. Many bacteria, viruses, and fungi are all capable of infecting the lungs, causing this disease. Just as we humans have "walking pneumonia," so can our canine friends and, just as we, our dogs may appear to have little congestion one day and be dying of it the next. The congestion is seen and the diagnosis is verified by chest radiographs.

As with so many diseases, most pneumonias are overcome by the dog, whereas other pneumonias are cured only with the correct antimicrobial or antifungal medication. You will note we omitted virus-caused pneumonia since we have no virus-destroying medication, but antibiotics are helpful to prevent secondary bacteria from developing in virus-damaged tissue.

The great lifesaver, penicillin, is used to cure most bacterial pneumonia, but bacteria are becoming resistant to many of our older tried-and-true drugs and many of the newer drugs are more specific for a few bacteria. It is difficult to obtain bacteria from the lungs of affected, critically ill dogs to find out which correct antibiotic should be used. It seems to us the mortality rate in pneumonia cases is rising in spite of the scores of drugs we have available.

Signs of pneumonia are usually a shortness of breath, frequently but not always a cough, fever, lassitude with loss of responsiveness, and a reduced desire for food. These signs are a good reason to seek veterinary help promptly. Many dogs are in such a critical condition they need oxygen for a few days while medications are working. Most cases should be hospitalized while they are receiving injectable medication, which seems to us to be currently more effective than the oral ones.

Warmth and restricted exercise are important, as are small amounts of high-quality food fed often or intravenous feeding.

Septicemia. We used to refer to septicemia as blood poisoning, and most people understand that this is a bacterial infection of the blood running rampant through the vascular system. Today broad-spectrum antibiotics usually cure such a problem in either humans or animals before the laboratory can identify one of the many microorganisms capable of causing it.

Abscesses. When an abscess, or infection, develops in or under the skin, the body is usually able to create a barrier around the area to prevent septicemia from developing. We say it is "walled off." Dogfight wounds often result in abscesses and may be left to nature; this will result in a protracted problem with eventual rupturing and draining and healing. We presume we may call the veterinarian part of "nature." He or she may lance, drain, and perhaps suture a rubber drain in the incision, thereby reducing the healing time by half.

Anal Gland Abscesses. The two small scent glands located on either side of the anus each have a duct that permits small quantities of the secretion of the glands to be discharged at the anal rim. If these glands become infected, a foul odor and a good deal of discomfort results. The infected glands should be expressed and packed with an antibiotic ointment. The treatment may have to be repeated several times. Infection is indicated by redness, heat, and a swelling over one of the glands which may be lanced, drained, and packed with antibiotics. More often, after a few days of misery for the dog, the abscess ruptures, leaving a draining opening in the skin that usually heals without treatment. This abscess is due to a blockage of a duct leading from the gland to the rim of the anus, and the condition rarely occurs in both glands simultaneously. With the blocked duct, the gland continues to secrete until it bursts causing the abscess.

If problems of the anal glands recur too often, ask your veterinarian of the advisability of surgically removing them.

Fistulas. A fistula is an abnormal draining tract from one area of the body to another. The majority of fistulas are caused by foreign bodies, such as gunshot wounds or splinters, but there are some inherited fistulas, such as a tract from the lower bowel to the vaginal area.

A fistula developed in one of our patients draining to the outside of the skin from the side at the flank area. X rays revealed a needle near the spine that we suspect had been swallowed and which worked its way through the bowel to its location. Unless the source is reached and removed, a fistula will usually heal and rupture every month or so for the remainder of the dog's life.

With a compound fracture a chip of bone may be infected, resulting in a tract from the chip through the skin. The chip must be removed to correct this problem.

Tonsillitis. Every veterinarian has heard the remark, "I didn't know a dog had tonsils." We would like to respond with, "Yes, and they have hearts and lungs and kidneys, too," but we hold our tongues and explain that inflammation of the tonsils is not an unusual finding. As is now the case in human medicine, we rarely remove them as was done in the past but utilize antibiotics to combat the infection that is the usual cause of tonsillitis.

Fungus or Mycotic Infections. There is no evidence that mycotic diseases other than ringworm are transmitted from dog to man or vice versa, and there is also little evidence that they are transmitted from dog to dog. Some of these diseases have specific geographical distribution, whereas others are found everywhere.

These agents may start as a localized infection and remain as such or

Table XIV
DISTRIBUTION AND SYMPTOMS OF MYCOTIC DISEASES

DISEASE	LOCATION	SIGNS
Blastomycosis	Eastern half of U.S. and Southeastern Canada	Weight loss, lung problems, eventually skin lesions and blindness
Histoplasmosis	Eastern half of U.S. and Southeastern Canada	Chest problems, fever, anemia, coughing, and eventual intractable diarrhea
Cryptococcosis	Metropolitan areas of the world	Nasal and lung problems, perhaps encephalitis, and discharging skin lesions
Coccidioidomycosis	California and Southwestern U.S.	Nonproductive cough
Actinomycosis	Worldwide, rural areas of U.S.	Nonproductive cough, sneezing, and skin ulcers
Nocardiosis	Worldwide, rural areas of U.S.	Nonproductive cough, sneezing, and emaciation
Aspergillosis	Worldwide (rare occurrence)	Infections of nasal passages, sinuses, and ears
Maduromycosis	Worldwide (rare occurrence), Southeastern U.S.	Discharging skin lesions and lameness
Sporotrichosis	Worldwide (rare occurrence)	Skin lesions that may discharge pus

spread to most of the tissues of the body including the bone marrow and even the brain. To identify the causative agent the bacteriologist uses specific media to grow specific fungal agents in and special stains to identify them.

When these diseases become generalized many infected animals will not survive even with treatment. Specific treatment is necessary for specific diseases and that is why the bacteriological identification is critical. When successful, treatment either with or without surgery is protracted, often extending over many months.

Canine Cushing's Syndrome (Hyperadrenocorticism). When either the pituitary or the adrenal glands secrete a cortisonelike material in excess over a period of many months or when cortisonelike drugs are given to a dog over a period of many months, physical changes take place. This condition is called Cushing's syndrome after a similar problem in humans. The causes are tumors of the pituitary gland or adrenal glands or, as we said, from medication.

The signs are a gradual loss of hair until the dog is almost hairless. For some reason the hair usually remains on the head. The abdomen becomes distended, the appetite is increased, the muscles become weak, and the skin becomes thin and perhaps wrinkled. There may be pigment changes. Although one dog may not have all the above signs, all have one symptom in common: they drink great quantities of water and, of course, urinate frequently.

There are blood tests that help verify a correct diagnosis and there are treatments dependent on the cause. One is sophisticated surgery of the adrenal glands. Another treatment is with chemotherapy and sometimes combinations of surgery and medication. Another method is applicable only to those dogs receiving cortisonelike drugs—and that is to stop the drugs.

Addison's Disease (Hypoadrenocorticism). Addison's disease or syndrome is the counterpart of Cushing's disease in that the body produces too little of a cortisonelike substance. It appears to take some weeks or even months of insufficiency before a sudden attack of weakness, abdominal pain, nausea, and vomiting are observed. Of course, these are symptoms we mention for many problems in this book and when they are severe let your veterinarian make the diagnosis.

With Addison's disease the coat will be dry and strawlike, with excess dandruff. A dog in this condition can progress quite suddenly from weakness to a coma and death. Hospitalization, tests, and treatments will often save a dog's life if started soon enough.

Of course, there are more hormonal problems than there are hormones with the possible combinations. There are hormones produced by diseased tissue. One example is a tumor of the testicle called a

Sertoli cell tumor, which causes feminization in a male. He develops enlarged nipples and may not raise a leg to urinate.

In a small percent of females the loss of the estrogens from a spaying operation results in urinary incontinence. This is thought to be due to the pituitary gland's loss of influence on the sphincter muscles of the urinary bladder. The condition is corrected by administration of diethylstilbestrol (DES). Although this hormone has been incriminated in problems in humans, DES has to our knowledge caused no problems in dogs unless given in excess. An excess will produce heat signs even in the spayed female.

Hypothyroidism. When underactive, the thyroid glands, located in the neck, cause a condition called hypothyroidism. This insidious disease of middle-aged or older dogs may, in the early stages, appear to an owner to be signs of aging, but with a few of the many manifestations of the disease it becomes clear that it is not just aging. Some dogs show thickening of the skin of the face, resulting in a change of expression to one of anxiousness. Some dogs gain a great deal of weight and others gain none. Many lose their coats starting on the ventral surfaces of the body and the lower areas of the legs. The undercoat sheds, leaving rough guard hairs. Some females cease to have heat periods and others mate and abort during the first five weeks of pregnancy. Anemia, if not severe, is usually present.

Since no dog has many of the varied signs mentioned, diagnosis is made by laboratory techniques. The success of the treatment is obvious by the rapid improvement of the patient.

Hyperparathyroidism. The parathyroid glands are attached to the thyroid glands. When one of these glands develops a lesion, it may secrete excess hormone, which eventually is the cause of a demineralization of bone, resulting in lameness and even fractures from minor stress. The bones of the jaws may become soft to the touch. A similar situation develops when other problems cause an enlargement and increase secretion of hormone. This is called secondary hyperparathyroidism.

Hypoparathyroidism. In the case of inactive parathyroid glands, hypoparathyroidism develops; which causes muscular tremors, depression, and eventually convulsions.

Laboratory tests for levels of hormones in the body may one day be developed. At present we have few such tests. There is little doubt that there are many dogs with borderline hormone deficiencies that would be helped with therapy.

Hyperkinesis. Some dogs become so abnormally overreactive and nervous as they reach adulthood that they are almost unmanageable. A dog of this kind may destroy a house if left alone. The cause of this problem is not understood, but strangely enough the administration of the drug, amphetamine, produces a calming effect. After some months the drug may be withdrawn and the dog remains calm for the remainder of its life. If they go untreated most hyperkinetic dogs are destroyed as misfits. If amphetamine does not work, the dog does not have this problem.

Pancreatitis. Many theories have been suggested as to the cause of pancreatitis, but other than injury and tumors we have few answers. It usually occurs in middle-aged, overweight animals and is obviously a painful experience for a dog. Necrosis or decomposition occurs, releasing into the gland enzymes that should be released into the small intestine by way of ducts. The enzymes literally digest parts of the pancreas. Initially there is vomiting with acute abdominal pain followed by depression, shock, and even convulsions in some cases. This is a problem requiring hospitalization and intensive care to relieve pain and to maintain hydration. With treatment the survival rate is good if the rare neoplasm is not present. If damage is excessive, it may be necessary to administer pancreatic enzymes to the dog with each meal for the rest of its life.

In young dogs under two years of age there is a less common form of this disease called juvenile pancreatic atrophy, which requires the same enzyme addition to the diet as the chronic form.

DEFICIENCY DISEASES

Negative as well as positive factors cause disease. Many pets have died from lack of oxygen. There are the obvious cases of suffocation; the carrying cage or shipping crate may be insufficiently ventilated, and when it is opened the pet is found dead. Lack of oxygen, obvious as it is, constitutes a deficiency disease. There are many more subtle deficiencies.

Some deficiencies produce what should be called conditions, not diseases. A disease is a morbid process with characteristic symptoms. Thirst is neither a disease nor the result of disease. The symptoms of dehydration are cured by water consumption. Anemia is a disease in one sense, a condition in another. Millions of humans go about in an anemic condition. In general, deficiency diseases are quite easily cured, simply by furnishing the body with missing nutritional elements.

Anemia. Anemia is a disease in the oxygen-carrying capacity of blood. We have considered the obvious form but not the symptoms. *When an animal suffocates, the pink color of the tissue turns blue.* A lack of oxygen in the tissues can be produced by many causes other than lack of air. The blood may simply be unable to carry it about the body. This, in turn, may result from a diminished supply of red cells in the blood. There may be too few, or the chemical composition of their components may be inadequate.

Hookworms are the most common cause of an inadequate supply of red cells. Their blood consumption strains the blood-building equipment, which cannot keep up with the loss. A hookworm-infested animal lacks animation and gets out of breath easily. It shows all the symptoms of anemia, as though blood had been drawn from its arteries or veins. Little puppies are frequently found to be anemic because of hookworm infestation. There is so little iron in milk that they cannot regain their losses despite deworming, and they frequently die because of their owner's ignorance of this fact.

Heavy infestations of sucking lice may also cause anemia. Some dogs harbor so many lice that the parasites touch one another in places. The animal's gums reveal a sickly pallor; it can't stand cold and loses its appetite. The basic condition is probably aggravated by toxins from the lice. Animals are often seriously weakened by these parasites. Dogs have actually been known to die from lice infestation.

Blood diseases, rare in animals, produce an altered blood picture. Some ordinary diseases alter the proportion of red and white cells, not by reducing the number of red cells but by increasing the number of white cells. This is not anemia. Diseases that produce toxins or attack the blood-building apparatus of the body produce anemia by reducing the number of red cells.

A lack of iron or copper or both causes anemia. Insufficient iron is responsible for a shortage of hemoglobin, and though there may be a full quota of red cells, they can't pick up and transport oxygen. Copper deficiency also causes anemia. Copper is not part of hemoglobin but is concerned with its formation.

Niacin deficiency, which causes black tongue; a shortage of vitamin B complex factors; and pyridoxin deficiency—all cause anemia.

Rickets. Once a common problem, rickets is almost unheard of today due to the presence of vitamin D, calcium, and phosphorus in dog foods.

Eclampsia. Also called puerperal tetany, eclampsia a disease of nursing mother animals caused by an inadequate amount of calcium or an inadequacy in the parathyroid glands.

Black Tongue. Black tongue is a disease almost unheard of where dogs eat commercial dog food or table scraps. A deficiency of niacin in the diet over a period of many weeks is at least one of the causes. The dog develops a general loss of condition and muscular incoordination. It slobbers constantly from the mouth, and its breath is obnoxious. Its gums and tongue appear inflamed. Associated with the disease is a great proliferation of spirochetal bacteria, such as cause trenchmouth. Injections of niacin (nicotinic acid) or the whole B complex will effect dramatic recovery. The term "black tongue" is misleading because that symptom is seen only in a dead dog. Soon after death the mouth, because of congestion in the tissues, turns deep purple.

Mineral Deficiencies. The only two minerals of great consequence to dogs are calcium and iron, but nevertheless in passing we must recognize that the absence of others causes dire consequences. Iodine is essential. Its lack causes goiter in animals, and when pregnant females are iodine-starved they may produce abnormal young called cretins. Common salt is also essential. Since 99 percent of the calcium in the body is found in the skeleton, obviously a calcium deficiency results in poor skeletal development, as we saw in the case of rickets. But calcium does more than develop bone. It is necessary to proper nerve function and acts almost like some vitamins as a catalyst or "marrying agent" between other minerals. Bad teeth may be traced to a fluorine deficiency. Cobalt and boron, though needed in minute quantities, produce sickness through their absence. Potassium deficiency causes paralysis, and so forth.

Vitamin Deficiencies. The subject of vitamins has been covered in Chapter 3. In raw eggs there is an inactivator, avertin, which inactivates biotin (one of the B complex vitamins) and prevents egg white digestion. Cooking destroys avertin also and prevents biotin deficiency.

Bloat. A condition that kills a great many dogs of the large breeds, especially Great Danes, St. Bernards, and Bloodhounds, is bloat. One will see his dog eat a satisfactory meal, appear to feel perfectly well, and be dead three hours later. The pressure generated in the stomach by the formation of gas by bacteria becomes too great for the organs to endure. The stomach distends like a balloon, and even the skin becomes so taut from the expansion that it resounds like a drum if you snap it with your finger. The gas presses the diaphragm forward against the heart and lungs. Besides the pressure, there seems to be a bacterial toxin developed.

TREATMENT: It is imperative to obtain veterinary assistance promptly when bloat is suspected. The first signs may be misleading. The dog seems restless, unable to be comfortable. It lies down, rises, and finds another spot, which is equally unacceptable. It has a stomachache. Only these actions suggest the problem early. Pat the dog on its side just behind the ribs; if you hear a resonance, as you would with a drum, bloat is the problem. Of course, when the stomach is greatly distended the condition is obvious.

Your veterinarian will work quickly and perhaps pass a stomach tube to relieve the pressure of the gas-filled stomach. He or she may have to resort to introducing a needle through the skin into the stomach to relieve the pressure. There are many variations and your veterinarian will use the technique that has given best results.

In our experience, after the dog is relieved and when it can handle the stress, surgery should be undertaken to correct any twisting, called torsion of the stomach, and perhaps an engorged spleen. Then the stomach, in its normal position, should be attached to the outer muscle wall of the abdomen. This may seem like drastic surgery but it will prevent future episodes and perhaps death if you don't observe the problem in time.

AFTEREFFECTS: A dog saved from bloat usually has little appetite for some time. The stomach has been so badly stretched that it is not uncommon to find brownish blood in the stool for several days. There are cases on record in which the stomach never did return to normal; postmortem examination years later revealed a thin-walled, greatly enlarged organ.

Autoimmunity. When a dog builds up a resistance and attempts to reject part of itself, we call the problem autoimmunity. There are a host of problems produced by this phenomenon and no doubt many we don't even recognize as yet. A dog may become immune to parts of the kidneys, to the blood platelets, to the red or the white blood cells. If diagnosed early enough, some cases are reversed and returned to normal by the administration of steroids. Rheumatoid and polyarthritis are thought to be the result of autoimmunity.

26

What You Can Catch from Your Dog

"Can I catch it from my dog?" is a question asked every day of every veterinarian in practice and the answer is almost always negative. Almost—but not always. Depending on the authority quoted, there are 165 to 300 diseases transmissible from lower animals to man. Why the discrepancy in numbers? If we consider one family of organisms, salmonella, as one disease, or the dozens of serotypes that dog and man may have, we see part of the reason.

Many years ago, a study was made of the dogs in our veterinary establishment and our own research kennel. The sampling was done monthly for eleven months. It indicated that over 28 percent had salmonella of one type or another in their intestinal tracts. The investigator thought the findings were so significant that he would not publish them for fear the owners would get rid of their dogs.

Of the imposing number of communicable diseases in Table XV on pages 420–22, we wonder how many you have even heard of, and of those, how many can be contracted by people from their pets.

We see an occasional case of scabies and ringworm in dogs, perhaps one of each a year, where some human in the family has the same problem. We always inquire as to who contracted it first. Ringworm may be brought home from school by the children and infect the dog, rather than vice versa.

On the list, less than half the diseases are found in North America and some have been reported so rarely that they make medical history when identified.

VIRUS DISEASES

Perhaps the best known virus disease transmitted from dogs to man is rabies. There is no doubt that it is the most serious disease, but preventive inoculations have made it a rarity in dogs. Wild animals are the chief vectors with skunks, foxes, bats, and raccoons leading the list of cases of this fatal disease (see Table XII). However, more humans die of infected ingrown toenails each year than of rabies.

Of the other virus diseases, measles and mumps are transmitted to dogs from a sick person in the house but once established, these viruses may be passed from the dog to another person in the house.

RICKETTSIAL DISEASES

In some areas of the world rickettsial diseases are represented by dogs as important hosts to infected ticks which may then transmit it to man.

Q fever does not appear to be a very serious problem in North America but blood tests indicate a significant part of the population has had and recovered from it. Since the symptoms in man are similar to those caused by many strains of flu, Q fever may be overlooked in the diagnostic process. It is estimated that 19 percent of all animals including man have had the disease. Lower animals show few signs of illness but it is thought they play some role in spreading the disease. Ticks and some other bloodsucking insects spread it but airborne organisms probably enter through the respiratory system in most cases of Q fever.

Another disease in this group is Rocky Mountain spotted fever, which is spread by ticks. This tick-borne disease is rarely reported but when it is it is usually found as headline news.

BACTERIAL DISEASES

The list of bacterial diseases is long, but dogs with any of them rarely transmit them to us. If dogs do have a high incidence of salmonella there does not appear to be a corresponding incidence in man.

There have been a few cases of brucellosis in dogs that were transmitted, it is thought, by pets to man.

SPIROCHETAL DISEASES

Many animals, perhaps most, are capable of contracting leptospirosis, a spirochetal disease, and there have been cases reported now and then of people contracting the disease from their pets.

Lime fever is spread by ticks and has been diagnosed in a few dogs but so far is thought to be primarily a human problem.

FUNGUS DISEASES

Ringworm heads the list of fungus diseases, but how many people do you know who have contracted it from their pets? Although cats have a much higher incidence of it than do dogs, few people have seen it in any pet. When contracted it's little more than a nuisance. All pets appear to develop an immunity upon recovery.

Many of the fungal diseases have an affinity for the lungs and once established are among the most difficult of diseases to treat in man and beast. They are contracted by inhalation of spores of dust in the air. The infected dog may cough up spores that dry up, become airborne, and can infect us.

PROTOZOAN DISEASES

Although dogs do have amoebic dysentery, a protozoan disease, they transmit it by contaminating food or drinking water, which man must ingest to become infected. Most of us, however, don't eat such food or drink such water.

The disease toxoplasmosis has had extensive reporting in the more sensational press. It is dangerous to developing embryos in pregnant humans and it may cause birth defects. Dogs do have the disease about as frequently as man and a majority of humans tested indicate they have had and recovered from the disease without demonstrating any symptoms.

NEMATODE DISEASES

The wormlike creatures in nematode diseases are at worst a nuisance except in the occasional rare case. When ingested by children, the eggs of the roundworm hatch, burrow through the intestinal wall, and migrate anywhere in the body. If one finds its way to an eye it may be misdiagnosed as a type of cancer.

Dirofilaria, or heartworm disease, in man may cause a lesion in the lungs that may appear as lung cancer. The dog hookworm may penetrate the skin and cause a skin rash called creeping eruption. Dogs and man do contract trichinosis, but only in areas of the world where lean dog meat is eaten could this disease be transmitted from dog to man.

CESTODE DISEASES

The flat worms and flukes of cestode diseases are more serious in lands far from North America. When a dog is affected it acts as an intermediate host to infect man. A parasitized dog passes feces with the parasite eggs into the water where fish, crabs, crayfish, and even plants are infected which, if eaten by man, can cause one of these diseases.

ARTHROPOD DISEASES

We mentioned scabies in man caused by contact with a dog with sarcoptic mange. There have been rare cases of so-called red or demodectic mange resulting from direct contact with a parasitized pet, and it is so infrequent that veterinarians don't mention the possibility to owners. Demodectic mange is commonly found on the human face, where it causes no problem.

Over the years, during the many outbreaks of influenza that have occurred in North America, veterinarians have observed the house dog with a condition similar to that of the flu-afflicted human members of the household.

POISON IVY

Another condition perhaps more common than all the others combined is poison ivy poisoning. Although dogs do not contract it they can run through the lush leaves and come home to be petted, thereby exposing humans in the household to the oil of the plant that causes the rash.

ALLERGY

There are people who say they are allergic to their dogs. They are really allergic to their dog's dander. It becomes airborne and is inhaled, resulting in a reaction in a susceptible person. We remember an asthmatic-sounding client who had to take many short breaths during each sentence. One day he arrived to leave his Boston Terrier in our care. He was going into the hospital for tests to determine the cause of his shortness of breath. When he returned three days later with a clean bill of health, his breathing was normal. He collected his dog and left. An hour later someone brought the little dog back. It seems that the owner was allergic to his dog and in the hospital, away from his pet, he had recovered from the allergy. With the dog in the car on the way home he had had a violent attack and had to be rushed to the hospital. When he returned two days later he told us the doctors wanted him to get rid of the dog but that he would rather die. We suggested he oil his palms with mineral oil and rub the oil over the dog's body daily. This "sealed" the skin, preventing the dander from becoming airborne, and our allergic client solved his problem.

Table XV
DISEASES COMMUNICABLE FROM DOGS TO HUMANS

VIRUS DISEASES	MEANS OF TRANSMISSION
Rabies	Bites
Lymphocytic choriomeningitis	Food, dust
Measles	Contact
Mumps	Contact
Rickettsial Diseases	
African tick fever	Tick bite
Boutonneuse fever	Tick bite

VIRUS DISEASES	MEANS OF TRANSMISSION
Brazilian typhus	Tick bite
Colombian typhus	Tick bite
Kenya typhus	Tick bite
Rocky Mountain spotted fever	Tick bite
Q fever	Tick bite, airborne
Colombian spotted fever	Tick bite
Bacterial Diseases	
Anthrax	Contact, contaminated food
Brucellosis	Inhalation, abrasion
Diptheria	Contact
Gas gangrene, clostridium	Through broken skin
Hemorrhagic septicemia	Animal bites, contact
Listeriosis	Uncertain
Melioidosis	
Plague	Flea bite, inhalation
Salmonellosis	Contact, feces
Scarlet fever	Contact
Tuberculosis, bovine type	Contact
Tuberculosis, human type	Contact
Tularemia	Inhalation, insect bite
Spirochetal Diseases	
Leptospirosis (both canicola and icterohalmorrhagic)	Water, feces, saliva
Fungus Diseases	
Actinomycosis	Unknown
Blastomycosis	Inhalation, trauma
Coccidiodyomycosis	Abrasion, inhalation
Cutaneous streptothricosis	Contact
Histoplasmosis	Inhalation, ingestion
Nocardiosis	Contact
Ringworm	Contact
Sporotrichosis	Through broken skin, animal bites
Protozoan Diseases	
Amebiasis	Food, water
Leishmaniasis	Sand fly bite
Toxoplasmosis (shares with many other animals)	Unknown
Trypanosomiasis	Insect fecal material
Balantidiasis	Food and water with feces

VIRUS DISEASES	MEANS OF TRANSMISSION
Nematode Diseases	
Ancylostomiasis	Through unbroken skin
Dirofilaria infection, heartworm	Mosquito
Dracontiasis*	Drinking water
Gnathostomiasis*	Infected fish, ingestion
Larva migrans, filarial	Mosquito
Larva migrans, cutaneous	Hookworms, through unbroken skin
Larva migrans, visceral	Ingestion of roundworm eggs
Strongyloidiasis	Through unbroken skin
Thelaziasis	Uncertain
Trichinosis	Ingestion of infected meat
Cestode Diseases	
Diphyllobatriasis	Raw fish
Dog tapeworm infection	Swallowing infected fleas
Echinococcosis, hydatid disease	Dog feces
Clonorchiasis, liver fluke	Raw fish
Echinostomiasis, snail-intest	Raw fish
Fasciolopsiasis	Raw aquatic plants
Heterophylasis, intest fluke	Raw fish
Opesthorchiasis	Raw fish
Paragenomiasis (lung)	Crabs, crayfish
Schistosomiasis, blood fluke	Through skin
Arthropod Diseases	
Chigre dermatitis	Contact
Sarcoptes scabiei	Contact
Demodex folliculorum	Contact

* Not in North America.

27

Cancer and Tumors

Of the major problems in dogs, cancer perhaps heads the list as being one of the most devastating. There has been a paucity of research in the field to specifically help dogs but fortunately millions of dollars have been spent to find answers for cancer in humans, which has resulted in also being beneficial to other animals, including dogs. It is our contention that solving the multiplicity of riddles of cancer in one species will help all species.

When a tumor or cancer is diagnosed by a veterinarian, it is surprising how frequently the owner will ask, "What causes cancer, Doctor?" To which we reply, "The person who can answer that question will go down in history." Research at this time indicates a myriad of causes. Perhaps cancer will be considered a heading for many diseases.

It is helpful to review the definitions of some of the common terms used to describe unusual swellings; the most frequently used is *tumor*, which originally meant a swelling but is now synonymous with *cancer* and *neoplasm*.

A *metastasis* refers to a new growth of cells that develop without control and resemble the healthy cells from which they arose; they serve no useful purpose. These cells are called *benign* when they grow in a local area and do not infiltrate surrounding tissue. Others, called *malignant*, do infiltrate surrounding tissue, even spreading through the body and establishing new growths elsewhere. This process of spreading is also called metastasis.

Carcinomas are malignant tumors that arise in the skin, in the intestinal linings, and in all tissues that develop from the same original embryonic sources. *Sarcomas* are tumors made up of connective tissue —the part of the dog's body that binds it together and supports it.

Studies indicate that repeated exposure to certain chemicals will eventually cause cancer just as repeated mechanical injury to an area will also cause it. Furthermore, we know some types and locations of cancer are more common in a particular geographical location. In the Philadelphia, Pennsylvania, area the most common body location for growths is in the mouth and throat. In Connecticut the most common sites are equally divided between the mammary glands, the skin, and under the skin.

Many otherwise concerned, dedicated dog owners fail to take the time to give their pets a thorough home physical examination from time to time. This results in the sudden discovery of a tumor that has been growing for months that is by then the size of a hen's egg. Try to develop the habit of running your fingers over every inch of your dog once a month as described in Chapter 9. If you find a lump or soft swelling, inform your veterinarian and ask his or her advice. If it is small, you may be asked to observe it over a period of time and to inform your veterinarian if it grows. There is no doubt it is easier to remove a small lesion than a large one, but some, such as warts, are not serious. They are nuisances but even a wart may be irritated by licking, in which case we like to remove them.

TYPES OF CANINE CANCER

Lipoma. A common growth is the fatty tumor, or lipoma, which is usually found in overfed animals. We often suggest nothing be done about a lipoma unless it becomes too large, in which case simple surgery is corrective. When a lipoma is located on the chest behind an elbow where the elbow strikes it with every step we suggest it be removed since the constant irritation often causes it to grow.

Mammary Cancers. The mammary cancers are usually one of two types. One is dangerous to life and the other is not. Unfortunately it is not possible to differentiate between them by palpation so we suggest they all be removed. We know breast tumors are much less common in females that have had an ovariohysterectomy; thus many females' lives are extended by the spaying operation before such tumors develop. If a dog has breast tumors, many veterinarians insist on performing both surgeries at once in the hope that removing the ovaries and uterus will prevent the development of more lesions in the future. We think this is a valid recommendation.

When the cancer spreads to the lungs, as it often does with malignancy, the case is hopeless. Many veterinarians urge owners of dogs with growths to have the dog's chest X-rayed before any surgery. Although radiographs cannot show every small lesion, if any at all are observed there is no point in surgery. A dog in this condition should be permitted to live until it is in discomfort and then humanely euthanized.

An exception is a condition with a name that is not exactly a household word—hypertrophic pulmonary osteoarthropathy. This condition is first observed as a progressive swelling of the forelegs. Radiographs show a typical bone proliferation. Further radiographs show that there is a tumor in the lungs. The removal of the lung tumor often corrects the bone lesions, resulting in an uneventful recovery. In this condition we think the initial lesion is in the lungs rather than having spread from another area in the body to the lungs, as malignancies may.

Lymphosarcoma. A busy veterinarian will encounter about one case of lymphosarcoma, or leukemia, in his or her patients in a year. In the early stages swelling in the glands of the neck and perhaps in those anterior to the shoulder blades may be observed but in a few days or a week all the lymph glands are enlarged. In addition to the neck and shoulder glands, enlarged glands behind the knees, or stifles, and those in the groin will be obvious. However, not as obvious are the glands in the abdomen and thoracic cavities.

The swollen glands in the neck may come close to strangling an affected pet and exert such pressure that breathing and heart action are not normal. A host of drugs work dramatically in reducing the glands initially but rarely does the dog remain in remission for long. Many consider this to be a virus disease but more research is needed both to determine that and to find a cure or a method of prevention.

In summary, examine your dog regularly. If you find an unusual swelling consult your veterinarian for his or her opinion; if you need a second opinion get it; and if surgery is the logical solution have it done promptly. Finally, examine the surgical area carefully for six months after surgery and follow your veterinarian's recommendations to the letter.

Cysts. In the growth category other than cancer are swellings called cysts, which we discuss here because they are often mistaken for cancer. These are caused by sebaceous glands, which produce a cheesy material, and are sometimes lanced, expressed, and have their linings removed. When left untreated they usually do no harm. Some appear to externalize with dry horny protuberances. These are not serious lesions. In our practice one dog stands out as a record holder with an estimated five hundred sebaceous cysts having been removed during its lifetime.

Small swellings of the eyelids are usually innocent but some irritate the outer surface of the eye, the cornea. If left unattended these irritating swellings may produce blindness from the constant blinking of the eyelid. They should be removed.

DIAGNOSIS AND TREATMENT

Biopsy. The determination of the type of cancer must be done by a trained animal pathologist, and the question may arise whether or not a biopsy should be done. A needle biopsy is a sensible approach: a needle is inserted into the growth and the removed tissue or fluid is sent to a pathologist. Frequently we prefer to operate no matter what the pathologist's report may be; benign or malignant, it should all be removed. After surgery the tissue is submitted and the findings tell us what the future is apt to hold. As there is no definite line of demarkation between benign and malignant, some tissues are difficult to classify. The pathologist will admit the quandary and one day we will tell him whether or not the tumor returned.

Surgery. That the incidence of cancer in older dogs is greater than that in younger dogs is a truism. The possibility of surgery to older dogs creates a dilemma to many owners. This is a situation with which veterinarians can be of great help. They have seen their rates of success in hundreds and perhaps thousands of similar situations and can and will be of great help in making a decision. We personally appreciate the owner asking us, "What would you do if it were your dog, Doctor?" If you have any doubts about your veterinarian's judgment ask for a suggestion about someone else for a second opinion or arrange an appointment with another doctor. If you do seek another's advice tell the new doctor you are looking for a second opinion. We are sure you realize this is no cat-and-mouse game. It is the well-being and perhaps the life of your pet hanging in the balance of your decision.

In old dogs cancer usually grows more slowly than the same type does in younger dogs. Very old dogs with very invasive lesions frequently keep the cancer so well under control they die of other causes. Whatever the reason, it might be valuable to know why. We don't. There is an old adage in surgery that the surgeon who removes it should not be the one who sews it up. The thought here is that if you leave enough skin to make a cosmetically acceptable result you may leave some of the cancer cells. That maxim crosses our minds when we contemplate surgery to remove a particularly large lesion.

Immunotherapy. So far we have mentioned surgery as a cancer treatment and to date it remains a lifesaving approach for a tremendous number of pets. But the future appears bright for another treatment, that of immunotherapy. A great deal of research is focused toward injections that will stimulate the immune system of the body to prevent or to reject the wild-growing cells of cancer.

X-Ray Therapy. At this time X-ray therapy is used with great success on certain types of cancer but you must be near someone who has this expensive equipment. The dog usually must have an anesthetic for each of many treatments.

Cryosurgery. Tumor cryosurgery is the exposure of the growth to extremely cold temperatures to destroy the cancer cells and perhaps some of the healthy cells around them.

Hyperthermia. Encouraging results are seen in overheating patients with total body immersion in hot water combined with X-ray therapy. Repeated treatments are necessary.

Chemotherapy. Chemotherapy has not produced the results in treating canine leukemia that it has in human leukemia but new treatments are being tried in the hope that a breakthrough discovery will be forthcoming soon. Laetrile was not effective on three dogs we treated nor has it been in the hands of others who treated dozens with hopeless cancer.

All too often owners find a tumor and decide, since the pet is old, to wait until it becomes too large and then, assuming the poor dog will be failing, request euthanasia. The problem arises when the tumor reaches a huge size—often larger than the dog's head—and the patient is just as happy and active as before the growth appeared. Many cases like this are brought into us and our attitude is that it is better to try and fail than not to try at all. It may be a surprise but a goodly percent of large growths can and are removed successfully. We successfully removed a three-and-a-half-pound tumor from a twelve-pound poodle.

In our opinion, old dogs, even with heart problems, tolerate modern anesthetics surprisingly well. It is a rare case that succumbs to anesthesia. When large abdominal masses are discovered we urge surgery with the stipulation that if it is a hopeless case the dog not be permitted to recover from the anesthesia but be given an overdose while still on the operating table. When the disease is hopeless, it is not fair to the patient or the owner for the pet to return home and die a slow, usually painful death. We often request that we be permitted to make such a decision as if the dog were our own. Most people agree. Those who do not we think are selfish in that they will not be parted from the poor animal no matter how much suffering is involved.

28

Geriatrics

If you have never had the luxury of living with an old dog that has grown old with you, you have missed a great adventure of life. The golden years in a dog's life vary with the individual animal as they do with the individual human being, but it's safe to say the last 25 percent of a dog's life represent its old age. An aged dog has long since forgotten its puppy antics and may have lost a good deal of physical alertness, but it knows your every mood, your schedule of arrivals and departures, the sound of your car, and it knows what pleases you and tries its best to oblige.

If your pet is a hunter it goes about its job with no lost motion—all business—and it knows by then where its chances of scenting a bird or a rabbit are and goes right to work. If your dog can no longer jog with you it watches your departure with a healthy concern and greets your return like a long-lost friend.

The aging process is involved with many and various factors. If one organ has been stressed by disease it may be a weak link. For example, if the kidneys had infections during the pet's earlier life they could be the weak link in the machine. The dog may not have the capability of eliminating normal wastes of metabolism as easily as in its younger days. Perhaps it must drink twice as much water to flush the same wastes it disposed of with no problem a year before. This situation requires the pumping of more blood through the tired kidneys by the heart. This is stressful to the heart.

And there are a myriad of similar problems, some of which we have good potential for alleviating and many of which are beyond our knowledge and control. Nevertheless, it seems to us an old dog has earned the right to be helped when problems arise. Where veterinary medicine can provide so many answers a loyal old dog should be given every opportunity.

THE IMPORTANCE OF HEALTH EXAMINATIONS

But this time above all times in a dog's life should not be taken for granted. Because the dog has always been healthy many devoted owners will try their best to overlook problems that may be the forerunners of disaster.

This is the time to overlook nothing. It is the time for an in-depth physical examination by your dog's friendly veterinarian. Not a cursory examination—but one that includes a battery of screening tests to see if all systems are normal. The urine should be studied for kidney function, the stool for parasites that no old-timer should have to coexist with, and the blood to determine that there is no anemia and that the numbers and ratio of cells are normal. The blood test will also indicate kidney function as well as liver function. When all the information is put together and if no problem is found you have accomplished two important goals. First, you know the old dog is still normal but, second, you have on file a set of your dog's laboratory values that may be more important than you think in the future.

Why? Because with each value of each test there is a low normal and a high normal. Let's say the kidney function test is low-normal and one day in the future the dog has a problem for which tests are indicated. If at that time the kidney function test is slightly above high-normal it is significant. If the pet's norm is high-normal and a subsequent test is slightly above that value it is not as significant.

A baseline of tests indicating its normal values is well worthwhile.

ARTERIOSCLEROSIS

What happens as an old dog ages is similar in all mammals to some degree. Arteriosclerosis, or hardening of the arteries, comes to all and is evidenced by the change in the color and perhaps size of the pupils of the eyes. Once dark black, they come to have a gray cast or even a milky appearance. Because of the structure of the eyes, the dog may still be able to see a fly on the wall and will experience no functional problems. This curse of aging in dogs frequently accompanies a loss of hearing for the same reason. The eye grayness is actually minute blood vessels that develop thick walls. If the density is too great the dog dilates the pupils to admit more light and the combination of larger and gray pupils is the result.

With arteriosclerosis some of the elasticity of the vessels is gone, resulting in an increase of effort on the part of the heart to circulate blood. The dog compensates by doing less of the type of activity that places stress on the heart. More and longer periods of sleep occur as this slow process develops over the years. The dog becomes obviously old. Blood is not circulated through the brain as well as in the past and the dog demonstrates the fact by being less sure of foot and perhaps a little dizzy on arising from a nap.

LIFE EXPECTANCY

The life expectancy of adult dogs is said to be about thirteen years. That is an average, as many die on the highways and, at a young age, by other unnatural causes. In our experience, most properly cared for canines live to fourteen or fifteen years. The giant breeds and Boxers are exceptions, with an average life expectancy of eight to nine years.

There is good evidence that life expectancy is a genetic trait; that during the development of the embryo the life span is predetermined and somehow imprinted on each individual animal. It has been observed that some strains in a given breed tend to live longer than others in that same breed.

If we assume life expectancy is hereditary we must not assume the quality of life is a stereotyped fact. There are many factors within our control which when applied enhance the quality of life for the geriatric pet: medications for the heart and lungs, for kidneys, and even arthritis, to name a few. Perhaps the most important consideration concerns nutrition. But you say the old dog has always been on one diet and has done well for so many years, what difference does the diet make? Depending on the individual animal, perhaps a great deal. It is true that commercial dog foods are nutritionally balanced and nourishing, but if certain problems develop, a change of nutrition can and does prolong the quality of life. If the kidneys have lost some of their capability of filtering wastes from the system then a change to a diet that produces less waste may be helpful. Likewise, if the heart is failing and the retention of fluid is a problem, a low sodium diet may be helpful. A favorite diet of ours for the geriatric animal consists of equal parts of lightly cooked inexpensive hamburger, boiled rice, and canned tomatoes. There is a minimum of nitrogenous waste produced in the dog for the kidneys to eliminate and this diet is reasonably low in sodium. We frequently suggest a change from a commercial food to this diet for a week's trial and it is a pleasure to hear from a significant number of owners that the old dog appears healthier on it. If this diet is to be used for a long while, we also add a vitamin-mineral supplement.

SENILITY

Many old dogs require a good deal of care as they reach the end. Some show signs of senility by ceasing to be housebroken. As sight, hearing, and reflexes are impaired, a pet must be watched over more carefully than previously. A deaf dog cannot hear danger approaching and if eyesight is failing cannot see it. There is no sadder event than a seventeen-year-old dog being struck by a car. After it has avoided this danger for a long lifetime, the protective signals just weren't there. The old dog deserves a better fate. Most of us are willing after a lifetime of loyalty and affection from it to give of ourselves to make the golden years as comfortable as possible.

One way to help is to find problems before they become serious. The home physical exam described in Chapter 9 should be employed on a regular basis. And when its last days approach, don't permit an old-timer to wander away aimlessly, to lose its way and die from exhaustion far from the security and love found in your home.

THREE CAUSES OF DEATH

The three most common causes of death in old dogs in descending order are, it seems to us, cancer, heart disease, and kidney disease. This statement is not the result of a statistical analysis but of a clinical evaluation that may be colored by the hideousness of cancer and by our helplessness to cure it in so many cases.

Many a terminally ill dog will have so many concurrent problems it is difficult to determine which single one is the cause of death. And perhaps it is not important.

The oldest dog we have seen was a twenty-three-year-old Cocker Spaniel but the *Guinness Book of World Records* mentions a spayed female black Labrador Retriever that lived to twenty-seven years and three months.

29

When the End Comes

The death of a dog is a very serious problem to a great many people. Too many otherwise intelligent pet owners simply can't bring themselves to realize that every life has a limit. When their conscientious veterinarian assures them it is time to say good-by to their pet, instead of taking this advice they say good-by to the veterinarian and take their pet to another.

It is interesting and helpful to consider the life expectancy of the breeds of dogs. If you know what to expect in advance, you will not be surprised at death, nor will you ask the impossible of your veterinarian.

In the table below, the average age at death means *from natural causes* in animals that have survived infanthood.

Table XVI
CANINE LONGEVITY

BREED	AVERAGE AGE AT DEATH	OLDEST KNOWN TO THE AUTHORS
Airedale	12 yrs.	20 yrs.
Chihuahua	13	15
Cocker Spaniel	12	23
French Poodle	12	22
Foxhound	12	20
Great Dane	9	14
St. Bernard	10	15

There comes a time when we must ask ourselves what's best. Shall we let our dog die of old age, general breakdown, a growth, kidney disease, or other causes? Or shall we bravely say, "He has led a good life, he's no longer enjoying what little is left of it, he's blind and deaf, he's in some pain; we'll have him put painlessly to sleep"?

It takes courage to make such a decision. When the time comes for the owner to decide what to do with his or her aging pet, there are some general facts which should be known. They may make the decision easier.

There is no pain to euthanasia if properly administered. A veterinarian can inject a few cc of an anesthetic into a pet's vein and he droops his eyes, nods his head, sighs as he feels release from pain, goes to sleep. He just never wakens.

An animal does not miss tomorrow. Suppose that you couldn't think ahead. If you had no imagination, you couldn't project yourself into the future. Mentally and physically you would live only in this moment— not even two seconds in the future. We can anticipate a fine dinner party and see images of it in our mind's eye. We can look forward in winter to next spring's flowers and thus make our winter more bearable. But an animal lives in the present alone, without any thought of the future. If he dies, his existence merely terminates. He is being deprived of nothing, for he has no conception of the future.

The death of a pet is not his loss so much as it is ours. The home will be empty without his presence. True, for the past year he probably hasn't been the friend we knew and loved; he's been ailing and not himself. But propinquity has endeared him to us and *we* see him as he used to be; we remember all the fine qualities he once had. When we hesitate to bring his life to an end, we are unconsciously thinking of ourselves. We may even allow him to suffer pain and discomfort because *we* don't want to lose him; we don't want our serene existence upset by no longer having our pet.

He's going to die someday. We must face this fact, even though we shrink from it. Isn't it better to stop his suffering by terminating his existence by our own volition than to allow him to linger in pain or extreme old age?

What might he say if he could think? He would probably say something like this: "I don't want to leave you anymore than you want to be without me, but please give me comfort and freedom from misery. I can't see, so I bump into furniture. I can't hear you. I no longer enjoy the meals you prepare for me. I'm a burden to you, and certainly no good to myself. If I go outside, I might be crushed by an automobile. What good am I, anyway? Couldn't you be unselfish and grant me a blessed release?" And he might well add: "And if I gave you so much fun and companionship, get yourself another pet to fill my place just as quickly as you can. Start giving him the attention you have me when I was young. It will give you lots to think about and help to keep you young."

METHODS OF EUTHANASIA

The methods employed in euthanasia in the past—and, unfortunately, even today in some places—are largely responsible for the fact that so many people simply refused to consider ending a pet's life. They were shocking, inhumane, and often clumsy. Usually the animal was shot, gassed, or electrocuted. The drugs that were occasionally used were unsatisfactory: the injection of strychnine was certainly inferior even to shooting; ether and chloroform brought a kinder death but even with these there was considerable distress.

If your local humane society or dog warden is still using the methods of a decade or so ago, you will be doing a service to both the pets and pet owners in your community by discussing with the proper authorities the possibilities of using pentobarbital.

There has been a heated debate over the use of the high altitude chamber for euthanasia and many states have seen fit to eliminate it by law. Although experiments with people indicate there is no discomfort, the animal euthanasia chambers we have seen in operation raise doubts in our minds. The animals do pass through at least an apprehensive period before unconsciousness. We have asked ourselves if we would permit a pet of our own to be destroyed in this manner and the answer is no. We doubt any other veterinarians would either.

Today there are a number of drugs available that are both quick and painless. When you decide that it is best to terminate your dog's existence you have every right to insist that drugs of this type be administered. The best of these, in our opinion, are the barbiturates; and of them we prefer sodium pentobarbital. When injected into a vein or directly into the heart, its effects are almost instantaneous. A sudden sleep overcomes the animal and in a matter of seconds it is completely unconscious. The heartbeat and breathing cease; the end comes quietly and quickly. We have administered this drug to many pets in the presence of their owners, and without exception they have been tremendously impressed by the humane and painless death it has brought.

The lethal dose of sodium pentobarbital is usually considered to be one and a half times the amount required for anesthesia. In nearly every case an injection of this amount is adequate, but we have known cases in which it produced only a prolonged deep sleep and a second injection was necessary. To eliminate even the possibility of such occurrences, we administer three grains for each five pounds of the animal's weight. A dose of this size is completely and immediately effective.

CARE OF THE REMAINS

Should you have your dog buried? If so, where? The backyard? This is illegal in many cities. In a cemetery for pets? A grave and perpetual care is available in some communities. Should the animal be embalmed? Why? What happens after death, anyway?

Slow oxidation is what takes place, oxidation being the chemical name for burning. Wood in a fire oxidizes with a visible flame. A decaying stump oxidizes slowly, with no such flagrance. An animal's body oxidizes slowly too. So it is actually a matter of deciding between quick or slow oxidation; burial or cremation is the choice. We unhesitatingly recommend the latter. What matters if the oxidation is quick? Isn't it better to know it is over in a few minutes rather than slowly taking place in the cold ground over a period of years? Chemically, there's little difference; aesthetically, choose cremation. If your dog has certain diseases there is no doubt that cremation is in order to prevent the surfacing of the disease-causing organisms from the buried remains.

POSTMORTEMS

Sometimes the question arises, "Shall I permit a postmortem examination?" A study made in a large hospital for humans to determine the percentage of persons who refused to allow free postmortems on their loved ones showed that 26 percent disdained the thought and refused permission. Even though the physician might have gleaned information from the examination to help treat similar cases in the future or might have indicated a hereditary problem of interest to the family, 26 percent still refused. A similar study at the Whitney Veterinary Clinic revealed the astounding fact that 24.3 percent of pet owners refused to allow free examinations on their dogs after death. Many of the findings could have been of great help to other dogs, if not always to their owners.

Occasionally pets die of diseases that are transmissible to their owners. If the veterinarian is willing to risk his or her health performing a necropsy, one would think the owner would comply with a request for a postmortem—especially when this examination could help the veterinarian to help other dogs, or when it would add to our knowledge of cancer, or parasites, or blood, or heredity.

When your veterinarian finds your pet's malady of sufficient interest to give his or her time to studying its body, you need an excellent reason to justify your refusing him permission. If you love pets, you love to see them well. You can hardly do less than to help the doctor to help other pets—and perhaps, incidentally, yourself.

Fifty Questions Frequently Asked by Dog Owners

1. Q. What causes a dog to start shedding?
   A. The lengthening of the day.

2. Q. What causes a dog to have worms?
   A. They are part of nature and are usually contracted from the dog's ingesting worm eggs.

3. Q. Does a dog need lean meat?
   A. No. It can live on dehydrated meat or without any meat at all.

4. Q. Could a dog live on a vegetable diet?
   A. Yes, with added vitamins and minerals.

5. Q. Does milk make worms in dogs?
   A. No. In fact, milk is an excellent food for dogs.

6. Q. Does garlic kill worms?
   A. There is no scientific evidence to substantiate this. Garlic seems to nourish tapeworms, causing them to shed more egg masses called segments than they would shed without it.

7. Q. At what age do bitches first come in heat?
   A. At six to twelve months, depending on the breed and rapidity of growth.

8. Q. Does ground glass kill dogs quickly?
   A. It usually doesn't even bother them and passes through without appreciably damaging the digestive tract.

9. Q. Can you tell the age of a dog by its teeth?
   A. Its second set starts to erupt at fourteen weeks of age and are all in by five and a half months. Beyond that, teeth are a poor indication of age.

10. Q. Is distemper the only disease that leaves pits in the tooth enamel?
    A. No. There are a number of febrile diseases puppies can have at teething time which leave pits.

11. Q. Do dogs have eczema?
    A. They have a skin disease that is called eczema.

12. Q. How can I improve my dog's coat?
    A. For each ten pounds of body weight, add a teaspoon of corn oil to its foods.

13. Q. When a dog sits down and drags itself along with its front legs, does it mean it has worms?
    A. Not necessarily. It may have worms, but this particular action means that the dog is trying to squeeze out some of the accumulation in its anal glands or that it itches in the area.

14. Q. Do worms cause anemia?
    A. Yes. Hookworms cause it by drawing blood; whipworms by their toxins.

15. Q. Do dogs have collarbones (clavicles)?
    A. No. Among pets, only birds have them.

16. Q. What is a roundworm?
    A. It may be any of a class of nematodes—hook, whip, ascarid—or it may be a specific ascarid usually called roundworm. It is three to five inches long, one sixteenth of an inch thick, and pointed at both ends.

17. Q. Are hookworms so named because their ends are shaped like hooks?
    A. No. They are called hookworms because of the microscopic hooks around their mouths by which they attach themselves to the intestinal lining. Hookworms are five eighths of an inch long and about as thick as heavy thread.

18. Q. How do dogs acquire tapeworms?
    A. Principally by eating fleas and rabbits, each of which is host for a specific kind of tapeworm.

19. Q. Can a veterinarian find tapeworm eggs by a fecal examination?
    A. The eggs of the flea-host worm are seldom found, but the eggs of the rabbit-host worm are always evident.

20. Q. Are dogs subject to any infectious liver disease?
    A. One type—leptospirosis—which is spread by rats.

21. Q. Should I feed my pet a vitamin supplement?
    A. Except a few rare instances, not if you feed it a complete commercial dog food.

22. Q. Does long hair covering the eyes in some breeds protect the eyes?
    A. No. Except in dogs to be shown, much of it should be trimmed to permit better vision.

23. Q. Is there any way to stop an old bitch from dribbling urine?
    A. Many spayed bitches have weak bladder sphincters. Small doses of stilbestrol given at regular intervals will usually cure the dribbling.

24. Q. How often should a dog's nails be trimmed?
    A. It varies with the individual animal. If a dog stands on a firm surface and its nails touch the surface, they need trimming.

25. Q. Do dogs get cavities in their teeth?
    A. Very rarely.

26. Q. How often should a dog be bathed?
    A. Perhaps never. If the dog has an offensive odor or if obviously dirty it should be bathed. Our house dogs are bathed twice a year.

27. Q. Do dogs get stomach ulcers, for example, from worry?
    A. Dogs very seldom have stomach ulcers from any cause.

28. Q. What causes a dog to drag a front leg? Is it curable?
    A. An injury to the radial nerve. If damage is extensive, the dragging seldom is curable; usually the nerve fails to regenerate.

29. Q. Is coccidiosis caught from chickens or rabbits?
    A. Neither. The dog has three common forms, none of which is contracted from chickens or rabbits.

30. Q. Is cancer very common in dogs?
    A. Cancer is one of the leading causes of death in dogs.

31. Q. Why are puppies of white breeds so frequently deaf?
    A. Usually from careless breeding. Deafness is not necessarily associated with color, except in pups from two harlequin-colored dogs.

32. Q. What is the average life expectancy of a dog?
    A. For most that have avoided accidents and puppyhood diseases, thirteen years; for giant breeds and a few others, it is closer to eight or nine years of age.

33. Q. How long should a bitch be allowed to attempt whelping before it is necessary to use instruments?
    A. Until a puppy is down in the pelvis and is obviously too large to be passed normally, usually two hours.

34. Q. Should a dog's ears be cleaned regularly?
    A. They should be examined and cleaned only if they need it. Many dogs never have the need of ear cleaning.

35. Q. When a dog's eyelids turn in and the hair rubs on the eyeballs, can that be corrected?
    A. Yes, by an operation that removes a crescent of skin below and above the eye, thus pulling the lids out to their proper position.

36. Q. What can be done to remove the small tumor so often seen in the inside corners of the eyes of Boston Terriers and Cocker Spaniels?
    A. It can be removed by surgery successfully and quite simply.

37. Q. How does a fecal examination determine the presence of worms?
    A. By demonstrating the eggs of worms. Knowing which worm lays the eggs that are found, the technician knows which worm the dog is harboring.

38. Q. Do fleas breed on a dog?
    A. Fleas copulate and the female lays eggs while on the dog. The eggs fall to the ground, into rug nap, overstuffed furniture, cracks in the floor, and hatch when the weather is warm and damp. A worm emerges and grows, eventually spins a cocoon, pupates, and emerges as a flea which jumps on the first thing moving past it—dog, cat, or person.

39. Q. Do lice breed on a dog?
    A. Yes.

40. Q. Is red mange curable?
    A. It is self-limiting in some dogs, curable in most, but seemingly incurable in a few.

41. Q. Is glaucoma hereditary?
    A. One type is. It never skips a generation.

42. Q. Do dogs have hernias?
    A. Yes. The most common is the small navel (umbilical) hernia.

43. Q. What makes some dogs' eyes reflect red at night?
    A. A rare hereditary characteristic. The eyes are like those of a raccoon in this respect.

44. Q. Do dogs have lockjaw?
    A. Yes, but it is so rare that preventive inoculations are not usually administered.

45. Q. Can humans contract heartworms?
    A. Yes, but the diagnosis can be made only if heartworm incysted in the lung is verified by a pathologist.

46. Q. Is mange transmissible from dog to man?
    A. Sarcoptic mange is transmissible from dog to man and also from man to dog.

47. Q. Do dogs have many forms of cancer?
    A. Probably as many forms as human beings have.

48. Q. Can a dog get fat in any way other than by eating too much? How about glands?
    A. Glands help to regulate the use a dog makes of the food it eats. Eating is the only way it can get fat.

49. Q. Do dogs have venereal diseases?
    A. Not the kinds human beings have, but there is a cancer transmissible by copulation, as well as a disease called brucellosis.

50. Q. Will a dog infect its wounds if it licks them?
    A. No. It licks any dead tissue away, along with bacteria. It may lick and chew sutures out that were placed to close a skin incision.

Diagnostic Table

The following table is designed to help you use this book easily and well. It will make it possible for you to identify many of the common diseases of dogs.

If your dog is sick it will exhibit certain symptoms—probably several. These symptoms are shown in boldface in the table, and under each of them there is a list of diseases or conditions with which they are most commonly associated. You will find in the book a detailed discussion of the symptoms, causes, prevention, and treatment of each of these diseases.

Here is an example of the way the table should be used. You notice that your dog is excessively thirsty, seems to be bloated about the abdomen, and shows signs of a soft swelling in his legs. *Coughing, abdominal enlargements*, and *swellings* are all shown in the table as symptoms. The diseases listed under each of these symptoms vary greatly, but *dropsy* appears under all of them. By reading the discussion of dropsy, you will be able to determine whether your dog has the disease and, if it has, what you can do about it.

This table is *not* a cureall chart. It will *not* make you a veterinarian. It *will* help you to recognize the signs of disease in your pet and show you where to get the information you need in order to decide whether you can treat the condition yourself or whether your pet needs expert veterinary attention.

ABDOMINAL ENLARGEMENTS
Anemia (in young)
Bladder ailments
Bloat
Dropsy
Excessive thirst
Fat
Infected Uterus
Organ enlargement (spleen, liver)
Overfeeding
Parasites (in young)
Pregnancy
Tumors

ABDOMINAL TENDERNESS
Abdominal infection
Adhesions
Colon impaction
Enteritis
Foreign bodies
Inflamed pancreas
Poisoning
Porcupine quills
Stomach inflammation
Telescoped intestine
Tumors
Ulcers

ANEMIA (Pale gums)
Hemorrhage
Injury
Iron deficiency
Lice
Parasites

Poisoning
Tumors

APPETITE
(Difficulty in Eating)
Foreign bodies in
mouth or throat
Gum disease
Insect stings
Lead poisoning
Mouth ailments
Swelling under tongue
Teeth loose
Tongue injuries
Tonsillitis
Tumors in mouth
Ulcers
(Loss of)
Change of diet
Disease
Fever
Overfeeding
Parasites
Poisoning
Toxins
Tumors
(Ravenous Appetite)
Encephalitis
Heat, onset of
Incipient diabetes
Lactation
Pregnancy
Sugar diabetes
(Undernourishment)
Heredity

BAD BREATH
Cancer
Constipation
Foreign bodies in or on
teeth
Gum disease
Kidney disease

Lip ailments
Poisoning, caustic or
acid
Tartar
Teeth
Tongue injuries
Ulcers in mouth

BLINDNESS
Cataract
Concussions
Cornea, opacity of
Distemper
Eye injuries
Glaucoma
Infectious hepatitis
Vitamins

BREATHING
ABNORMAL
(Loss of breath from
exertion)
Anemia
Emphysema
Heart ailments
Heartworm
Hernia of diaphram
Pleurisy
Pneumonia
Snorting
Water, air, or pus in
chest

CONVULSIONS
Calcium-arsenate
poisoning
Eclampsia
Encephalitis
Epilepsy
Foreign bodies in
stomach
Hypoglycemia
Strychnine poisoning
Sugar diabetes

Uremia
Worms

COUGHING
Allergy
Bronchitis
Distemper
Emphysema
Esophageal worms
Foreign object
Heartworm
Kennel cough
Laryngitis
Pharyngitis
Pleurisy
Pneumonia
Worms

DIARRHEA
Allergy
Diet
Exercise
Fiber, excessive
Inflamed intestine
Malabsorption
Parasites
Poisoning
Skim milk

DIZZINESS
Accidents
Cerebral hemorrhage
Ear canker
Ear mites
Encephalitis
Middle-ear infection

EMACIATION
Allergy
Diabetes
Diarrhea
Kidney disease
Liver disease
Malabsorption

Tuberculosis
Tumors
Undernourishment

GAGGING
Distemper
Foreign body in throat
Kennel cough
Tonsillitis
Worms

HEAD SHAKING
Blood clot in ear flap
Canker in ear
Ear, ailments of
Ear flap torn
Ear mites
Fleas
Lice
Middle-ear infection

HOARSENESS
Asthma
Cancer
Foreign body in throat
Injuries to throat
Laryngitis
Paralysis
Throat ailments
 Streptococcus
 Virus
Tonsillitis

LUMPS
Abscesses
Blood clot
Bone tumors
Dropsy
Goiter
Hernia, anal
Hernia, groin
Hernia, navel
Leukemia
Salivary duct blockage
Tumors—cancer

Warts

**MOANING OR
 CRYING**
Anal gland abscesses
Constipation
Ear ailments
Encephalitis
Fleas
Foreign bodies
Pancreatitis
Poisoning
Skin disease
Tooth abscess
Urinary obstruction

NOSE, RUNNING
Allergy
Distemper
Nasal discharge
Nasal tumors
Noseworms
Pneumonia
Salmon poisoning

PARALYSIS
Back broken or injured
Diet
Disk
Nerve degeneration
Nerve injury
Rabies
Stroke
Toxins

**SHEDDING,
 ABNORMAL**
Burns
Insipient diabetes
Hormonal
Malnutrition
Mange
Nursing puppies
Skin diseases

**SHIVERING,
 TREMBLING**
Cold
Milk fever
Poisoning
 Caffeine
 Calcium arsenate
 Food
 Nicotine
 Strychnine
 Theobromine (in
 chocolate)
Shock

SKIN AILMENTS
Acne
Allergy
Alopecia
Burns
Dandruff
Fleas
Mange, three types

SLOBBERING
Convulsions
Encephalitis
Foreign bodies in
 mouth
Insect stings
Lip ailments
Poison
Teeth, loose or broken
Tongue injuries
Warts

**SNEEZING,
 SNORTING**
Allergy
Distemper
Inflammation of nasal
 passages
Nasal mites
Nose, ailments of
 (sinus)

Noseworm

Pneumonia

Sniffles

Tumors

SWELLINGS THAT
LEAVE PITS
WHEN
SQUEEZED

Dropsy

Effusion of serous fluid
into the interstices of
cells in tissues

Heart ailments

Index